Shojo Beat

VAMPIRE KNIGHT MEMORIES

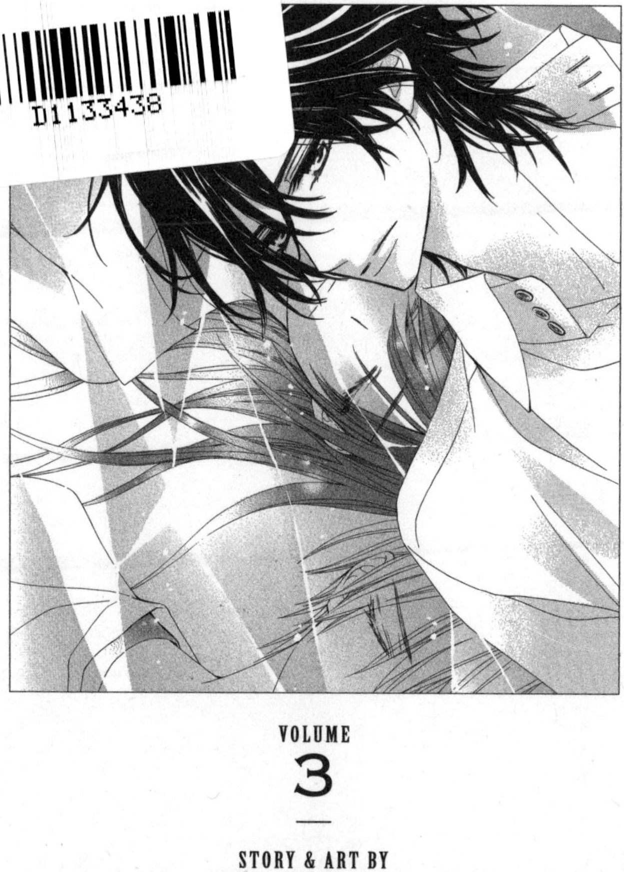

VOLUME

3

STORY & ART BY

Matsuri Hino

The Story of VAMPIRE KNIGHT

Previously...

Vampire Knight is the story of Yuki Kuran, a pureblood vampire princess, who was brought up as a human.
A moment of peace has arrived after a fierce battle between humans and vampires. But Kaname Kuran, whose heart became the Ancestor Metal for weapons capable of killing vampires, continues to sleep within the coffin of ice. A thousand years later, Yuki gives Kaname her heart, and he is revived as a human. Yuki and Kaname's daughter, Ai, begins to tell him about the days that have passed...
Yuki and Zero Kiryu have decided to start over, but choose to only meet on the bench at Cross Academy until everyone's anger has subsided. Meanwhile, young Ai has realized her love for Zero, and though she knows it will remain unrequited, she confesses her feelings to him. Sayori Wakaba passes away, proud that Hanabusa Aido had loved her human self.

CHARACTERS

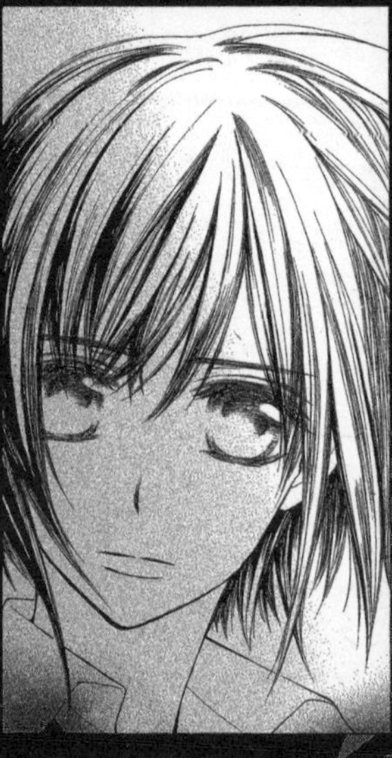

YUKI KURAN (CROSS)

The adopted daughter of the headmaster of Cross Academy. She is a pureblood vampire and the princess of the noble Kuran family. She has always adored Kaname, even when she did not have her memory.

KANAME KURAN

A pureblood vampire and the progenitor of the Kurans. He is Yuki's fiancé and was raised as her sibling. He knows Yuki's true identity and cares for her...

ZERO KIRYU

He was born into a family of vampire hunters and later was turned into a vampire. His parents were killed by a pureblood. He has agonized over his feelings for Yuki and his role as a vampire hunter.

REN AND AI

Yuki's children

HANABUSA AIDO

He was an upperclassman in the Night Class. He is working to create a medicine that will turn vampires into humans...

VAMPIRE KNIGHT
MEMORIES

CONTENTS

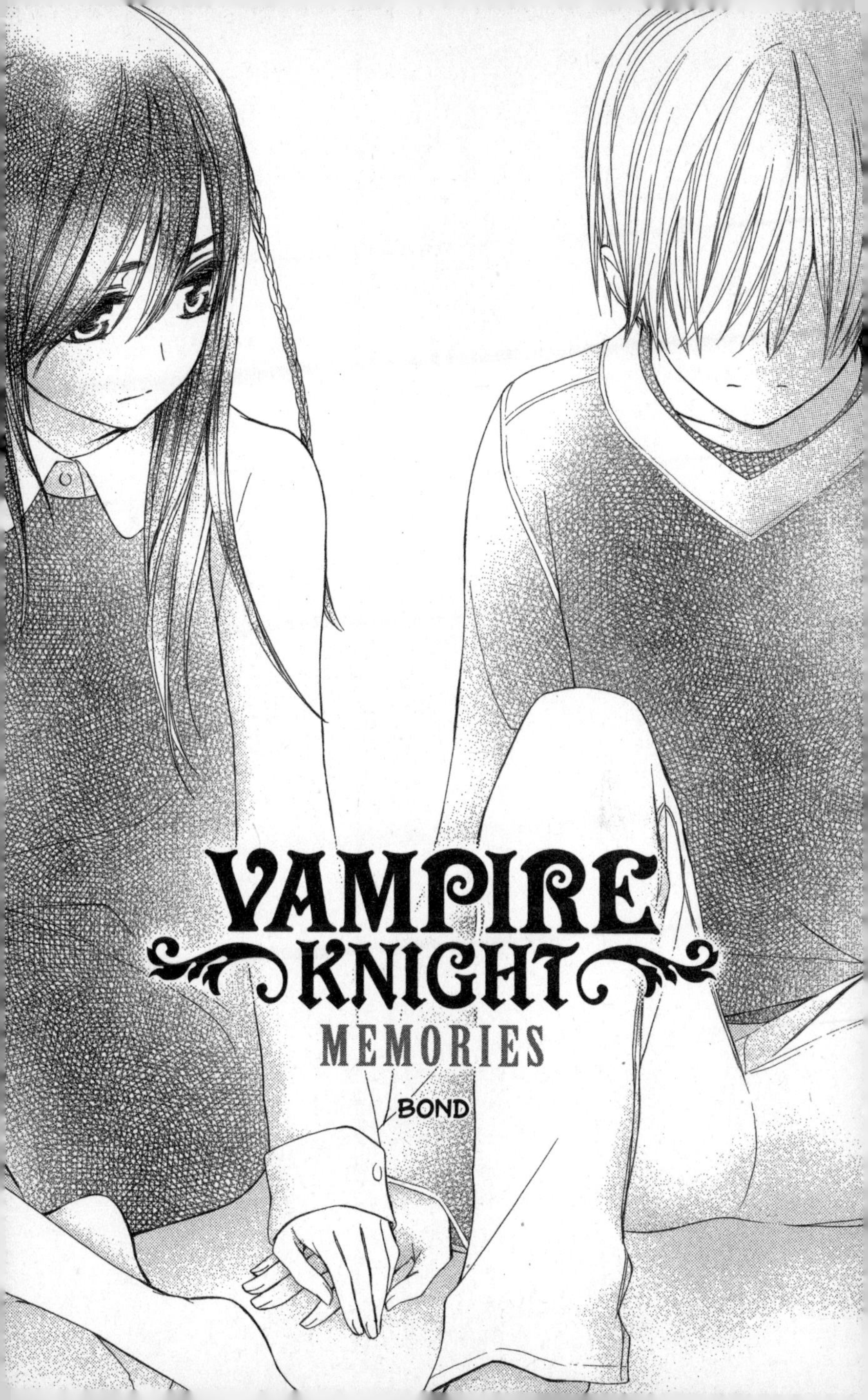
VAMPIRE KNIGHT
MEMORIES
BOND

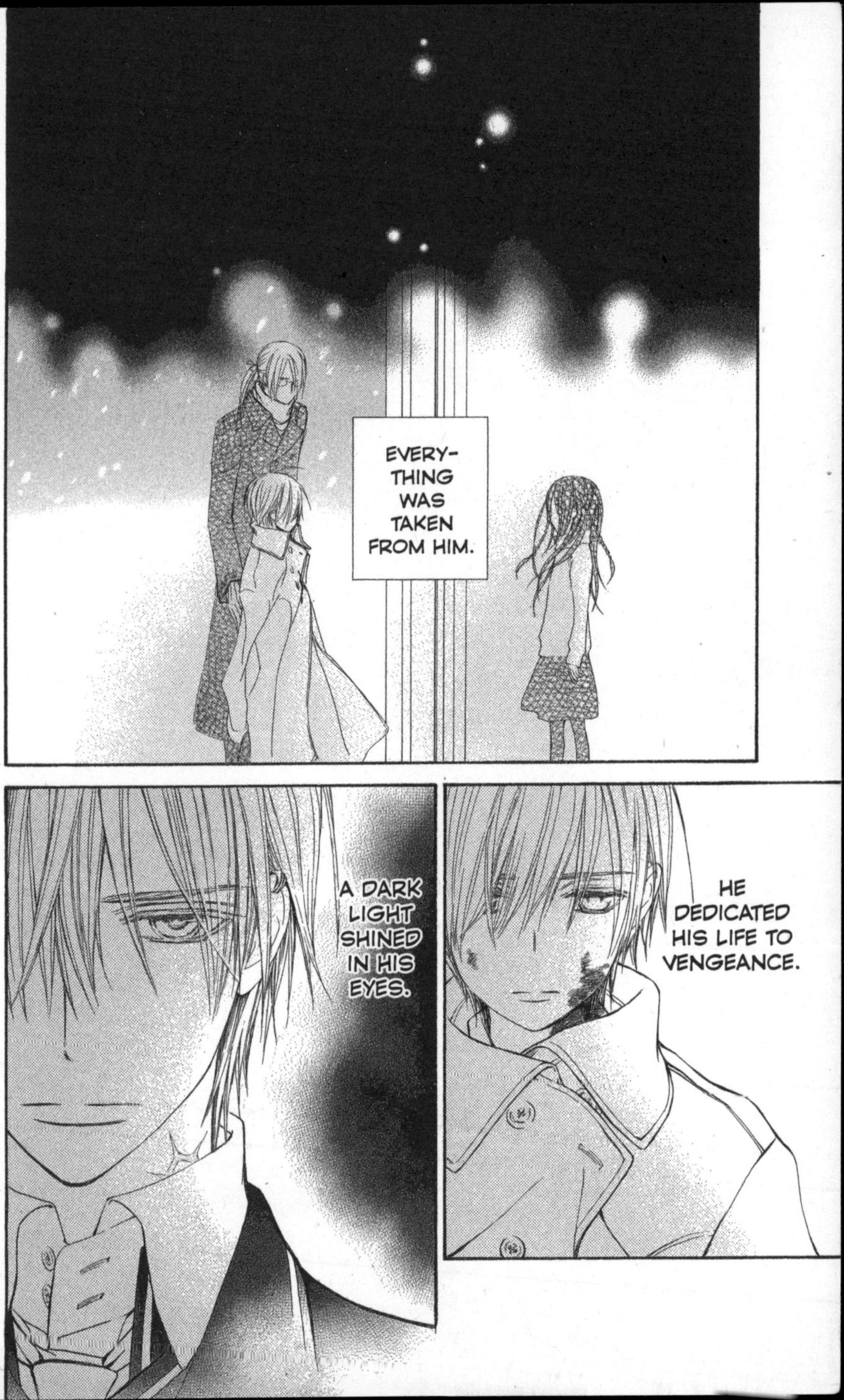
EVERY-THING WAS TAKEN FROM HIM.
HE DEDICATED HIS LIFE TO VENGEANCE.
A DARK LIGHT SHINED IN HIS EYES.

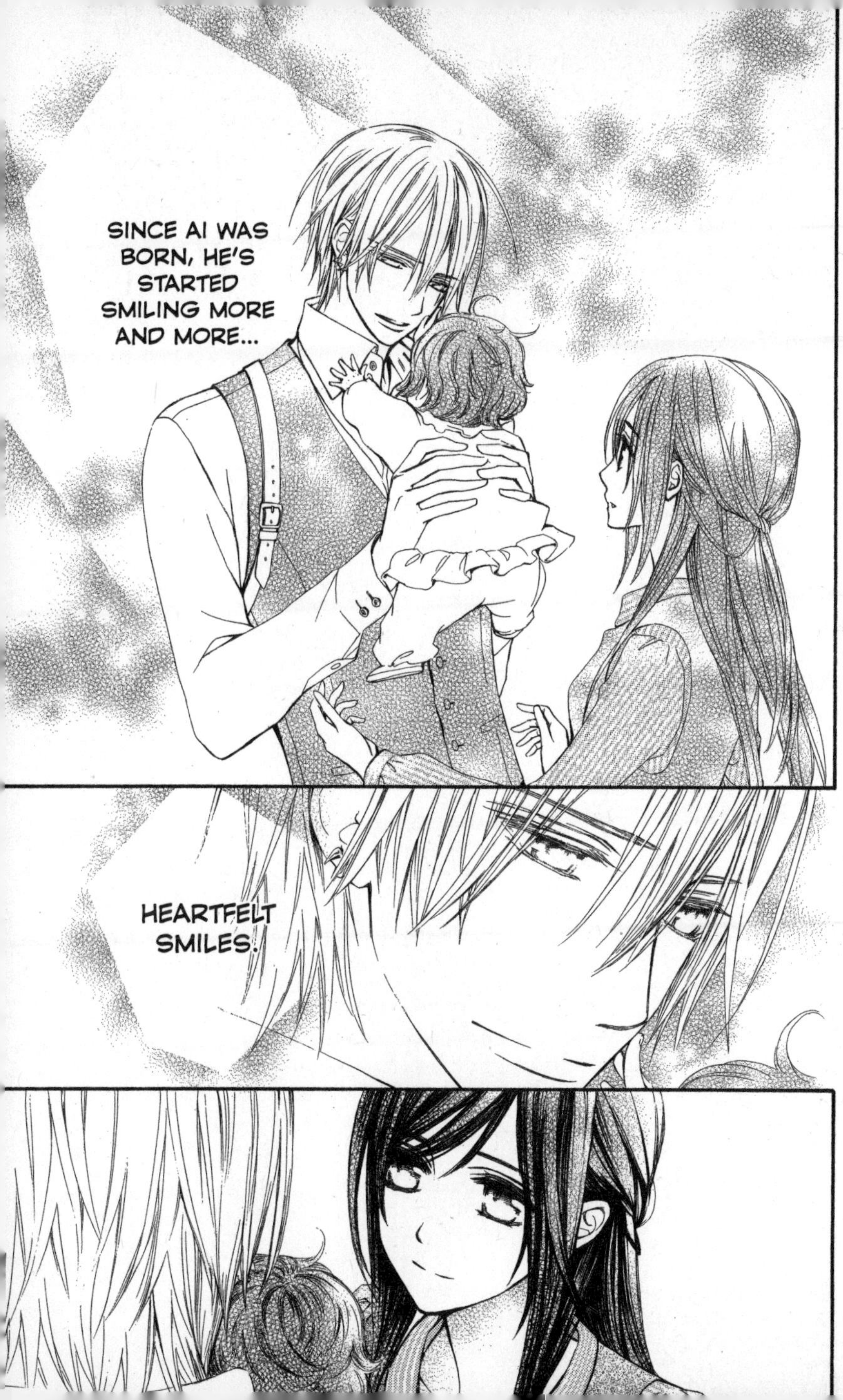
SINCE AI WAS BORN, HE'S STARTED SMILING MORE AND MORE...
HEARTFELT SMILES.

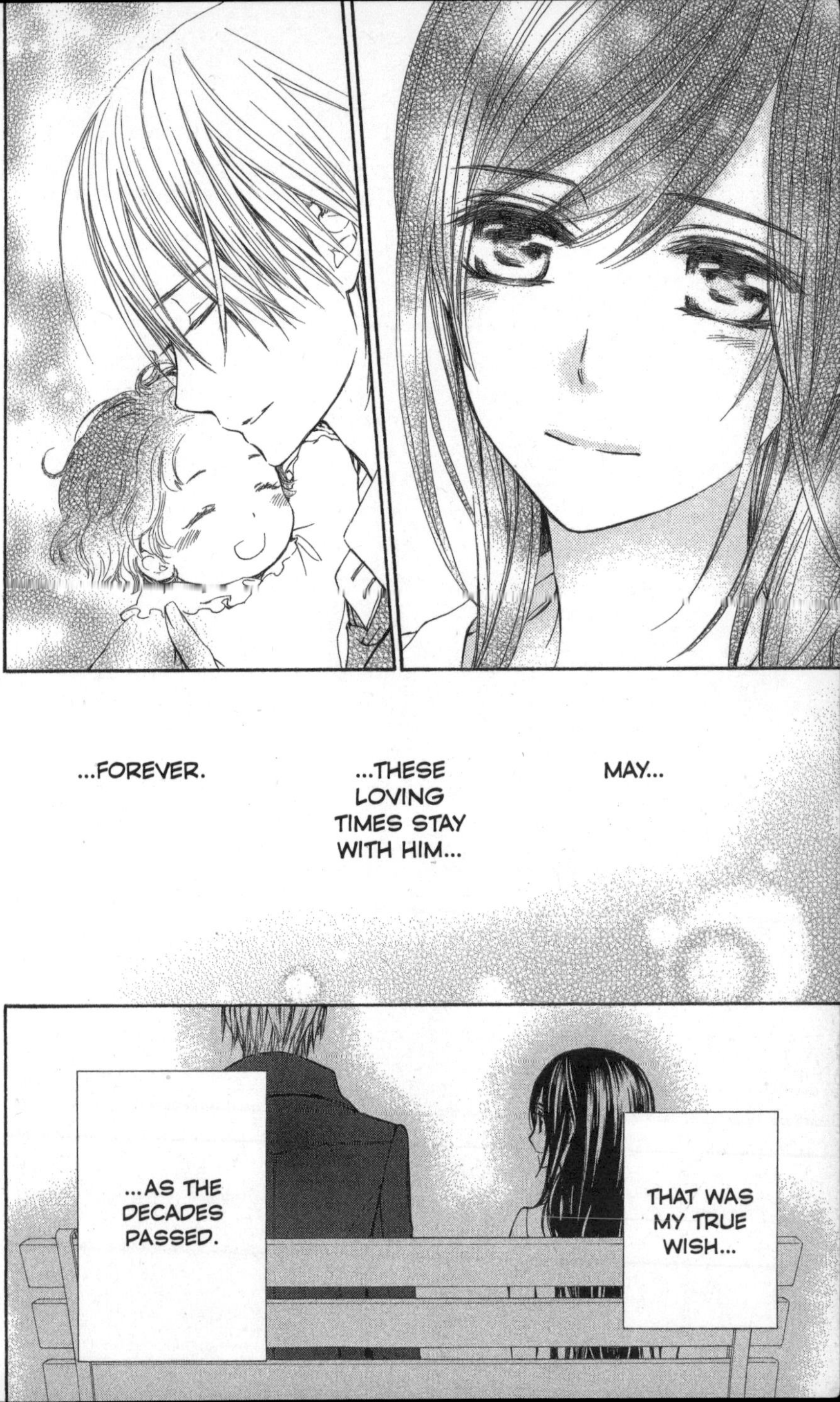
MAY...
...THESE LOVING TIMES STAY WITH HIM...
...FOREVER.
THAT WAS MY TRUE WISH...
...AS THE DECADES PASSED.

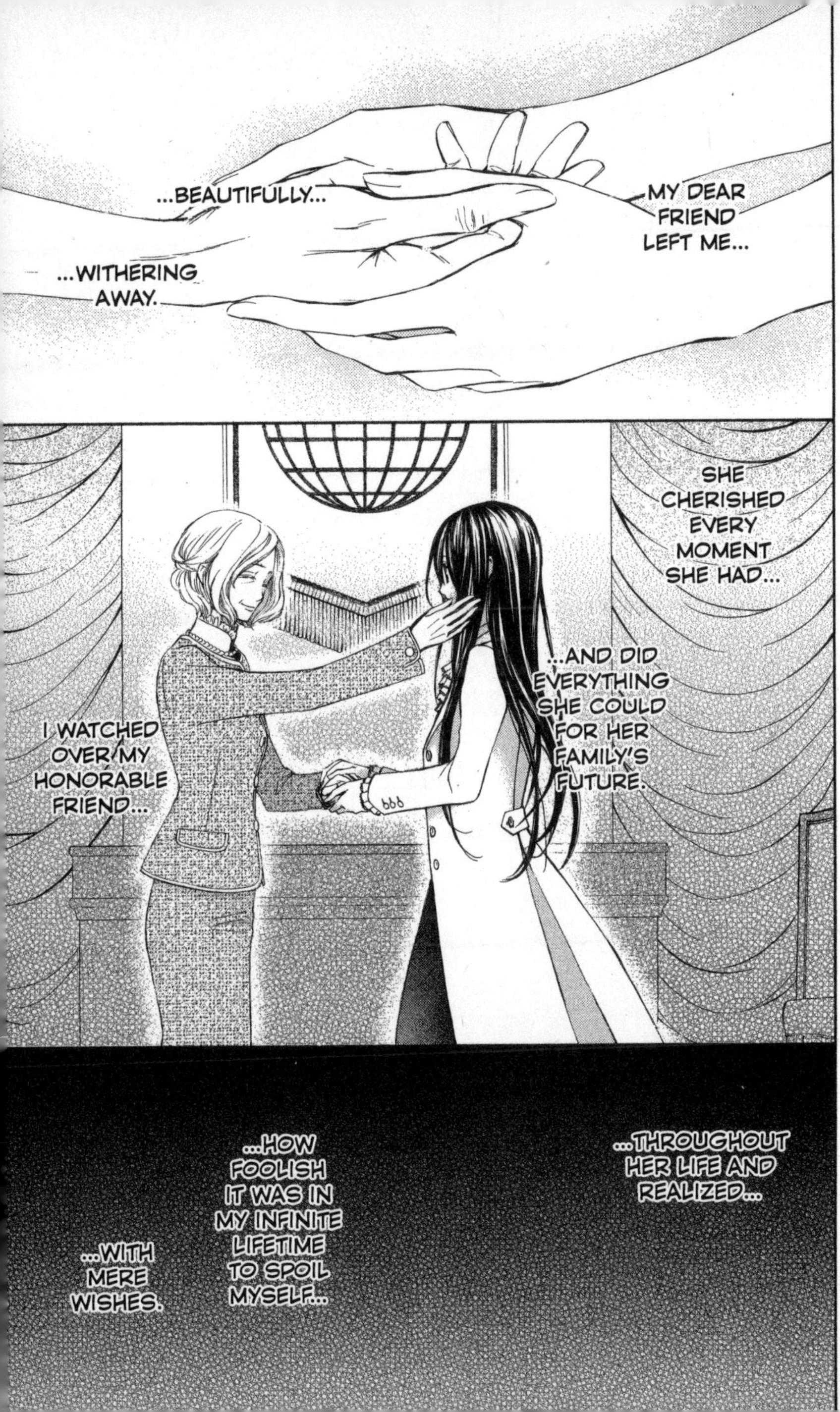
MY DEAR FRIEND LEFT ME...
...BEAUTIFULLY...
...WITHERING AWAY.
SHE CHERISHED EVERY MOMENT SHE HAD...
...AND DID EVERYTHING SHE COULD FOR HER FAMILY'S FUTURE.
I WATCHED OVER MY HONORABLE FRIEND...
...THROUGHOUT HER LIFE AND REALIZED...
...HOW FOOLISH IT WAS IN MY INFINITE LIFETIME TO SPOIL MYSELF...
...WITH MERE WISHES.

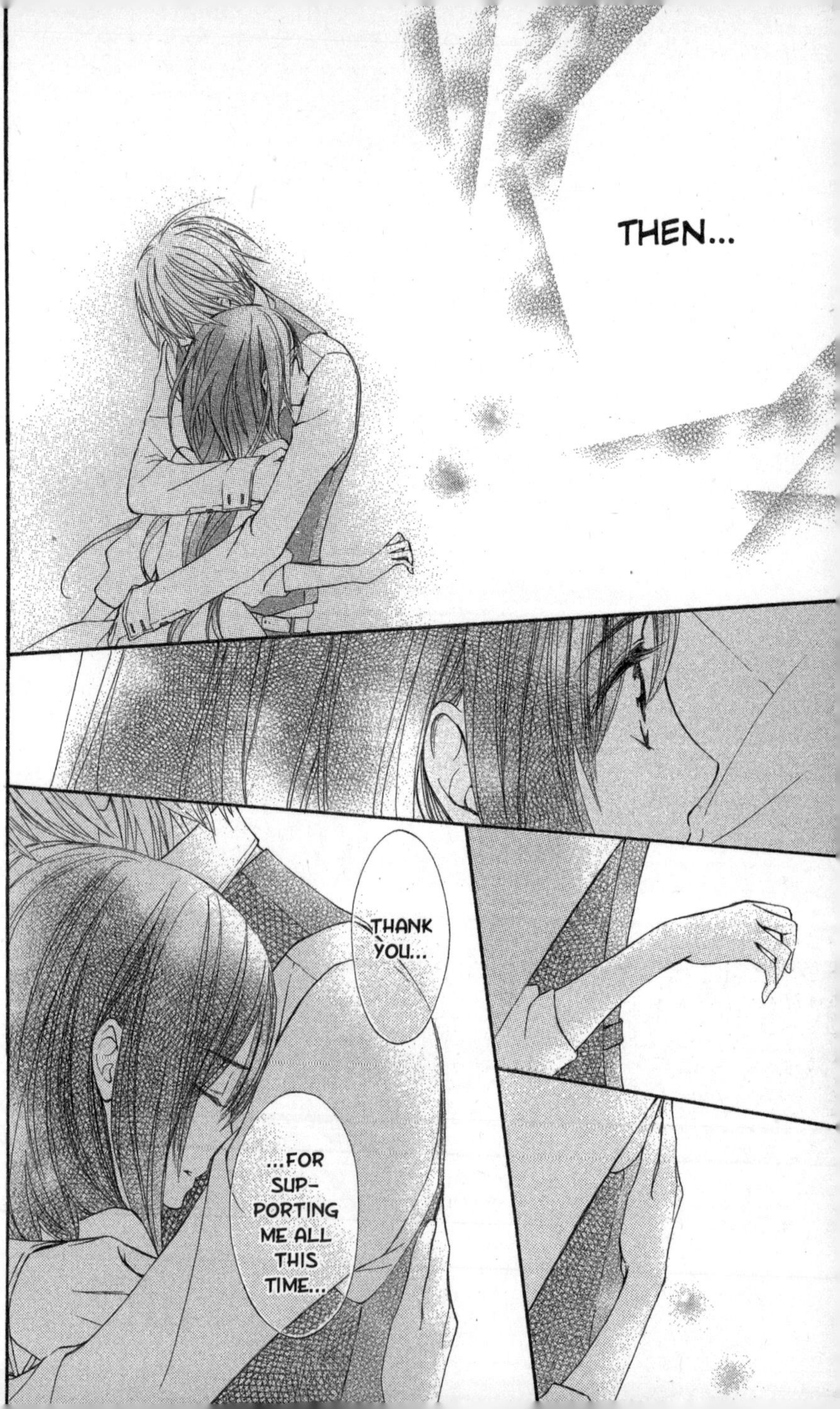
THEN...
THANK YOU...
...FOR SUPPORTING ME ALL THIS TIME...

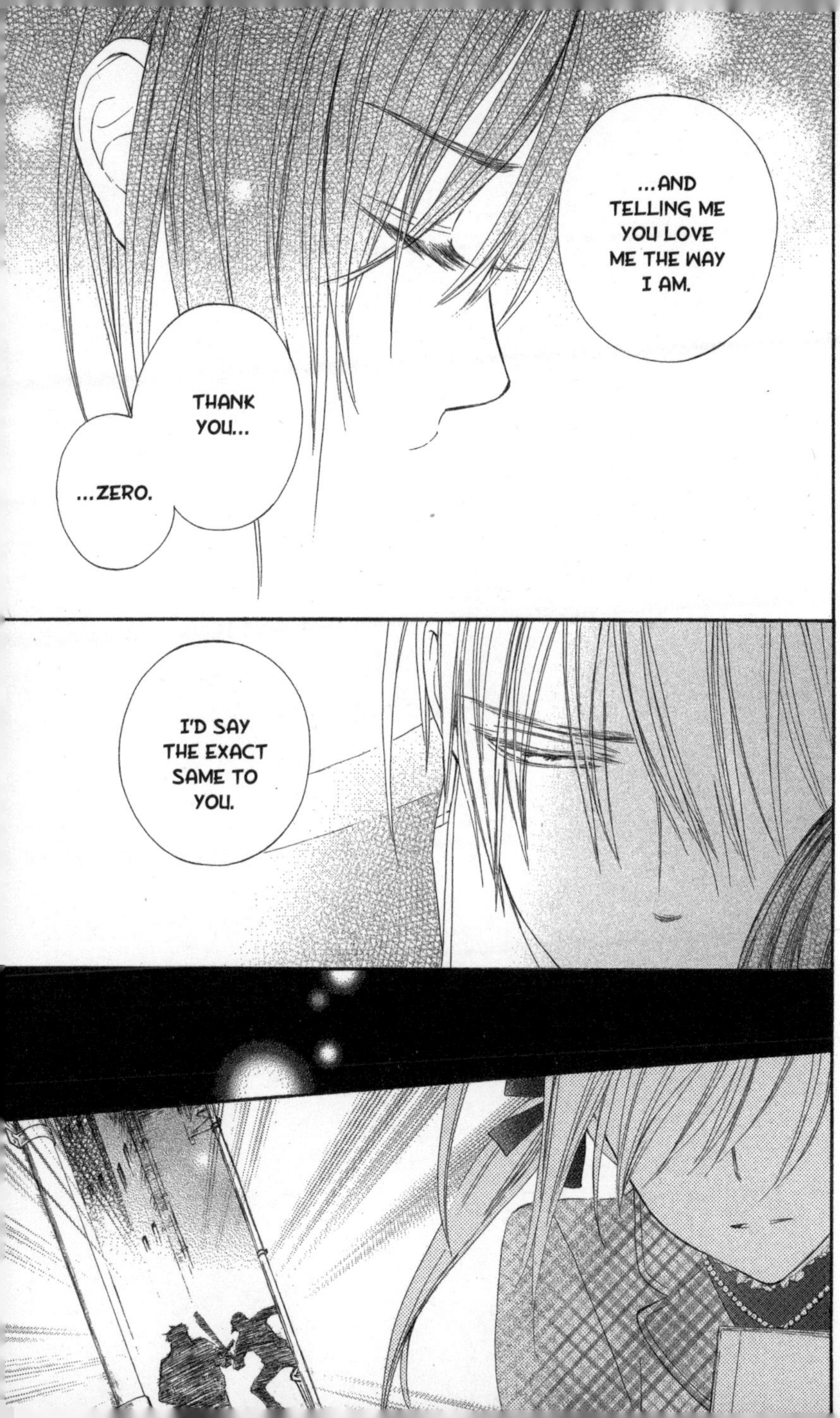
...AND TELLING ME YOU LOVE ME THE WAY I AM.
THANK YOU...
...ZERO.
I'D SAY THE EXACT SAME TO YOU.

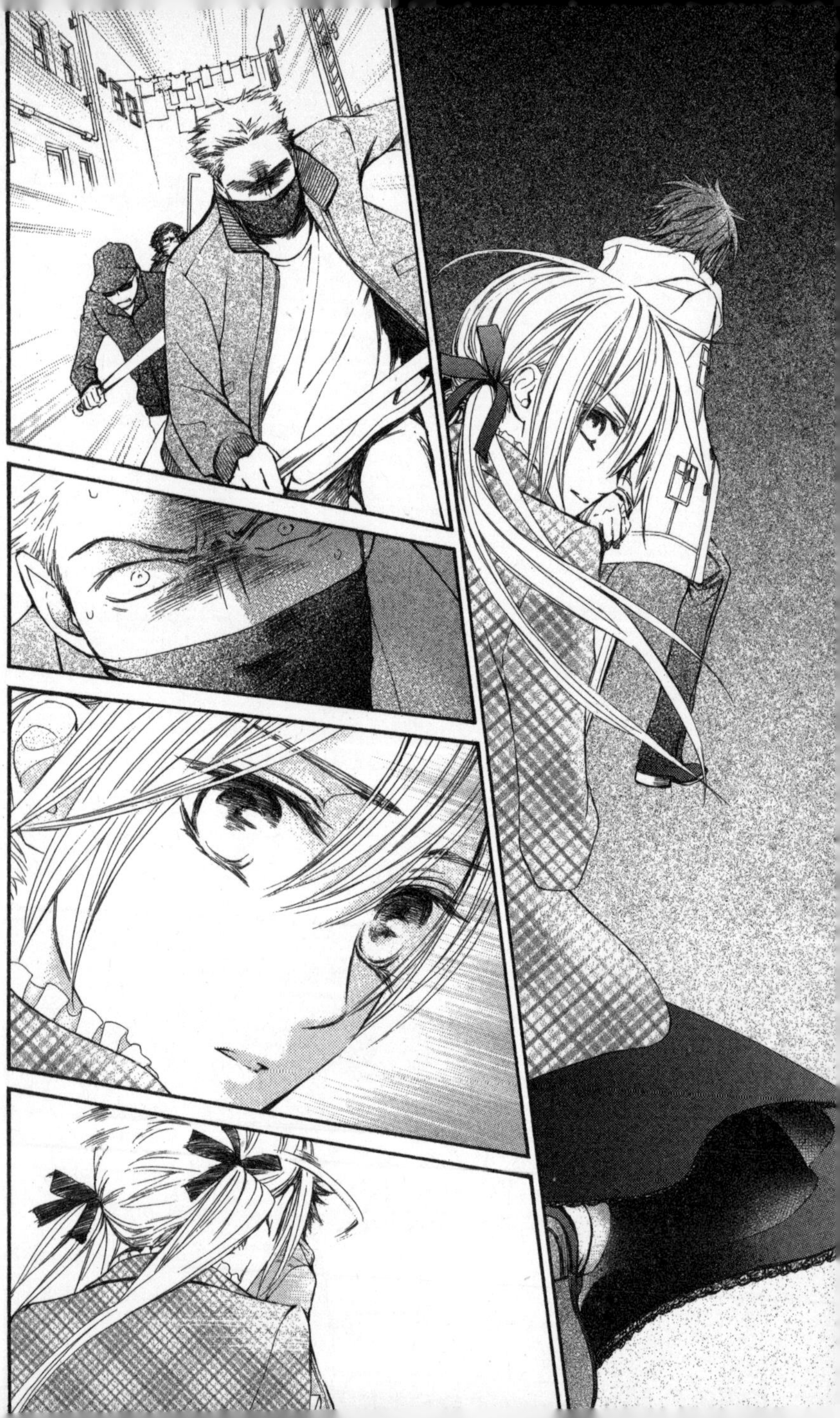

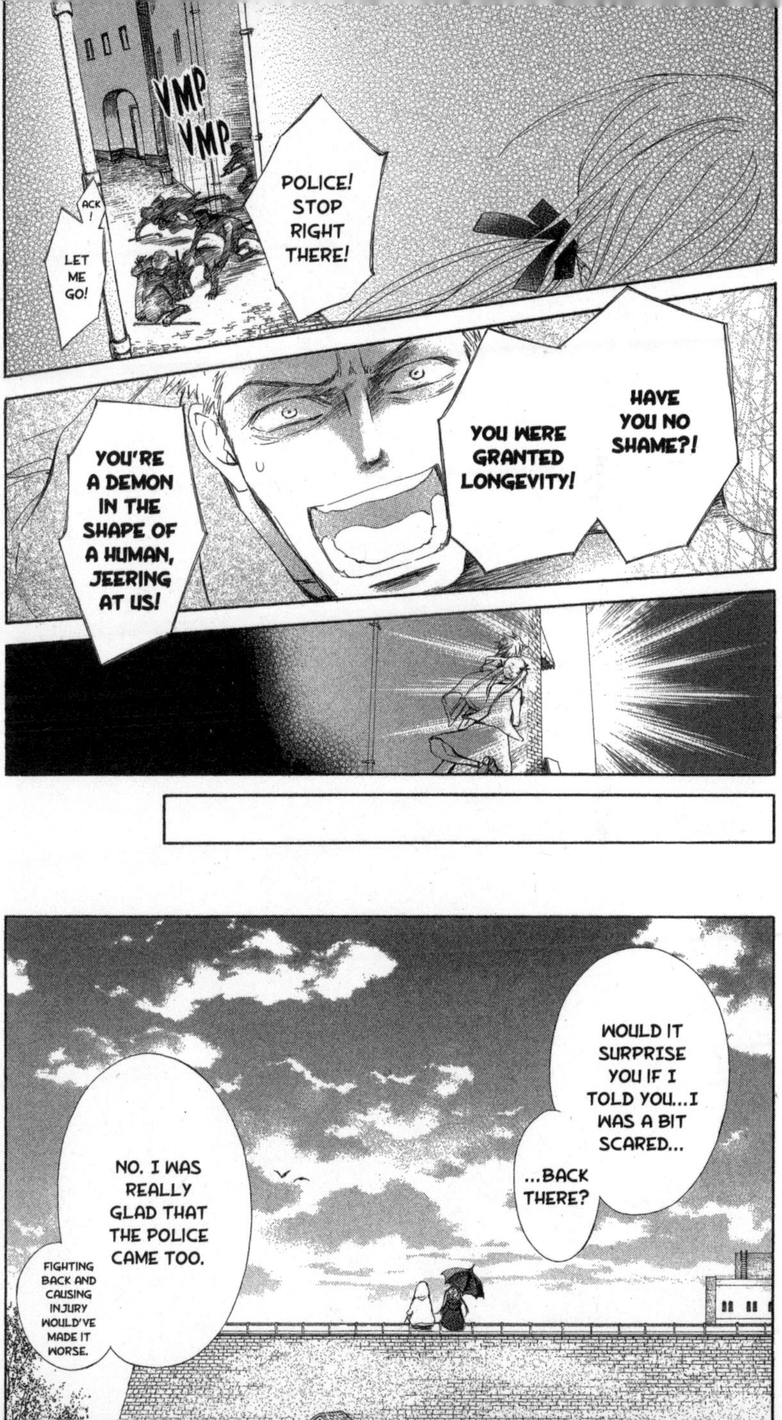
POLICE! STOP RIGHT THERE!
VMP VMP
ACK!
LET ME GO!
HAVE YOU NO SHAME?!
YOU WERE GRANTED LONGEVITY!
YOU'RE A DEMON IN THE SHAPE OF A HUMAN, JEERING AT US!
WOULD IT SURPRISE YOU IF I TOLD YOU...I WAS A BIT SCARED...
...BACK THERE?
NO. I WAS REALLY GLAD THAT THE POLICE CAME TOO.
FIGHTING BACK AND CAUSING INJURY WOULD'VE MADE IT WORSE.

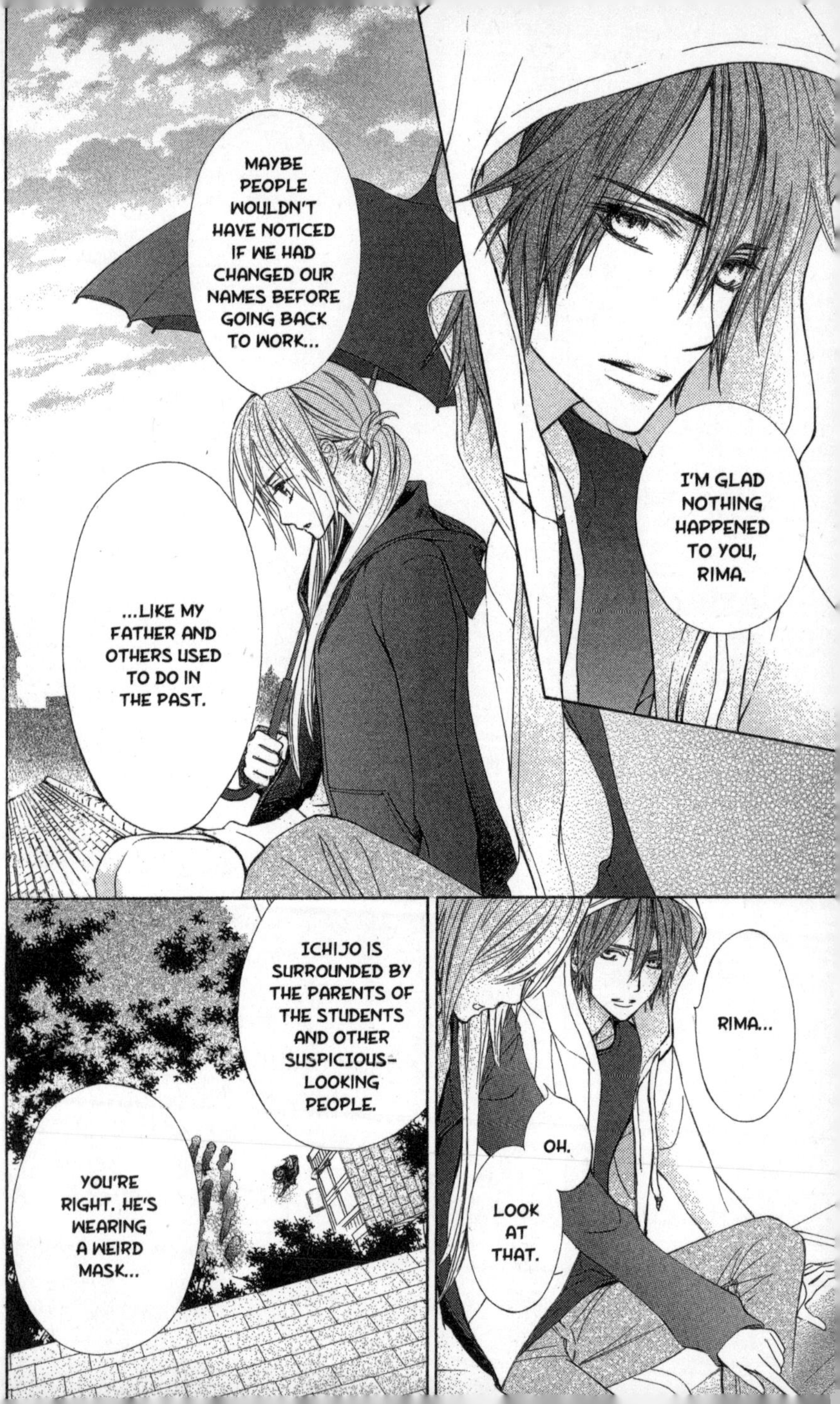
I'M GLAD NOTHING HAPPENED TO YOU, RIMA.
MAYBE PEOPLE WOULDN'T HAVE NOTICED IF WE HAD CHANGED OUR NAMES BEFORE GOING BACK TO WORK...
...LIKE MY FATHER AND OTHERS USED TO DO IN THE PAST.
RIMA...
OH.
LOOK AT THAT.
ICHIJO IS SURROUNDED BY THE PARENTS OF THE STUDENTS AND OTHER SUSPICIOUS-LOOKING PEOPLE.
YOU'RE RIGHT. HE'S WEARING A WEIRD MASK...

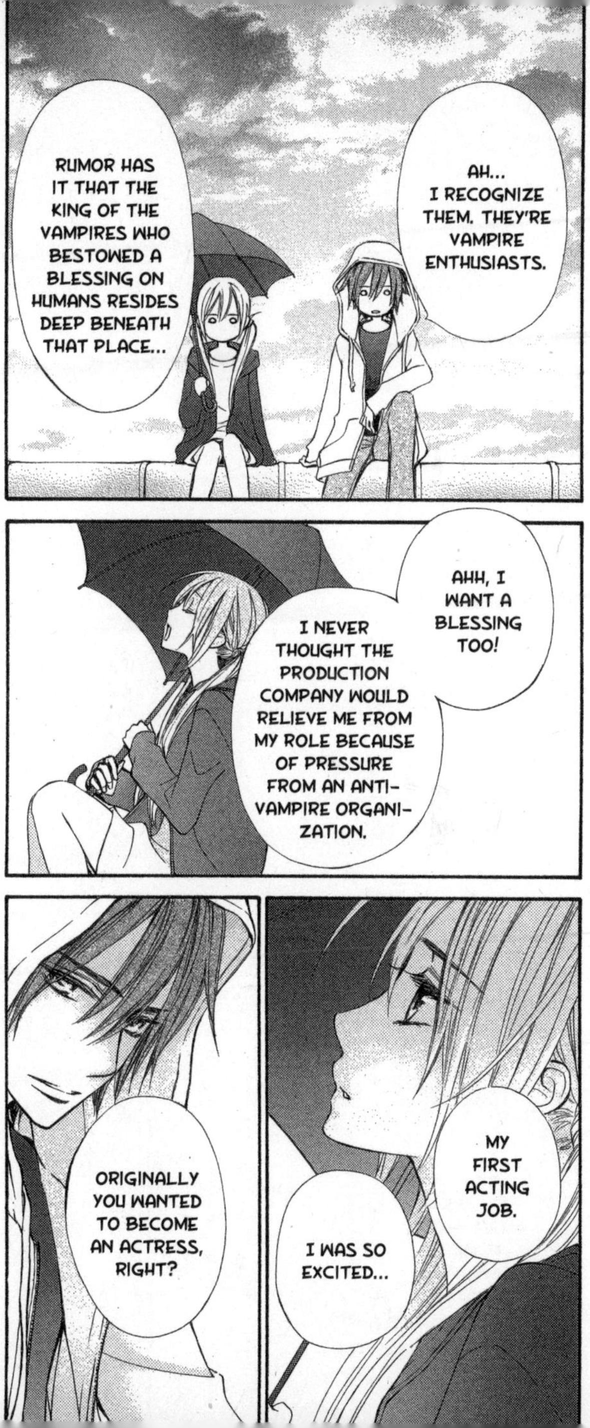
AH... I RECOGNIZE THEM. THEY'RE VAMPIRE ENTHUSIASTS.
RUMOR HAS IT THAT THE KING OF THE VAMPIRES WHO BESTOWED A BLESSING ON HUMANS RESIDES DEEP BENEATH THAT PLACE...
AHH, I WANT A BLESSING TOO!
I NEVER THOUGHT THE PRODUCTION COMPANY WOULD RELIEVE ME FROM MY ROLE BECAUSE OF PRESSURE FROM AN ANTI-VAMPIRE ORGANI-ZATION.
MY FIRST ACTING JOB.
I WAS SO EXCITED...
ORIGINALLY YOU WANTED TO BECOME AN ACTRESS, RIGHT?

—1—

Vampire Knight: Memories volume 3

Thank you very much for picking up this volume.

As usual, my drawing skills are not good enough to draw what I truly envision, so I'm continuing to struggle as I work on this. But I'm so happy if you're enjoying it!

The volumes are published slowly, at a pace of one per year. We've finally reached volume 3. Now that I read it over, it looks like I am paving the way for the next volume... I'll work on volume 4 with all my heart... ☺

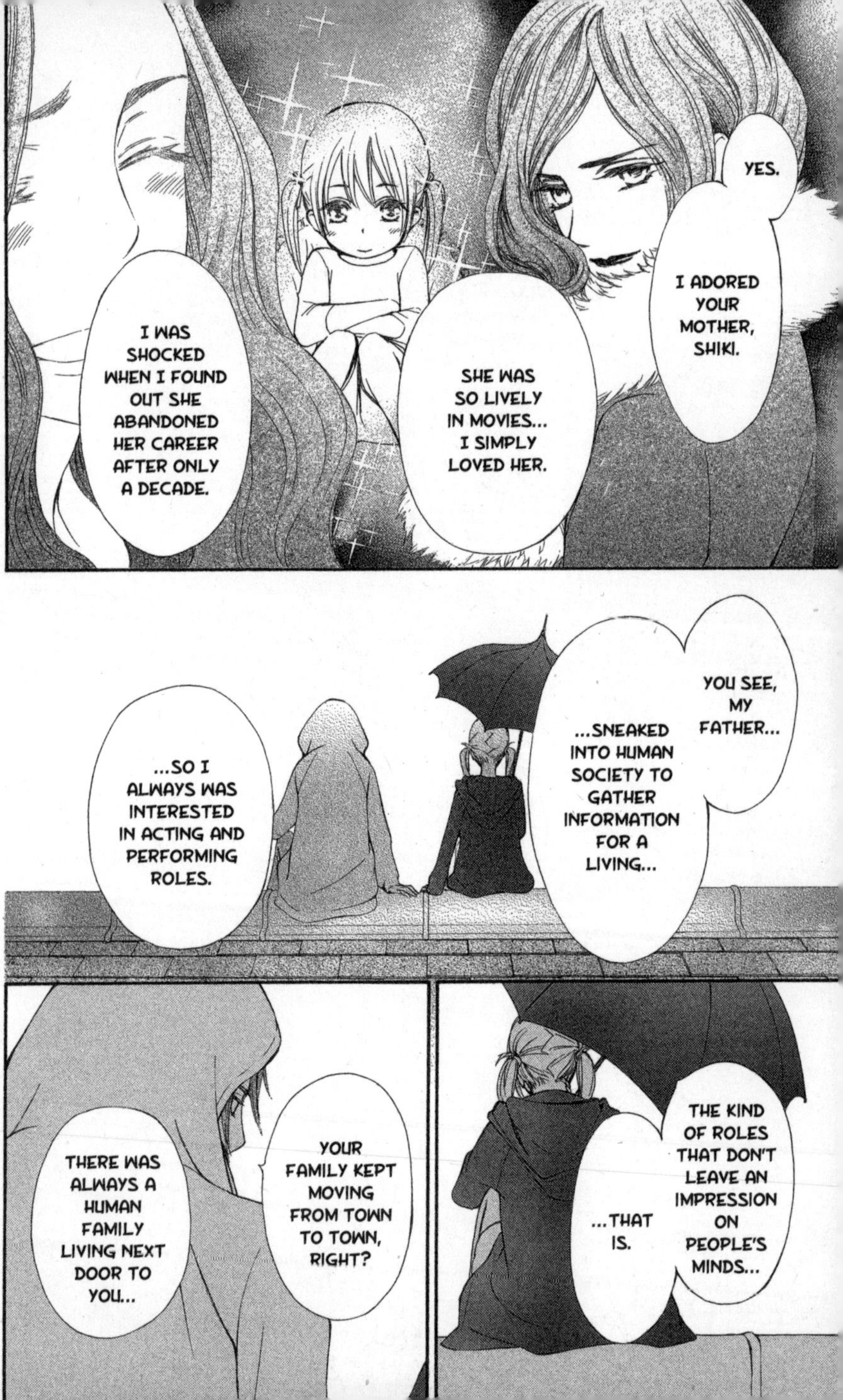
YES.
I ADORED YOUR MOTHER, SHIKI.
SHE WAS SO LIVELY IN MOVIES... I SIMPLY LOVED HER.
I WAS SHOCKED WHEN I FOUND OUT SHE ABANDONED HER CAREER AFTER ONLY A DECADE.
YOU SEE, MY FATHER...
...SNEAKED INTO HUMAN SOCIETY TO GATHER INFORMATION FOR A LIVING...
...SO I ALWAYS WAS INTERESTED IN ACTING AND PERFORMING ROLES.
THE KIND OF ROLES THAT DON'T LEAVE AN IMPRESSION ON PEOPLE'S MINDS...
...THAT IS.
YOUR FAMILY KEPT MOVING FROM TOWN TO TOWN, RIGHT?
THERE WAS ALWAYS A HUMAN FAMILY LIVING NEXT DOOR TO YOU...

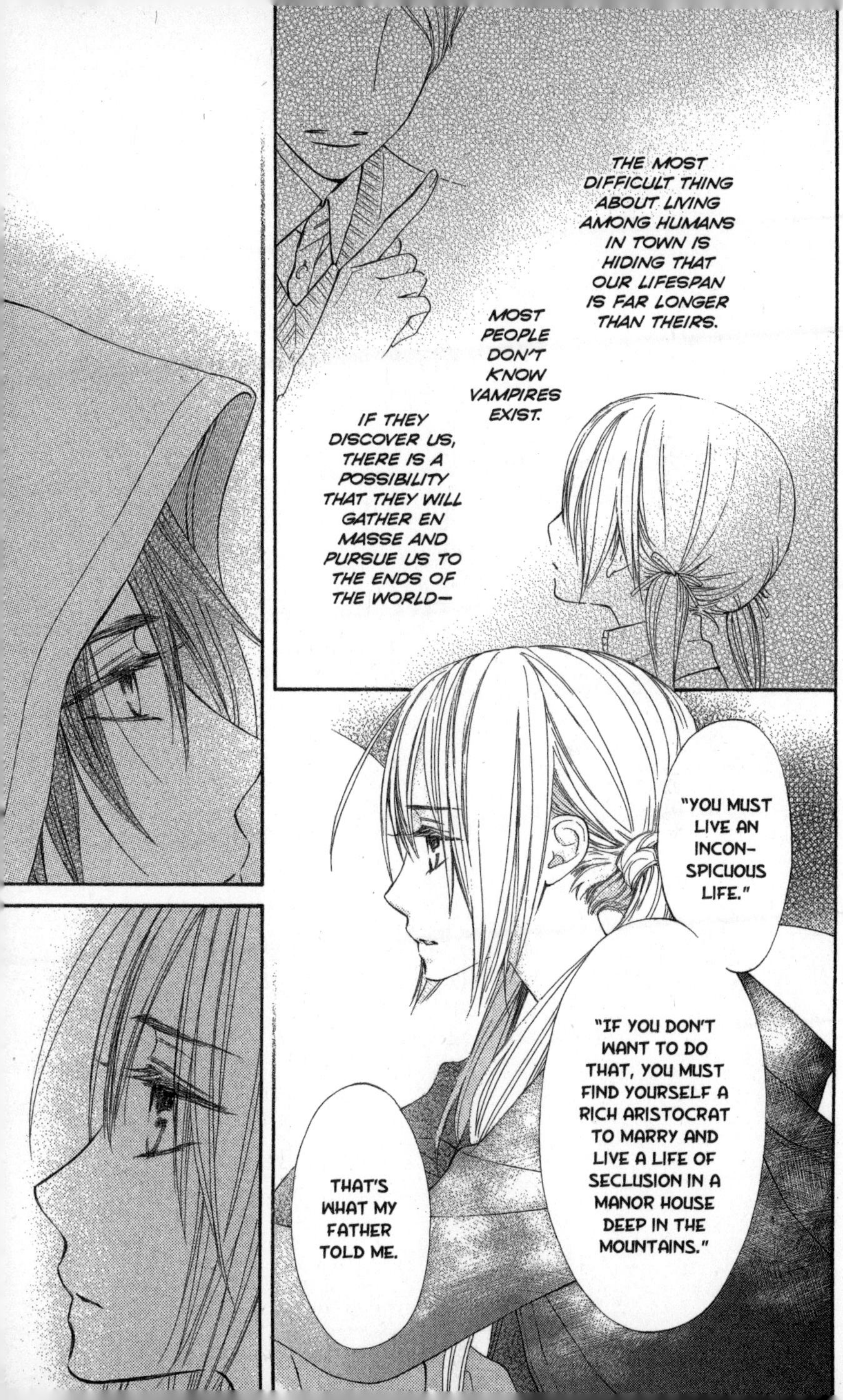
THE MOST DIFFICULT THING ABOUT LIVING AMONG HUMANS IN TOWN IS HIDING THAT OUR LIFESPAN IS FAR LONGER THAN THEIRS.
MOST PEOPLE DON'T KNOW VAMPIRES EXIST.
IF THEY DISCOVER US, THERE IS A POSSIBILITY THAT THEY WILL GATHER EN MASSE AND PURSUE US TO THE ENDS OF THE WORLD—
"YOU MUST LIVE AN INCON-SPICUOUS LIFE."
"IF YOU DON'T WANT TO DO THAT, YOU MUST FIND YOURSELF A RICH ARISTOCRAT TO MARRY AND LIVE A LIFE OF SECLUSION IN A MANOR HOUSE DEEP IN THE MOUNTAINS."
THAT'S WHAT MY FATHER TOLD ME.

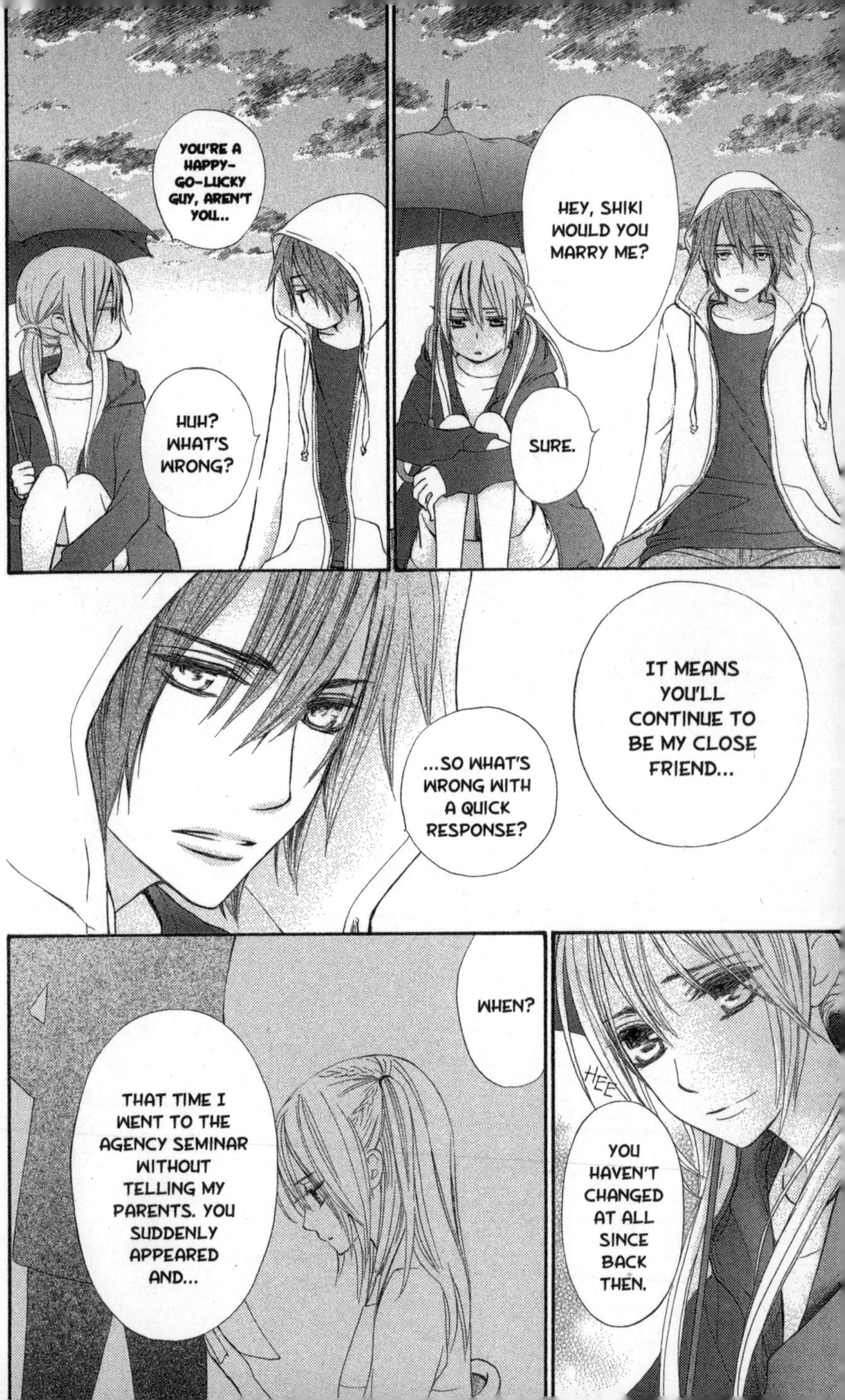
HEY, SHIKI WOULD YOU MARRY ME?
SURE.
YOU'RE A HAPPY-GO-LUCKY GUY, AREN'T YOU...
HUH? WHAT'S WRONG?
IT MEANS YOU'LL CONTINUE TO BE MY CLOSE FRIEND...
...SO WHAT'S WRONG WITH A QUICK RESPONSE?
HEE
YOU HAVEN'T CHANGED AT ALL SINCE BACK THEN.
WHEN?
THAT TIME I WENT TO THE AGENCY SEMINAR WITHOUT TELLING MY PARENTS. YOU SUDDENLY APPEARED AND...

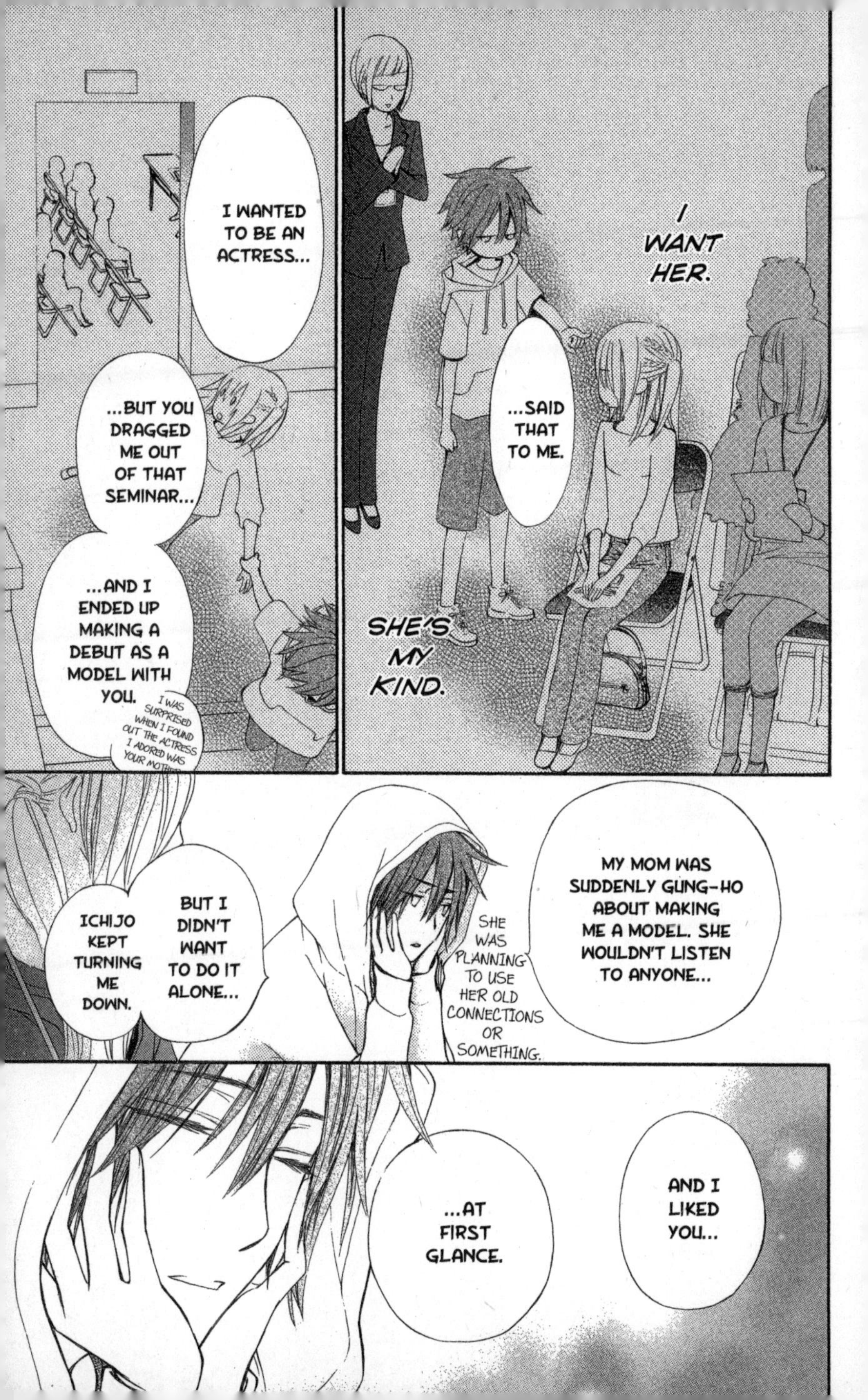
I WANT HER.
...SAID THAT TO ME.
SHE'S MY KIND.
I WANTED TO BE AN ACTRESS...
...BUT YOU DRAGGED ME OUT OF THAT SEMINAR...
...AND I ENDED UP MAKING A DEBUT AS A MODEL WITH YOU.
I WAS SURPRISED WHEN I FOUND OUT THE ACTRESS I ADORED WAS YOUR MOTHE
MY MOM WAS SUDDENLY GUNG-HO ABOUT MAKING ME A MODEL. SHE WOULDN'T LISTEN TO ANYONE...
SHE WAS PLANNING TO USE HER OLD CONNECTIONS OR SOMETHING.
BUT I DIDN'T WANT TO DO IT ALONE...
ICHIJO KEPT TURNING ME DOWN.
AND I LIKED YOU...
...AT FIRST GLANCE.

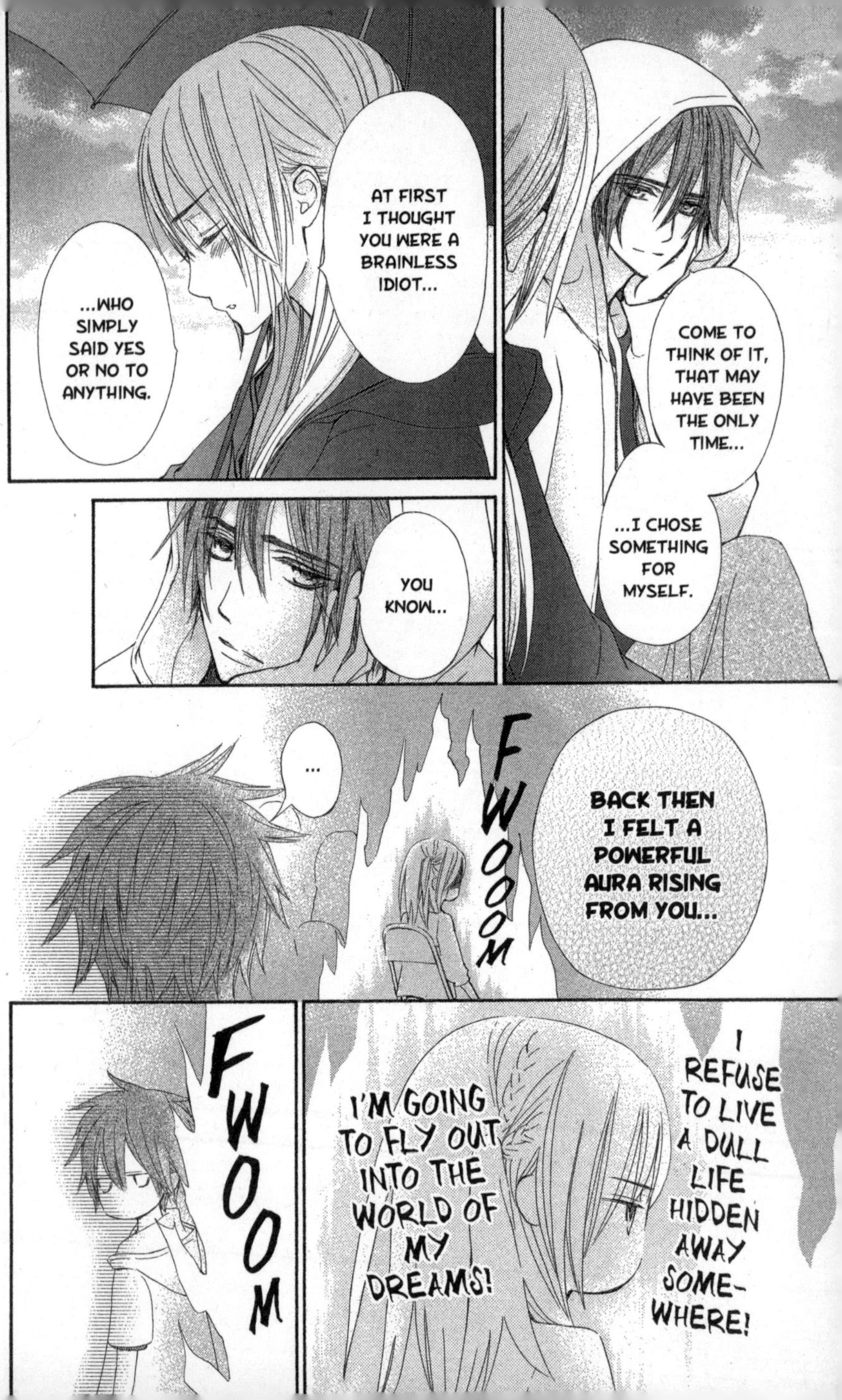
COME TO THINK OF IT, THAT MAY HAVE BEEN THE ONLY TIME...
...I CHOSE SOMETHING FOR MYSELF.
AT FIRST I THOUGHT YOU WERE A BRAINLESS IDIOT...
...WHO SIMPLY SAID YES OR NO TO ANYTHING.
YOU KNOW...
BACK THEN I FELT A POWERFUL AURA RISING FROM YOU...
FWOOOM
...
I REFUSE TO LIVE A DULL LIFE HIDDEN AWAY SOME-WHERE!
I'M GOING TO FLY OUT INTO THE WORLD OF MY DREAMS!
FWOOM

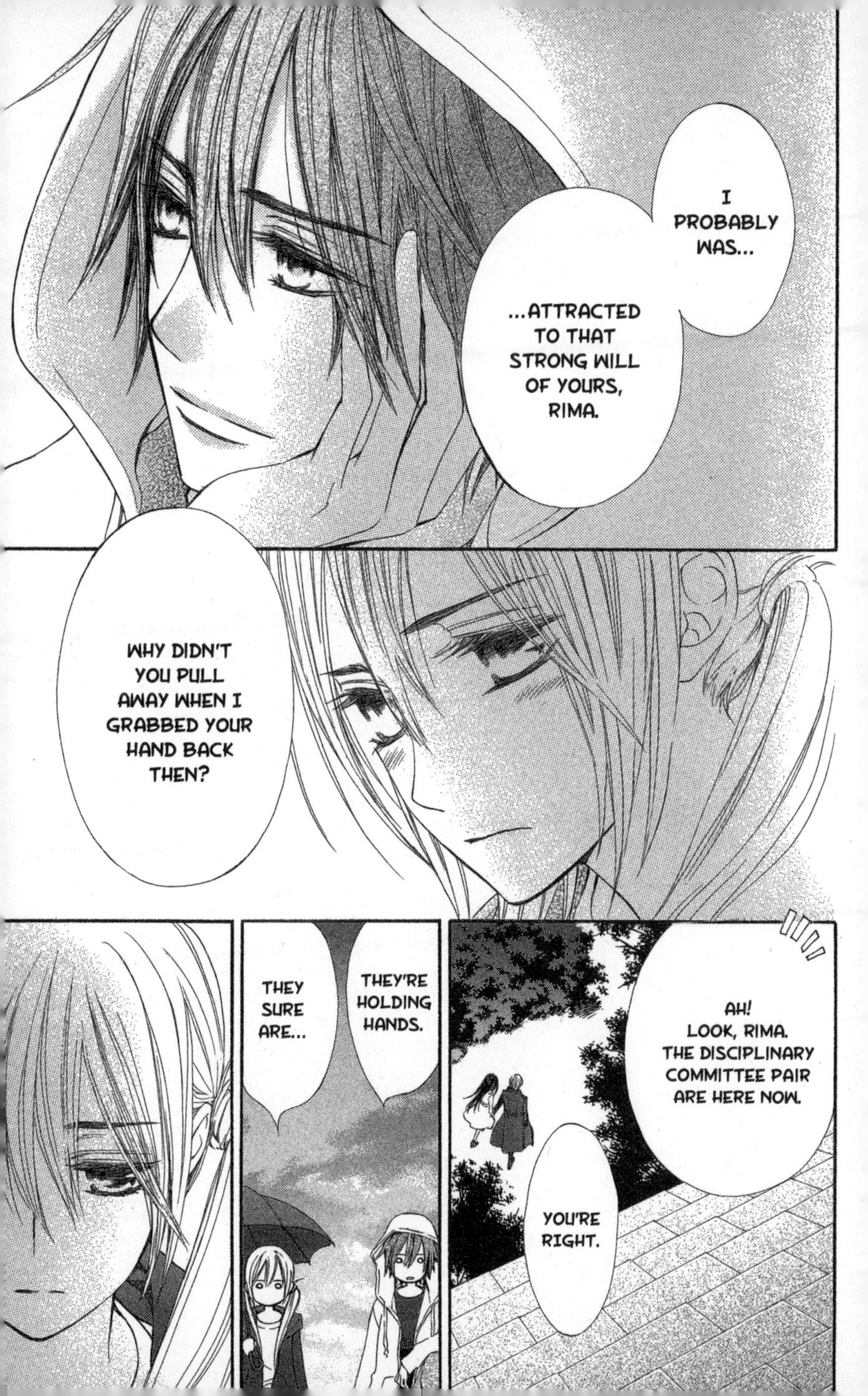
I PROBABLY WAS...
...ATTRACTED TO THAT STRONG WILL OF YOURS, RIMA.
WHY DIDN'T YOU PULL AWAY WHEN I GRABBED YOUR HAND BACK THEN?
AH! LOOK, RIMA. THE DISCIPLINARY COMMITTEE PAIR ARE HERE NOW.
YOU'RE RIGHT.
THEY'RE HOLDING HANDS.
THEY SURE ARE...

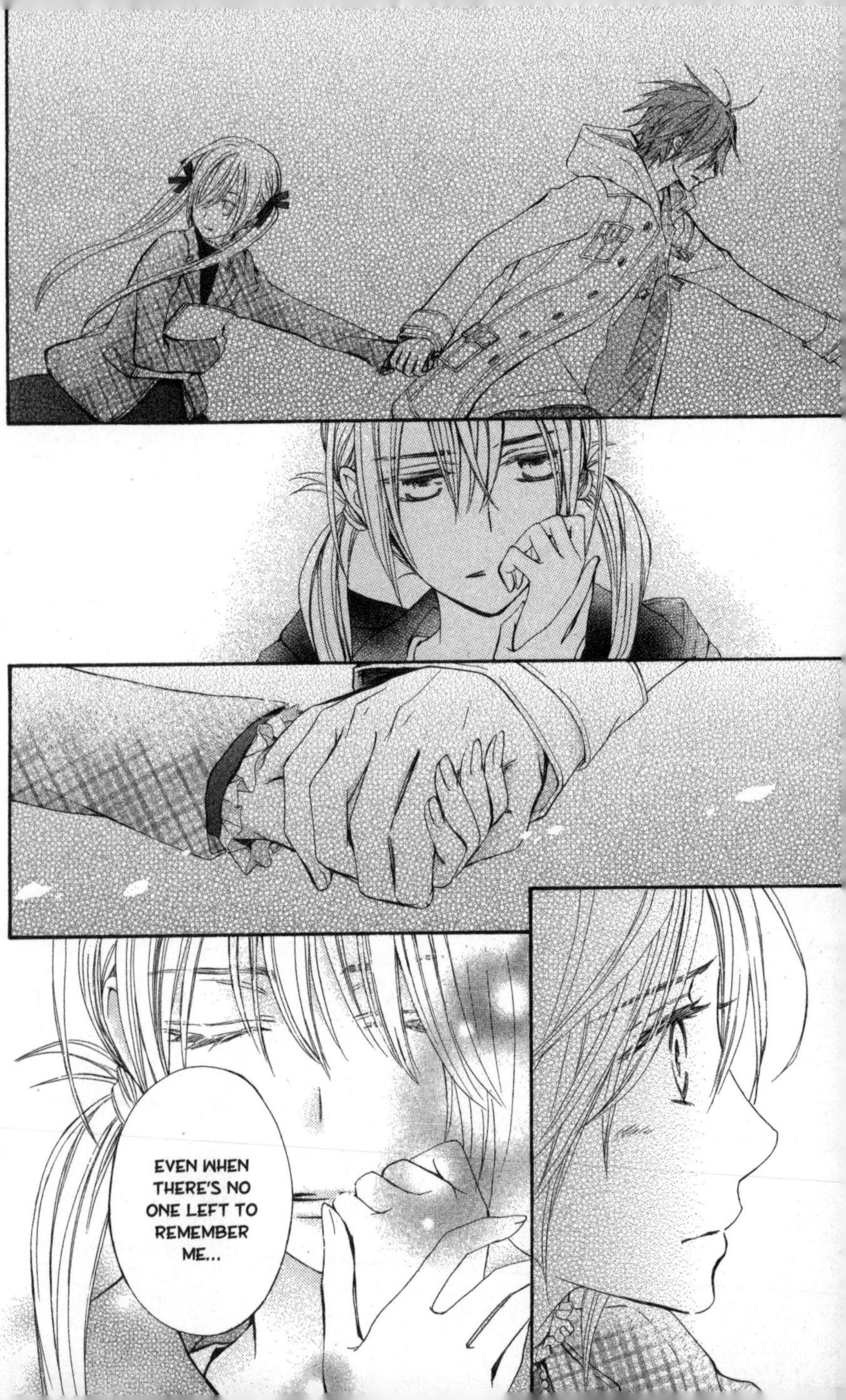
EVEN WHEN THERE'S NO ONE LEFT TO REMEMBER ME...

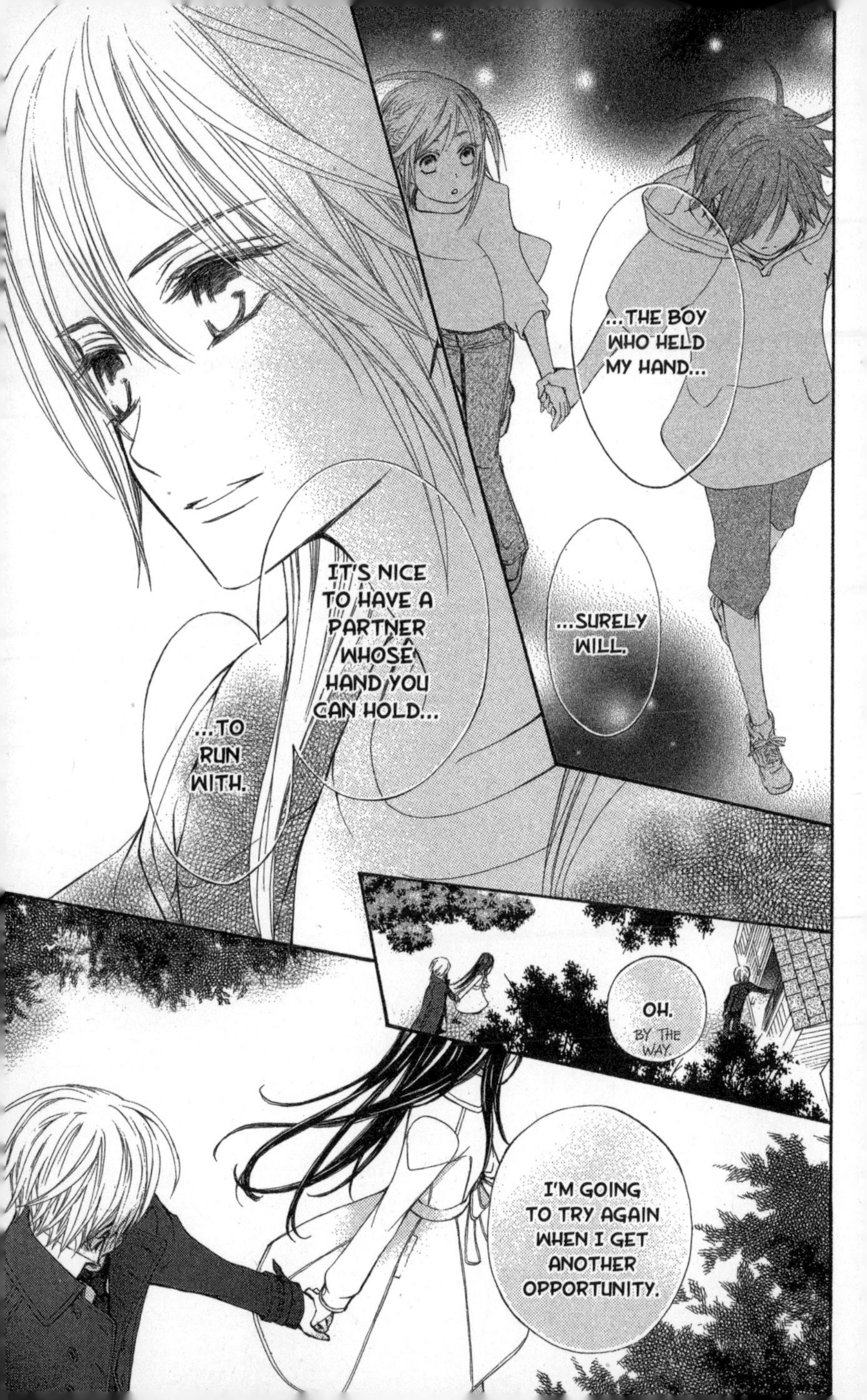
...THE BOY WHO HELD MY HAND...
...SURELY WILL.
IT'S NICE TO HAVE A PARTNER WHOSE HAND YOU CAN HOLD...
...TO RUN WITH.
OH.
BY THE WAY
I'M GOING TO TRY AGAIN WHEN I GET ANOTHER OPPORTUNITY.

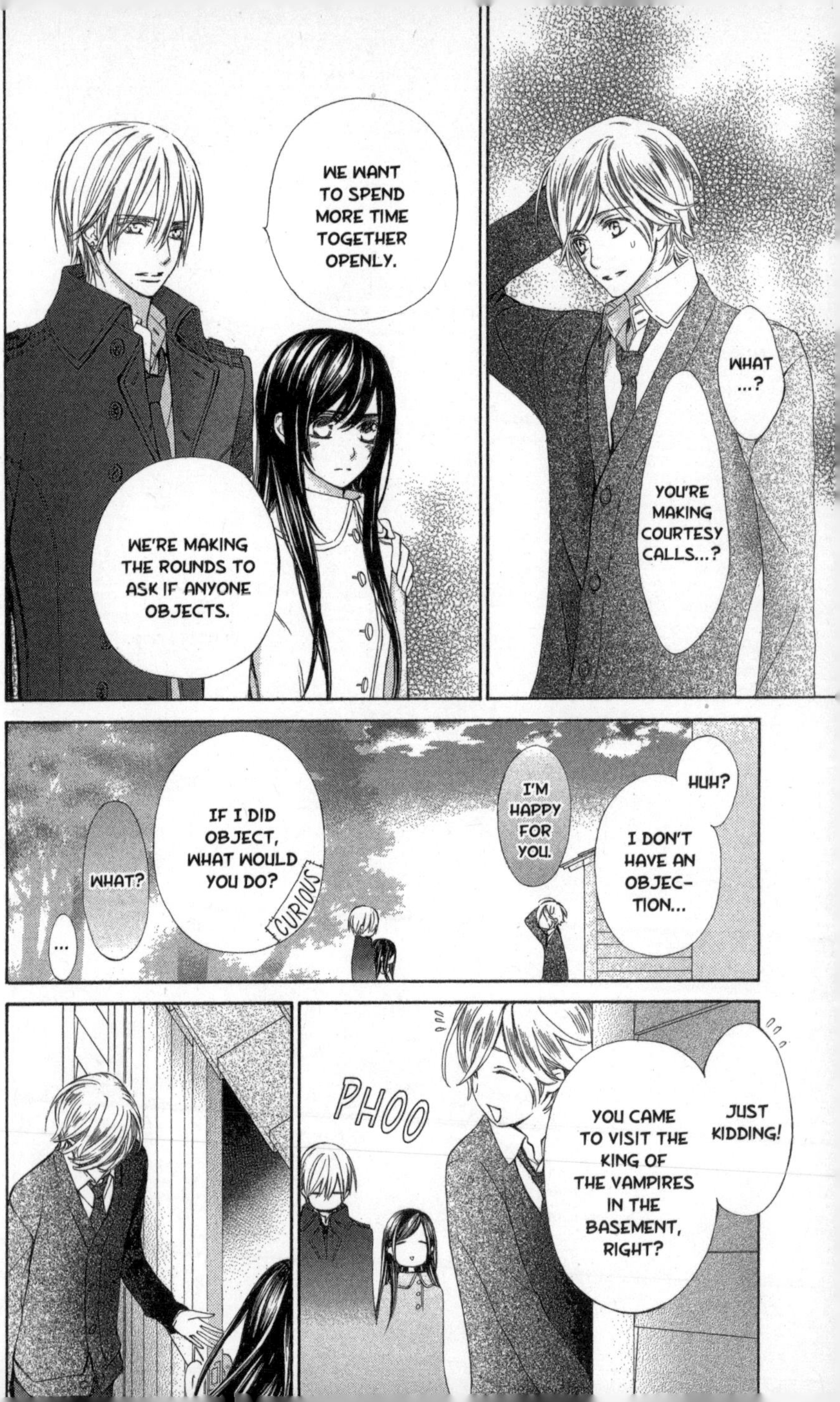
WHAT ...?
YOU'RE MAKING COURTESY CALLS...?
WE WANT TO SPEND MORE TIME TOGETHER OPENLY.
WE'RE MAKING THE ROUNDS TO ASK IF ANYONE OBJECTS.
HUH?
I DON'T HAVE AN OBJEC-TION...
I'M HAPPY FOR YOU.
IF I DID OBJECT, WHAT WOULD YOU DO?
CURIOUS
WHAT?
...
JUST KIDDING!
YOU CAME TO VISIT THE KING OF THE VAMPIRES IN THE BASEMENT, RIGHT?
PHOO

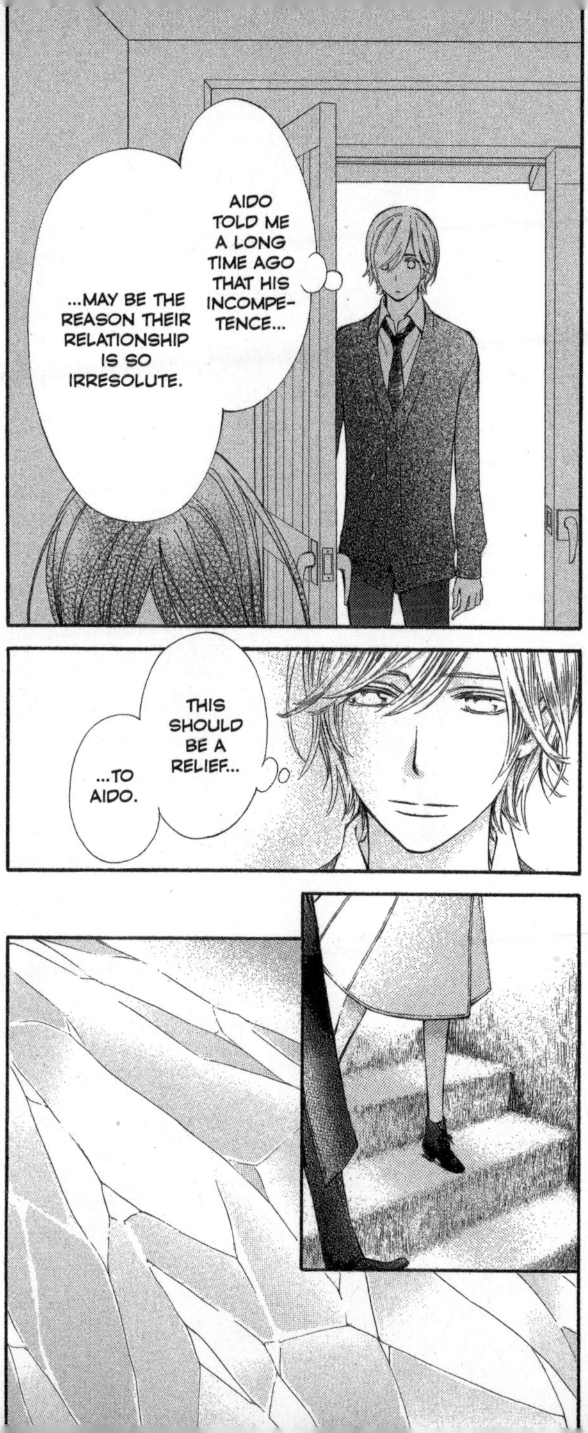
AIDO TOLD ME A LONG TIME AGO THAT HIS INCOMPE-TENCE...
...MAY BE THE REASON THEIR RELATIONSHIP IS SO IRRESOLUTE.
THIS SHOULD BE A RELIEF...
...TO AIDO.

— 2 —

Regarding volume 4...

I am grateful that there will be a drama CD version in Japan for the next volume. I am very fidgety about it...

And it's quite refreshing to find myself nervous. In the past I was just desperately trying to get through the immense work-load.

But my hope that it will be something everyone can enjoy is the same as before.

(As a matter of fact, I'm very excited and have stomach pain because I can afford to be fidgety about it...) (*laugh*)

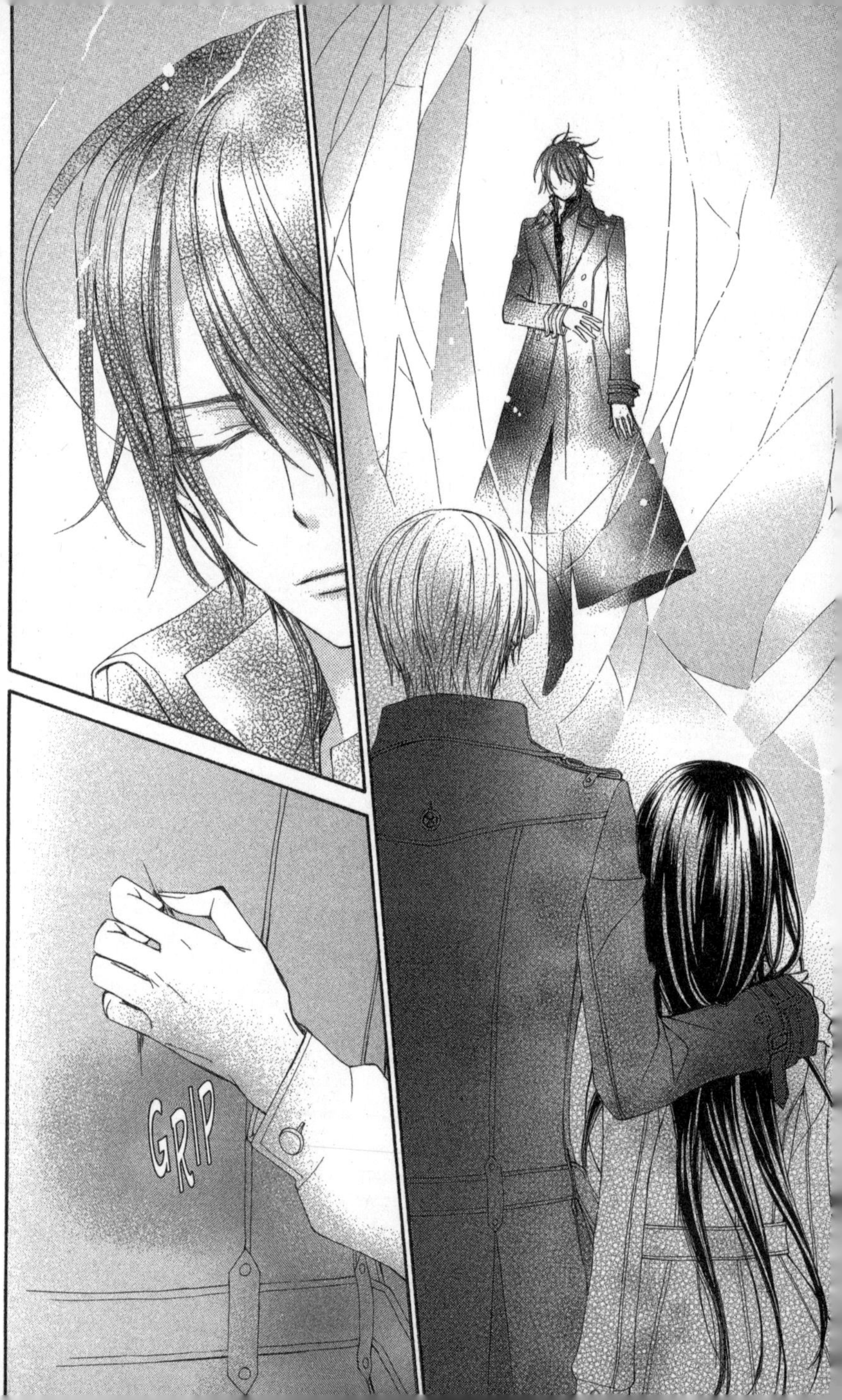
GRIP

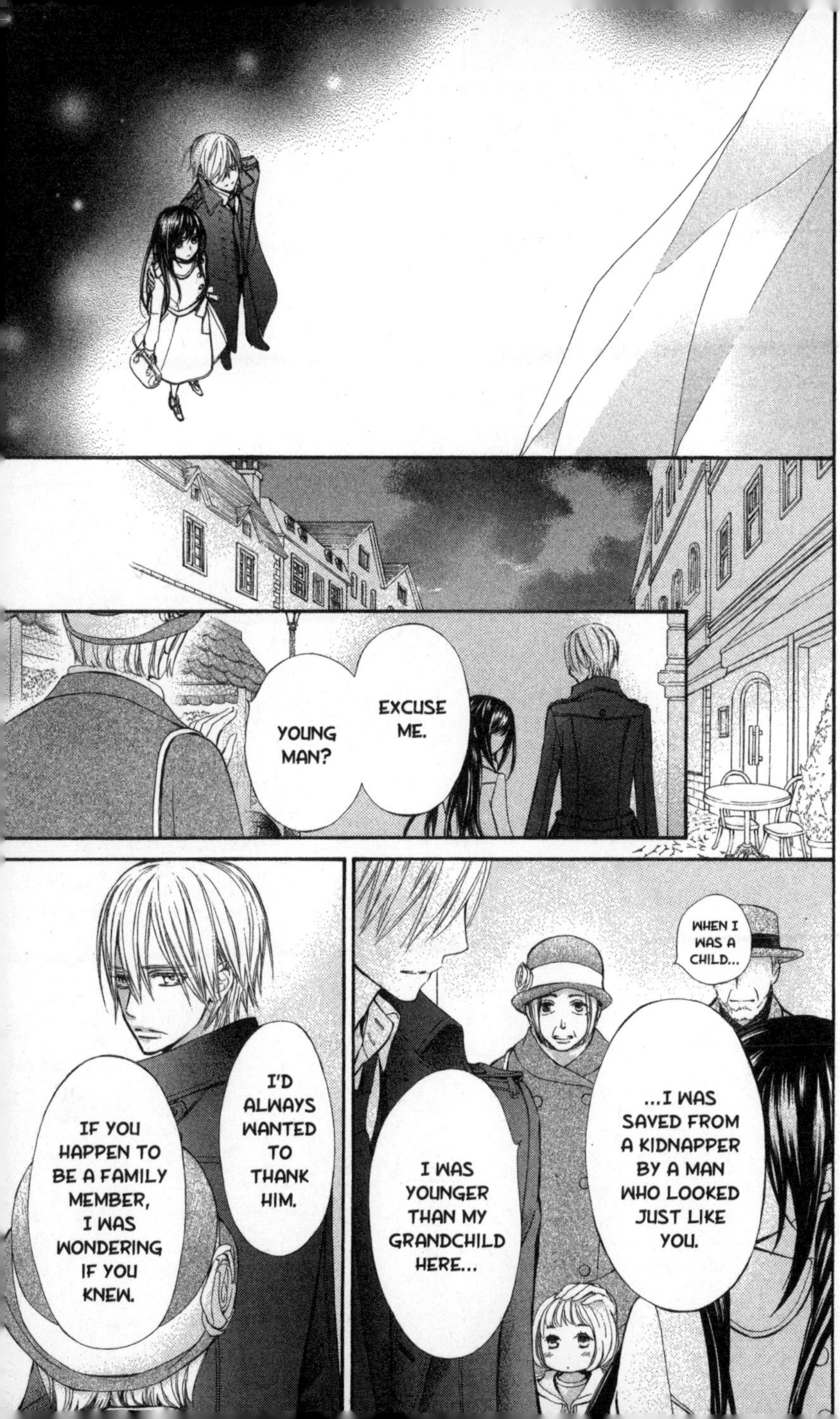
EXCUSE ME.
YOUNG MAN?
WHEN I WAS A CHILD...
...I WAS SAVED FROM A KIDNAPPER BY A MAN WHO LOOKED JUST LIKE YOU.
I WAS YOUNGER THAN MY GRANDCHILD HERE...
I'D ALWAYS WANTED TO THANK HIM.
IF YOU HAPPEN TO BE A FAMILY MEMBER, I WAS WONDERING IF YOU KNEW.

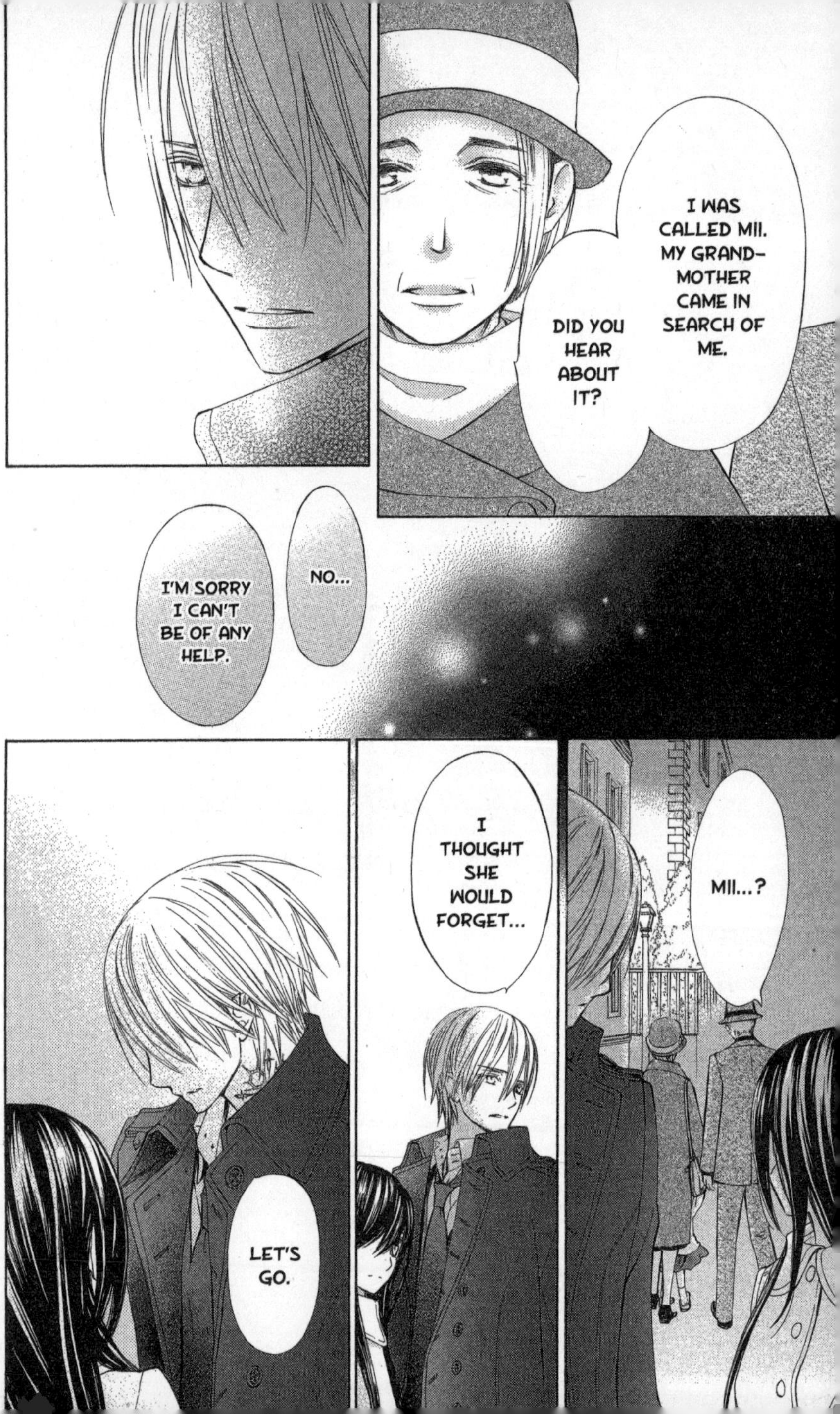
I WAS CALLED MII. MY GRAND-MOTHER CAME IN SEARCH OF ME.
DID YOU HEAR ABOUT IT?
NO...
I'M SORRY I CAN'T BE OF ANY HELP.
MII...?
I THOUGHT SHE WOULD FORGET...
LET'S GO.

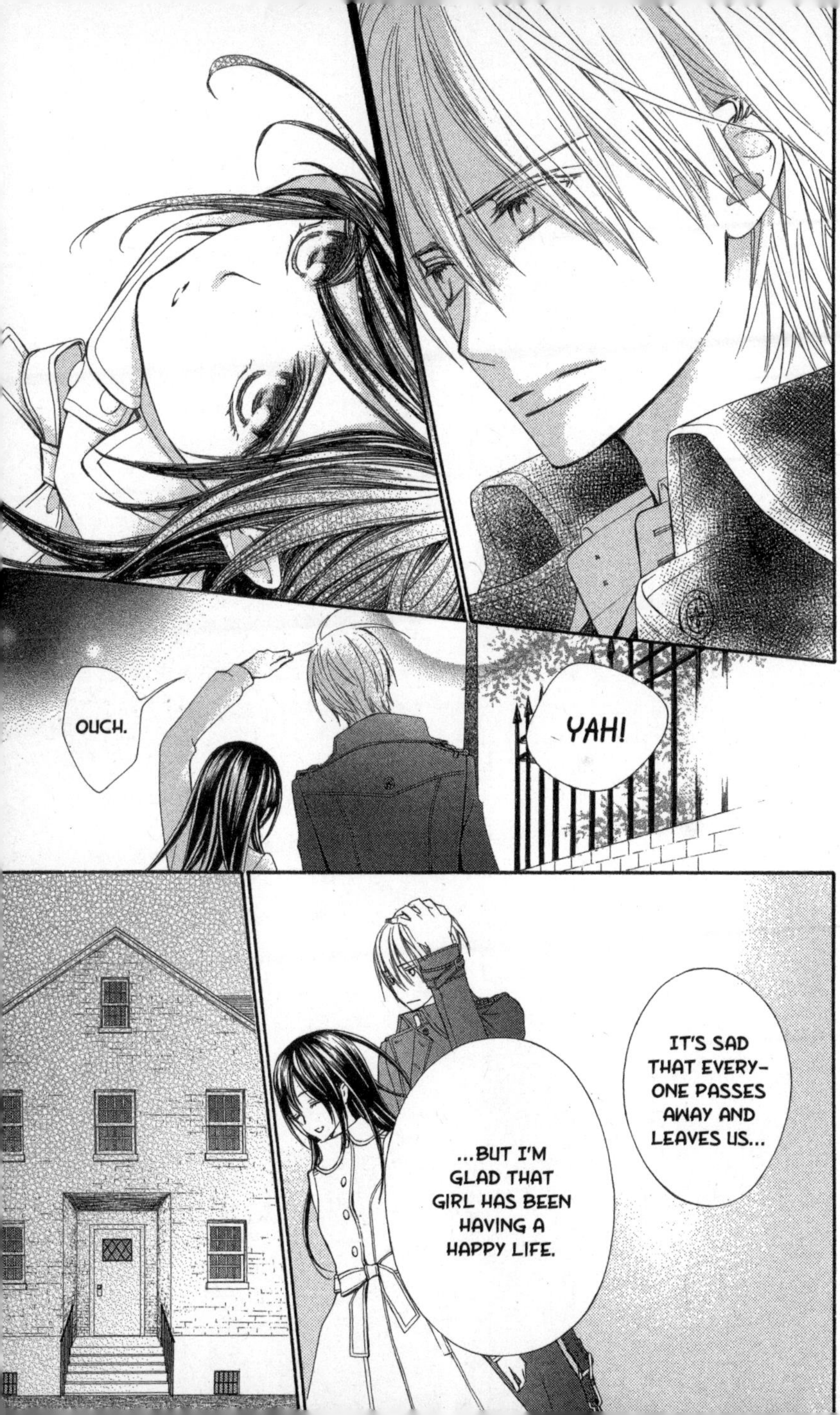
YAH!
OUCH.
IT'S SAD THAT EVERY-ONE PASSES AWAY AND LEAVES US...
...BUT I'M GLAD THAT GIRL HAS BEEN HAVING A HAPPY LIFE.

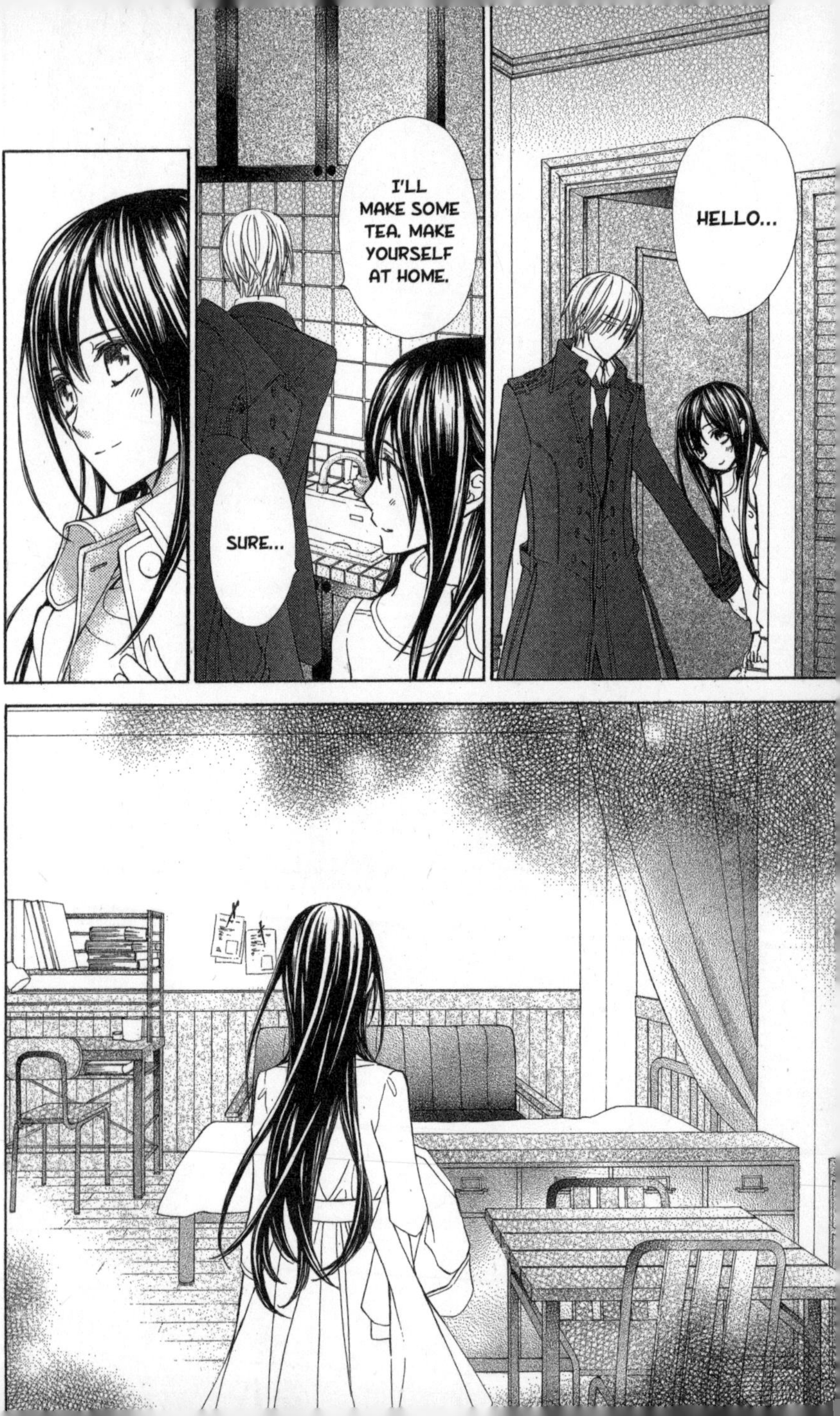
HELLO...
I'LL MAKE SOME TEA. MAKE YOURSELF AT HOME.
SURE...

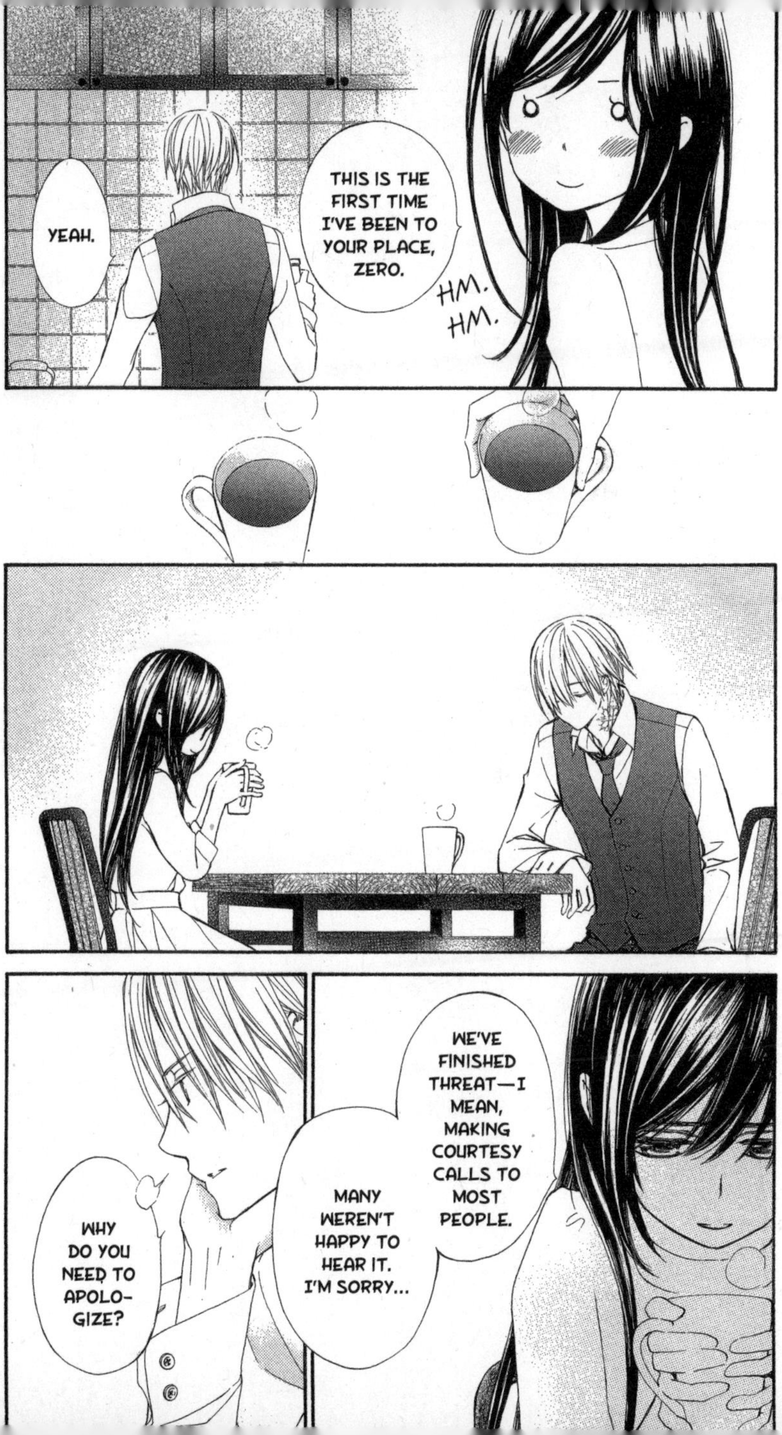
THIS IS THE FIRST TIME I'VE BEEN TO YOUR PLACE, ZERO.
HM. HM.
YEAH.
WE'VE FINISHED THREAT—I MEAN, MAKING COURTESY CALLS TO MOST PEOPLE.
MANY WEREN'T HAPPY TO HEAR IT. I'M SORRY...
WHY DO YOU NEED TO APOLO-GIZE?

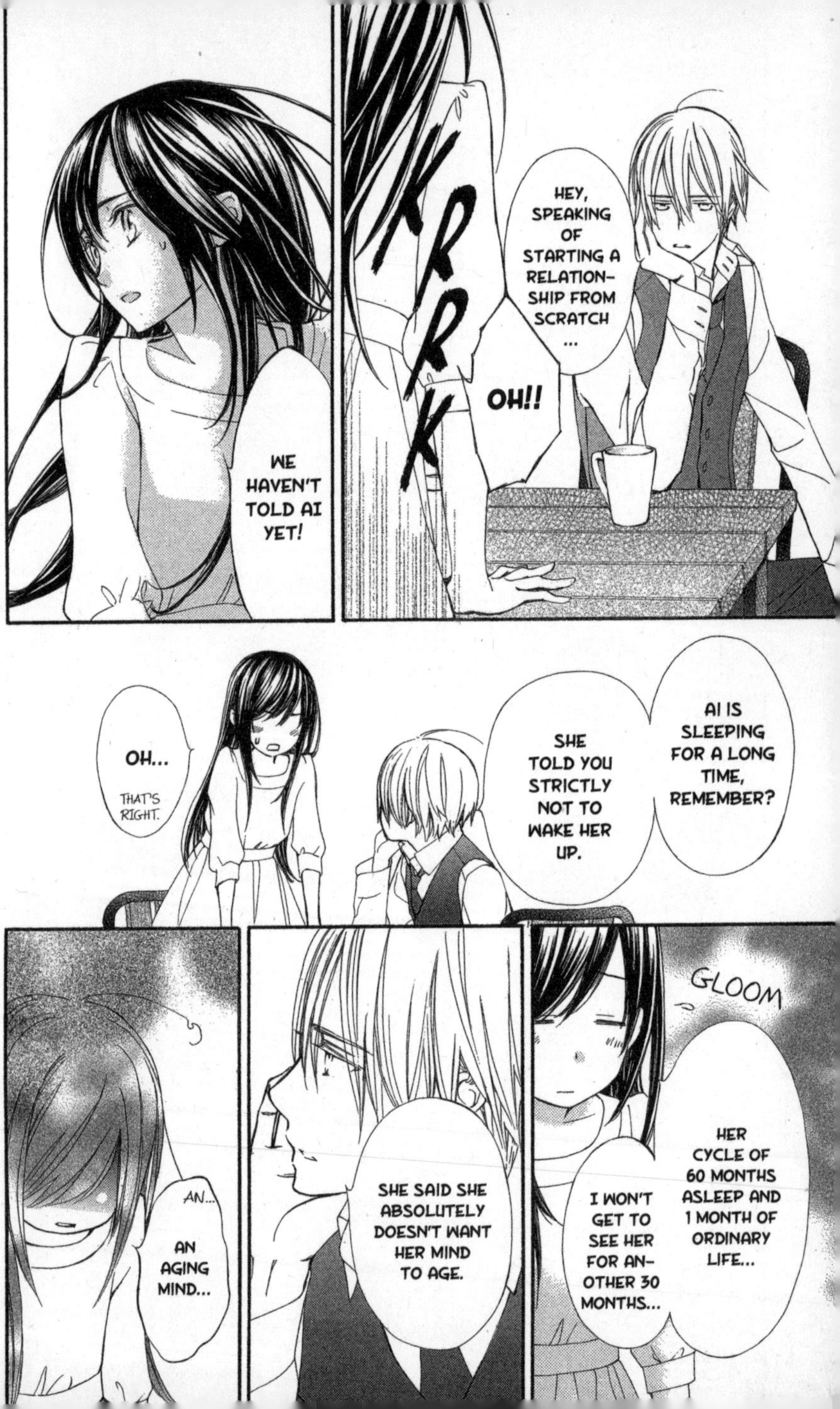
HEY, SPEAKING OF STARTING A RELATION-SHIP FROM SCRATCH ...
KRRK
OH!!
WE HAVEN'T TOLD AI YET!
AI IS SLEEPING FOR A LONG TIME, REMEMBER?
SHE TOLD YOU STRICTLY NOT TO WAKE HER UP.
OH...
THAT'S RIGHT.
GLOOM
HER CYCLE OF 60 MONTHS ASLEEP AND 1 MONTH OF ORDINARY LIFE...
I WON'T GET TO SEE HER FOR AN-OTHER 30 MONTHS...
SHE SAID SHE ABSOLUTELY DOESN'T WANT HER MIND TO AGE.
AN...
AN AGING MIND...

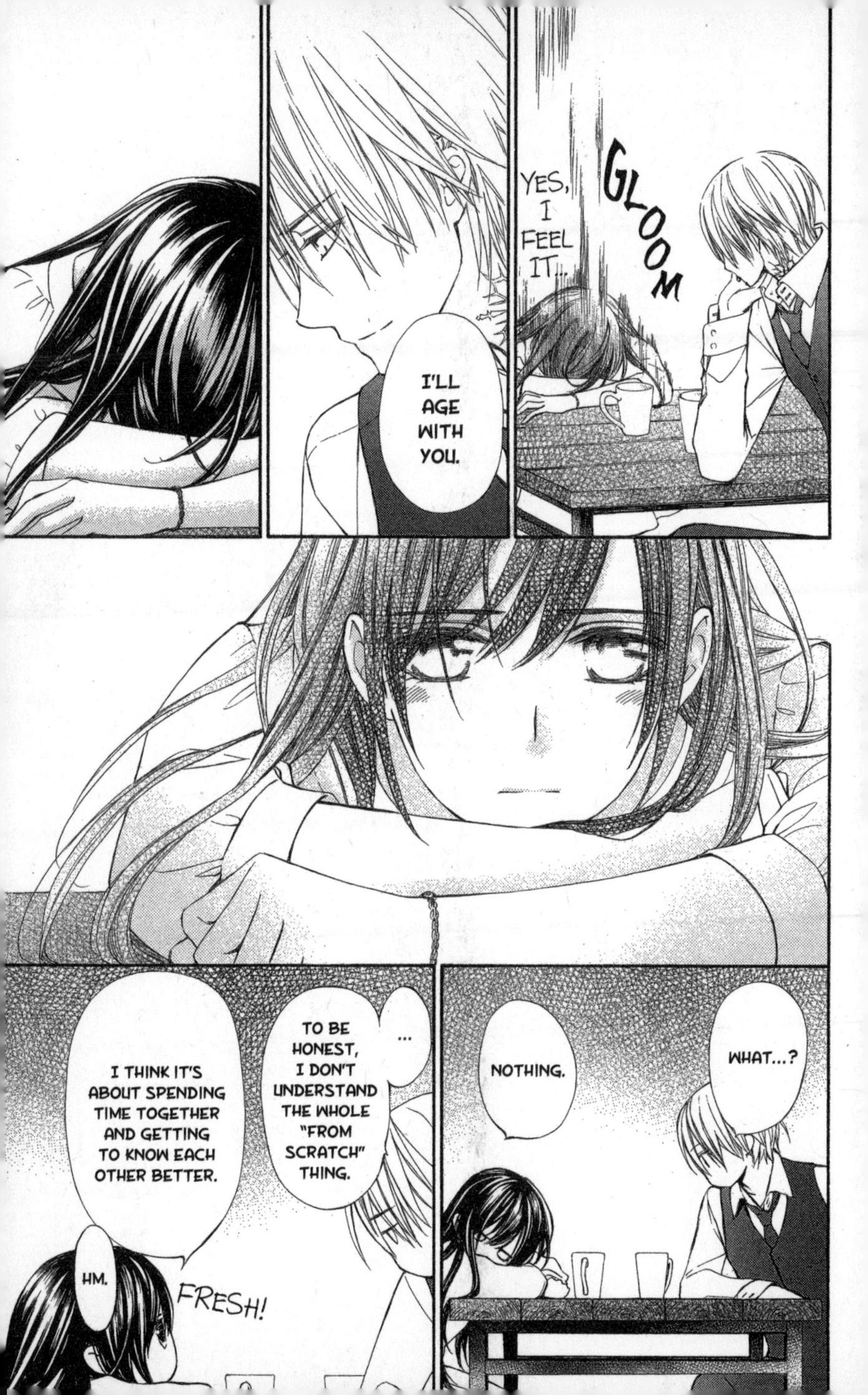
GLOOM
YES, I FEEL IT...
I'LL AGE WITH YOU.
WHAT...?
NOTHING.
...
TO BE HONEST, I DON'T UNDERSTAND THE WHOLE "FROM SCRATCH" THING.
I THINK IT'S ABOUT SPENDING TIME TOGETHER AND GETTING TO KNOW EACH OTHER BETTER.
HM.
FRESH!

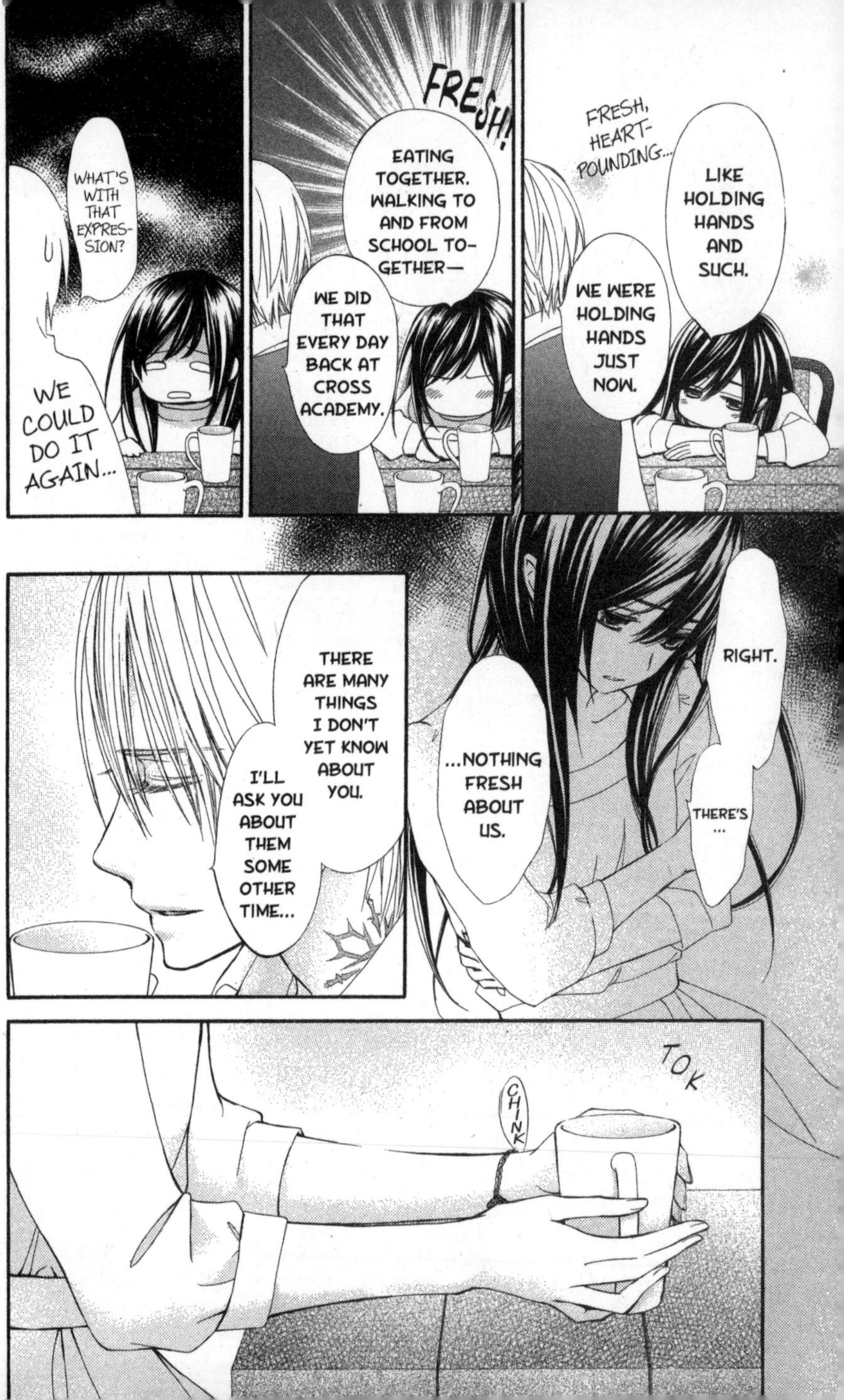
FRESH, HEART-POUNDING...
LIKE HOLDING HANDS AND SUCH.
WE WERE HOLDING HANDS JUST NOW.
FRESH!
EATING TOGETHER. WALKING TO AND FROM SCHOOL TO-GETHER—
WE DID THAT EVERY DAY BACK AT CROSS ACADEMY.
WHAT'S WITH THAT EXPRES-SION?
WE COULD DO IT AGAIN...
RIGHT.
THERE'S...
...NOTHING FRESH ABOUT US.
THERE ARE MANY THINGS I DON'T YET KNOW ABOUT YOU.
I'LL ASK YOU ABOUT THEM SOME OTHER TIME...
TOK
CHINK

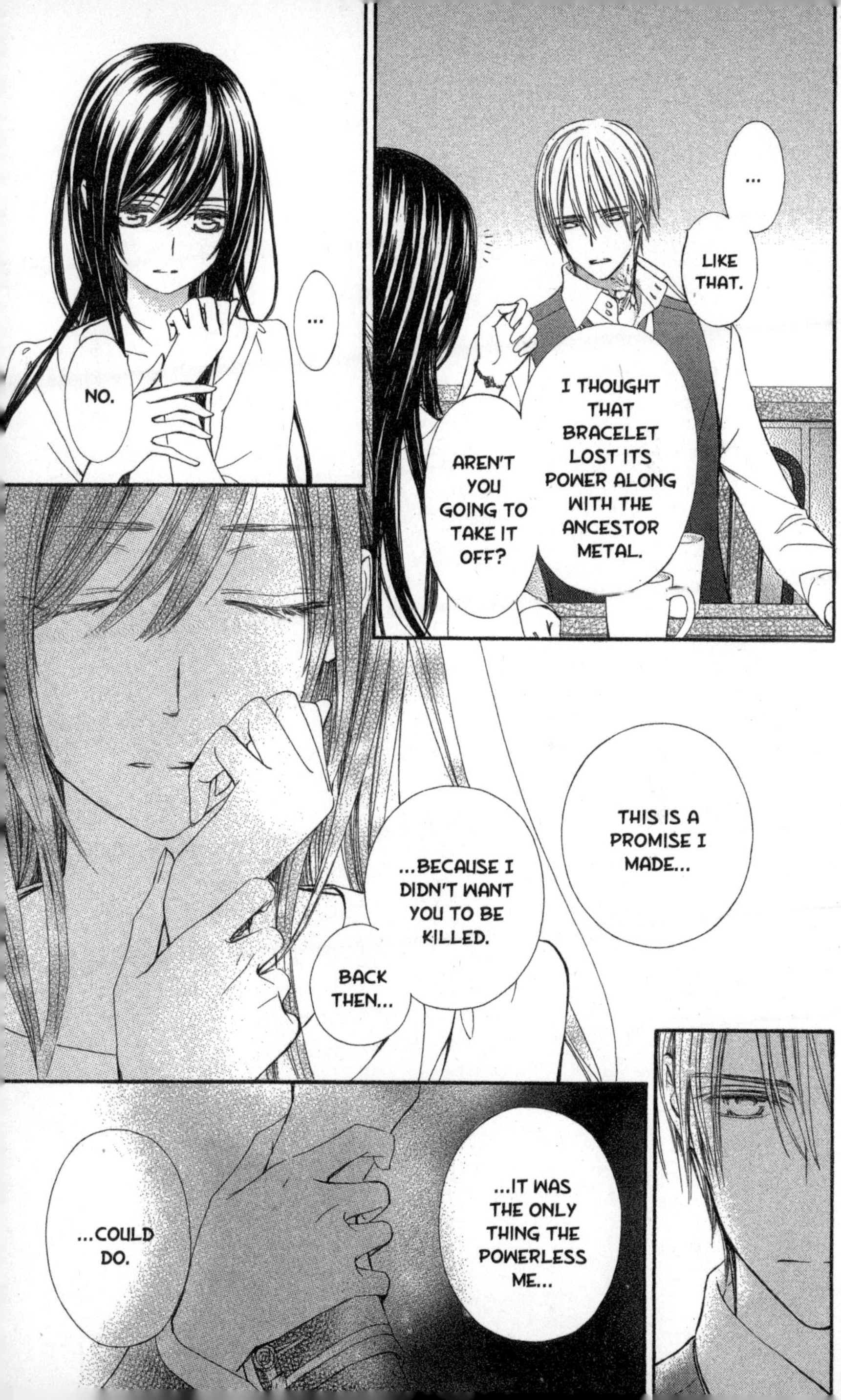
...
LIKE THAT.
I THOUGHT THAT BRACELET LOST ITS POWER ALONG WITH THE ANCESTOR METAL.
AREN'T YOU GOING TO TAKE IT OFF?
...
NO.
THIS IS A PROMISE I MADE...
...BECAUSE I DIDN'T WANT YOU TO BE KILLED.
BACK THEN...
...IT WAS THE ONLY THING THE POWERLESS ME...
...COULD DO.

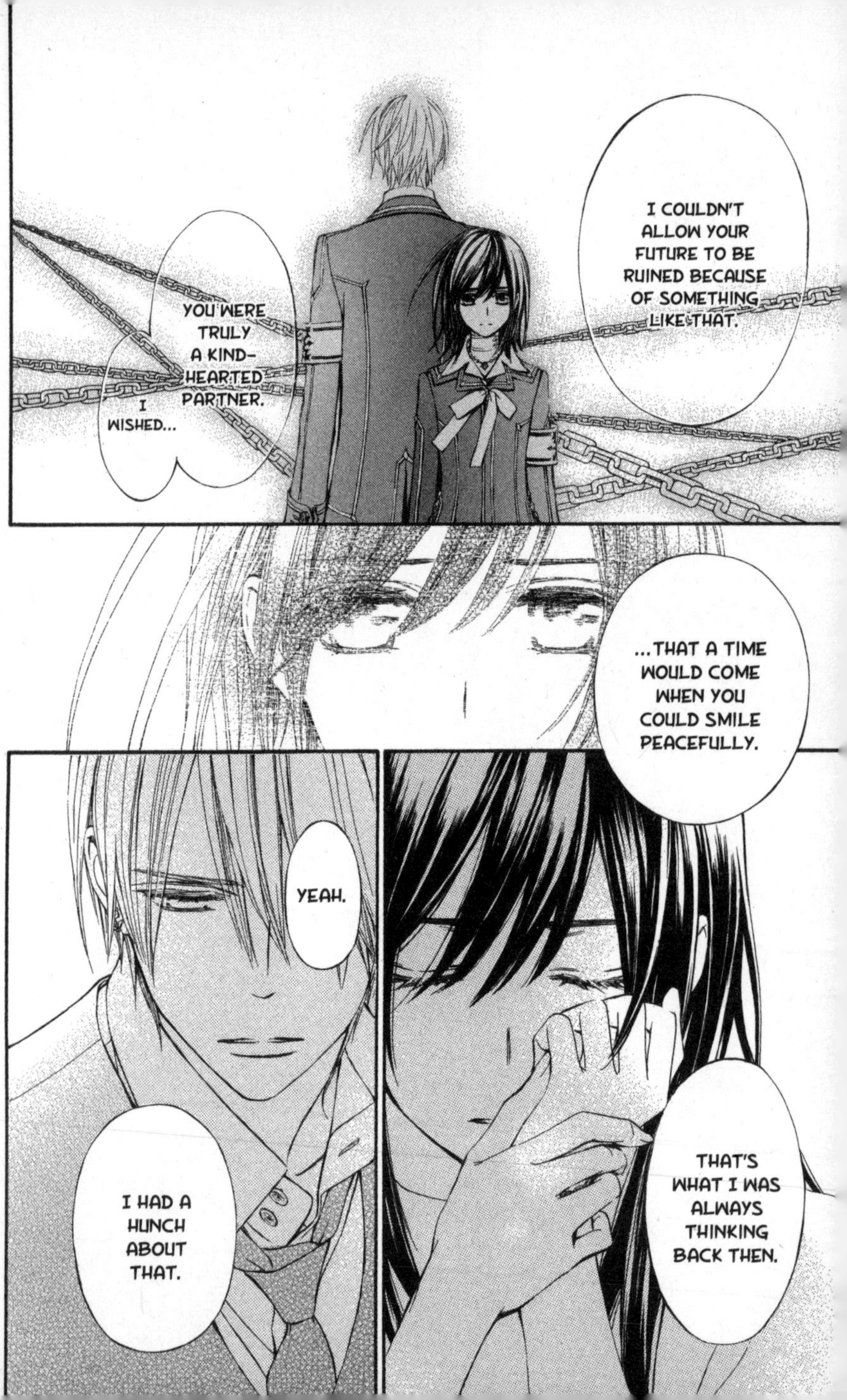
I COULDN'T ALLOW YOUR FUTURE TO BE RUINED BECAUSE OF SOMETHING LIKE THAT.
YOU WERE TRULY A KIND-HEARTED PARTNER.
I WISHED...
...THAT A TIME WOULD COME WHEN YOU COULD SMILE PEACEFULLY.
THAT'S WHAT I WAS ALWAYS THINKING BACK THEN.
YEAH.
I HAD A HUNCH ABOUT THAT.

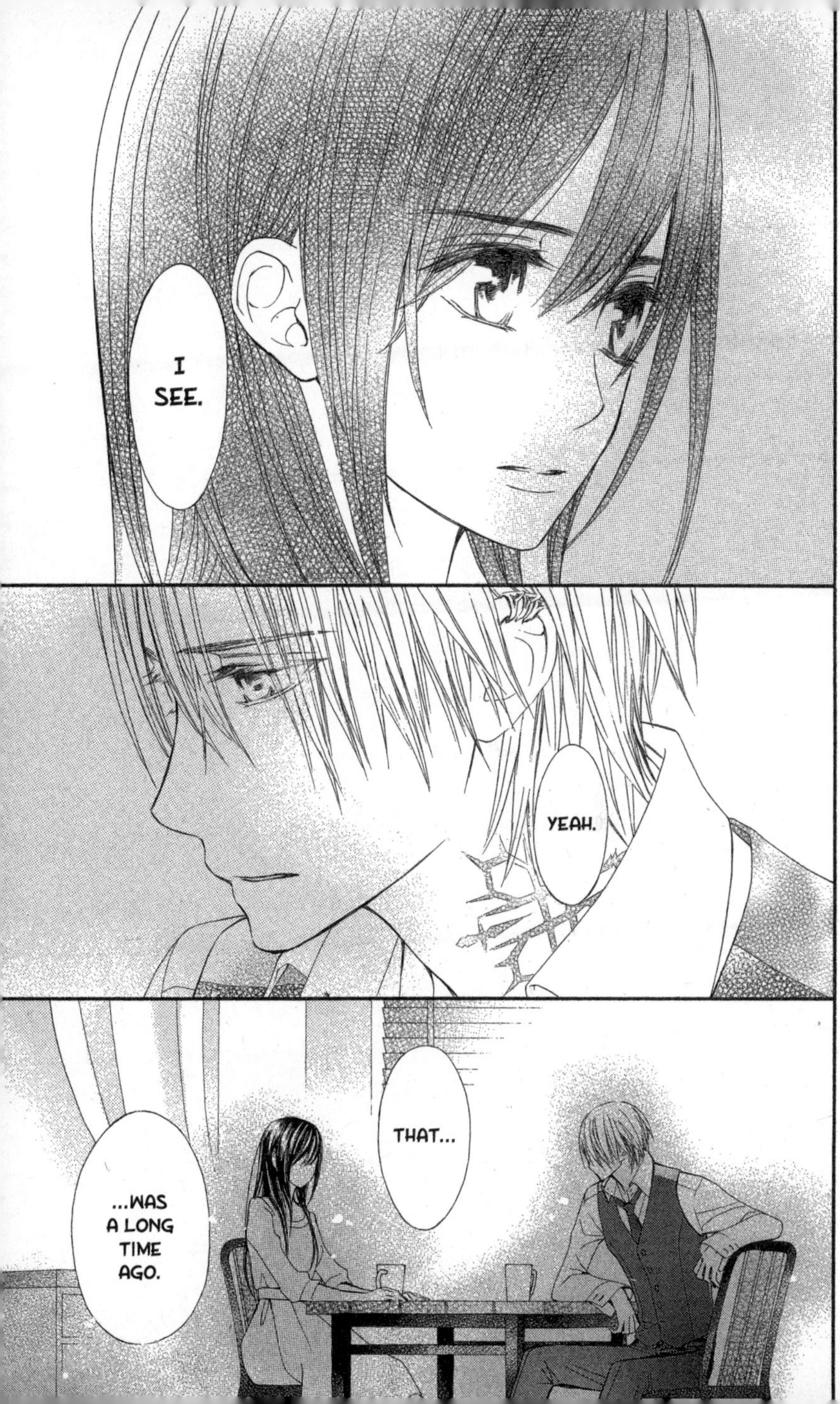
I SEE.
YEAH.
THAT...
...WAS A LONG TIME AGO.

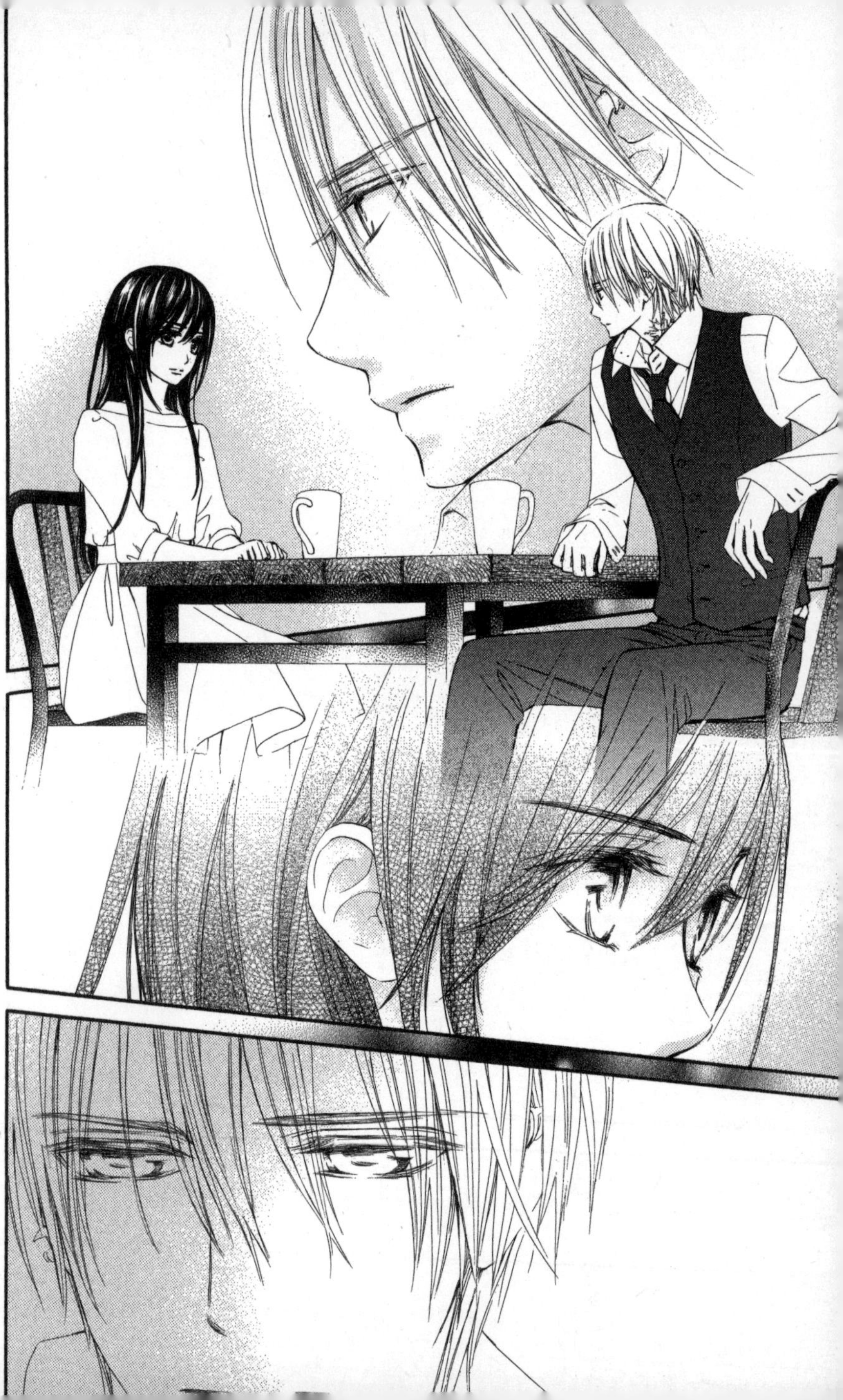

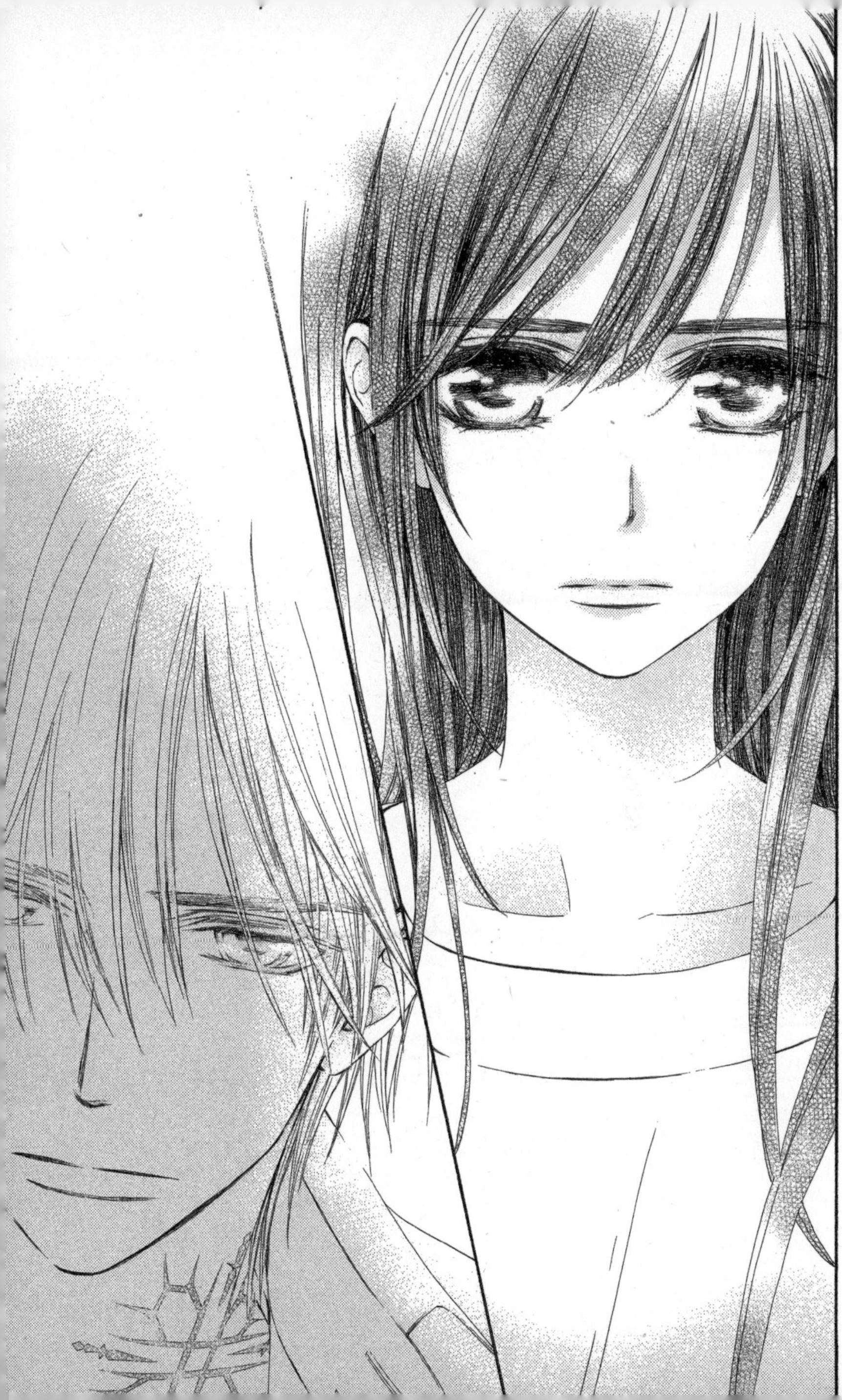

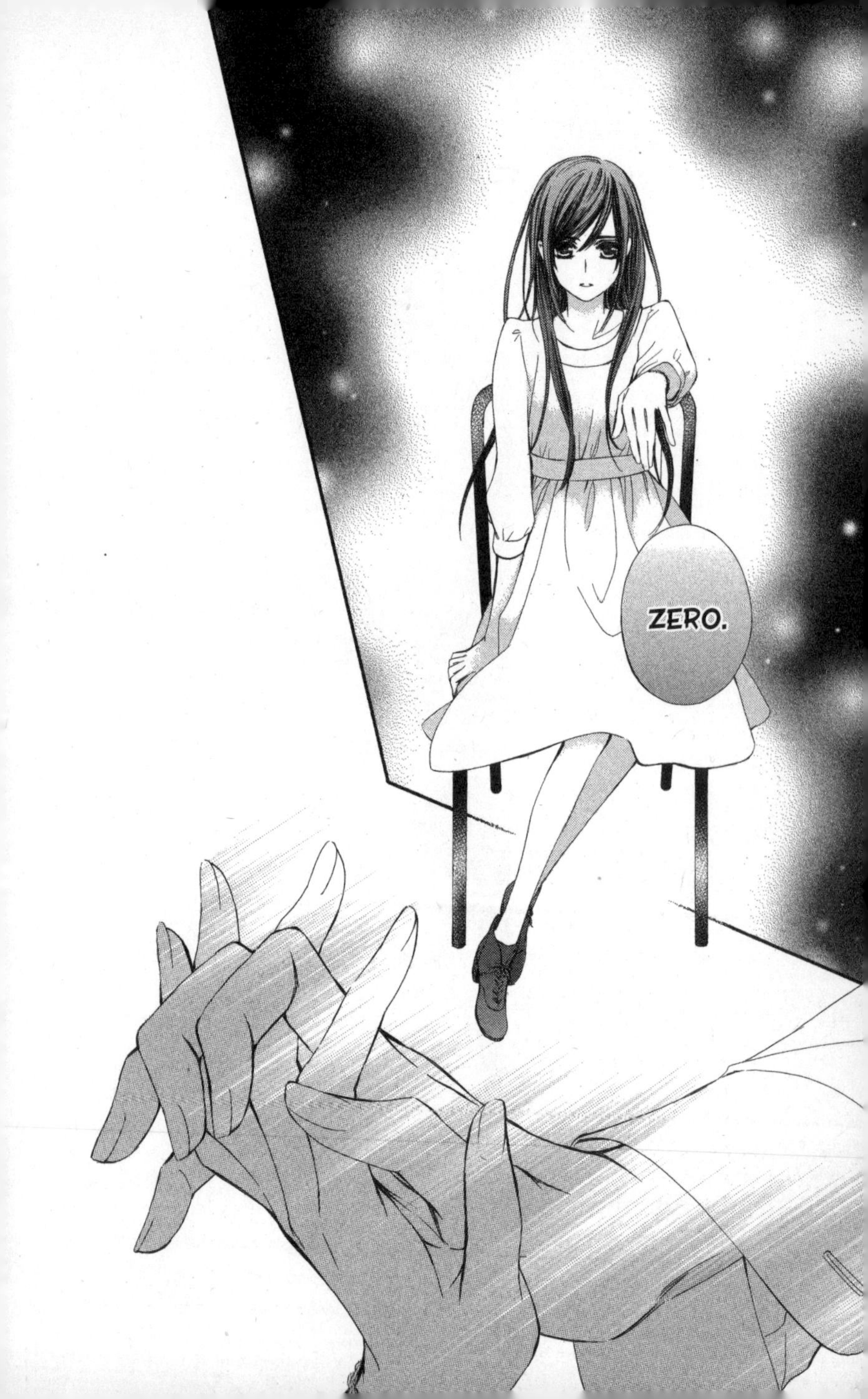
ZERO.

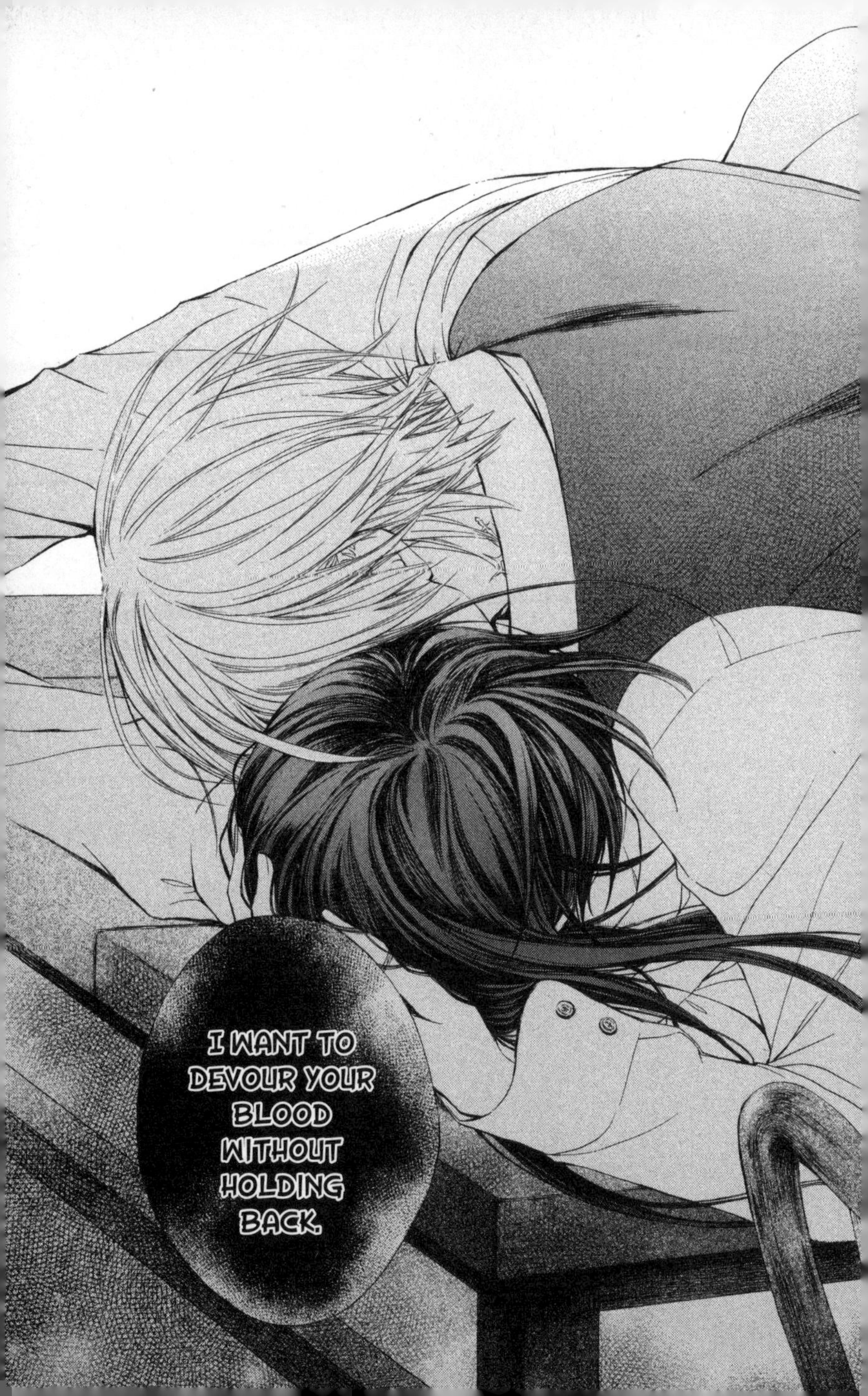
I WANT TO DEVOUR YOUR BLOOD WITHOUT HOLDING BACK.

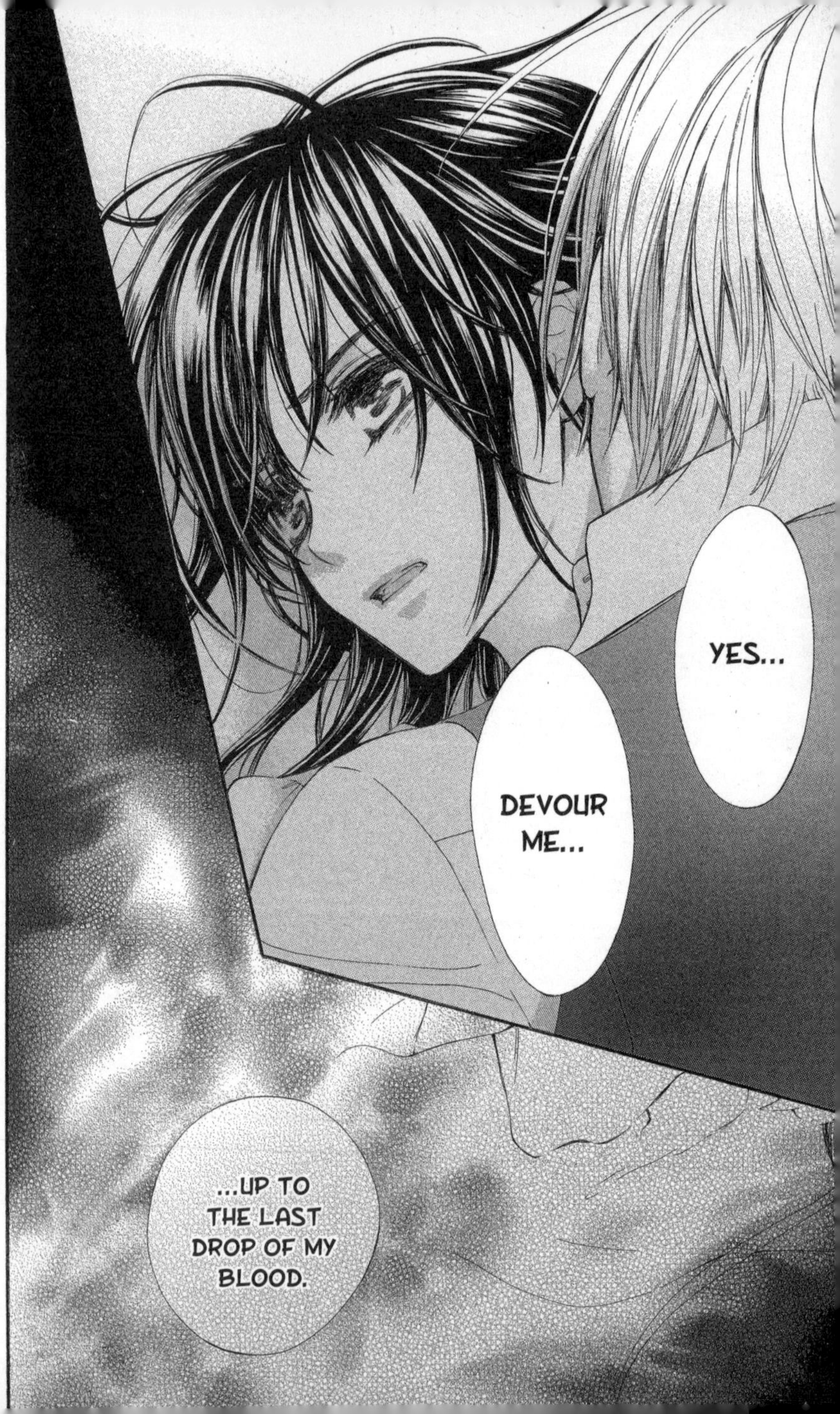
YES...
DEVOUR ME...
...UP TO THE LAST DROP OF MY BLOOD.

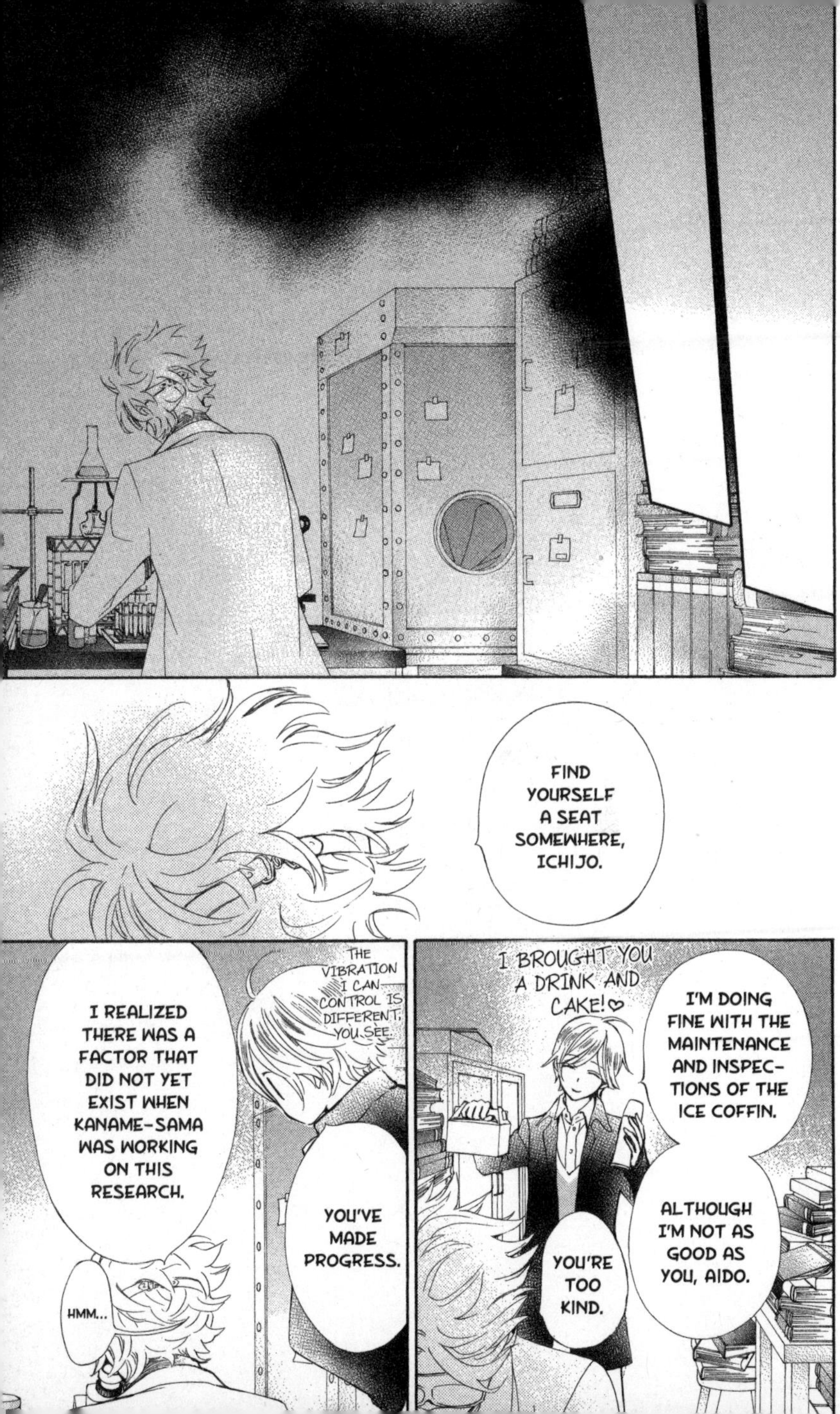
FIND YOURSELF A SEAT SOMEWHERE, ICHIJO.
I BROUGHT YOU A DRINK AND CAKE!♡
I'M DOING FINE WITH THE MAINTENANCE AND INSPECTIONS OF THE ICE COFFIN.
ALTHOUGH I'M NOT AS GOOD AS YOU, AIDO.
YOU'RE TOO KIND.
THE VIBRATION I CAN CONTROL IS DIFFERENT, YOU SEE.
I REALIZED THERE WAS A FACTOR THAT DID NOT YET EXIST WHEN KANAME-SAMA WAS WORKING ON THIS RESEARCH.
YOU'VE MADE PROGRESS.
HMM...

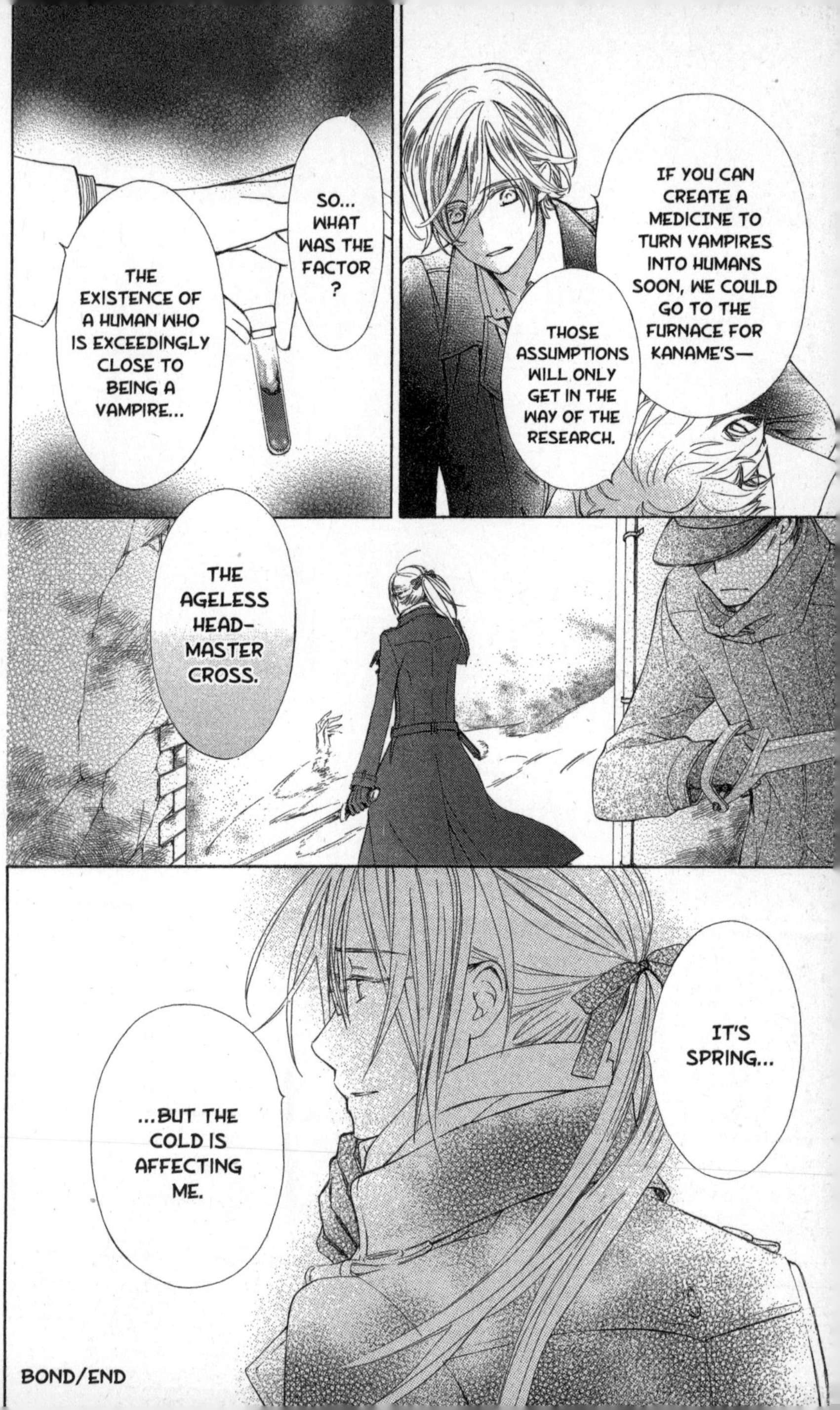
IF YOU CAN CREATE A MEDICINE TO TURN VAMPIRES INTO HUMANS SOON, WE COULD GO TO THE FURNACE FOR KANAME'S—
THOSE ASSUMPTIONS WILL ONLY GET IN THE WAY OF THE RESEARCH.
SO... WHAT WAS THE FACTOR?
THE EXISTENCE OF A HUMAN WHO IS EXCEEDINGLY CLOSE TO BEING A VAMPIRE...
THE AGELESS HEAD-MASTER CROSS.
IT'S SPRING...
...BUT THE COLD IS AFFECTING ME.
BOND/END

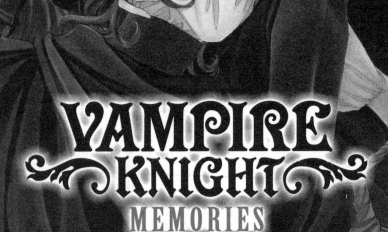

VAMPIRE KNIGHT
MEMORIES

MEMORIES OF THOSE WHO HAVE GONE

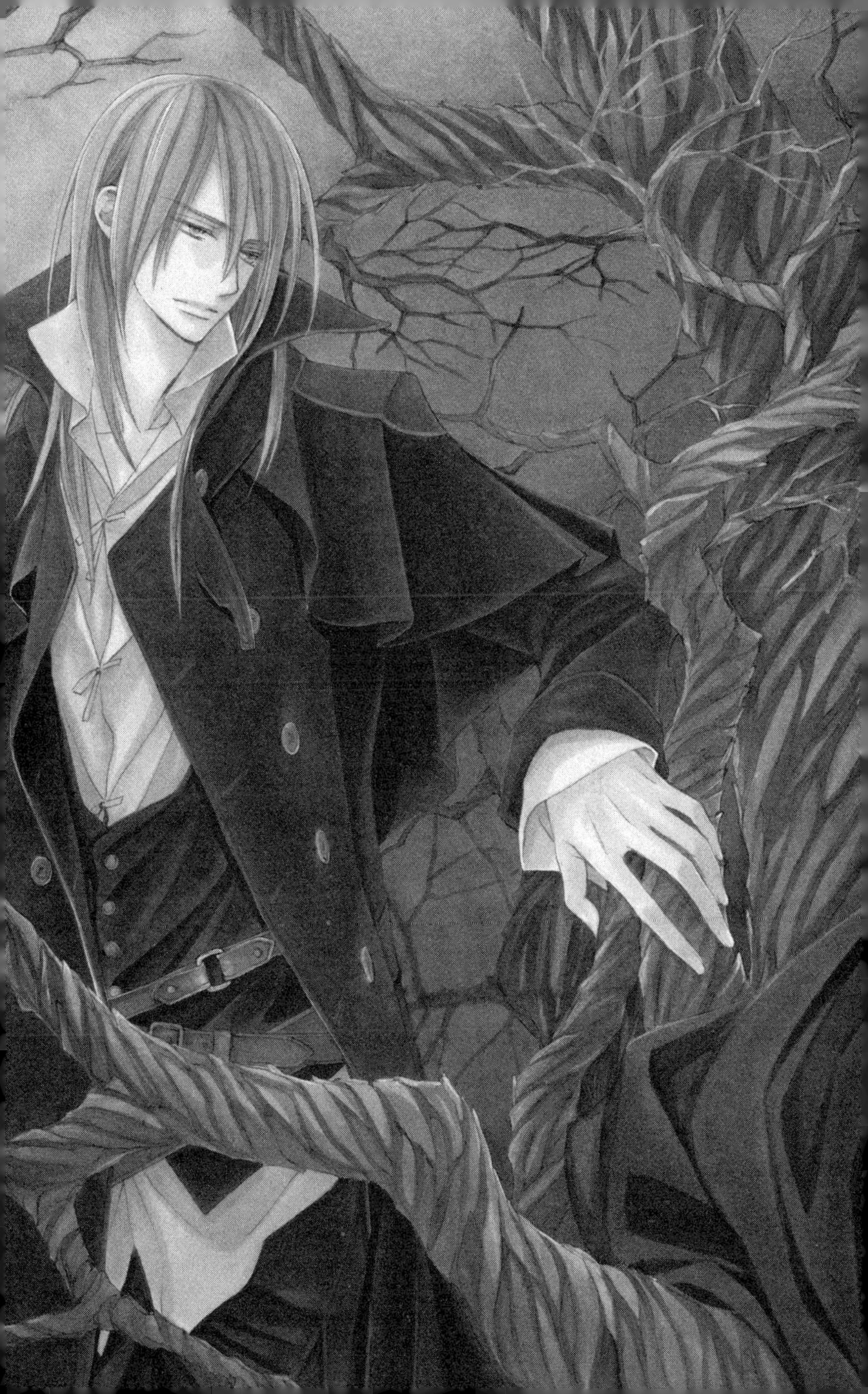

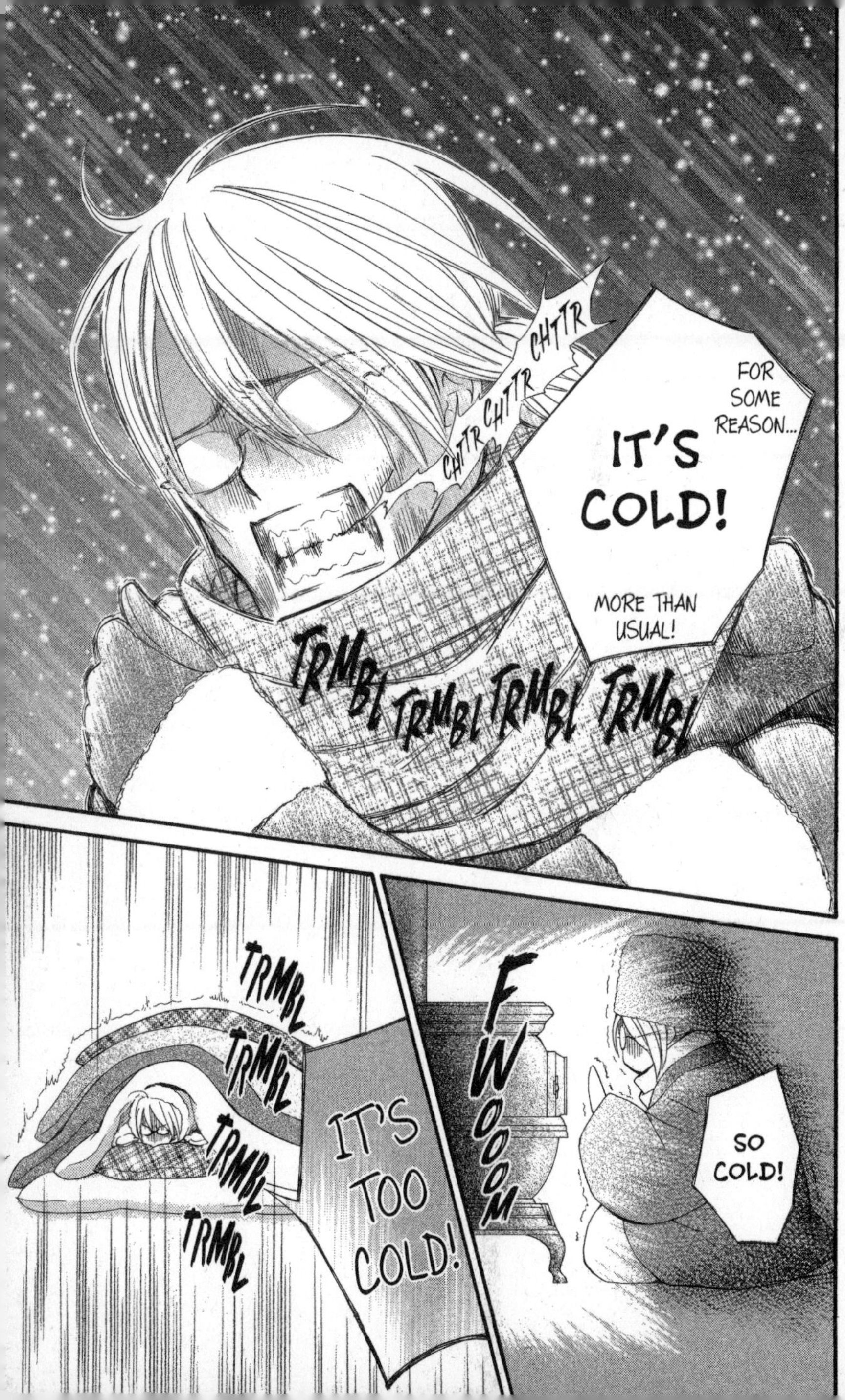
CHTTR CHTTR CHTTR
FOR SOME REASON...
IT'S COLD!
MORE THAN USUAL!
TRMBL TRMBL TRMBL TRMBL
FWOOOM
SO COLD!
TRMBL TRMBL TRMBL TRMBL
IT'S TOO COLD!

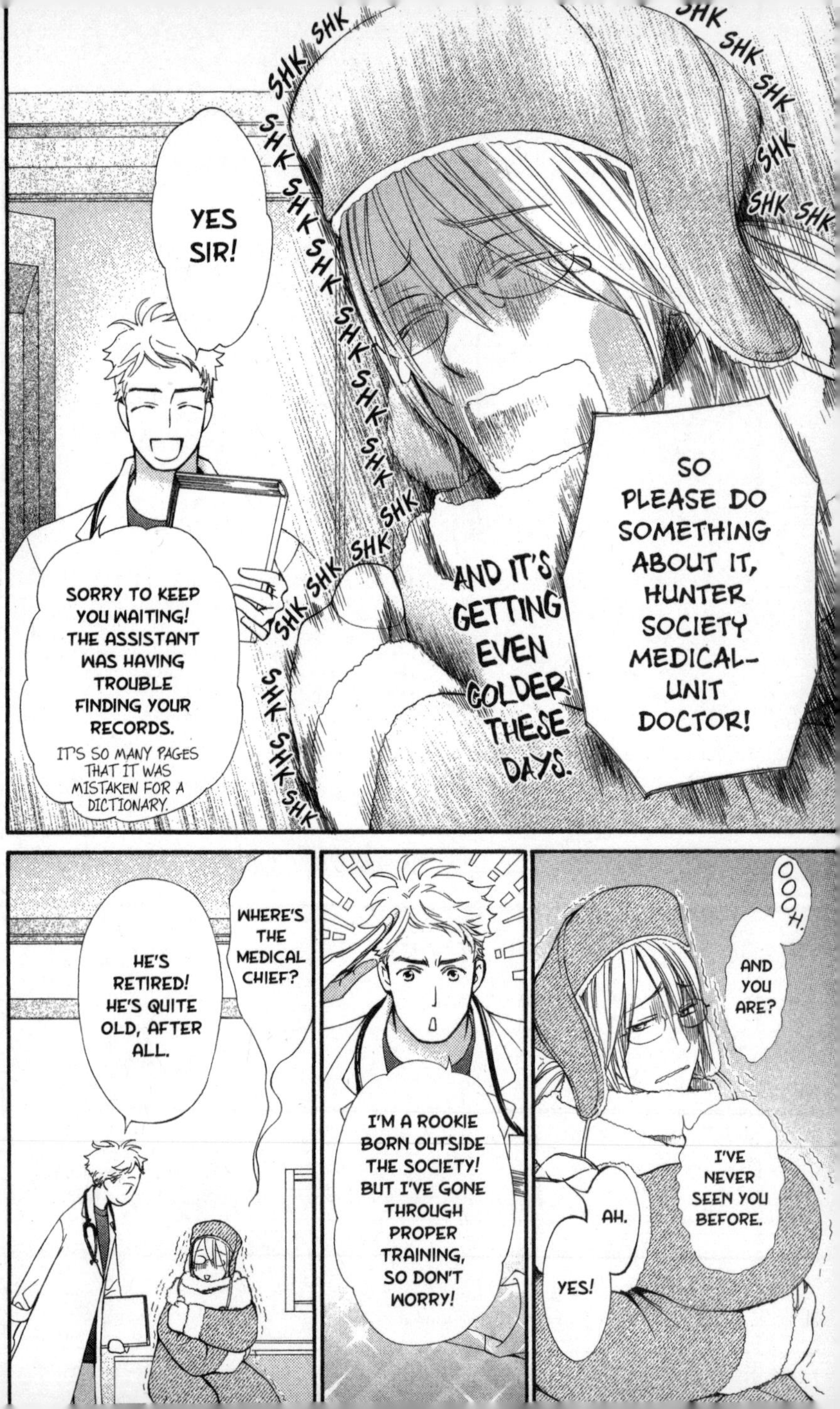
SHK SHK SHK SHK SHK SHK SHK
SHK SHK SHK SHK SHK SHK SHK SHK SHK SHK SHK SHK SHK SHK SHK SHK SHK SHK SHK
SO PLEASE DO SOMETHING ABOUT IT, HUNTER SOCIETY MEDICAL-UNIT DOCTOR!
AND IT'S GETTING EVEN COLDER THESE DAYS.
YES SIR!
SORRY TO KEEP YOU WAITING! THE ASSISTANT WAS HAVING TROUBLE FINDING YOUR RECORDS.
IT'S SO MANY PAGES THAT IT WAS MISTAKEN FOR A DICTIONARY.
OOOH.
AND YOU ARE?
I'VE NEVER SEEN YOU BEFORE.
AH.
YES!
I'M A ROOKIE BORN OUTSIDE THE SOCIETY! BUT I'VE GONE THROUGH PROPER TRAINING, SO DON'T WORRY!
WHERE'S THE MEDICAL CHIEF?
HE'S RETIRED! HE'S QUITE OLD, AFTER ALL.

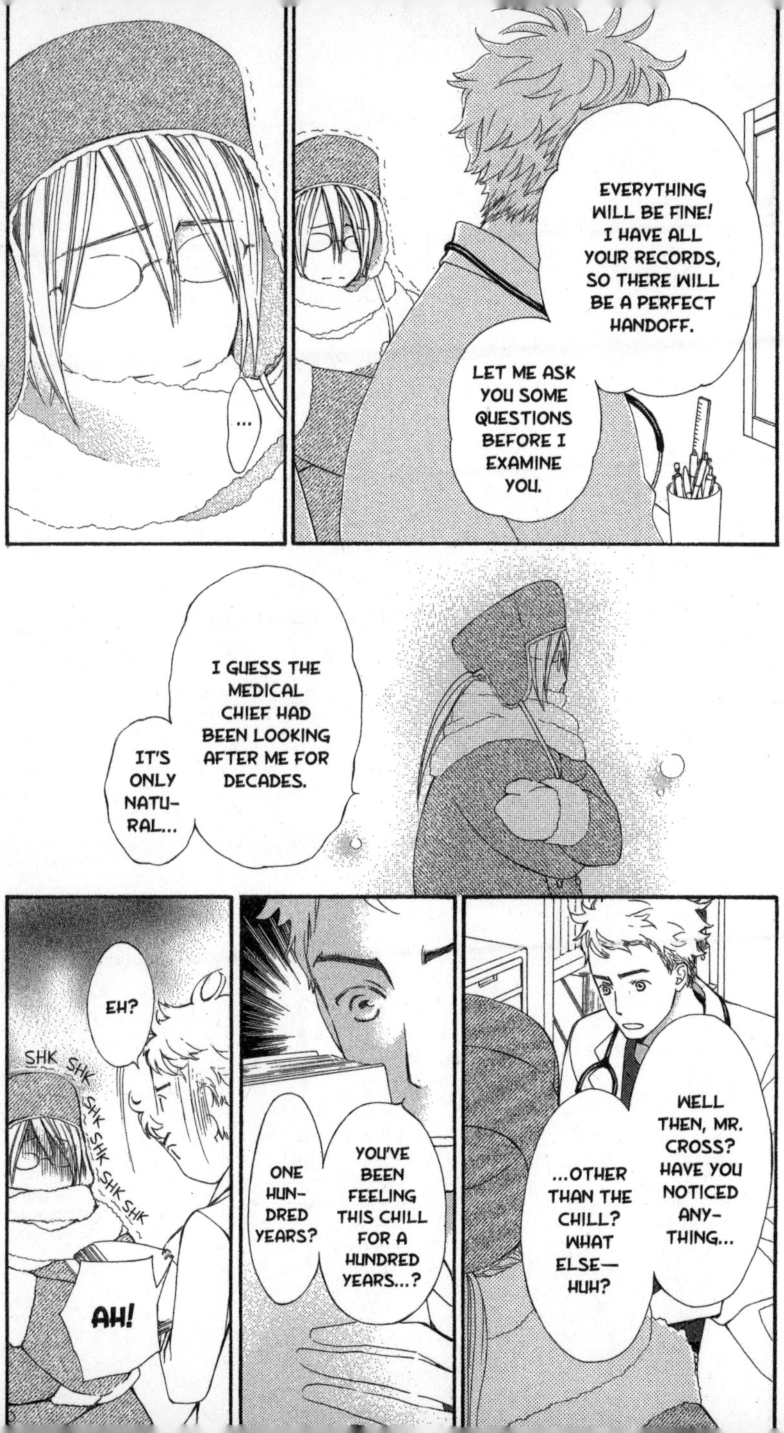
EVERYTHING WILL BE FINE! I HAVE ALL YOUR RECORDS, SO THERE WILL BE A PERFECT HANDOFF.
LET ME ASK YOU SOME QUESTIONS BEFORE I EXAMINE YOU.
...
I GUESS THE MEDICAL CHIEF HAD BEEN LOOKING AFTER ME FOR DECADES.
IT'S ONLY NATU-RAL...
WELL THEN, MR. CROSS? HAVE YOU NOTICED ANY-THING...
...OTHER THAN THE CHILL? WHAT ELSE— HUH?
YOU'VE BEEN FEELING THIS CHILL FOR A HUNDRED YEARS...?
ONE HUN-DRED YEARS?
EH?
SHK SHK SHK SHK SHK SHK
AH!

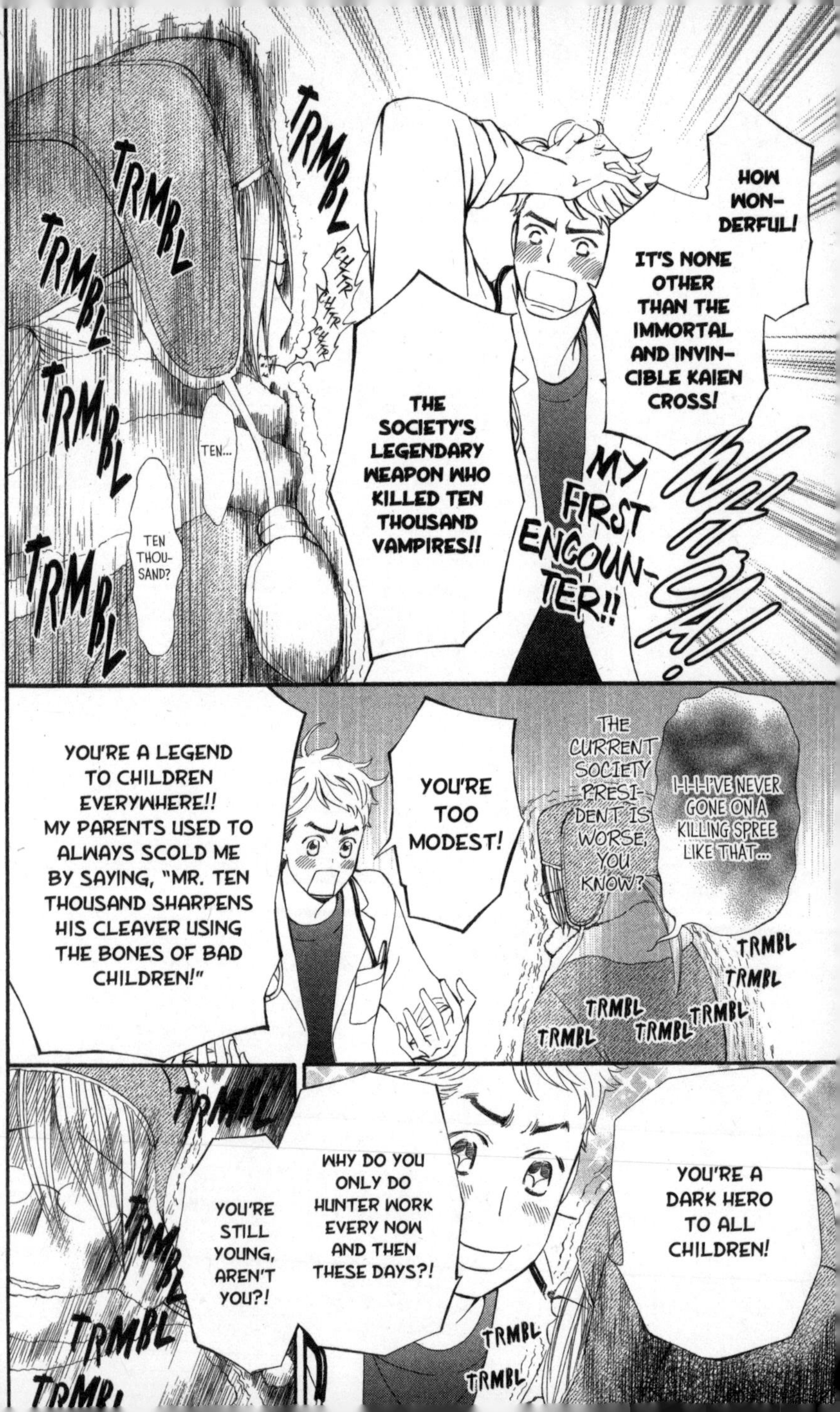
HOW WON-DERFUL!
IT'S NONE OTHER THAN THE IMMORTAL AND INVINCIBLE KAIEN CROSS!
MY FIRST ENCOUN-TER!!
WHOA!
THE SOCIETY'S LEGENDARY WEAPON WHO KILLED TEN THOUSAND VAMPIRES!!
CHTTR CHTTR CHTTR
TRMBL TRMBL TRMBL TRMBL TRMBL
TEN...
TEN THOU-SAND?
THE CURRENT SOCIETY PRESI-DENT IS WORSE, YOU KNOW?
I-I-I-I'VE NEVER GONE ON A KILLING SPREE LIKE THAT...
TRMBL TRMBL TRMBL TRMBL TRMBL TRMBL
YOU'RE TOO MODEST!
YOU'RE A LEGEND TO CHILDREN EVERYWHERE!! MY PARENTS USED TO ALWAYS SCOLD ME BY SAYING, "MR. TEN THOUSAND SHARPENS HIS CLEAVER USING THE BONES OF BAD CHILDREN!"
YOU'RE A DARK HERO TO ALL CHILDREN!
WHY DO YOU ONLY DO HUNTER WORK EVERY NOW AND THEN THESE DAYS?!
YOU'RE STILL YOUNG, AREN'T YOU?!
TRMBL TRMBL
TRMBL TRMBL TRMBL

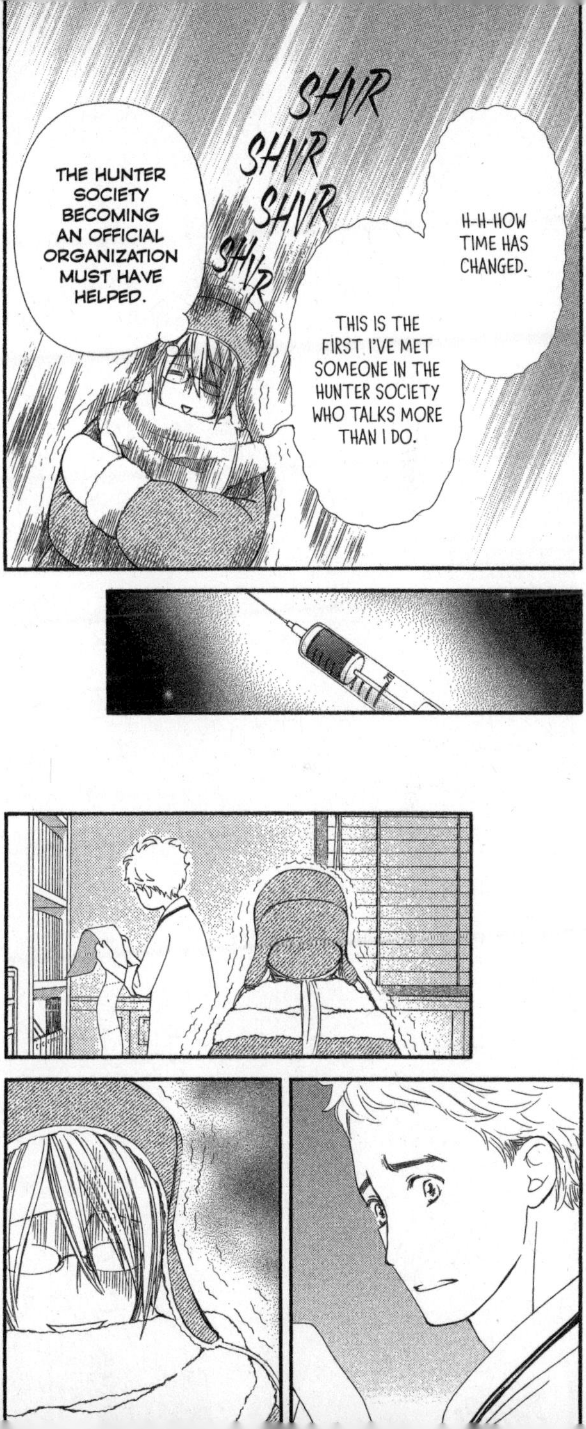
H-H-HOW TIME HAS CHANGED.
THIS IS THE FIRST I'VE MET SOMEONE IN THE HUNTER SOCIETY WHO TALKS MORE THAN I DO.
SHVR
SHVR
SHVR
SHVR
THE HUNTER SOCIETY BECOMING AN OFFICIAL ORGANIZATION MUST HAVE HELPED.

— 3 —

Thank you very much for all the touching letters you have sent me. I take my time to read through every one of them.

Ever since I've slowed down my pace of work, many people have asked after my health in their letters. I am very sorry to have worried you. And thank you very much for asking. (After all, I did keep mentioning how my body was falling apart... 3)

These days I have more free time on my hands, so I am visiting the doctor to get my head and stomach treated. ✧

(continues ↓)

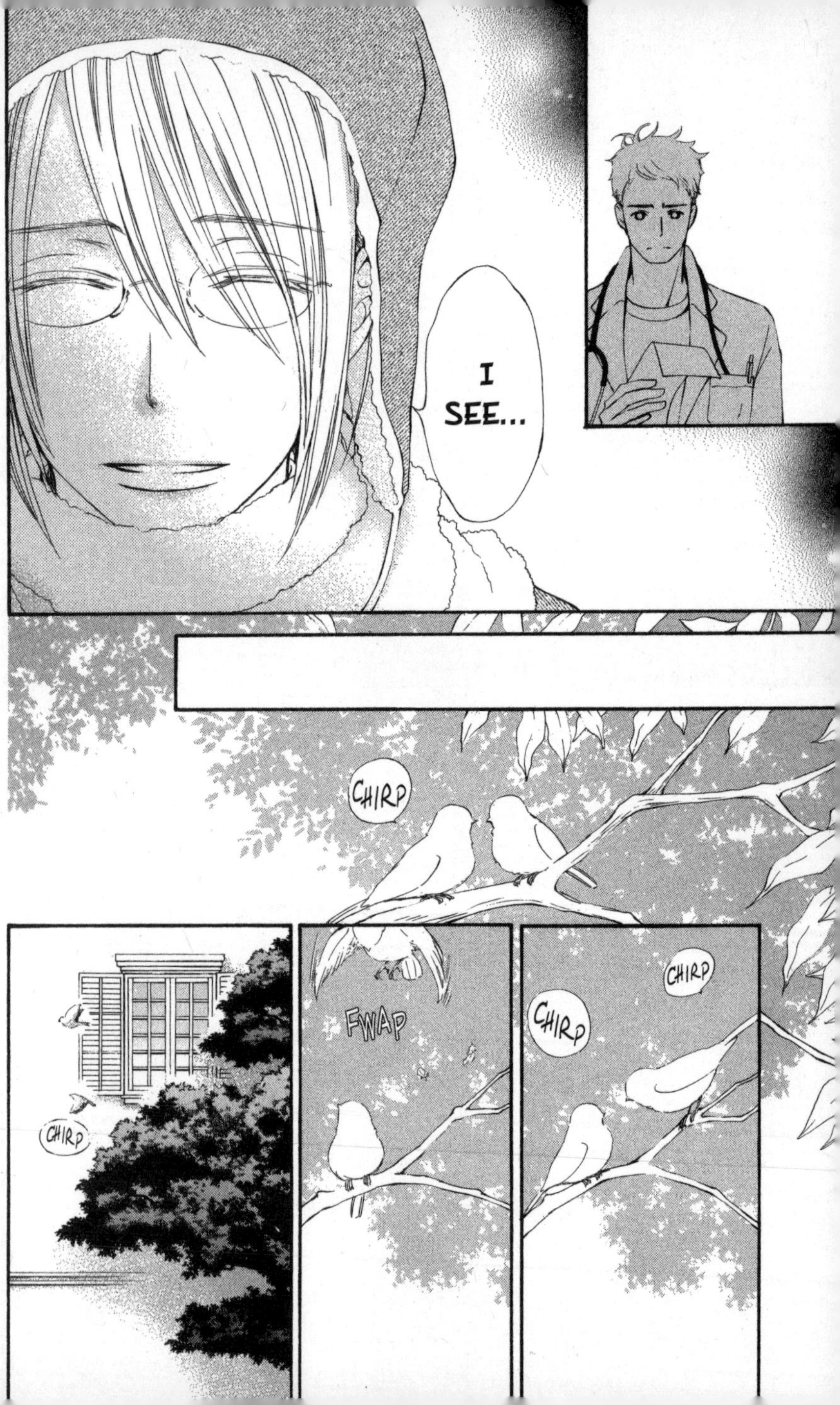
I SEE...
CHIRP
CHIRP
CHIRP
FWAP
CHIRP

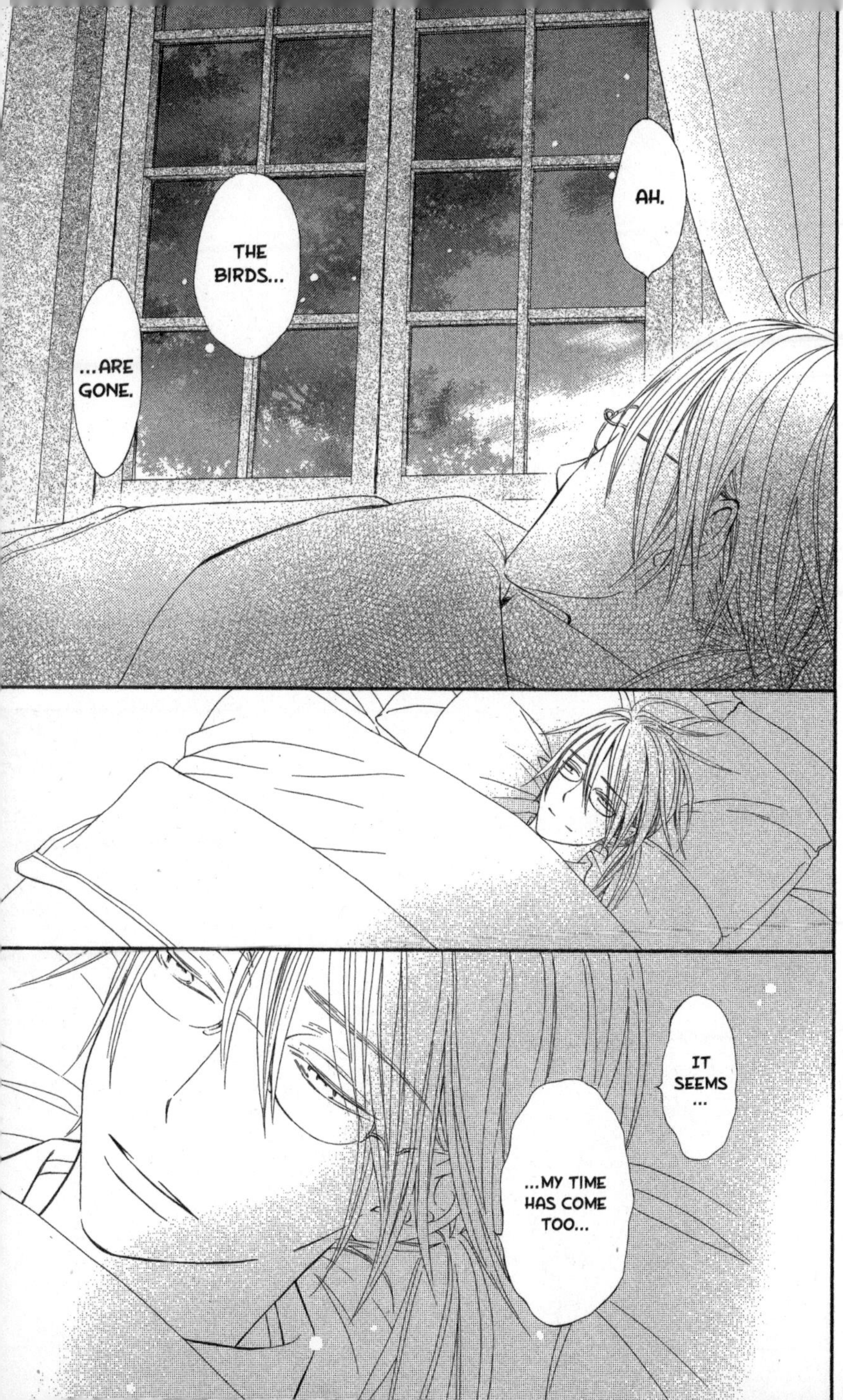
AH.
THE BIRDS...
...ARE GONE.
IT SEEMS ...
...MY TIME HAS COME TOO...

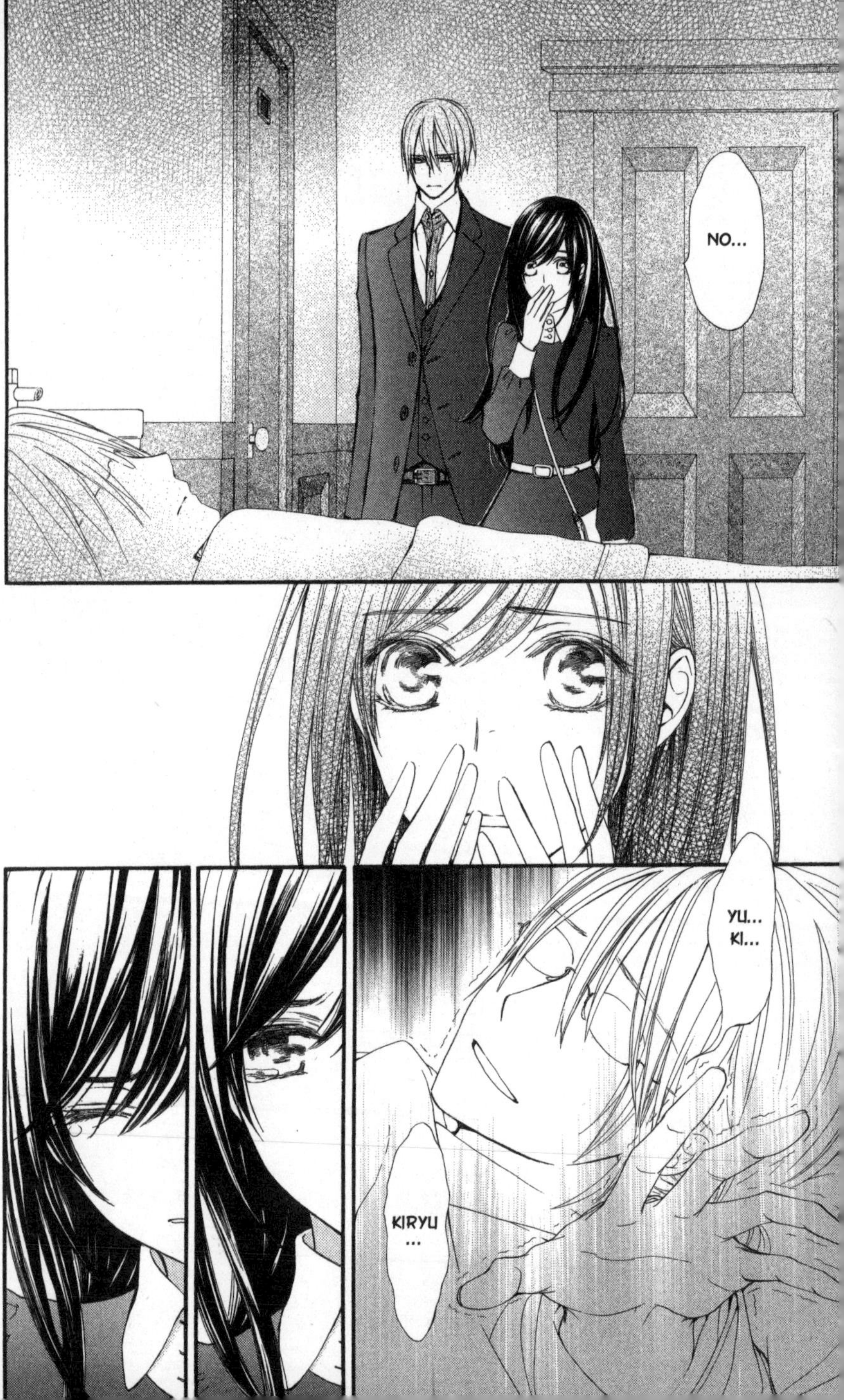
NO...
YU... KI...
KIRYU ...

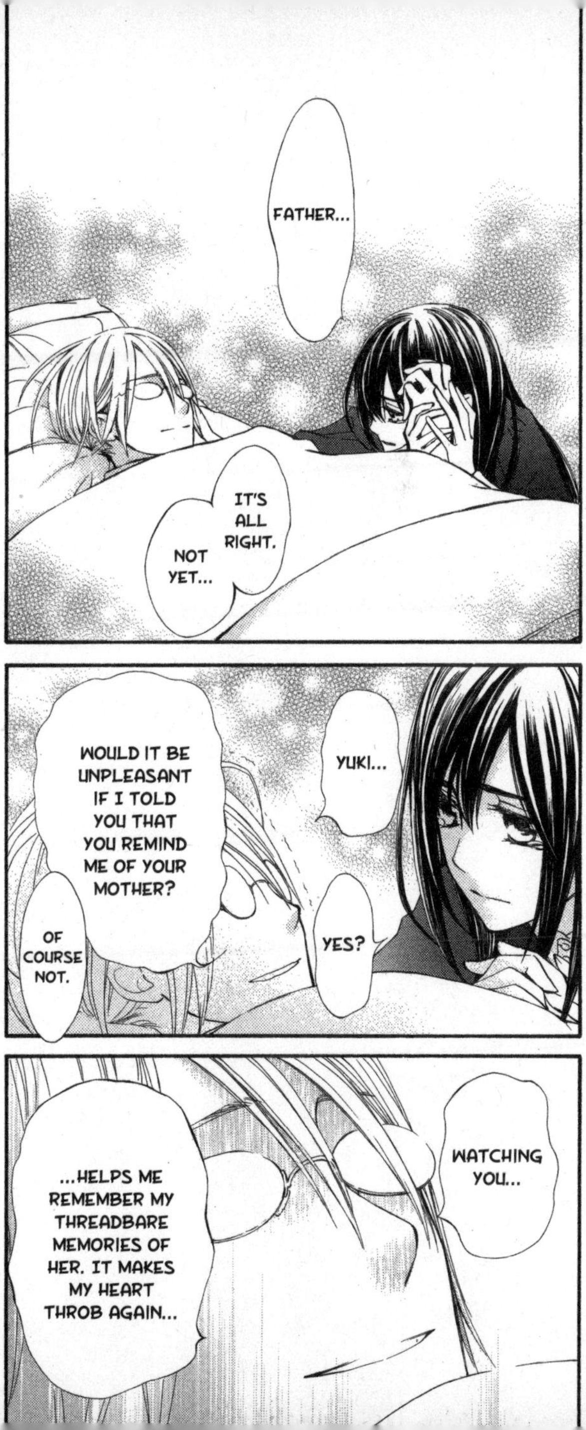
FATHER...
IT'S ALL RIGHT.
NOT YET...
YUKI...
WOULD IT BE UNPLEASANT IF I TOLD YOU THAT YOU REMIND ME OF YOUR MOTHER?
YES?
OF COURSE NOT.
WATCHING YOU...
...HELPS ME REMEMBER MY THREADBARE MEMORIES OF HER. IT MAKES MY HEART THROB AGAIN...

— 4 —

(continued ↓)

This is nothing but a funny story now, so I'm going to reveal it. When I was working on *Captive Hearts*, I was hospitalized and had stomach surgery without going on hiatus. I was working on the final draft for the series in the hospital room with a 104° fever because didn't have a good reaction to the antibiotics after the surgery. ^^;

I did inform the editorial office that I was going to get an operation because it might cause them trouble if something happened. But being a rookie mangaka, I didn't have the nerve to ask for a hiatus. And I actually managed to pull it off because I was young. I'd never be able to do it now.

(continues ↓)

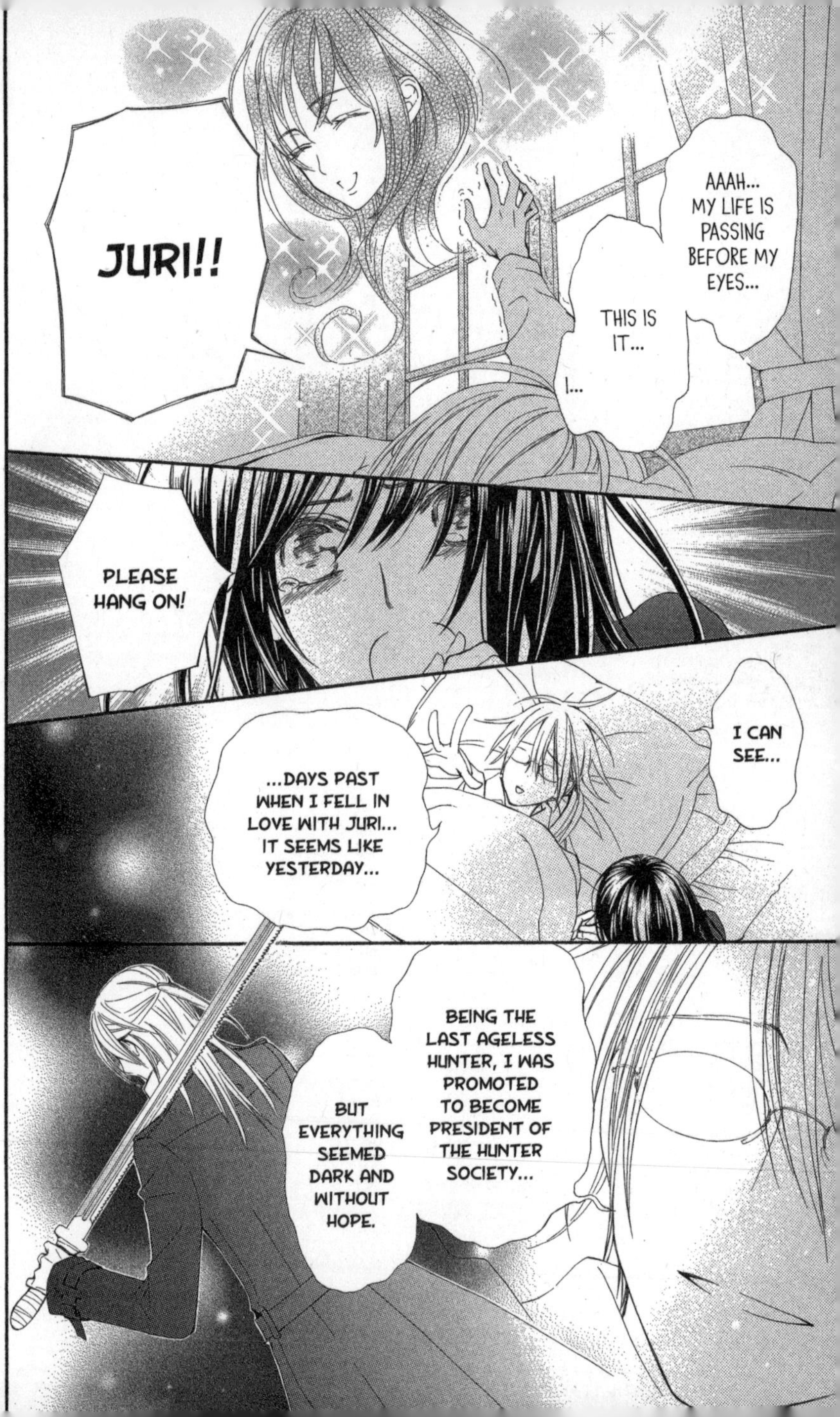
AAAH... MY LIFE IS PASSING BEFORE MY EYES...
THIS IS IT...
I...
JURI!!
PLEASE HANG ON!
I CAN SEE...
...DAYS PAST WHEN I FELL IN LOVE WITH JURI... IT SEEMS LIKE YESTERDAY...
BEING THE LAST AGELESS HUNTER, I WAS PROMOTED TO BECOME PRESIDENT OF THE HUNTER SOCIETY...
BUT EVERYTHING SEEMED DARK AND WITHOUT HOPE.

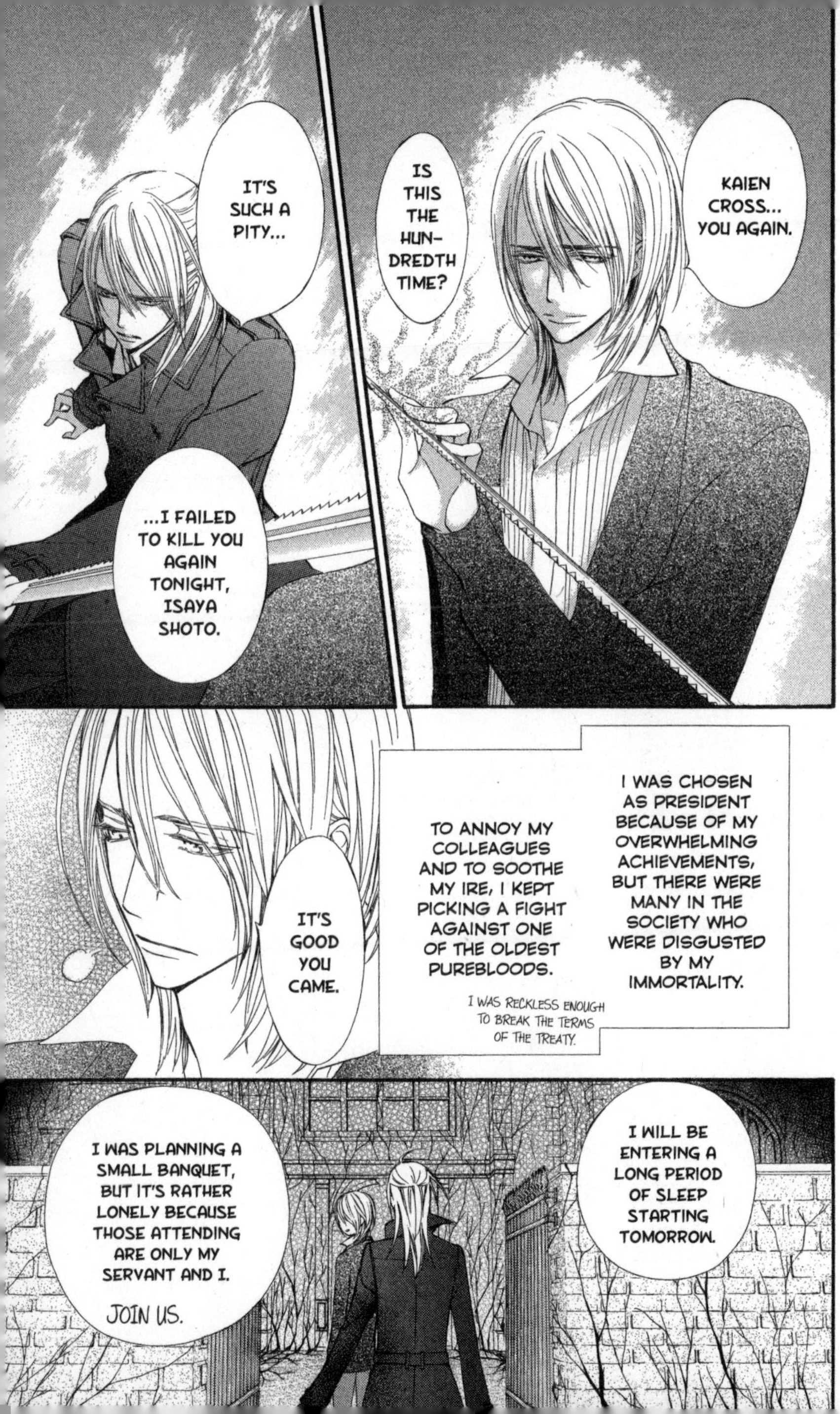
KAIEN CROSS... YOU AGAIN.
IS THIS THE HUN-DREDTH TIME?
IT'S SUCH A PITY...
...I FAILED TO KILL YOU AGAIN TONIGHT, ISAYA SHOTO.
I WAS CHOSEN AS PRESIDENT BECAUSE OF MY OVERWHELMING ACHIEVEMENTS, BUT THERE WERE MANY IN THE SOCIETY WHO WERE DISGUSTED BY MY IMMORTALITY.
TO ANNOY MY COLLEAGUES AND TO SOOTHE MY IRE, I KEPT PICKING A FIGHT AGAINST ONE OF THE OLDEST PUREBLOODS.
I WAS RECKLESS ENOUGH TO BREAK THE TERMS OF THE TREATY.
IT'S GOOD YOU CAME.
I WILL BE ENTERING A LONG PERIOD OF SLEEP STARTING TOMORROW.
I WAS PLANNING A SMALL BANQUET, BUT IT'S RATHER LONELY BECAUSE THOSE ATTENDING ARE ONLY MY SERVANT AND I.
JOIN US.

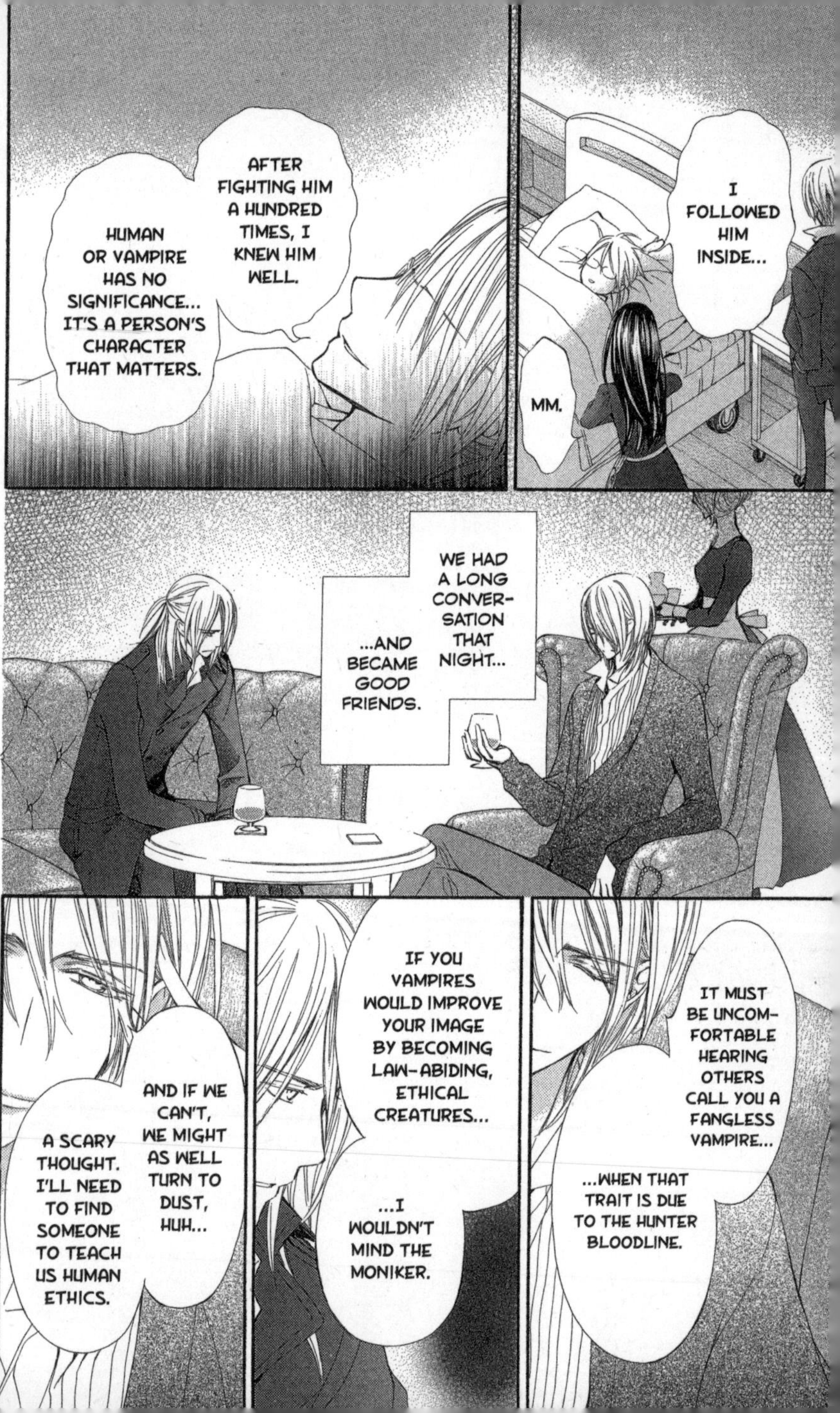
I FOLLOWED HIM INSIDE...
MM.
AFTER FIGHTING HIM A HUNDRED TIMES, I KNEW HIM WELL.
HUMAN OR VAMPIRE HAS NO SIGNIFICANCE... IT'S A PERSON'S CHARACTER THAT MATTERS.
WE HAD A LONG CONVERSATION THAT NIGHT...
...AND BECAME GOOD FRIENDS.
IT MUST BE UNCOMFORTABLE HEARING OTHERS CALL YOU A FANGLESS VAMPIRE...
...WHEN THAT TRAIT IS DUE TO THE HUNTER BLOODLINE.
IF YOU VAMPIRES WOULD IMPROVE YOUR IMAGE BY BECOMING LAW-ABIDING, ETHICAL CREATURES...
...I WOULDN'T MIND THE MONIKER.
AND IF WE CAN'T, WE MIGHT AS WELL TURN TO DUST, HUH...
A SCARY THOUGHT. I'LL NEED TO FIND SOMEONE TO TEACH US HUMAN ETHICS.

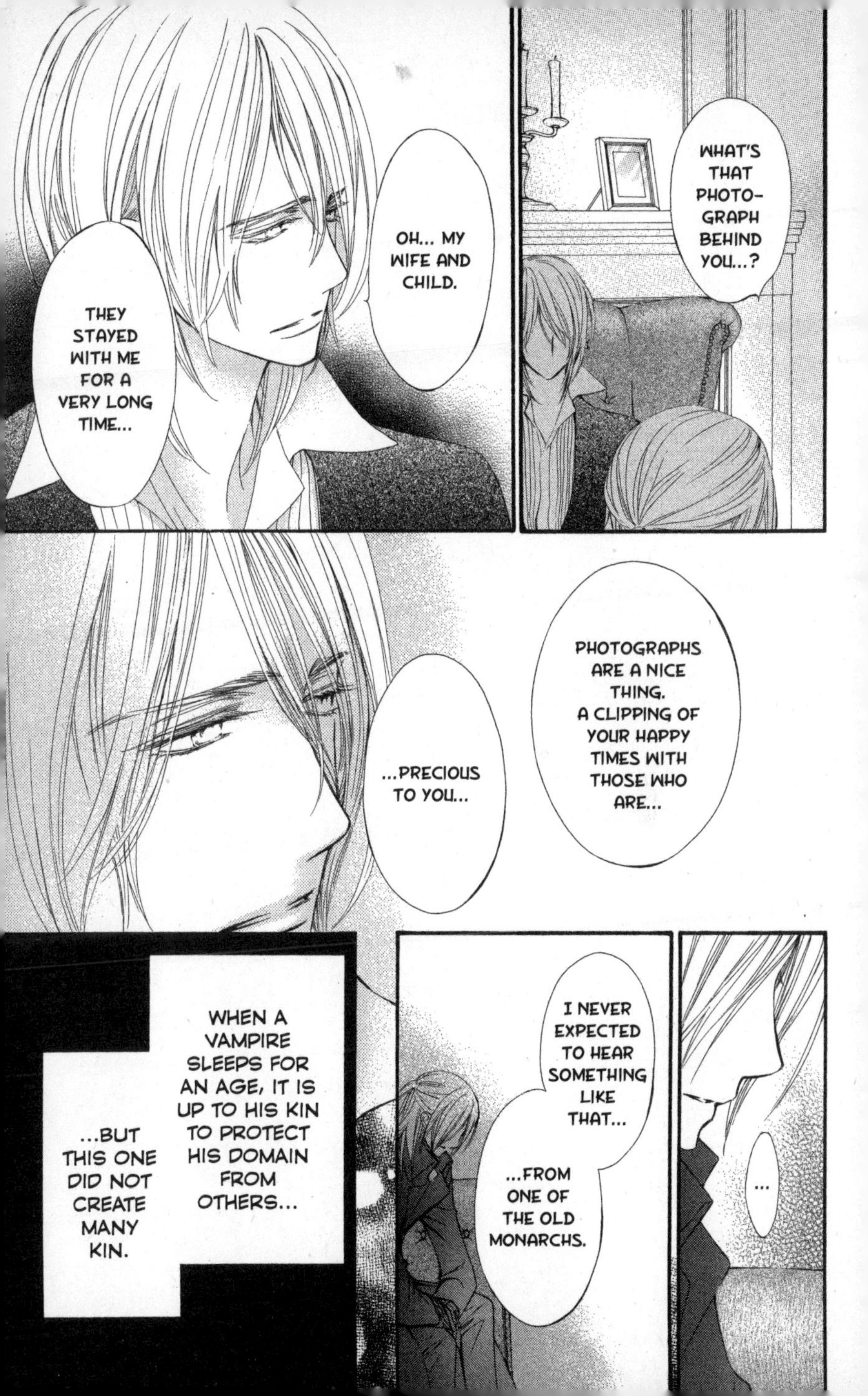
WHAT'S THAT PHOTOGRAPH BEHIND YOU...?
OH... MY WIFE AND CHILD.
THEY STAYED WITH ME FOR A VERY LONG TIME...
PHOTOGRAPHS ARE A NICE THING. A CLIPPING OF YOUR HAPPY TIMES WITH THOSE WHO ARE...
...PRECIOUS TO YOU...
...
I NEVER EXPECTED TO HEAR SOMETHING LIKE THAT...
...FROM ONE OF THE OLD MONARCHS.
WHEN A VAMPIRE SLEEPS FOR AN AGE, IT IS UP TO HIS KIN TO PROTECT HIS DOMAIN FROM OTHERS...
...BUT THIS ONE DID NOT CREATE MANY KIN.

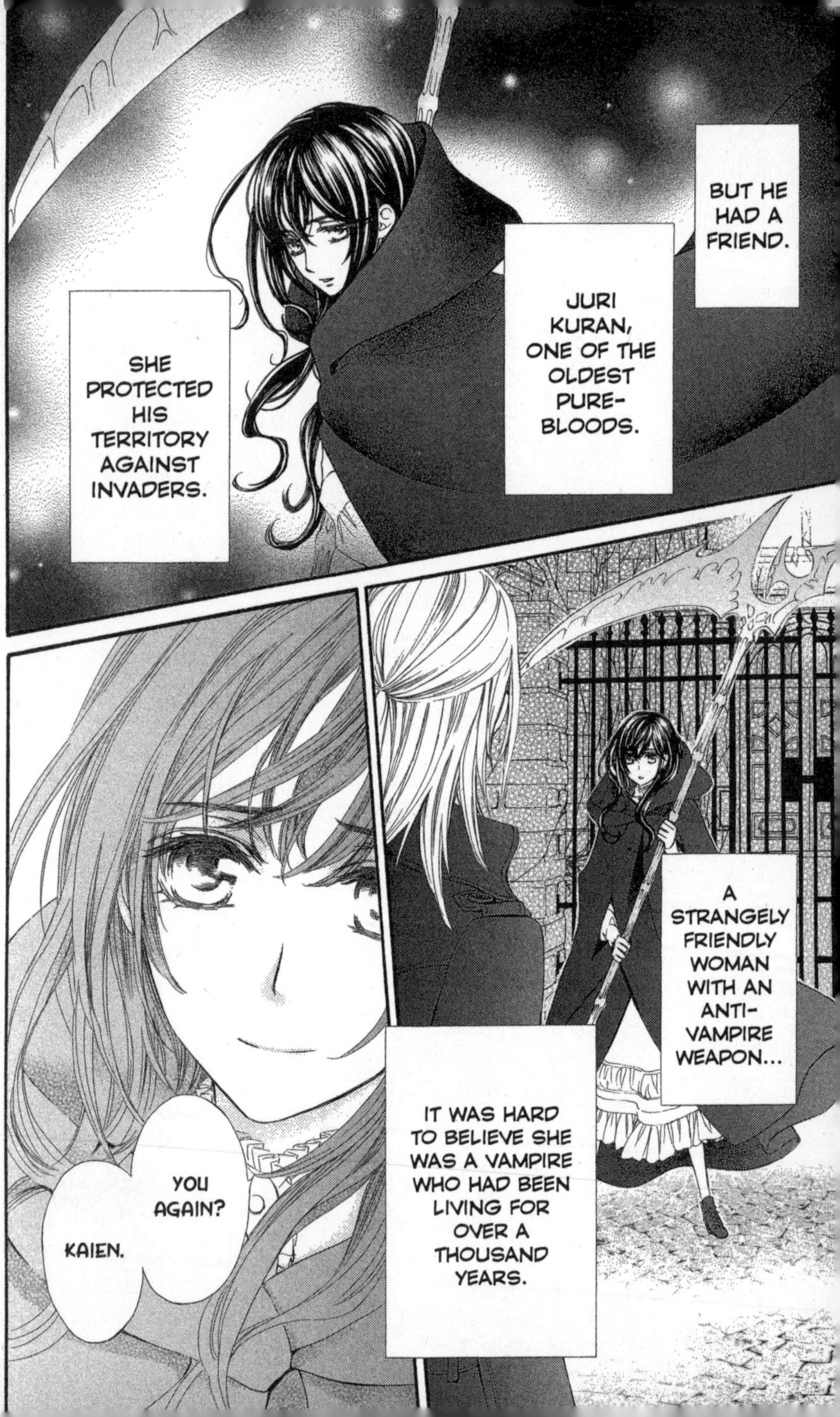
BUT HE HAD A FRIEND.
JURI KURAN, ONE OF THE OLDEST PURE-BLOODS.
SHE PROTECTED HIS TERRITORY AGAINST INVADERS.
A STRANGELY FRIENDLY WOMAN WITH AN ANTI-VAMPIRE WEAPON...
IT WAS HARD TO BELIEVE SHE WAS A VAMPIRE WHO HAD BEEN LIVING FOR OVER A THOUSAND YEARS.
YOU AGAIN?
KAIEN.

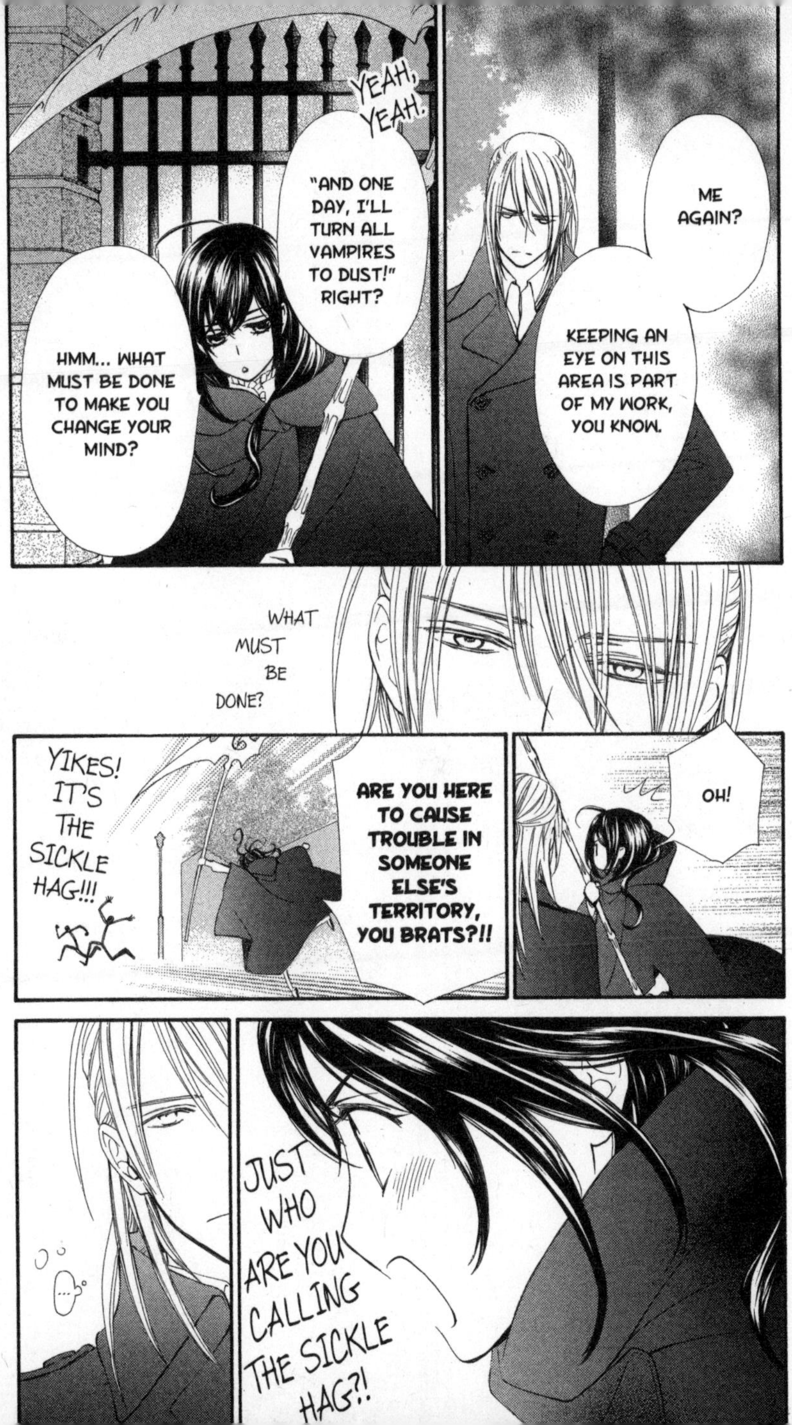
ME AGAIN?
KEEPING AN EYE ON THIS AREA IS PART OF MY WORK, YOU KNOW.
YEAH, YEAH.
"AND ONE DAY, I'LL TURN ALL VAMPIRES TO DUST!" RIGHT?
HMM... WHAT MUST BE DONE TO MAKE YOU CHANGE YOUR MIND?
WHAT MUST BE DONE?
OH!
ARE YOU HERE TO CAUSE TROUBLE IN SOMEONE ELSE'S TERRITORY, YOU BRATS?!!
YIKES! IT'S THE SICKLE HAG!!!
JUST WHO ARE YOU CALLING THE SICKLE HAG?!
...

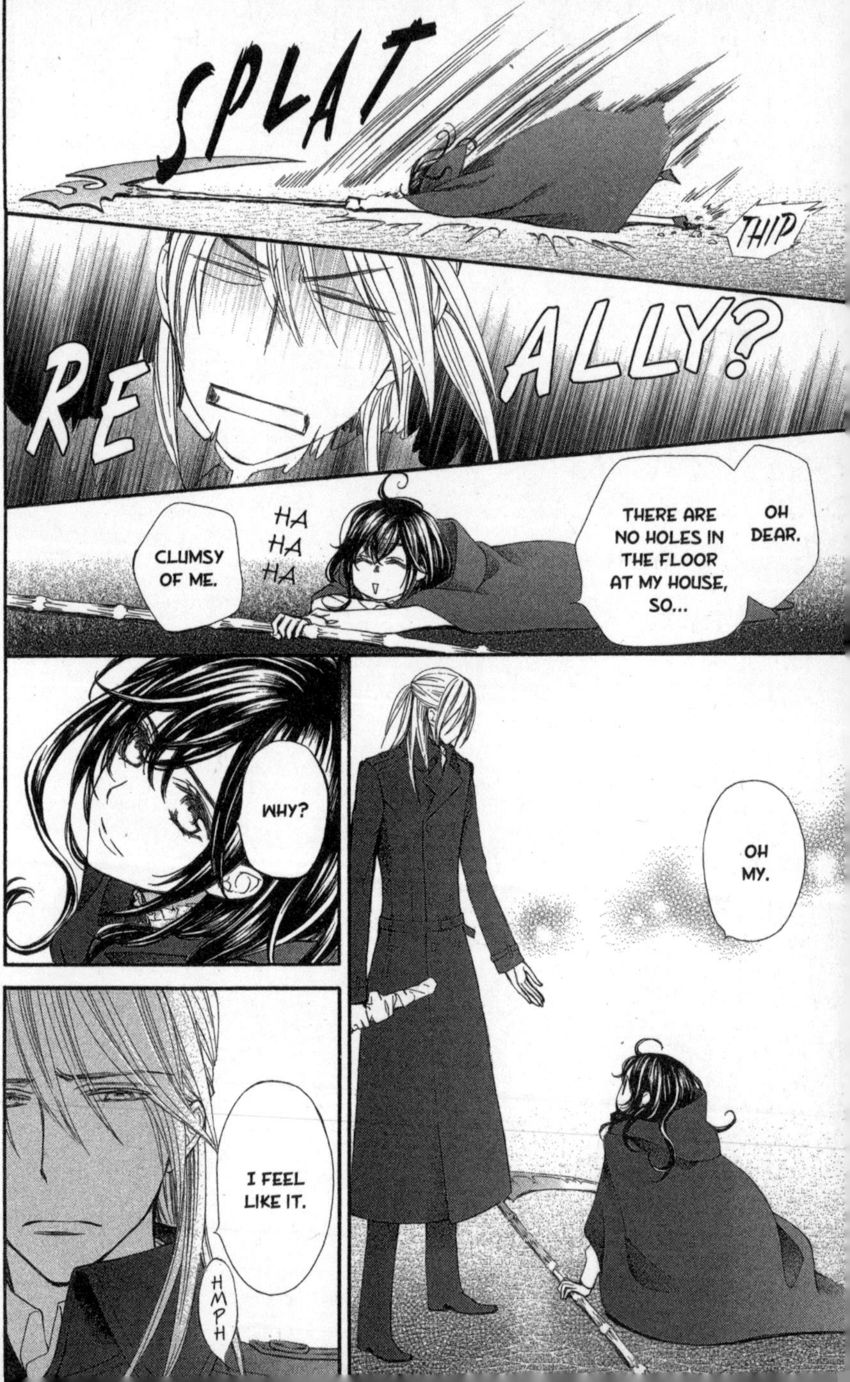
SPLAT
THIP
REALLY?
OH DEAR.
THERE ARE NO HOLES IN THE FLOOR AT MY HOUSE, SO...
HA HA HA
CLUMSY OF ME.
OH MY.
WHY?
I FEEL LIKE IT.
HMPH

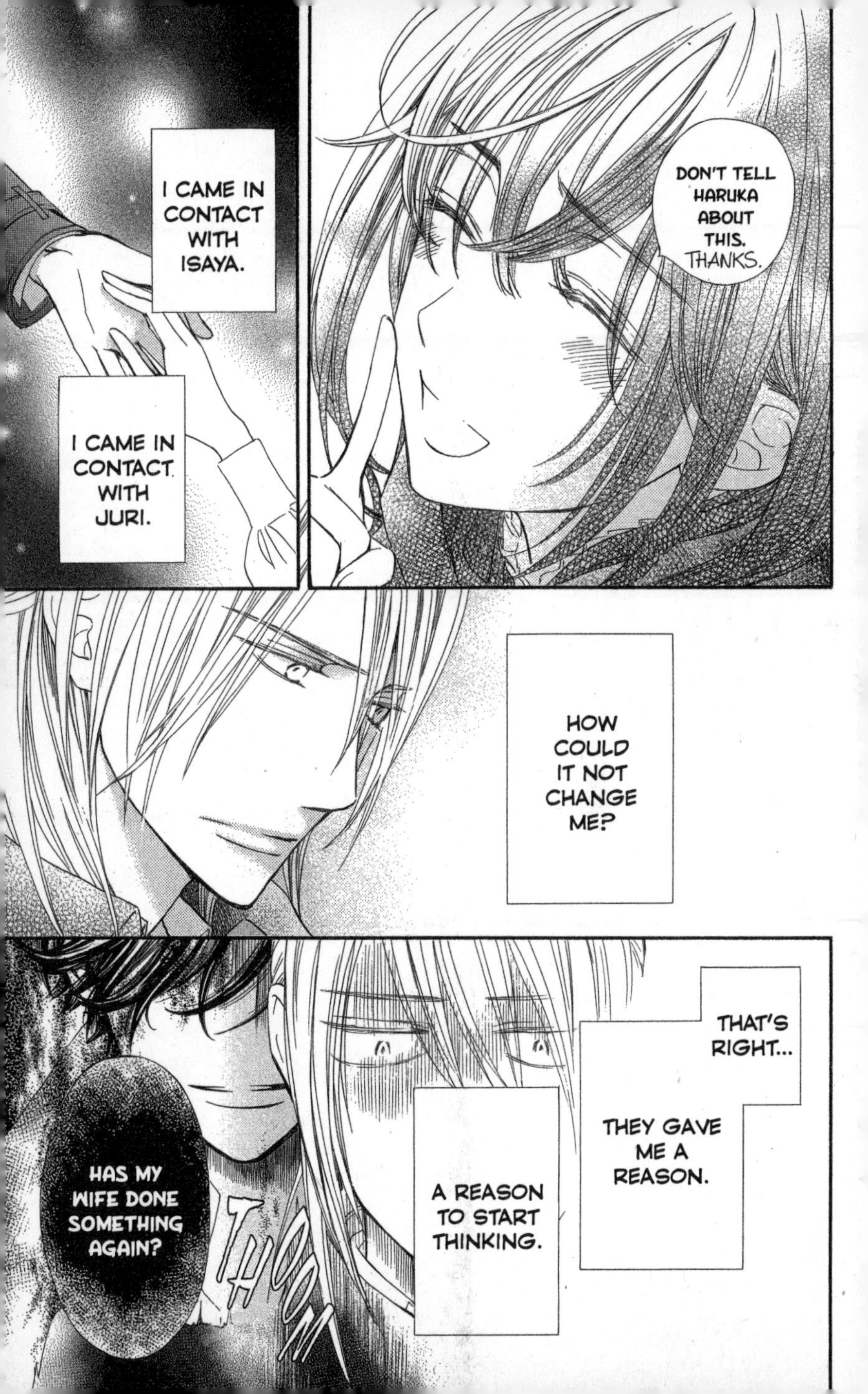
DON'T TELL HARUKA ABOUT THIS. THANKS.
I CAME IN CONTACT WITH ISAYA.
I CAME IN CONTACT WITH JURI.
HOW COULD IT NOT CHANGE ME?
THAT'S RIGHT...
THEY GAVE ME A REASON.
A REASON TO START THINKING.
HAS MY WIFE DONE SOMETHING AGAIN?
THOOM

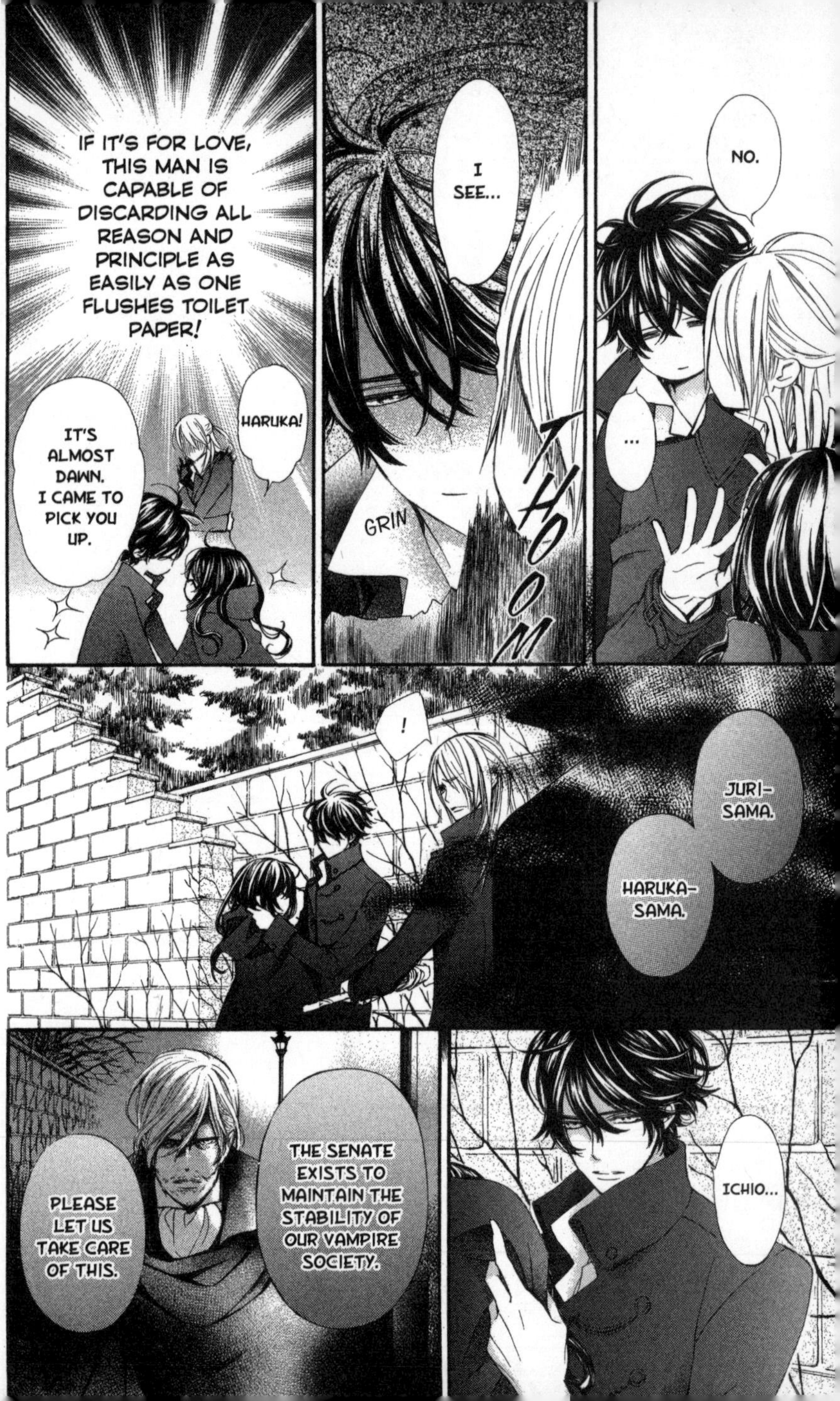
NO.
...
I SEE...
GRIN
THOOM
IF IT'S FOR LOVE, THIS MAN IS CAPABLE OF DISCARDING ALL REASON AND PRINCIPLE AS EASILY AS ONE FLUSHES TOILET PAPER!
HARUKA!
IT'S ALMOST DAWN. I CAME TO PICK YOU UP.
JURI-SAMA.
HARUKA-SAMA.
!
ICHIO...
THE SENATE EXISTS TO MAINTAIN THE STABILITY OF OUR VAMPIRE SOCIETY.
PLEASE LET US TAKE CARE OF THIS.

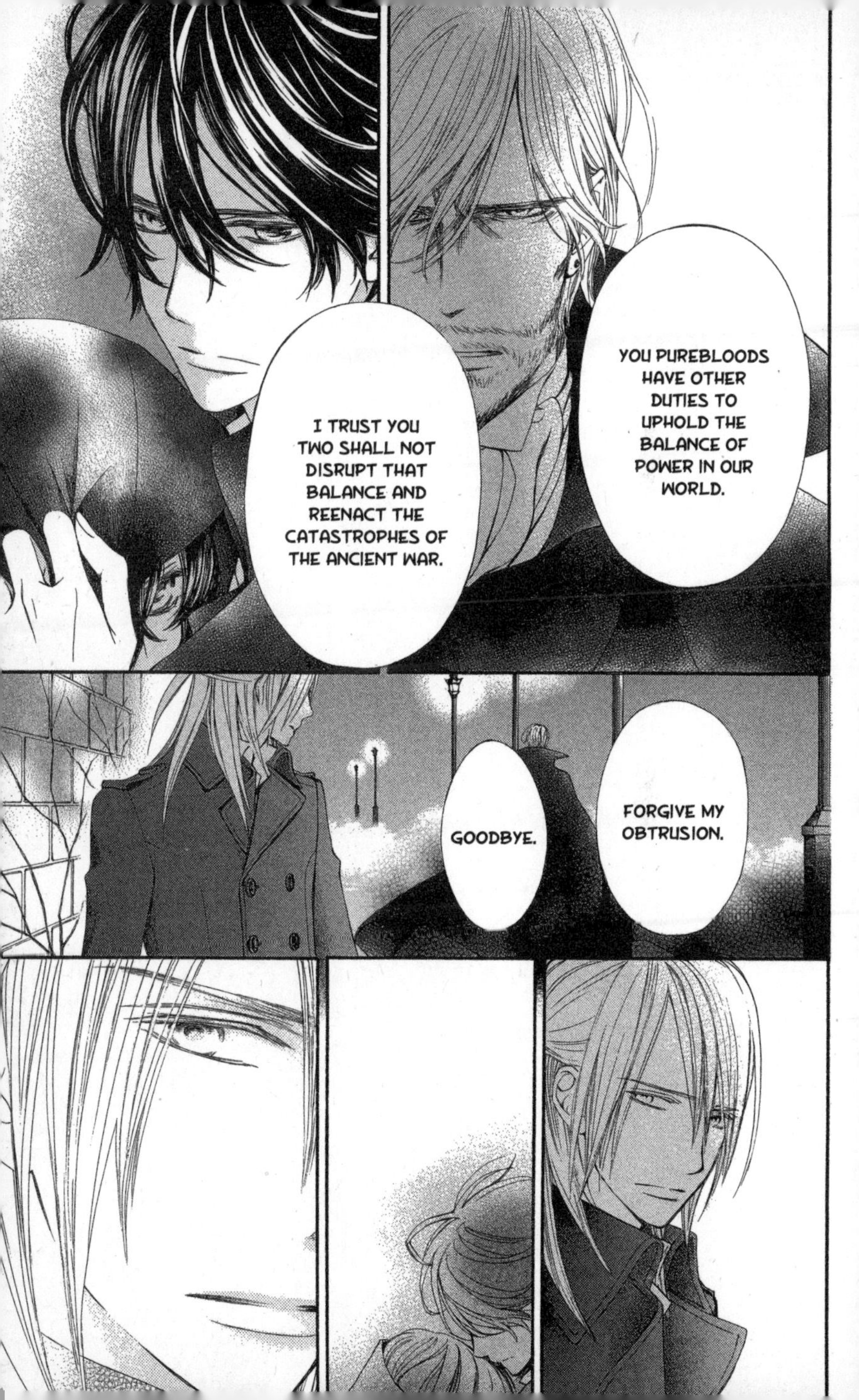
YOU PUREBLOODS HAVE OTHER DUTIES TO UPHOLD THE BALANCE OF POWER IN OUR WORLD.
I TRUST YOU TWO SHALL NOT DISRUPT THAT BALANCE AND REENACT THE CATASTROPHES OF THE ANCIENT WAR.
FORGIVE MY OBTRUSION.
GOODBYE.

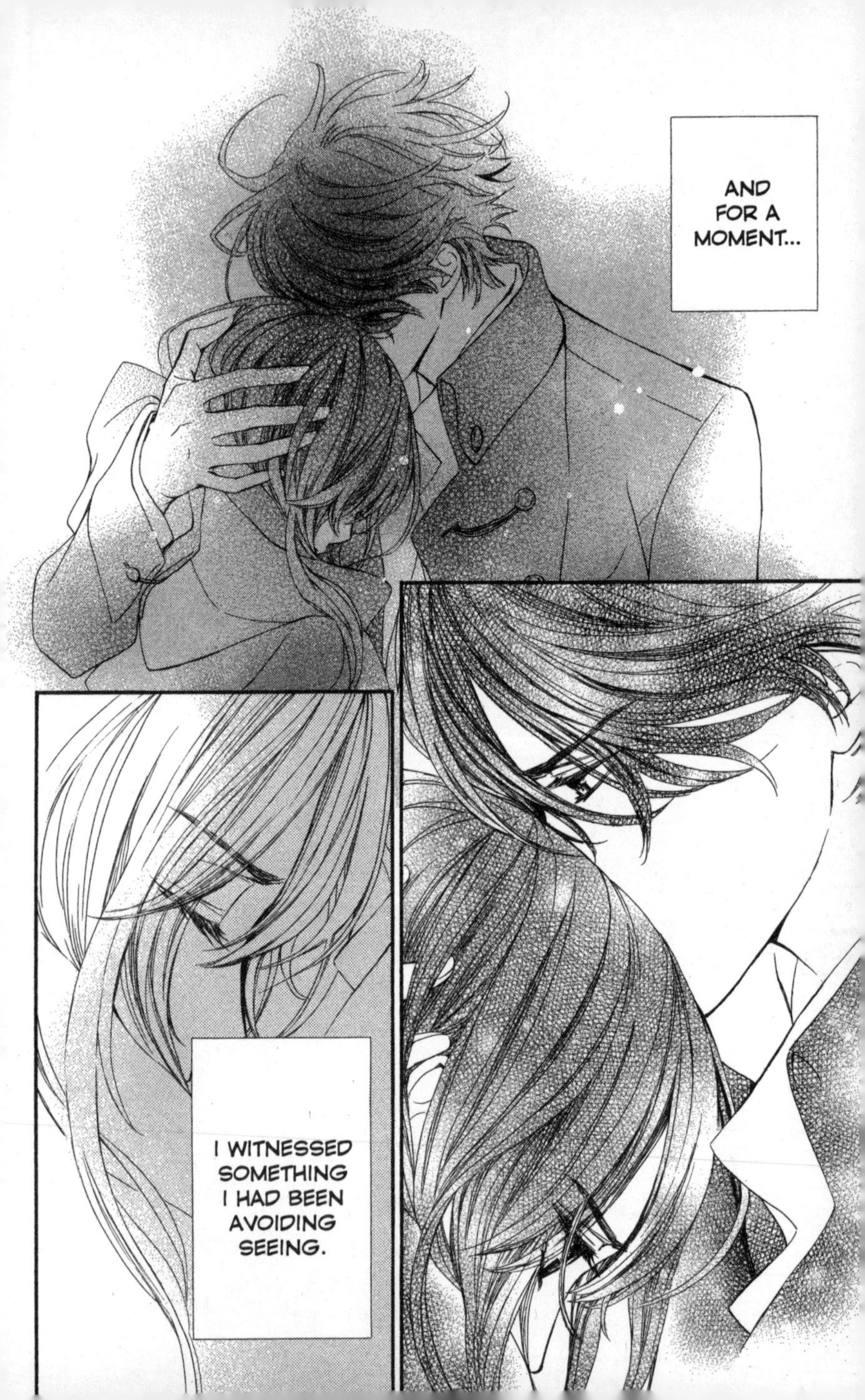
AND FOR A MOMENT...
I WITNESSED SOMETHING I HAD BEEN AVOIDING SEEING.

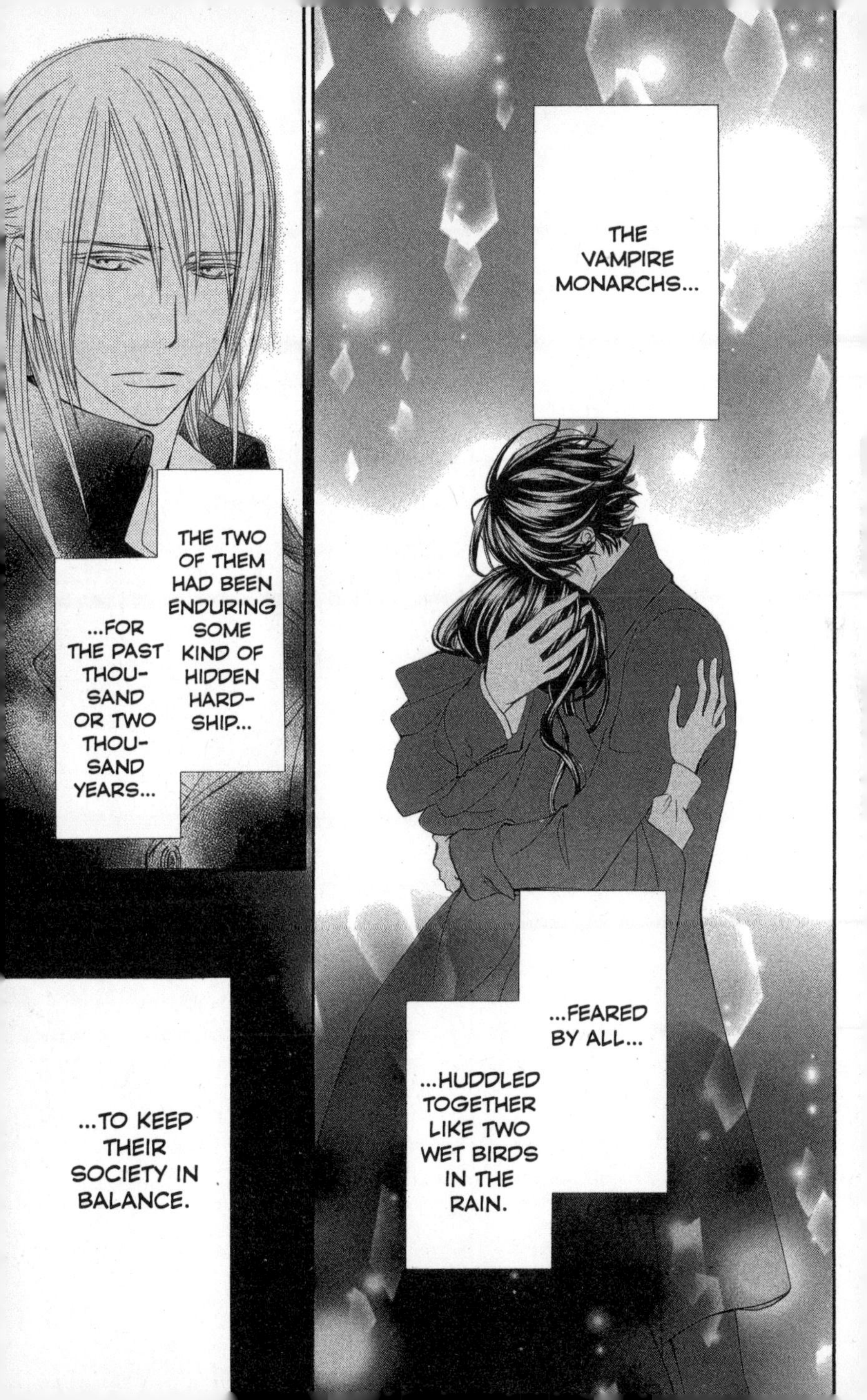
THE VAMPIRE MONARCHS...
...FEARED BY ALL...
...HUDDLED TOGETHER LIKE TWO WET BIRDS IN THE RAIN.
THE TWO OF THEM HAD BEEN ENDURING SOME KIND OF HIDDEN HARDSHIP...
...FOR THE PAST THOUSAND OR TWO THOUSAND YEARS...
...TO KEEP THEIR SOCIETY IN BALANCE.

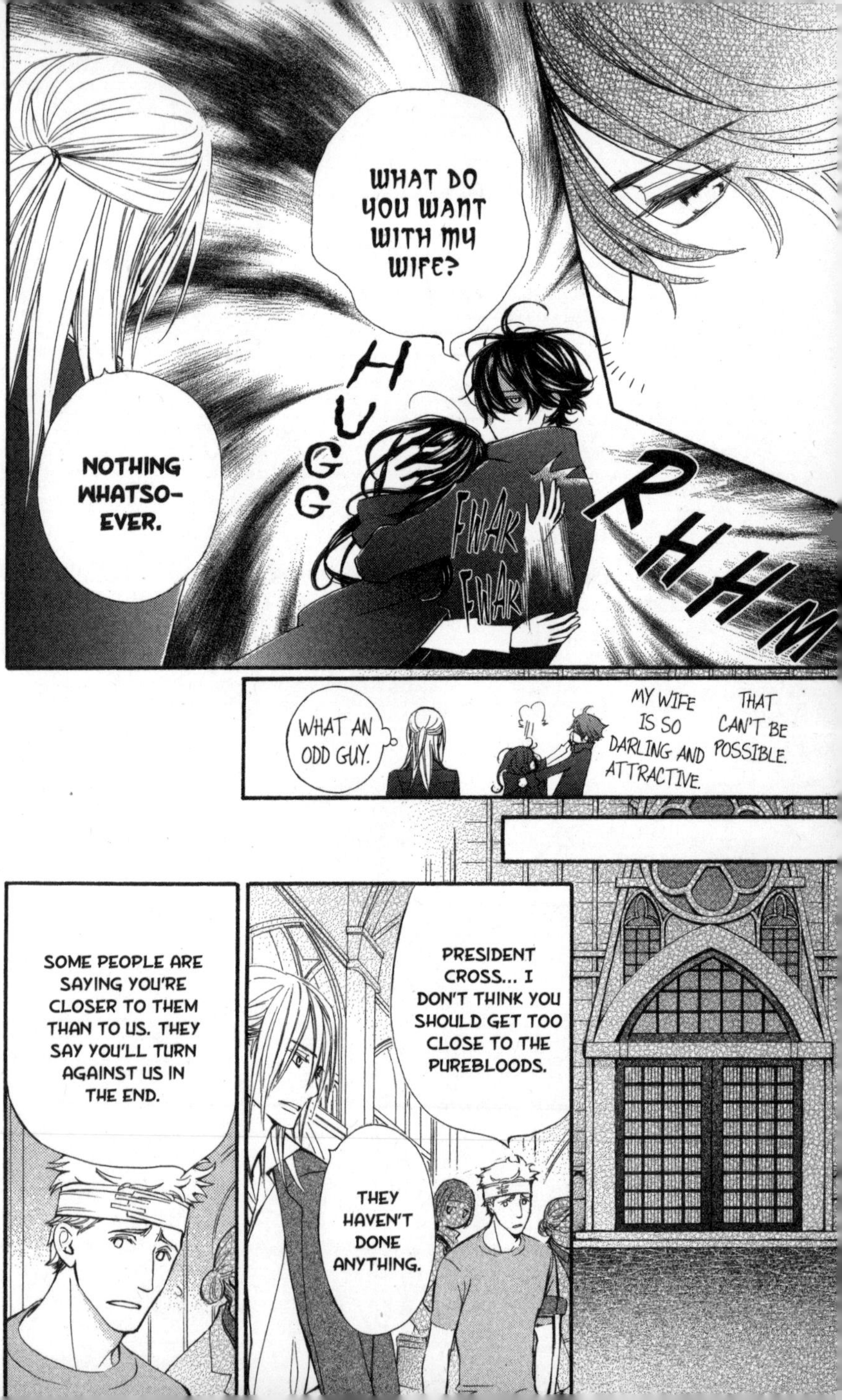
WHAT DO YOU WANT WITH MY WIFE?
RHHM
HUGG
FWAR FWAR
NOTHING WHATSO-EVER.
THAT CAN'T BE POSSIBLE.
MY WIFE IS SO DARLING AND ATTRACTIVE.
WHAT AN ODD GUY.
PRESIDENT CROSS... I DON'T THINK YOU SHOULD GET TOO CLOSE TO THE PUREBLOODS.
THEY HAVEN'T DONE ANYTHING.
SOME PEOPLE ARE SAYING YOU'RE CLOSER TO THEM THAN TO US. THEY SAY YOU'LL TURN AGAINST US IN THE END.

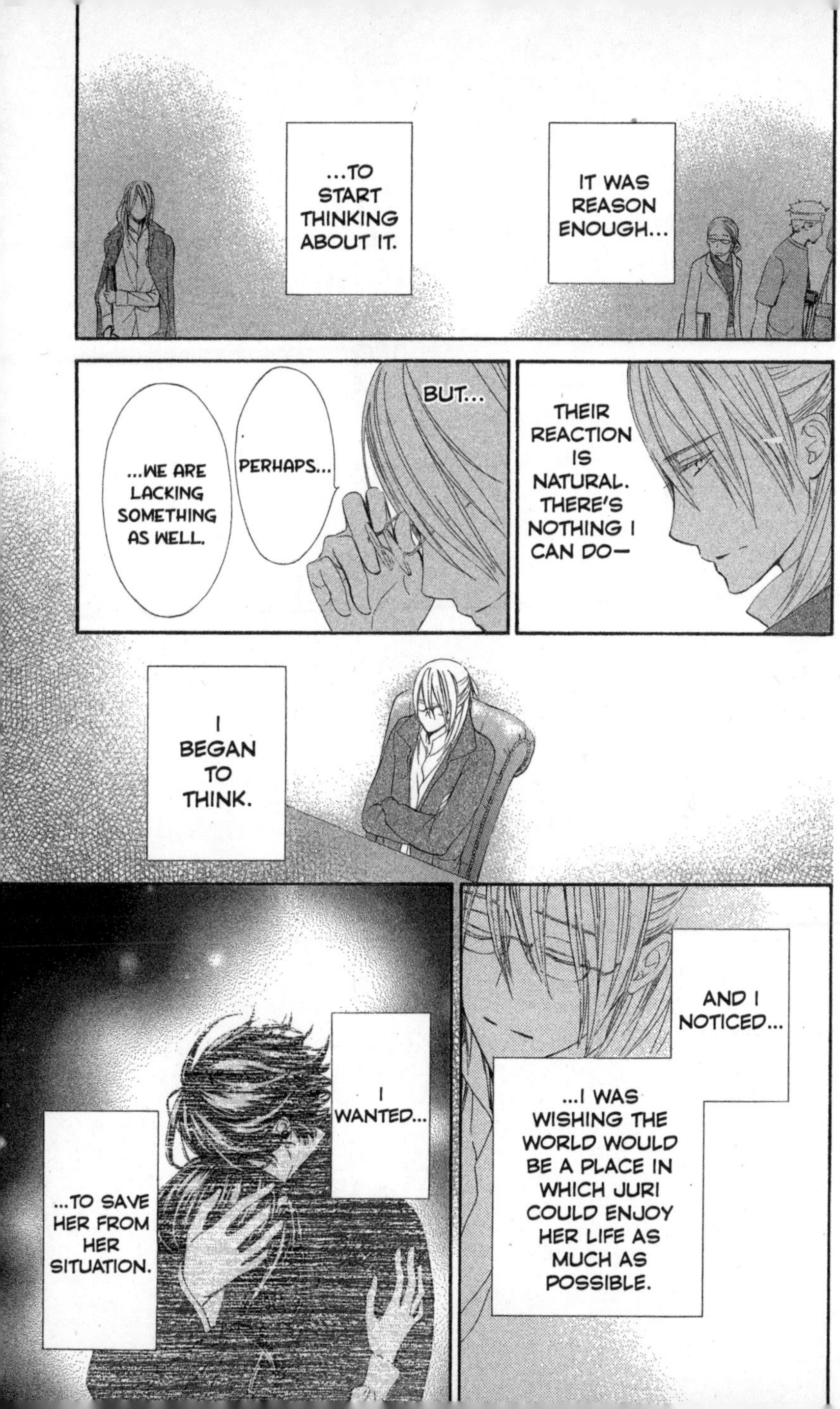
IT WAS REASON ENOUGH...
...TO START THINKING ABOUT IT.
THEIR REACTION IS NATURAL. THERE'S NOTHING I CAN DO—
BUT...
PERHAPS...
...WE ARE LACKING SOMETHING AS WELL.
I BEGAN TO THINK.
AND I NOTICED...
...I WAS WISHING THE WORLD WOULD BE A PLACE IN WHICH JURI COULD ENJOY HER LIFE AS MUCH AS POSSIBLE.
I WANTED...
...TO SAVE HER FROM HER SITUATION.

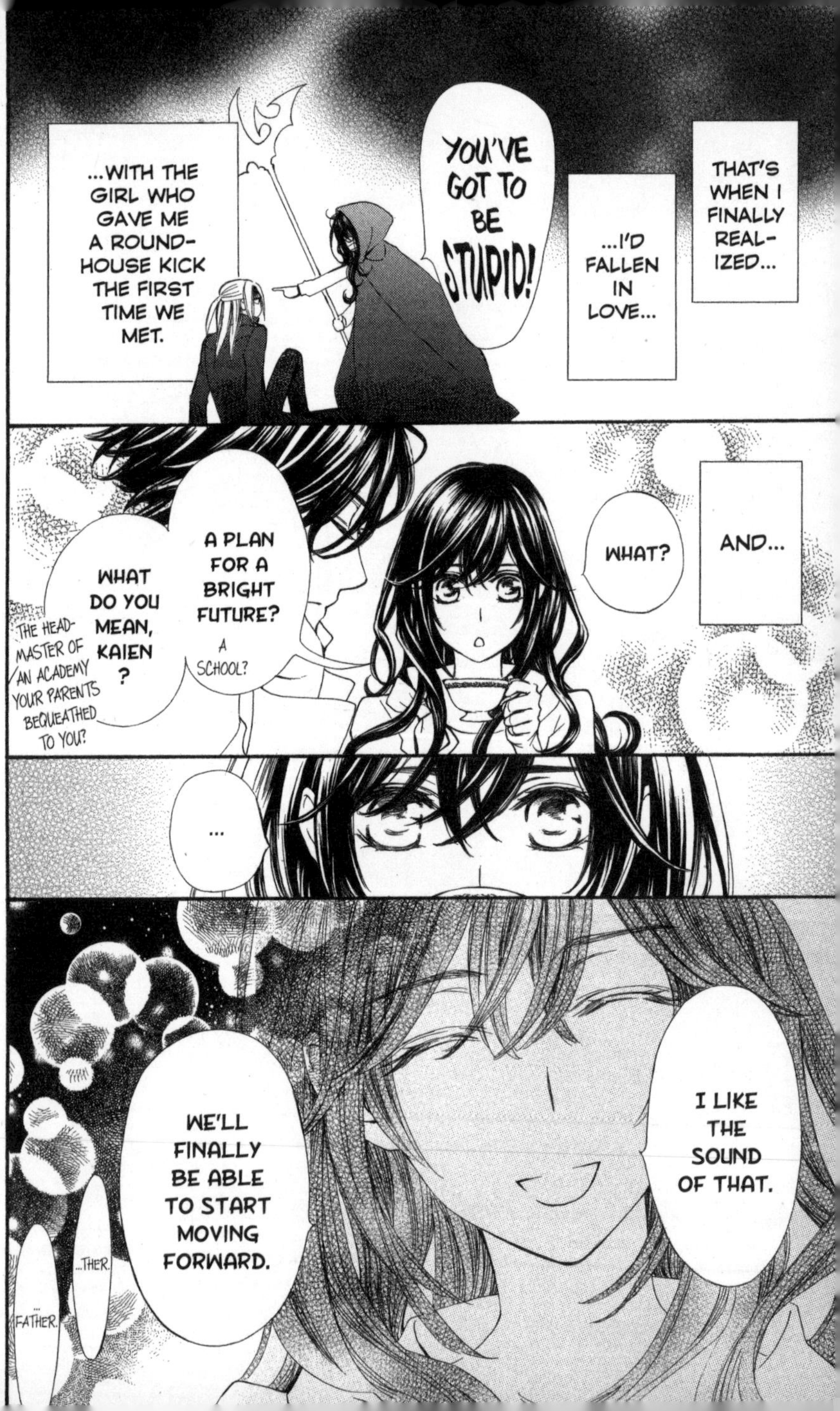
THAT'S WHEN I FINALLY REAL-IZED...
...I'D FALLEN IN LOVE...
YOU'VE GOT TO BE STUPID!
...WITH THE GIRL WHO GAVE ME A ROUND-HOUSE KICK THE FIRST TIME WE MET.
AND...
WHAT?
A PLAN FOR A BRIGHT FUTURE?
A SCHOOL?
WHAT DO YOU MEAN, KAIEN?
THE HEAD-MASTER OF AN ACADEMY YOUR PARENTS BEQUEATHED TO YOU?
...
I LIKE THE SOUND OF THAT.
WE'LL FINALLY BE ABLE TO START MOVING FORWARD.
...THER.
...FATHER.

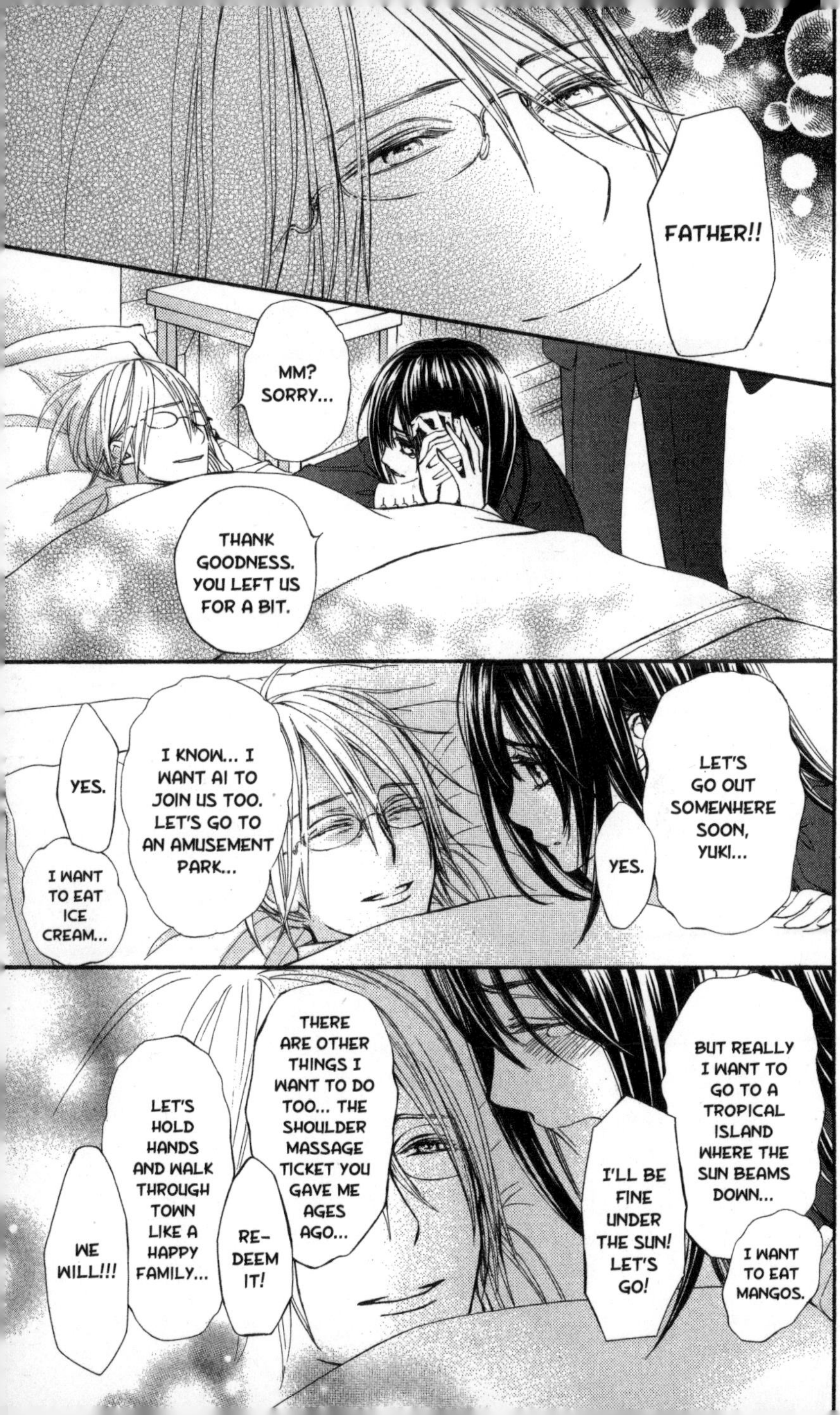
FATHER!!
MM? SORRY...
THANK GOODNESS. YOU LEFT US FOR A BIT.
LET'S GO OUT SOMEWHERE SOON, YUKI...
YES.
I KNOW... I WANT AI TO JOIN US TOO. LET'S GO TO AN AMUSEMENT PARK...
YES.
I WANT TO EAT ICE CREAM...
BUT REALLY I WANT TO GO TO A TROPICAL ISLAND WHERE THE SUN BEAMS DOWN...
I WANT TO EAT MANGOS.
I'LL BE FINE UNDER THE SUN! LET'S GO!
THERE ARE OTHER THINGS I WANT TO DO TOO... THE SHOULDER MASSAGE TICKET YOU GAVE ME AGES AGO...
RE-DEEM IT!
LET'S HOLD HANDS AND WALK THROUGH TOWN LIKE A HAPPY FAMILY...
WE WILL!!!

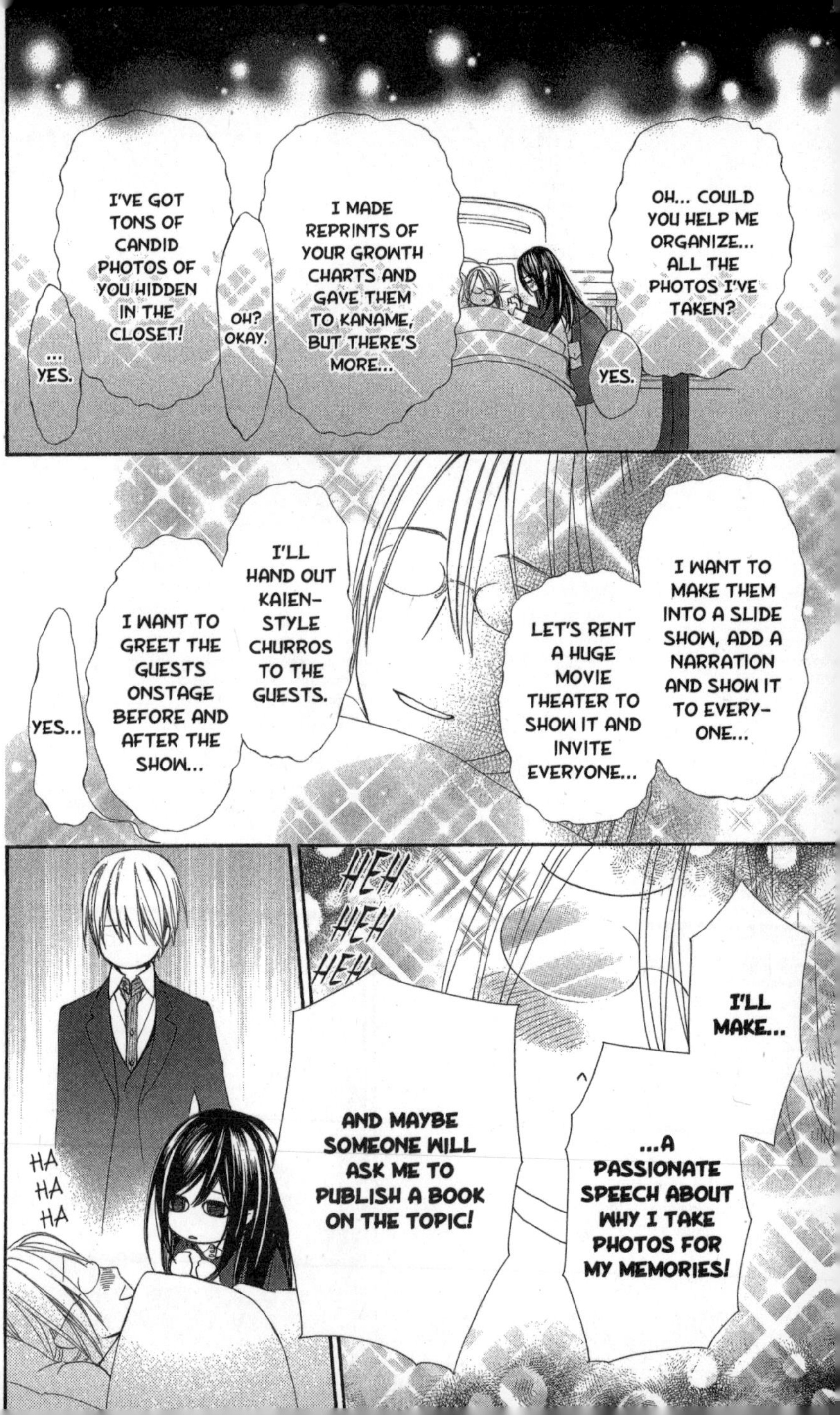
OH... COULD YOU HELP ME ORGANIZE... ALL THE PHOTOS I'VE TAKEN?
YES.
I MADE REPRINTS OF YOUR GROWTH CHARTS AND GAVE THEM TO KANAME, BUT THERE'S MORE...
OH? OKAY.
I'VE GOT TONS OF CANDID PHOTOS OF YOU HIDDEN IN THE CLOSET!
... YES.
I WANT TO MAKE THEM INTO A SLIDE SHOW, ADD A NARRATION AND SHOW IT TO EVERY-ONE...
LET'S RENT A HUGE MOVIE THEATER TO SHOW IT AND INVITE EVERYONE...
I'LL HAND OUT KAIEN-STYLE CHURROS TO THE GUESTS.
I WANT TO GREET THE GUESTS ONSTAGE BEFORE AND AFTER THE SHOW...
YES...
HEH HEH HEH
I'LL MAKE...
...A PASSIONATE SPEECH ABOUT WHY I TAKE PHOTOS FOR MY MEMORIES!
AND MAYBE SOMEONE WILL ASK ME TO PUBLISH A BOOK ON THE TOPIC!
HA HA HA

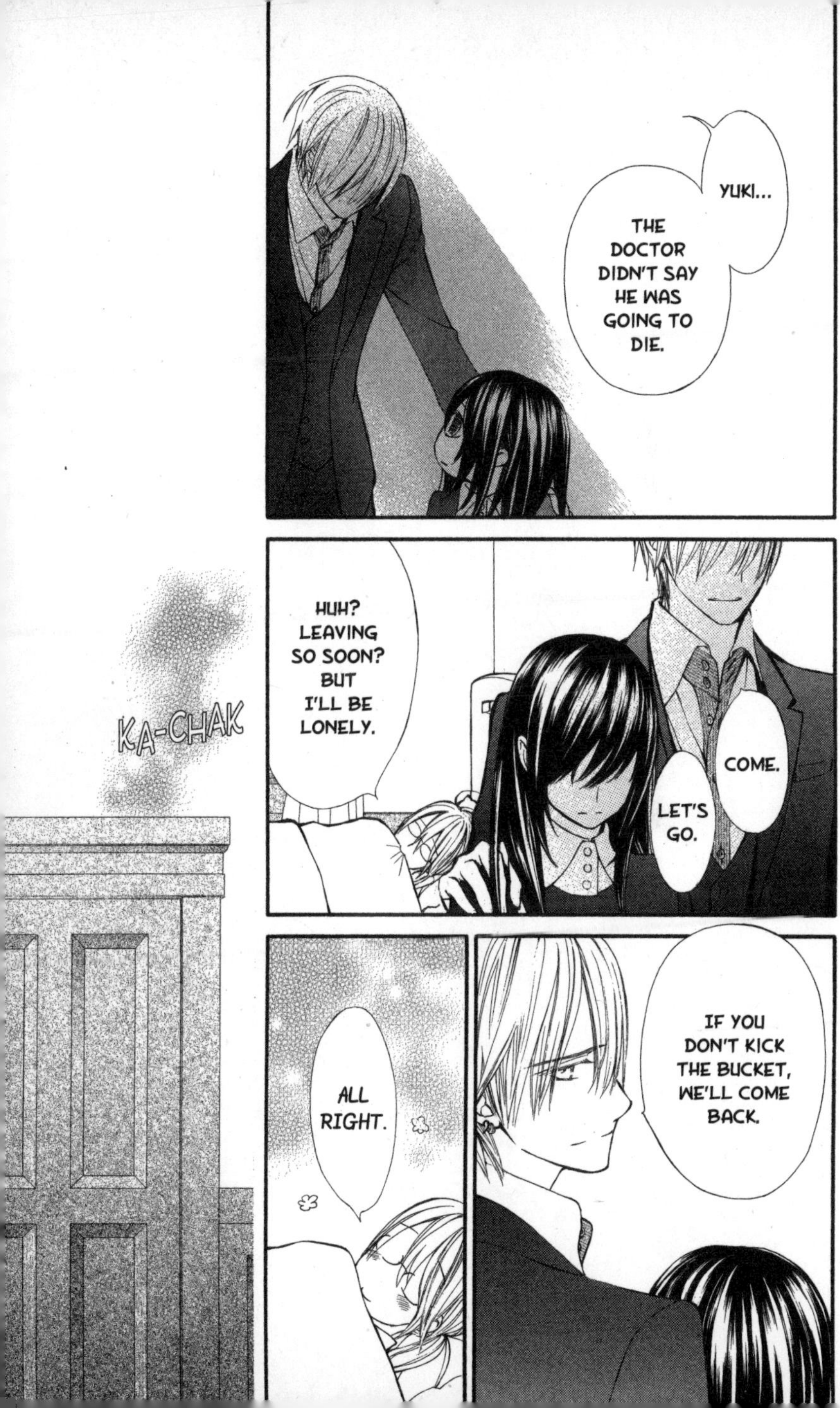
YUKI...
THE DOCTOR DIDN'T SAY HE WAS GOING TO DIE.
COME.
LET'S GO.
HUH? LEAVING SO SOON? BUT I'LL BE LONELY.
IF YOU DON'T KICK THE BUCKET, WE'LL COME BACK.
ALL RIGHT.
KA-CHAK

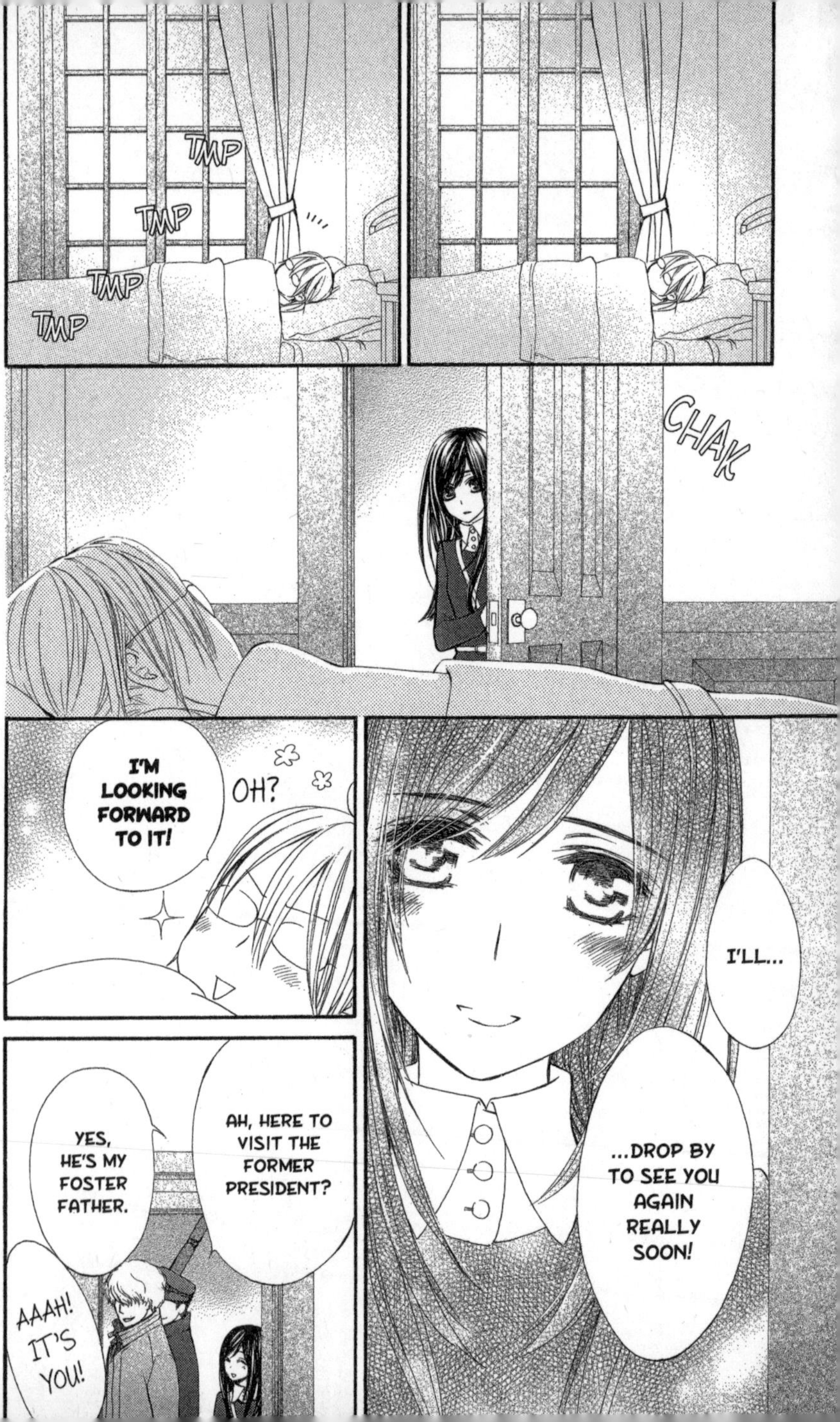
TMP
TMP
TMP
TMP
CHAK
I'LL...
...DROP BY TO SEE YOU AGAIN REALLY SOON!
OH?
I'M LOOKING FORWARD TO IT!
AH, HERE TO VISIT THE FORMER PRESIDENT?
YES, HE'S MY FOSTER FATHER.
AAAH! IT'S YOU!

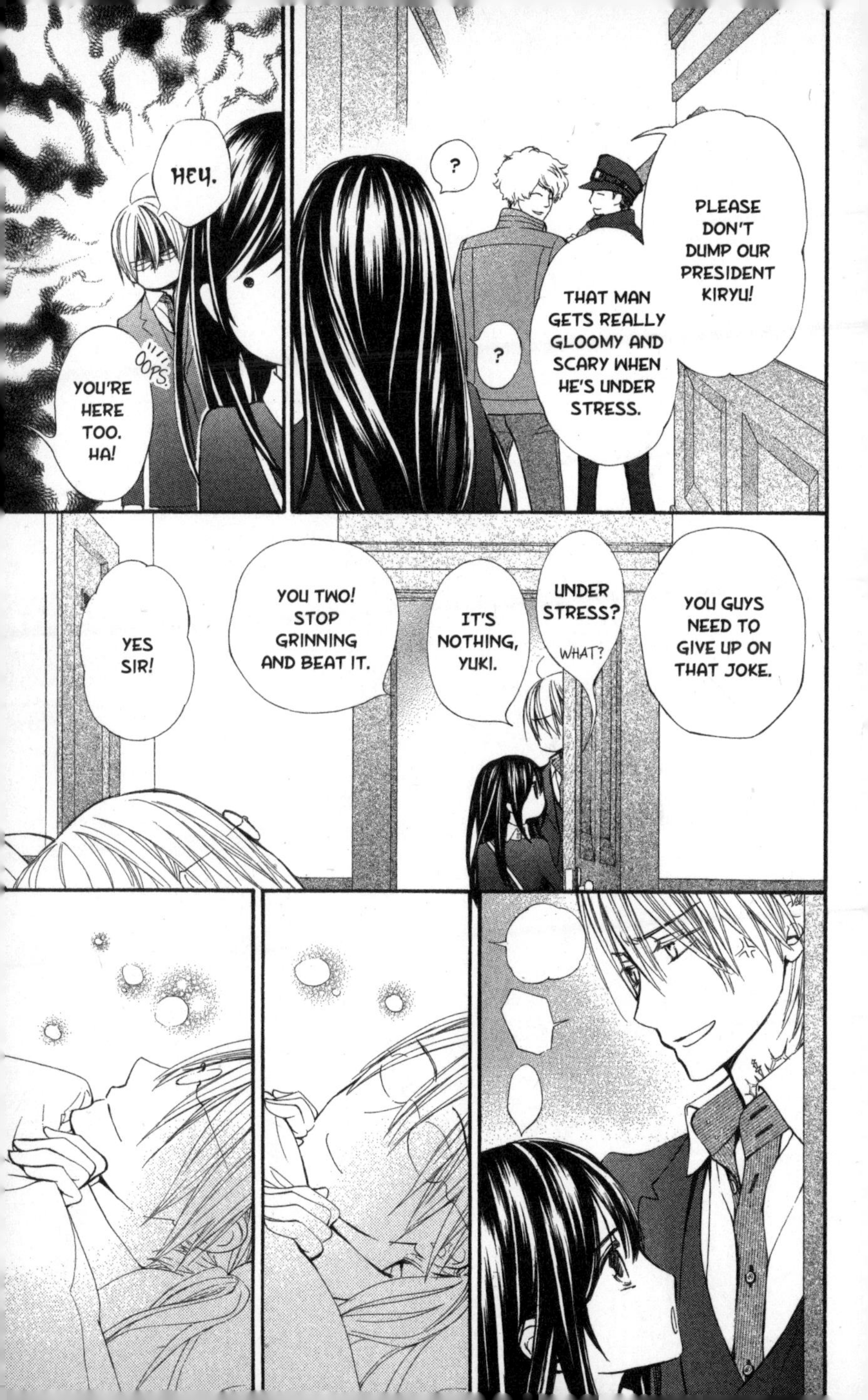
PLEASE DON'T DUMP OUR PRESIDENT KIRYU!
THAT MAN GETS REALLY GLOOMY AND SCARY WHEN HE'S UNDER STRESS.
?
?
HEY.
OOPS.
YOU'RE HERE TOO. HA!
YOU GUYS NEED TO GIVE UP ON THAT JOKE.
UNDER STRESS?
WHAT?
IT'S NOTHING, YUKI.
YOU TWO! STOP GRINNING AND BEAT IT.
YES SIR!

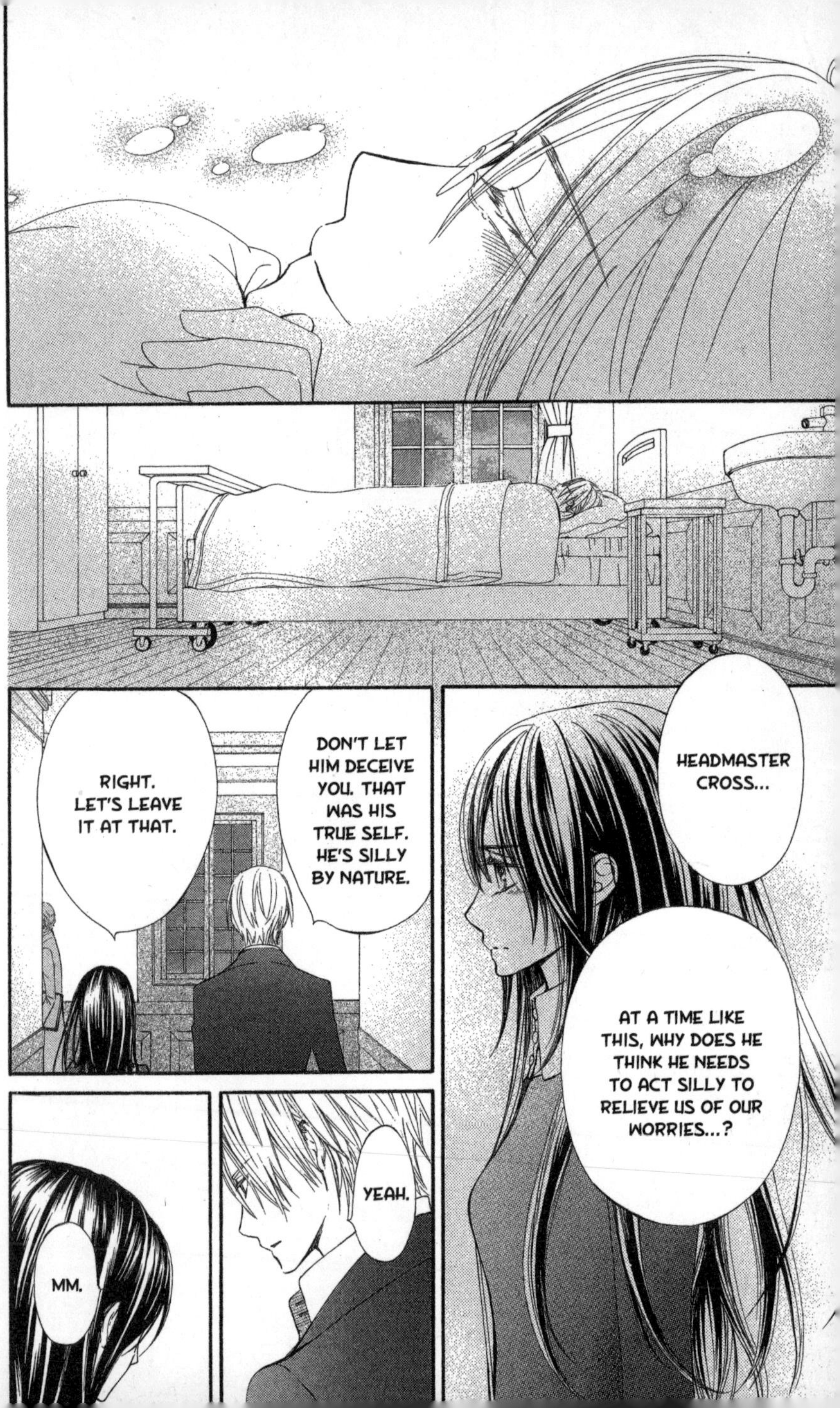
HEADMASTER CROSS...
AT A TIME LIKE THIS, WHY DOES HE THINK HE NEEDS TO ACT SILLY TO RELIEVE US OF OUR WORRIES...?
DON'T LET HIM DECEIVE YOU. THAT WAS HIS TRUE SELF. HE'S SILLY BY NATURE.
RIGHT. LET'S LEAVE IT AT THAT.
YEAH.
MM.

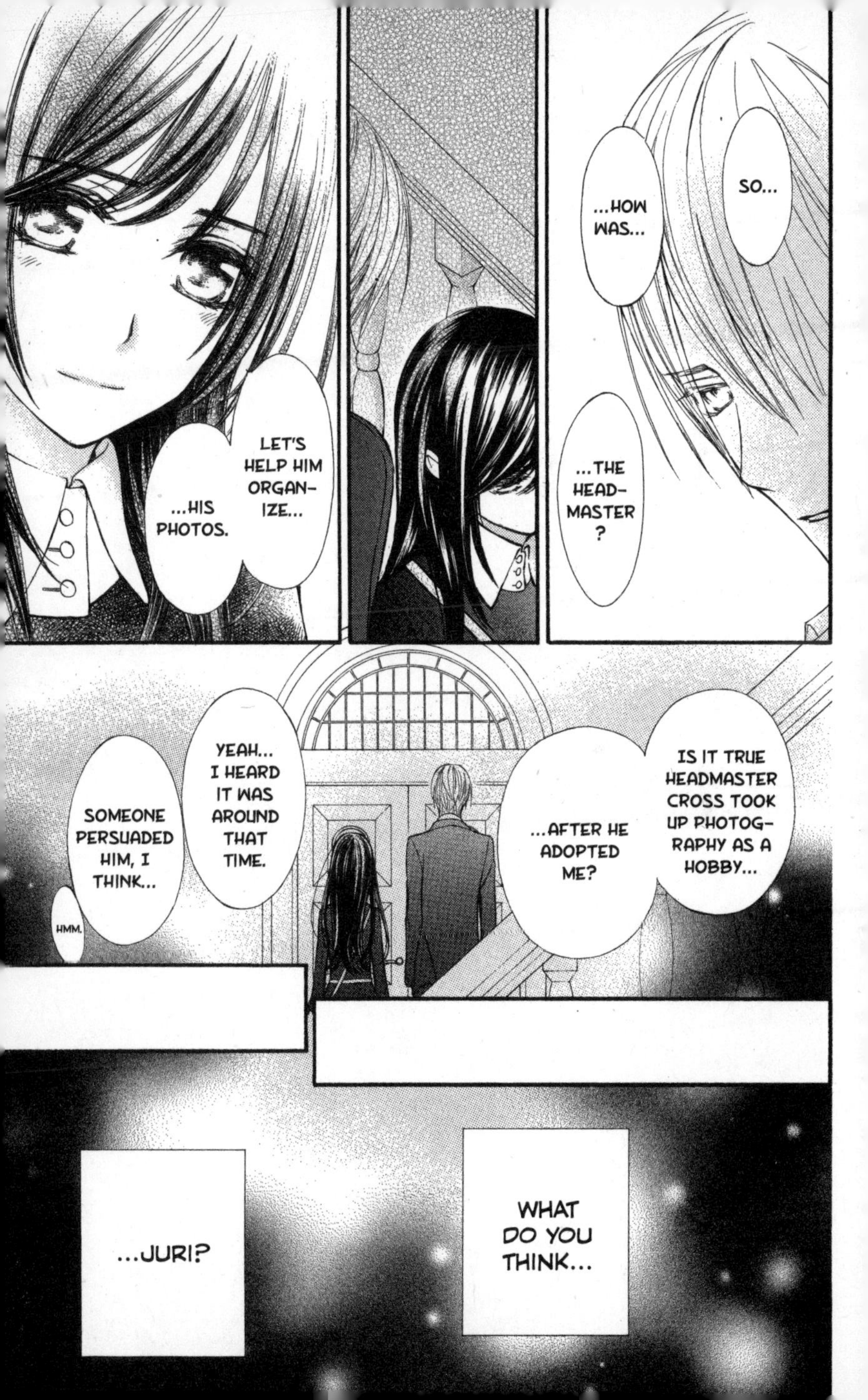
SO...
...HOW WAS...
...THE HEAD-MASTER?
LET'S HELP HIM ORGAN-IZE...
...HIS PHOTOS.
IS IT TRUE HEADMASTER CROSS TOOK UP PHOTOG-RAPHY AS A HOBBY...
...AFTER HE ADOPTED ME?
YEAH... I HEARD IT WAS AROUND THAT TIME.
SOMEONE PERSUADED HIM, I THINK...
HMM.
WHAT DO YOU THINK...
...JURI?

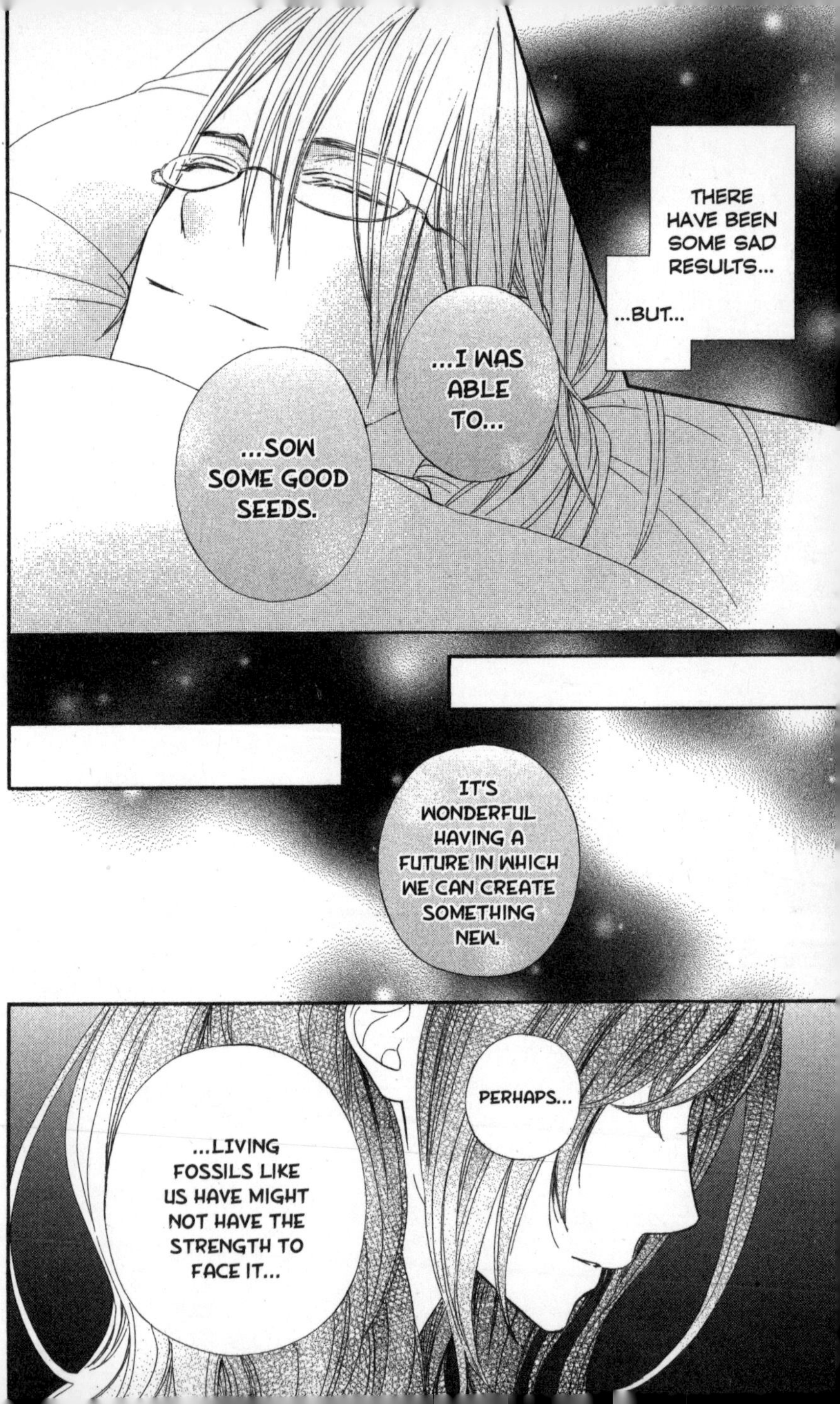
THERE HAVE BEEN SOME SAD RESULTS...
...BUT...
...I WAS ABLE TO...
...SOW SOME GOOD SEEDS.
IT'S WONDERFUL HAVING A FUTURE IN WHICH WE CAN CREATE SOMETHING NEW.
PERHAPS...
...LIVING FOSSILS LIKE US HAVE MIGHT NOT HAVE THE STRENGTH TO FACE IT...

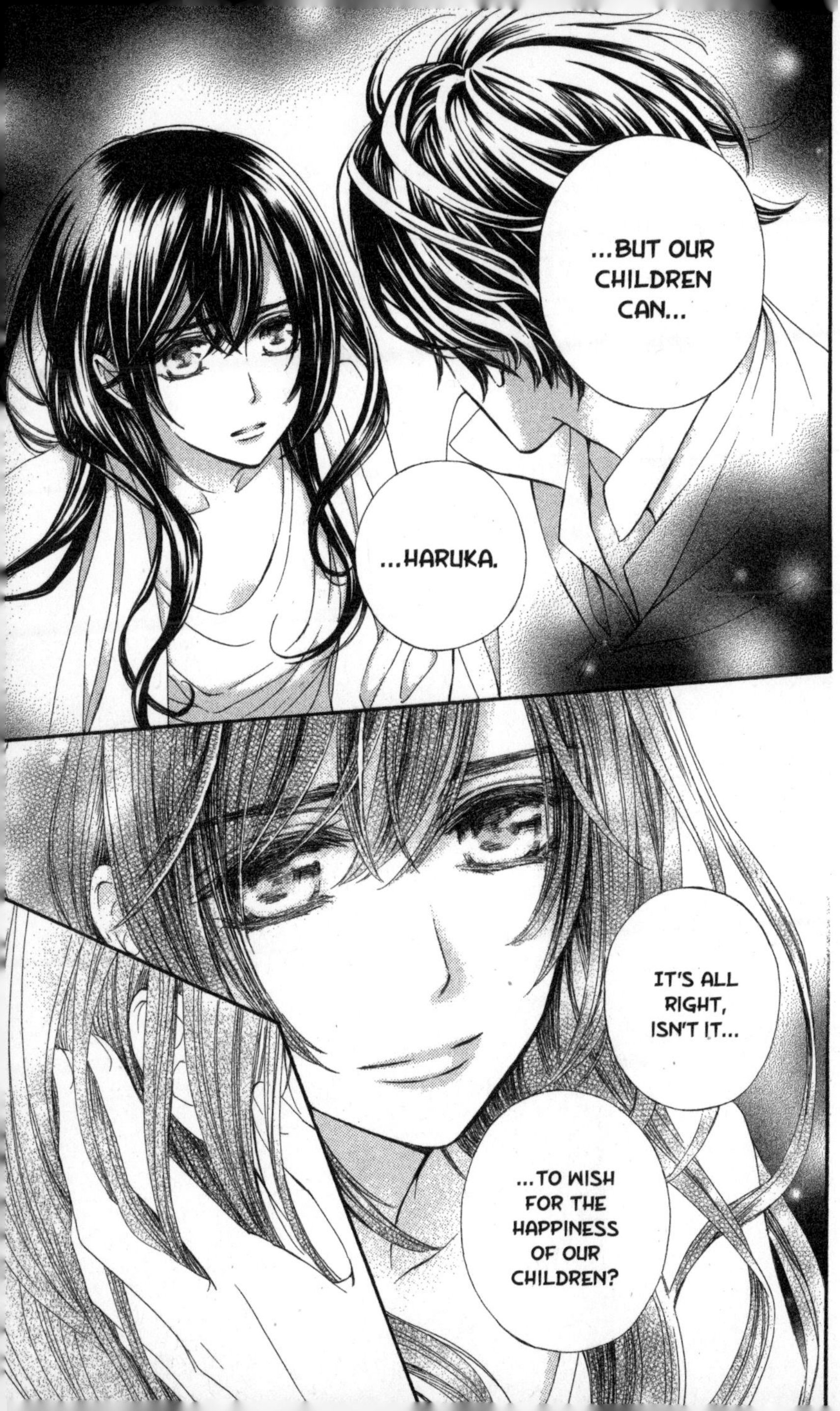
...BUT OUR CHILDREN CAN...
...HARUKA.
IT'S ALL RIGHT, ISN'T IT...
...TO WISH FOR THE HAPPINESS OF OUR CHILDREN?

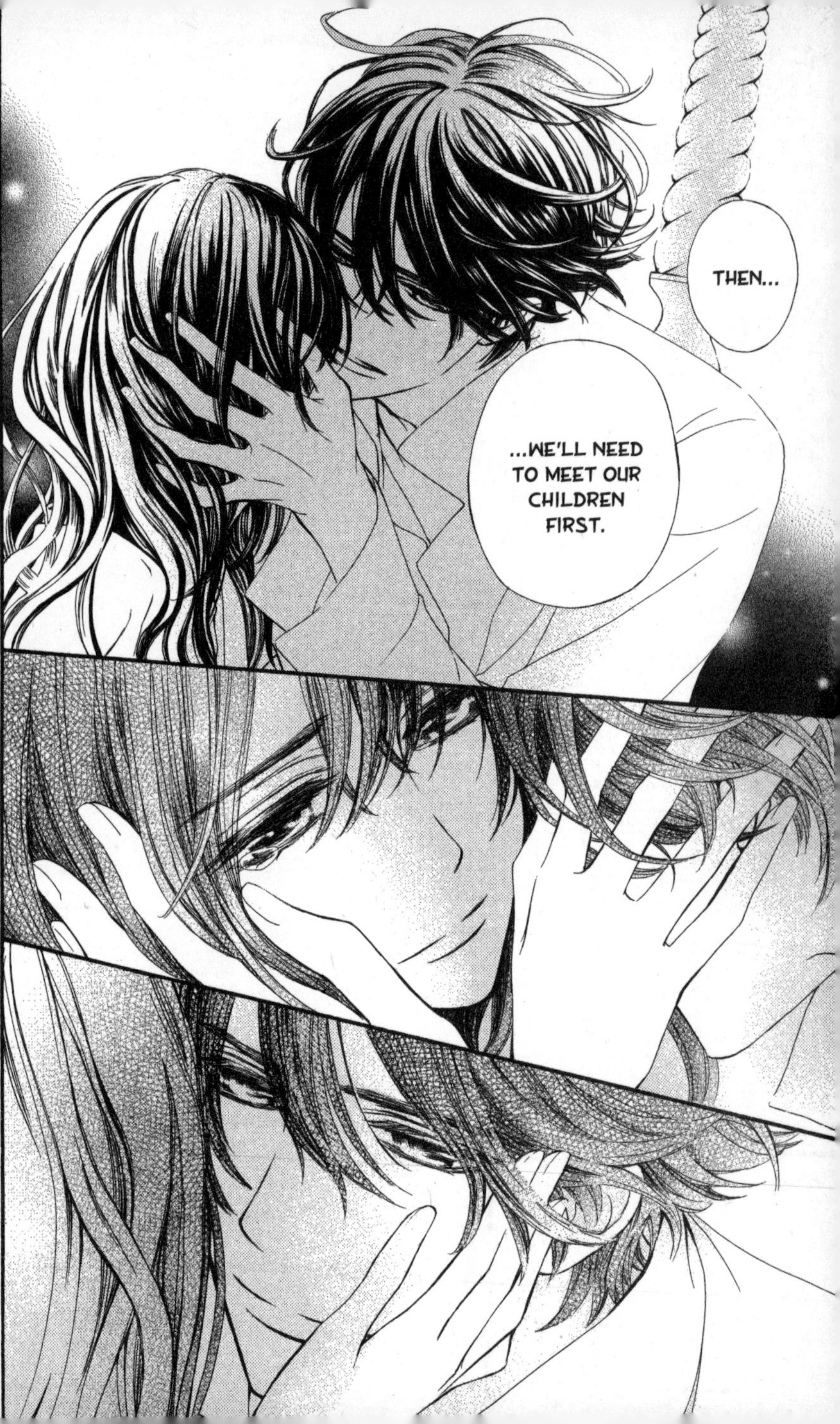
THEN...
...WE'LL NEED TO MEET OUR CHILDREN FIRST.

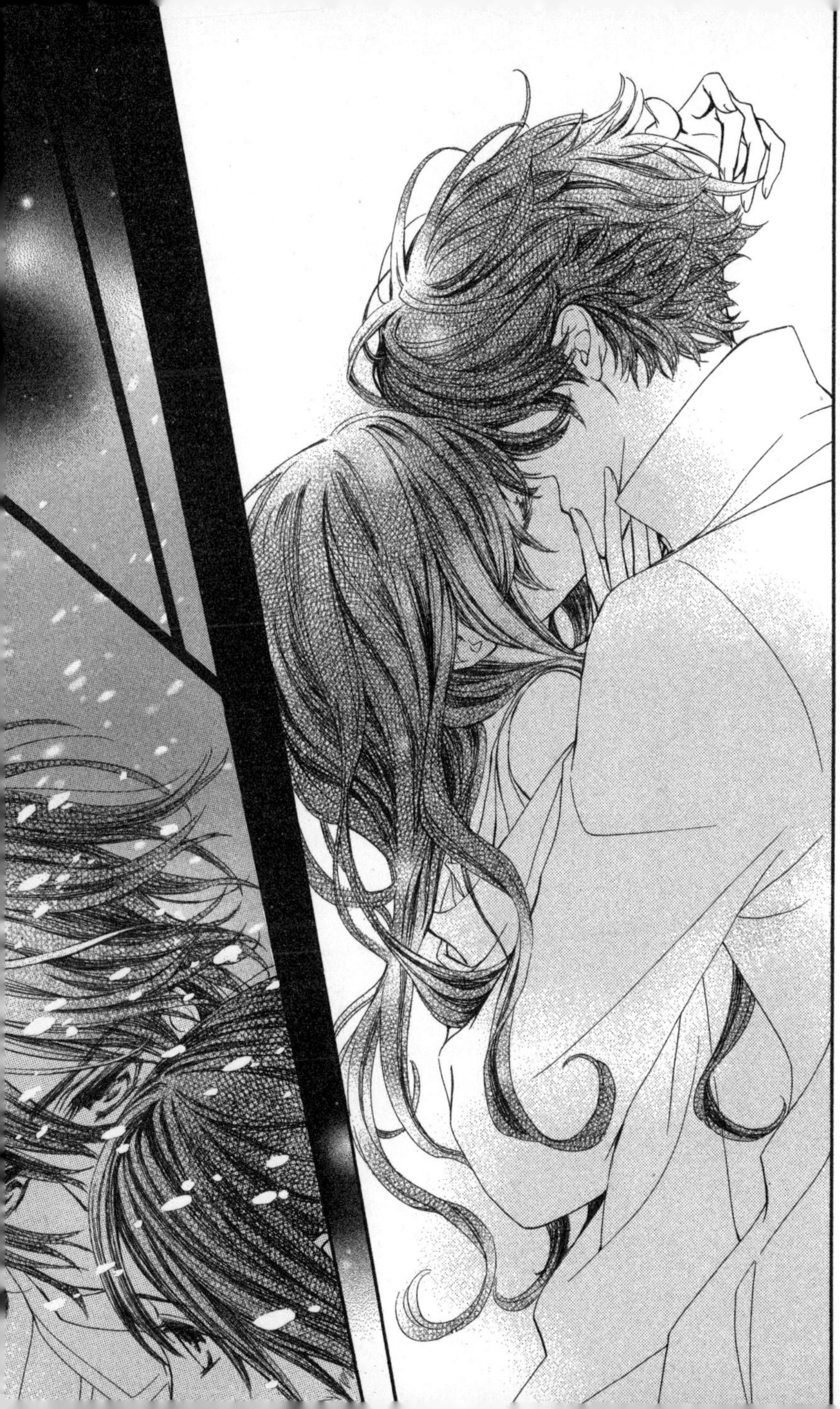

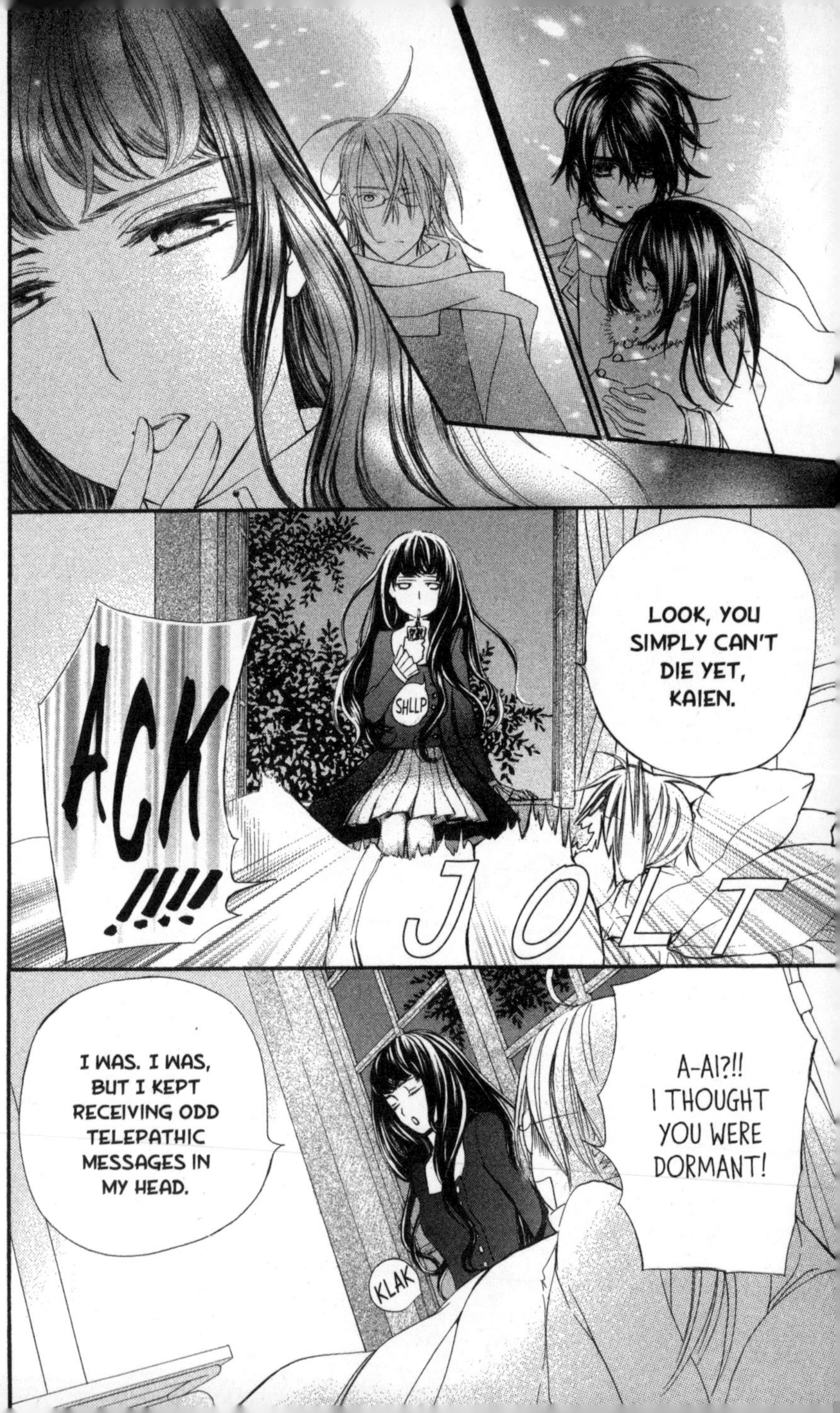
LOOK, YOU SIMPLY CAN'T DIE YET, KAIEN.
SHLLP
JOLT
ACK !!!!
A-AI?!! I THOUGHT YOU WERE DORMANT!
I WAS. I WAS, BUT I KEPT RECEIVING ODD TELEPATHIC MESSAGES IN MY HEAD.
KLAK

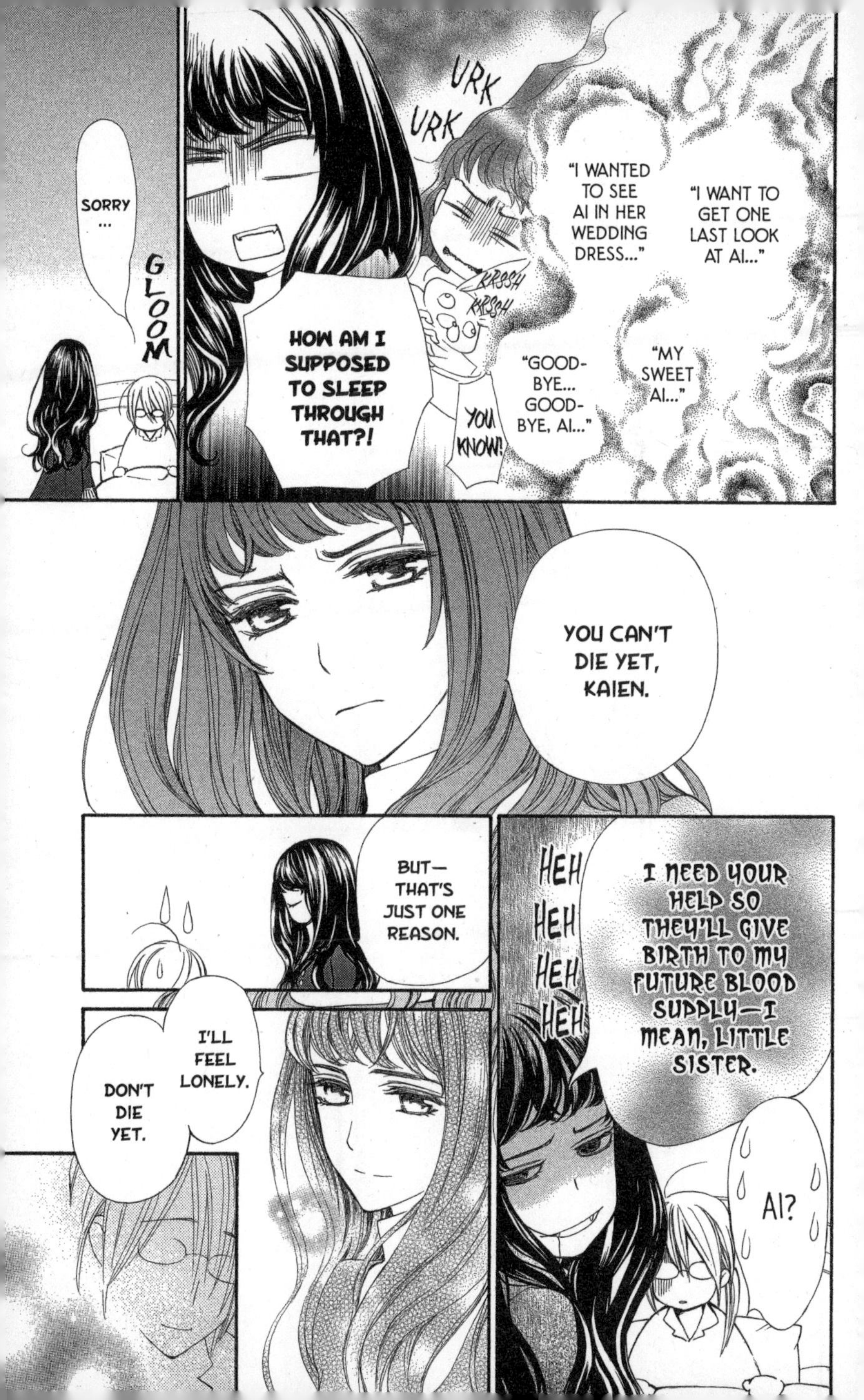
"I WANT TO GET ONE LAST LOOK AT AI..."
"I WANTED TO SEE AI IN HER WEDDING DRESS..."
URK
URK
"MY SWEET AI..."
"GOOD-BYE... GOOD-BYE, AI..."
KRSSH
KRSSH
YOU KNOW!
HOW AM I SUPPOSED TO SLEEP THROUGH THAT?!
GLOOM
SORRY...
YOU CAN'T DIE YET, KAIEN.
HEH
HEH
HEH
HEH
I NEED YOUR HELP SO THEY'LL GIVE BIRTH TO MY FUTURE BLOOD SUPPLY—I MEAN, LITTLE SISTER.
AI?
BUT— THAT'S JUST ONE REASON.
I'LL FEEL LONELY.
DON'T DIE YET.

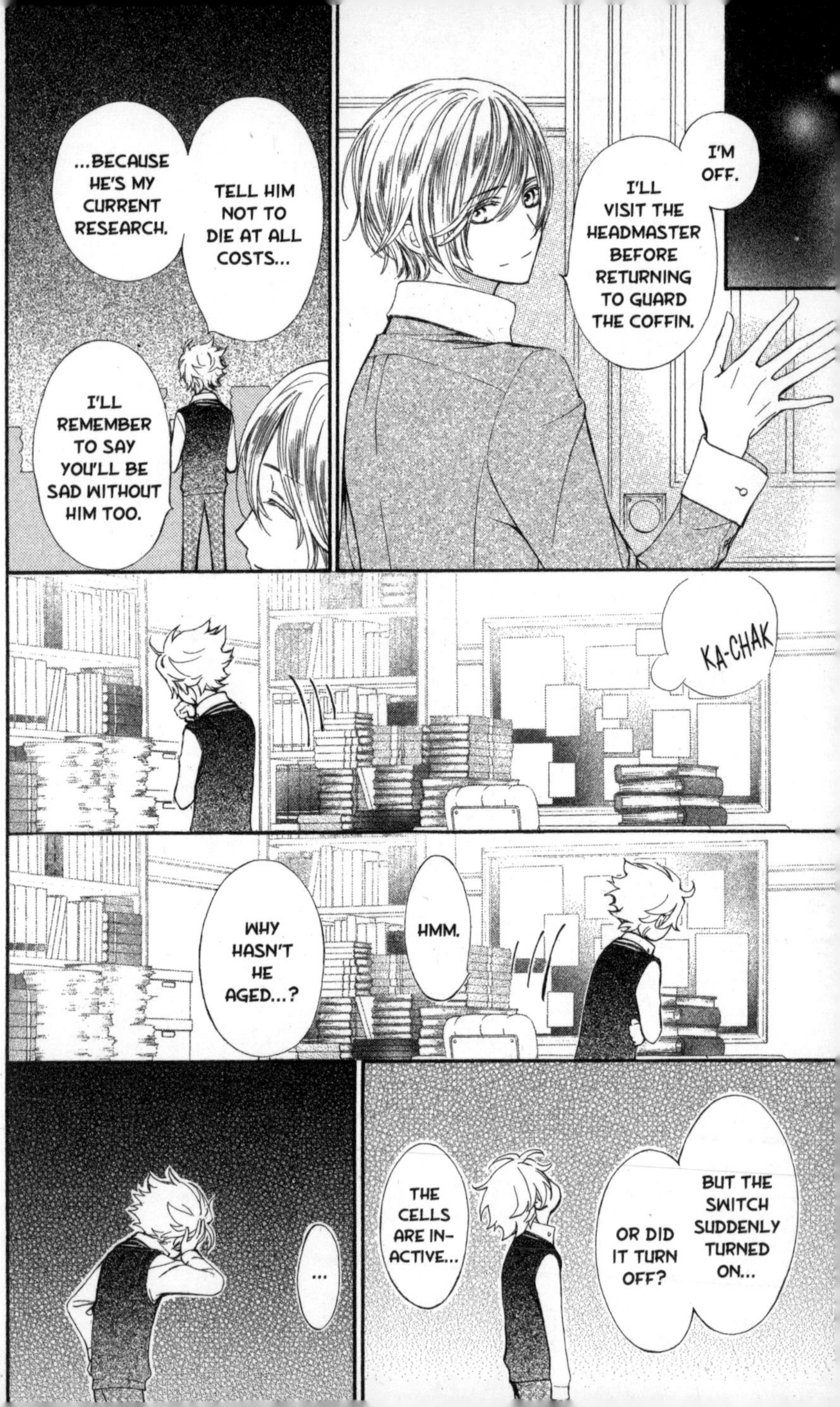
I'M OFF.
I'LL VISIT THE HEADMASTER BEFORE RETURNING TO GUARD THE COFFIN.
TELL HIM NOT TO DIE AT ALL COSTS...
...BECAUSE HE'S MY CURRENT RESEARCH.
I'LL REMEMBER TO SAY YOU'LL BE SAD WITHOUT HIM TOO.
KA-CHAK
HMM.
WHY HASN'T HE AGED...?
BUT THE SWITCH SUDDENLY TURNED ON...
OR DID IT TURN OFF?
THE CELLS ARE IN-ACTIVE...
...

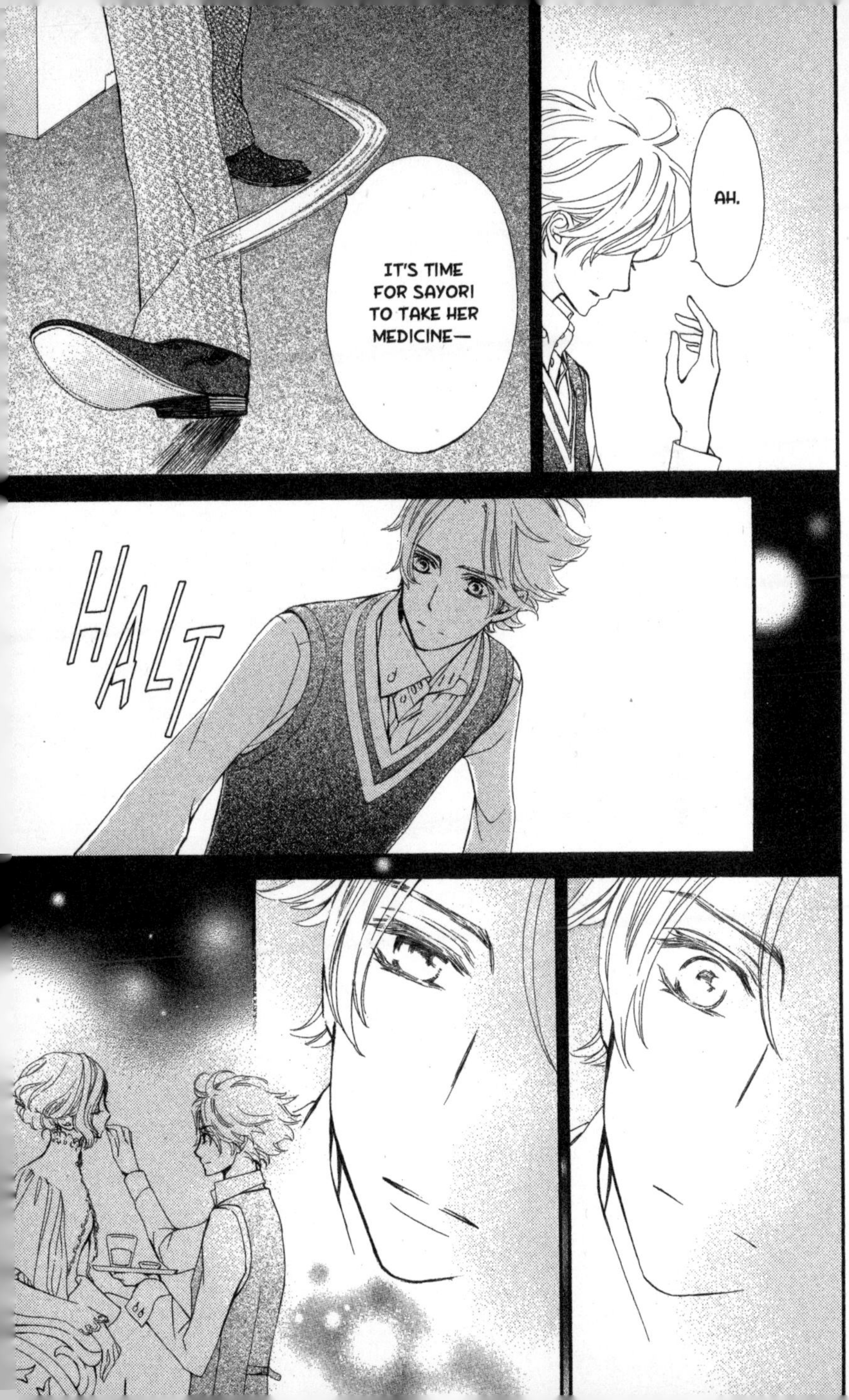
AH.
IT'S TIME FOR SAYORI TO TAKE HER MEDICINE—
HALT

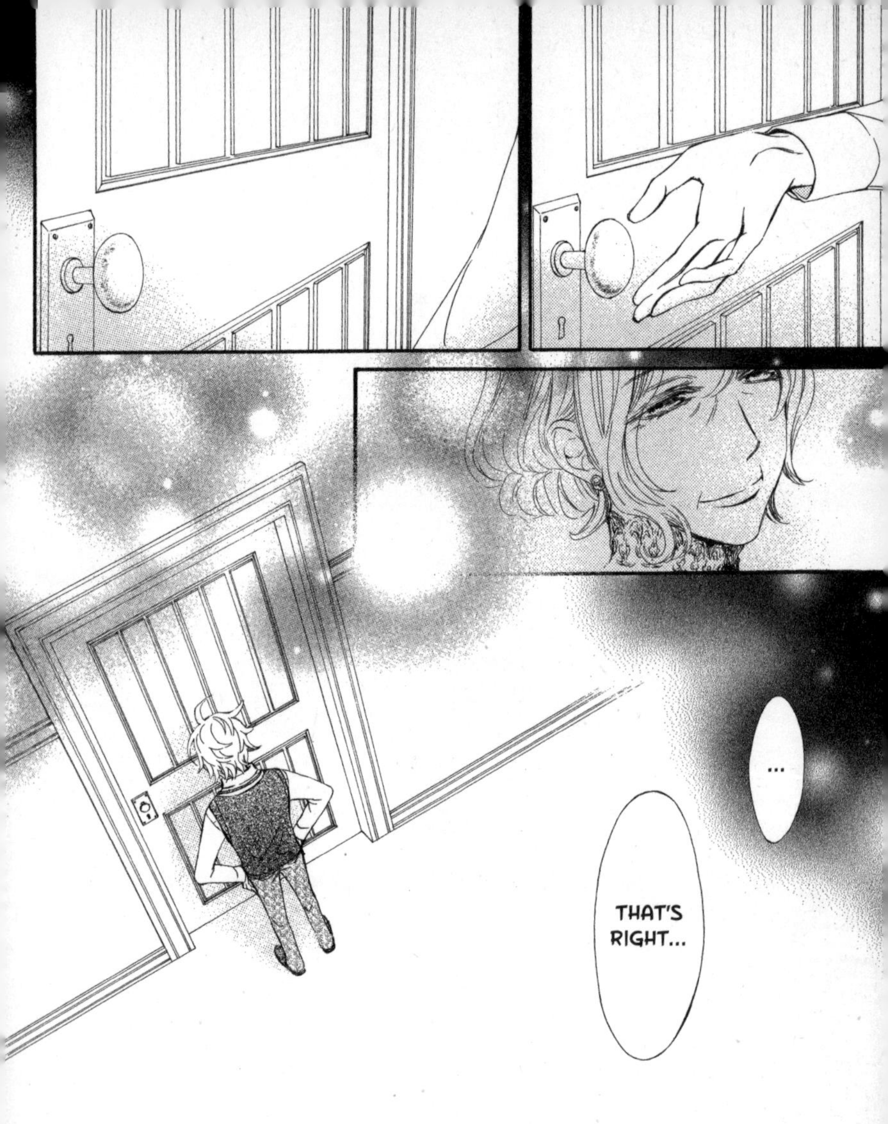
...
THAT'S RIGHT...

MEMORIES OF THOSE WHO HAVE GONE/END

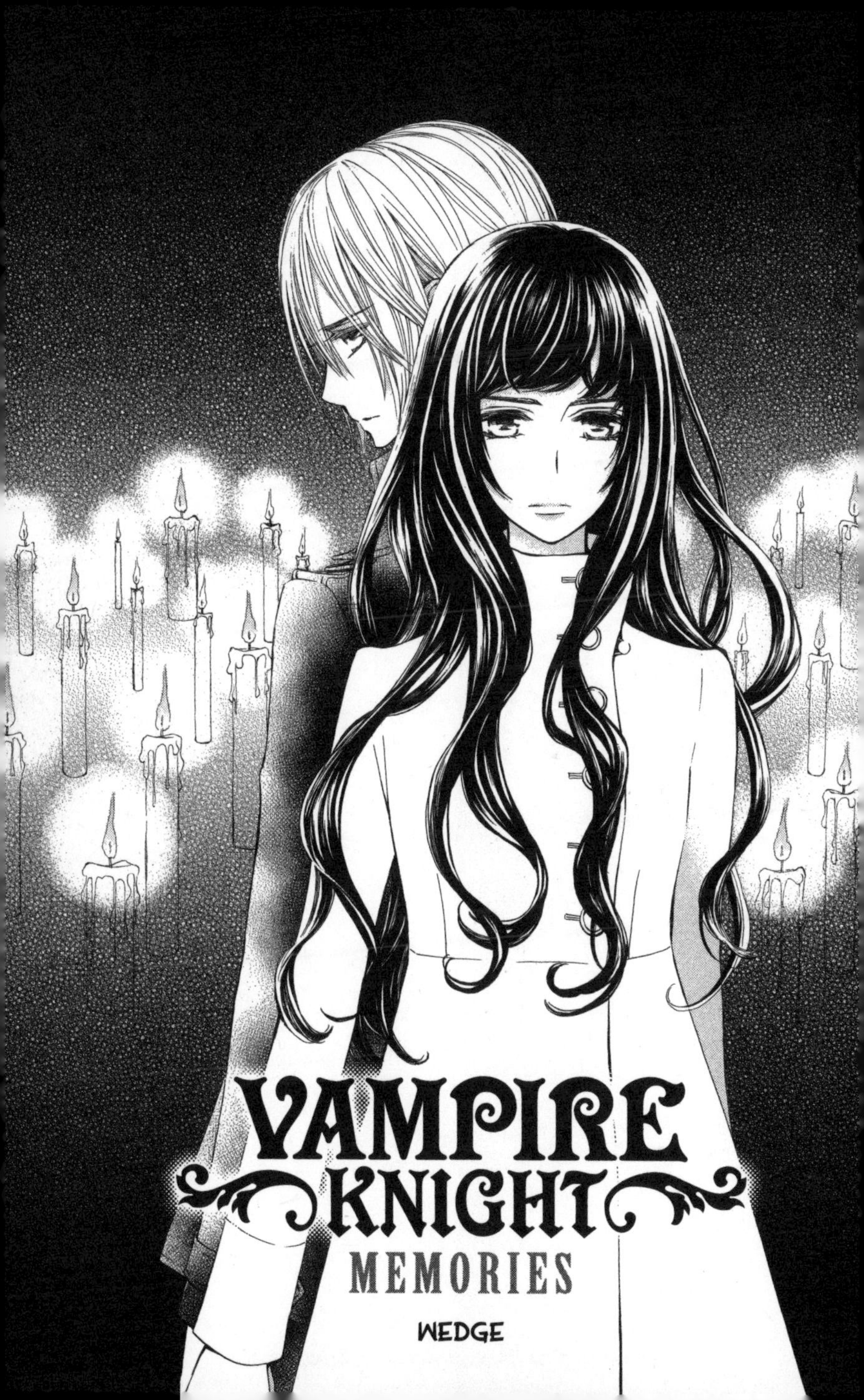
VAMPIRE KNIGHT
MEMORIES
WEDGE

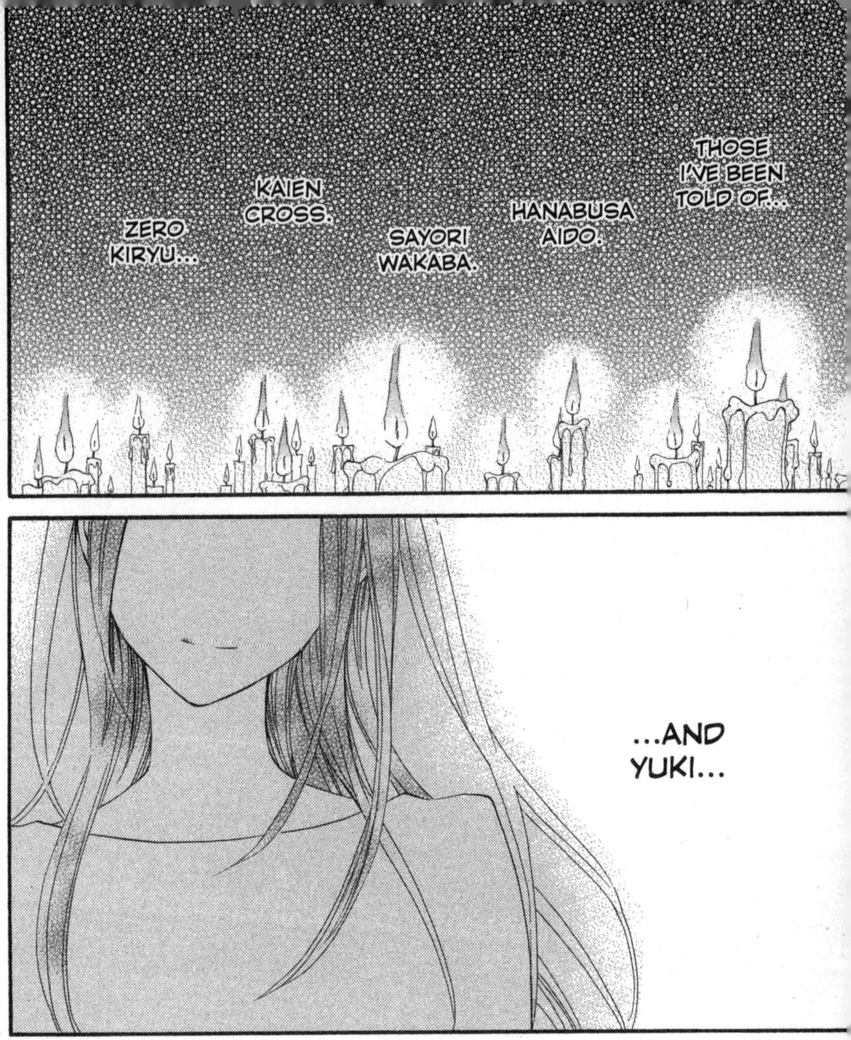
THOSE I'VE BEEN TOLD OF...
HANABUSA AIDO.
SAYORI WAKABA.
KAIEN CROSS.
ZERO KIRYU...
...AND YUKI...

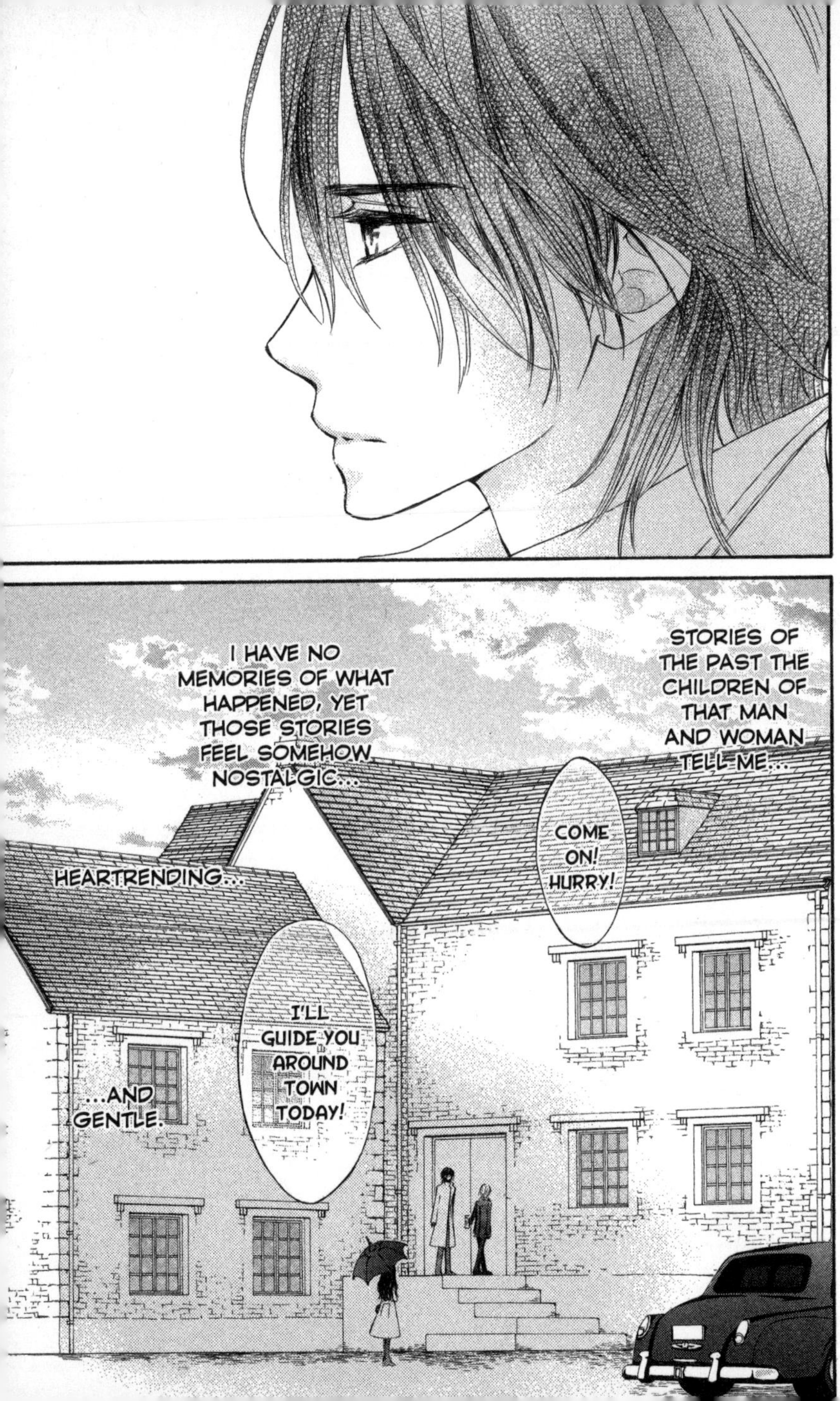
STORIES OF THE PAST THE CHILDREN OF THAT MAN AND WOMAN TELL ME...
I HAVE NO MEMORIES OF WHAT HAPPENED, YET THOSE STORIES FEEL SOMEHOW NOSTALGIC...
COME ON! HURRY!
HEARTRENDING...
I'LL GUIDE YOU AROUND TOWN TODAY!
...AND GENTLE.

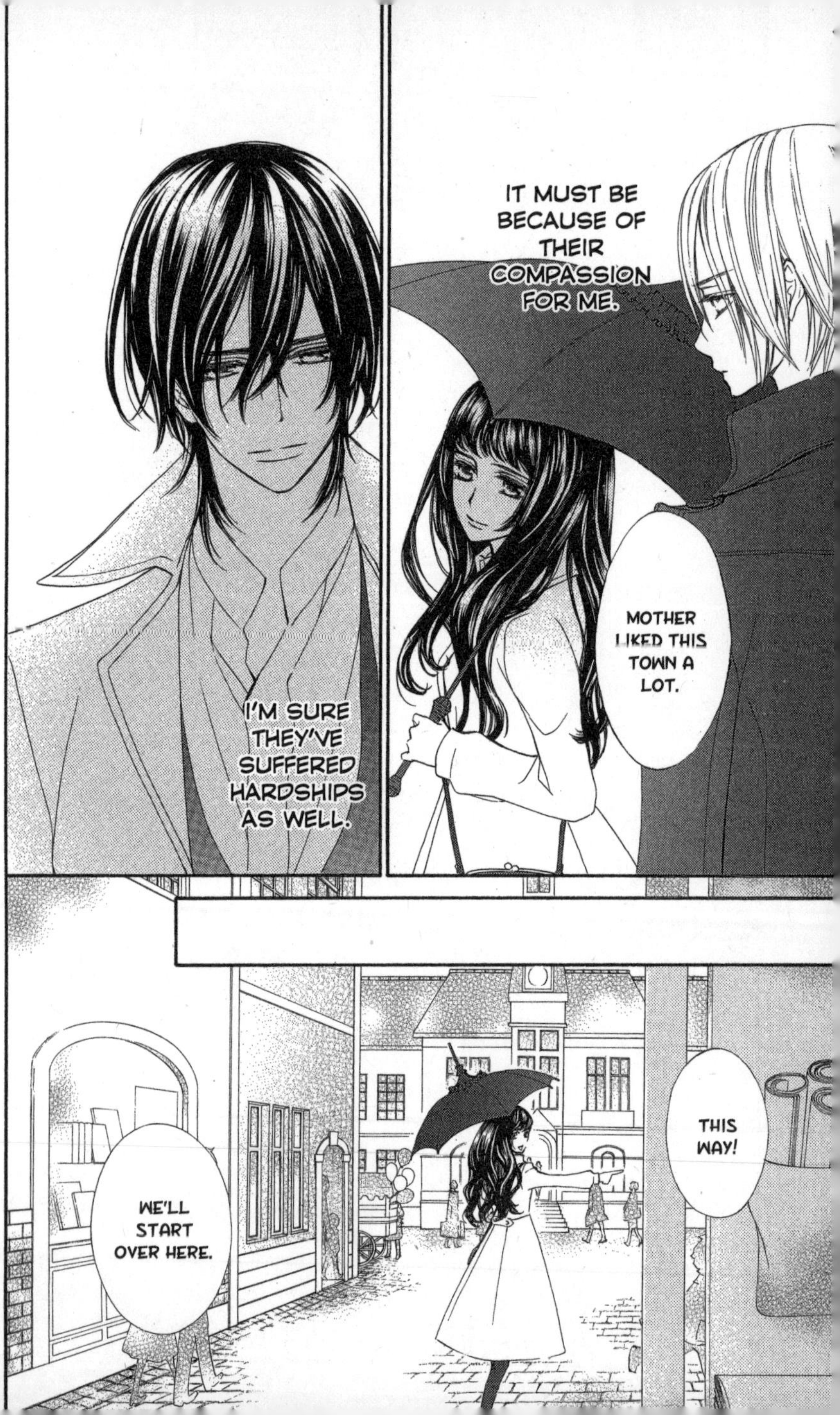
IT MUST BE BECAUSE OF THEIR COMPASSION FOR ME.
MOTHER LIKED THIS TOWN A LOT.
I'M SURE THEY'VE SUFFERED HARDSHIPS AS WELL.
THIS WAY!
WE'LL START OVER HERE.

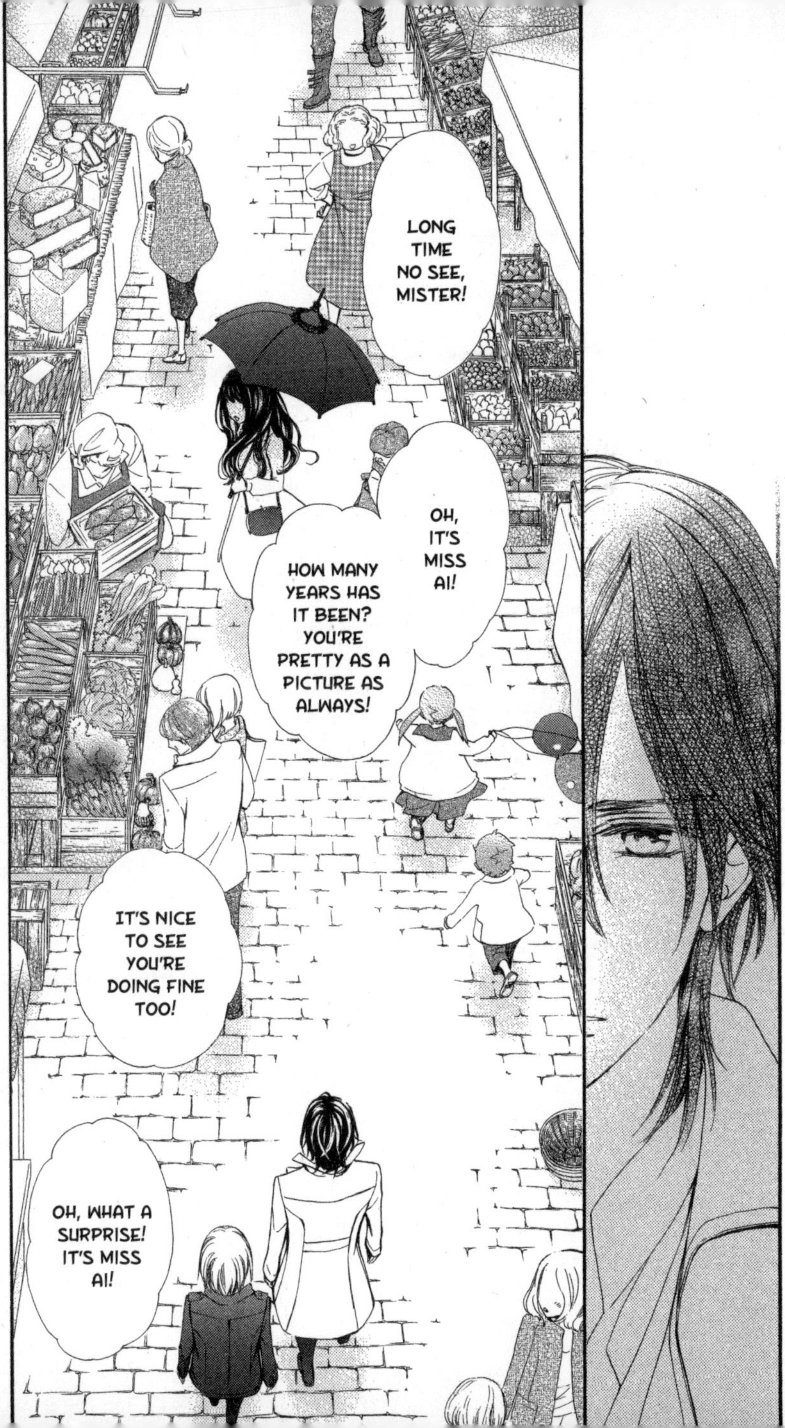
LONG TIME NO SEE, MISTER!
OH, IT'S MISS AI!
HOW MANY YEARS HAS IT BEEN? YOU'RE PRETTY AS A PICTURE AS ALWAYS!
IT'S NICE TO SEE YOU'RE DOING FINE TOO!
OH, WHAT A SURPRISE! IT'S MISS AI!

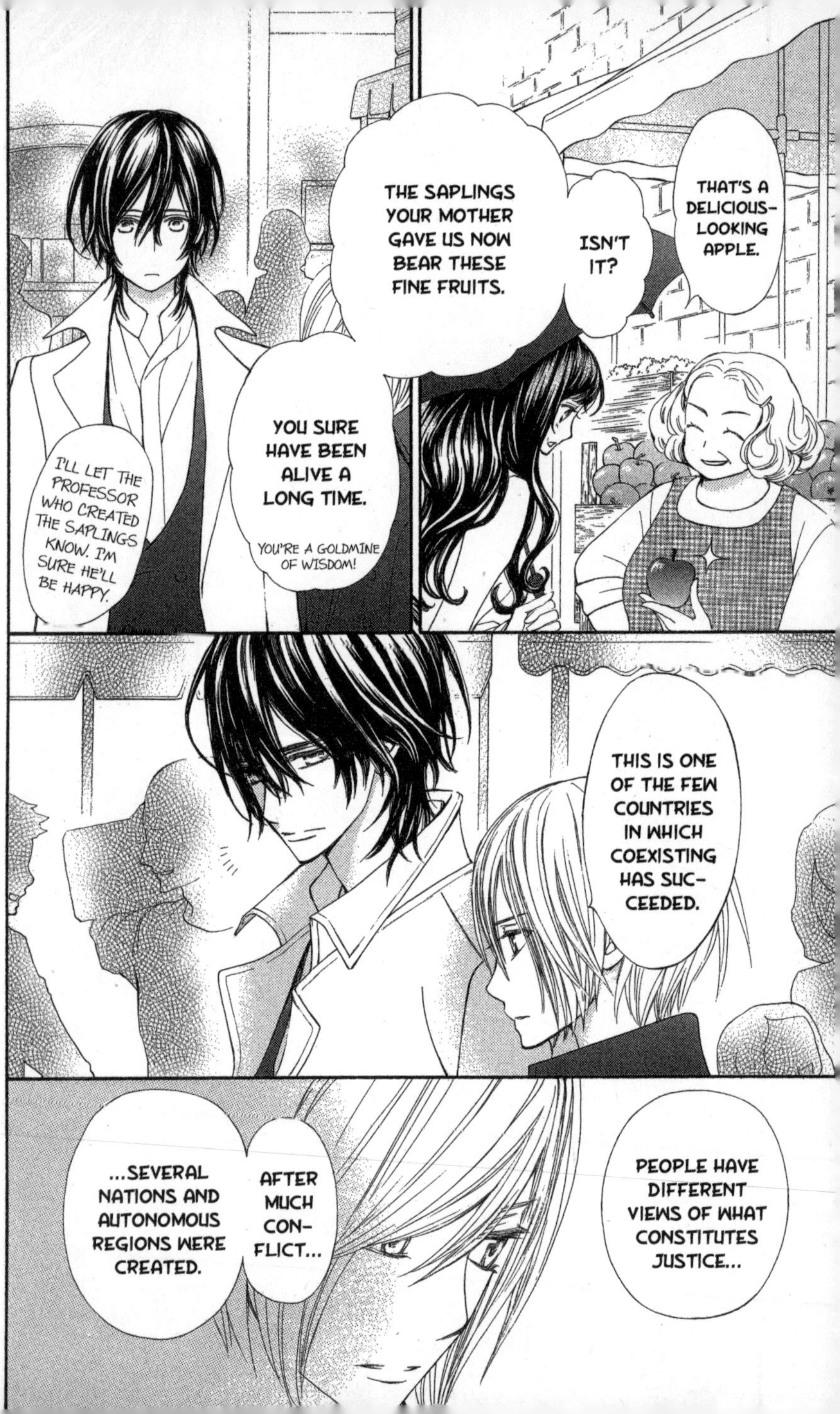
THAT'S A DELICIOUS-LOOKING APPLE.
ISN'T IT?
THE SAPLINGS YOUR MOTHER GAVE US NOW BEAR THESE FINE FRUITS.
YOU SURE HAVE BEEN ALIVE A LONG TIME.
YOU'RE A GOLDMINE OF WISDOM!
I'LL LET THE PROFESSOR WHO CREATED THE SAPLINGS KNOW. I'M SURE HE'LL BE HAPPY.
THIS IS ONE OF THE FEW COUNTRIES IN WHICH COEXISTING HAS SUC-CEEDED.
PEOPLE HAVE DIFFERENT VIEWS OF WHAT CONSTITUTES JUSTICE...
AFTER MUCH CON-FLICT...
...SEVERAL NATIONS AND AUTONOMOUS REGIONS WERE CREATED.

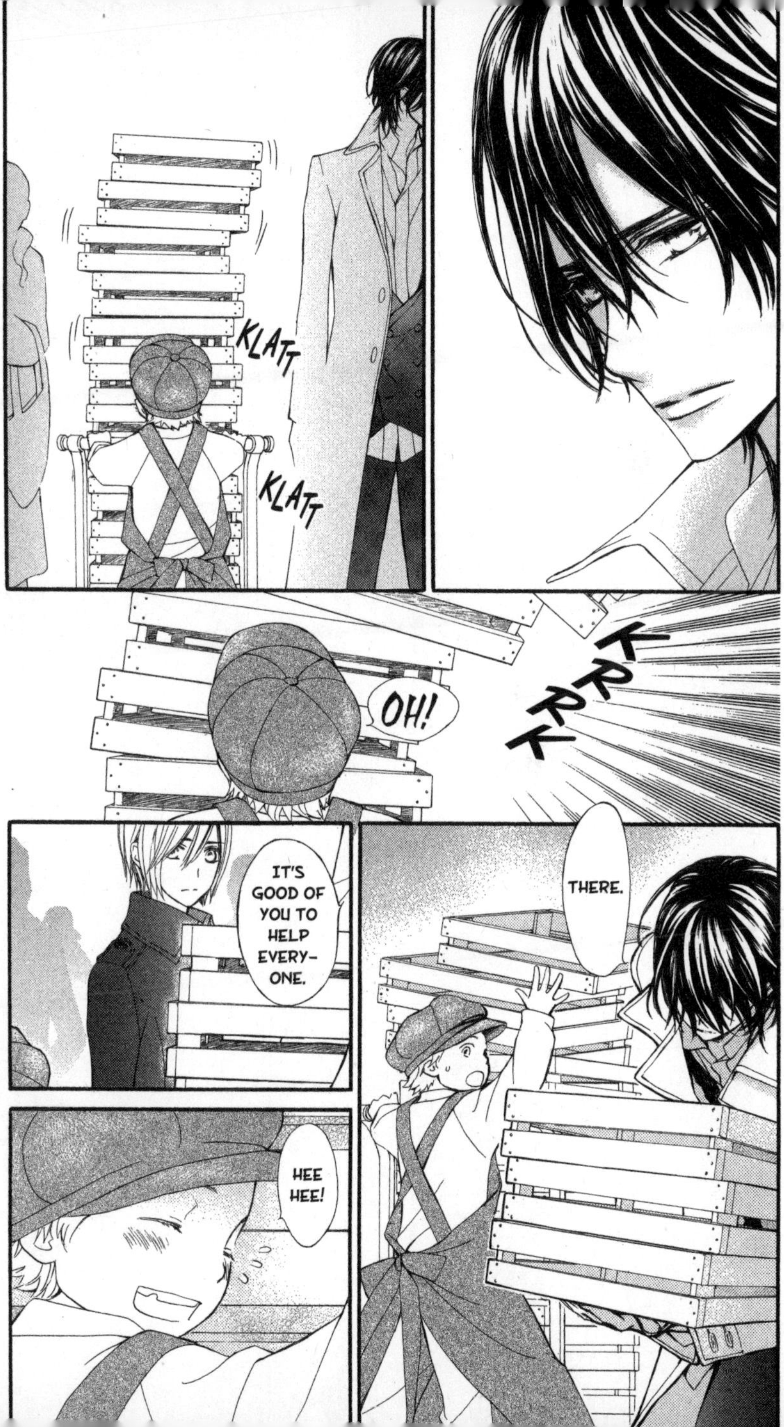
KLATT
KLATT
KRRK
OH!
THERE.
IT'S GOOD OF YOU TO HELP EVERYONE.
HEE HEE!

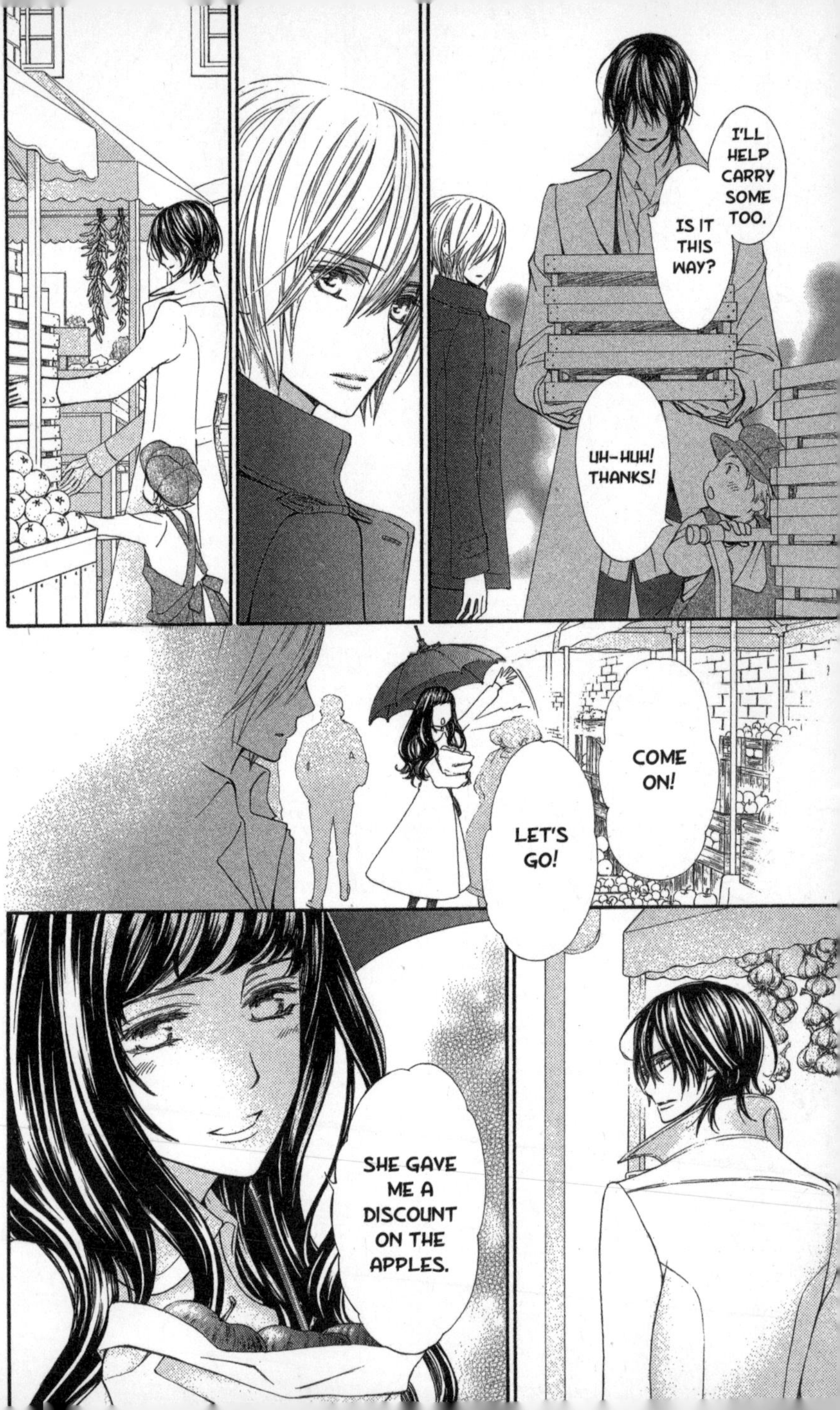
I'LL HELP CARRY SOME TOO.
IS IT THIS WAY?
UH-HUH! THANKS!
COME ON!
LET'S GO!
SHE GAVE ME A DISCOUNT ON THE APPLES.

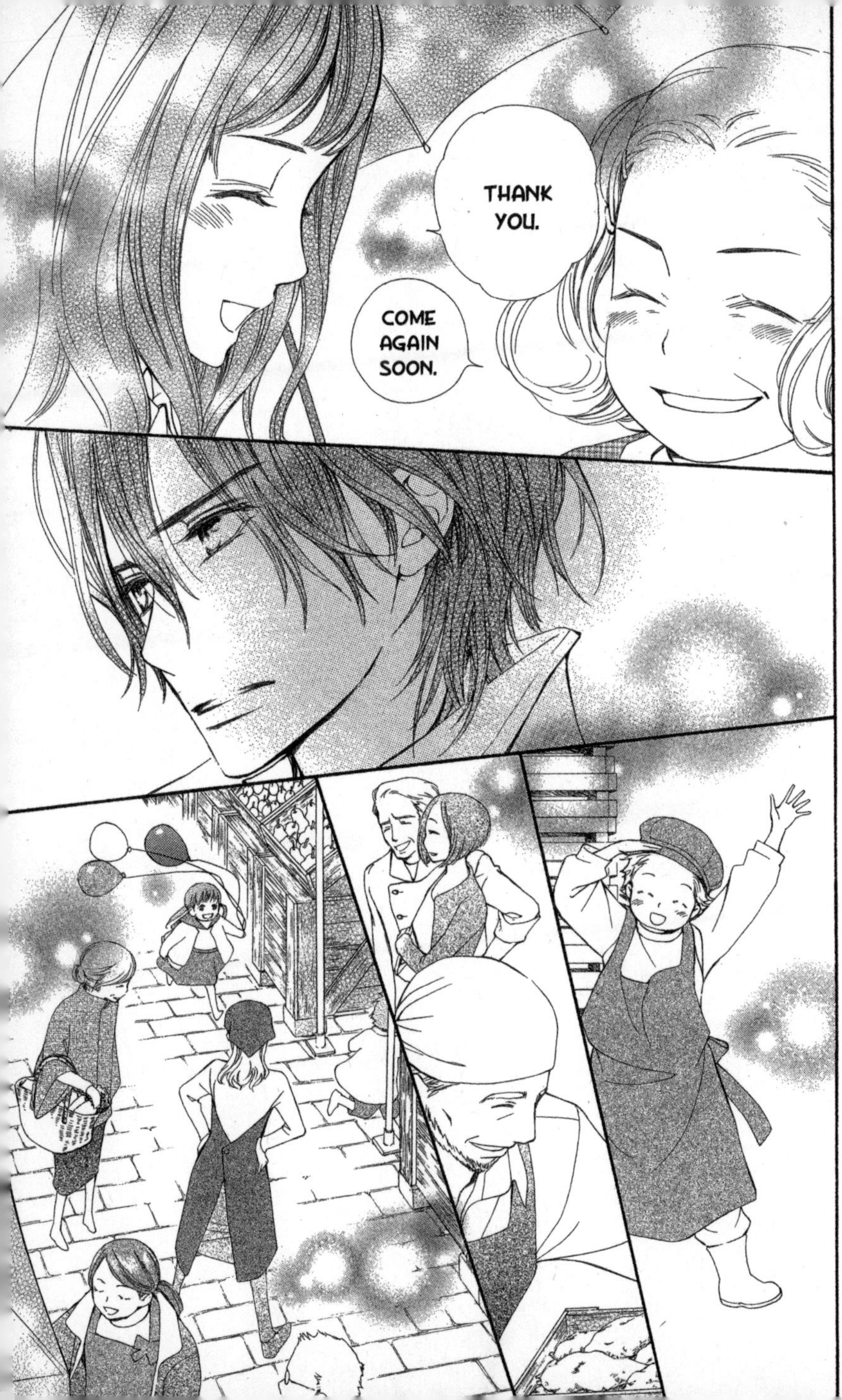
THANK YOU.
COME AGAIN SOON.

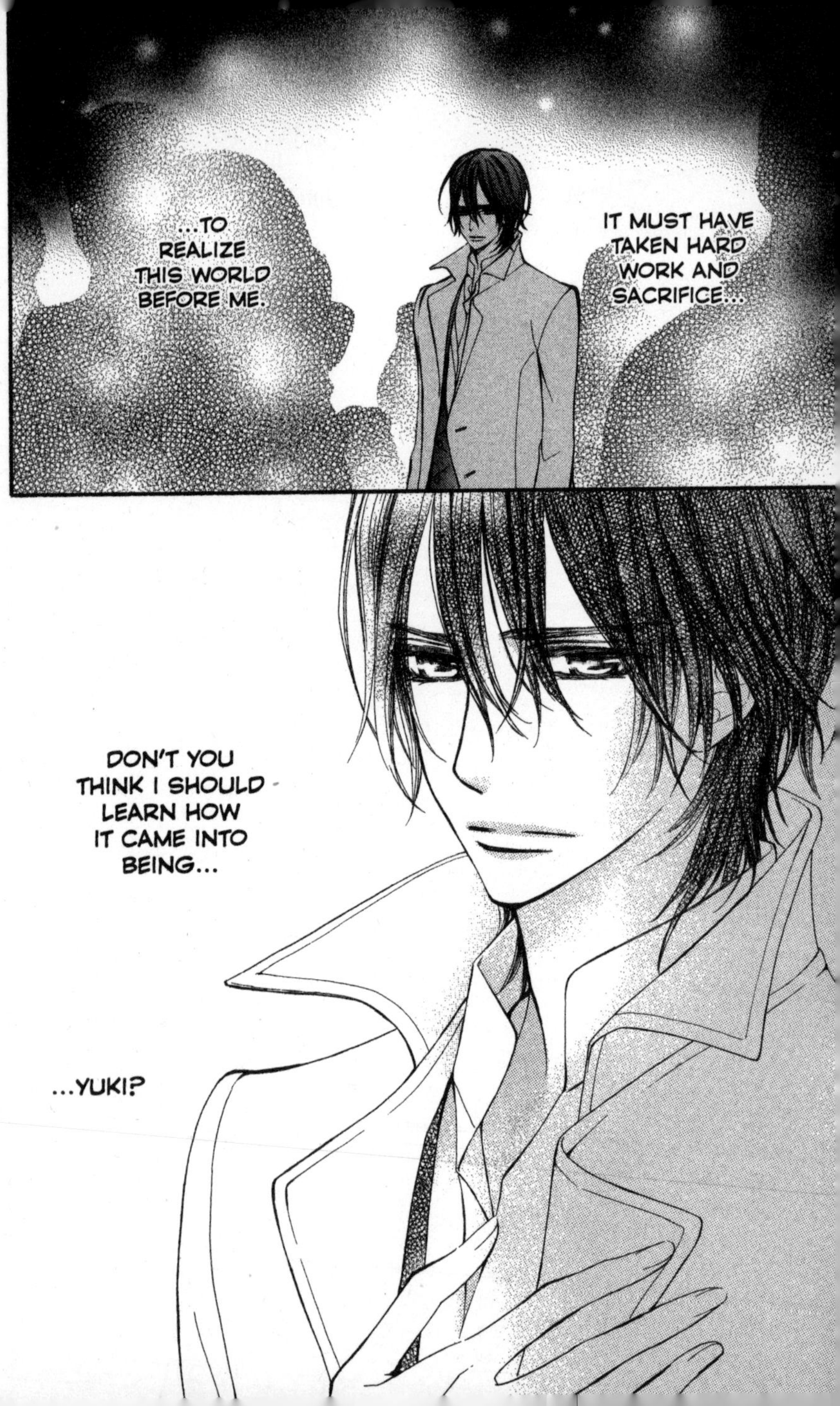
IT MUST HAVE TAKEN HARD WORK AND SACRIFICE...
...TO REALIZE THIS WORLD BEFORE ME.
DON'T YOU THINK I SHOULD LEARN HOW IT CAME INTO BEING...
...YUKI?

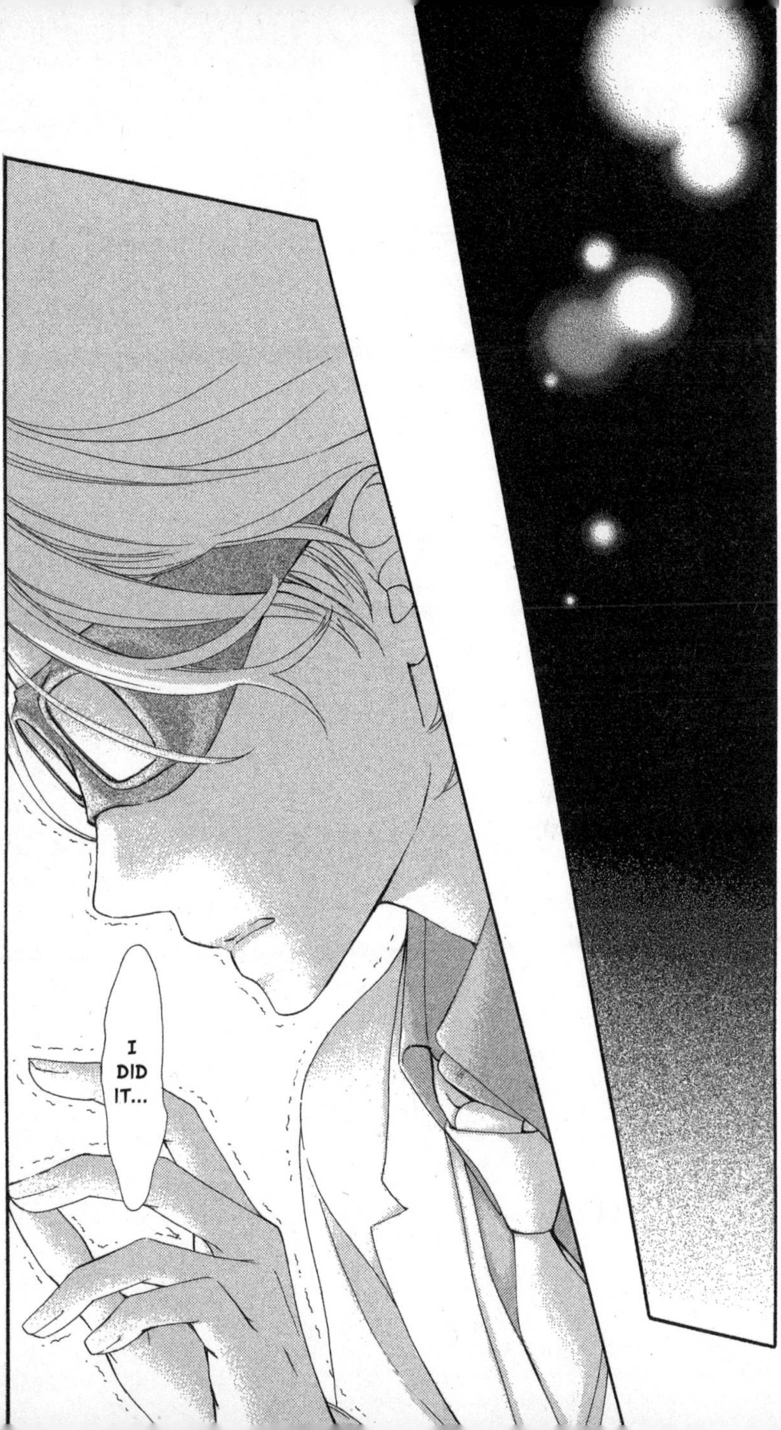
I DID IT...

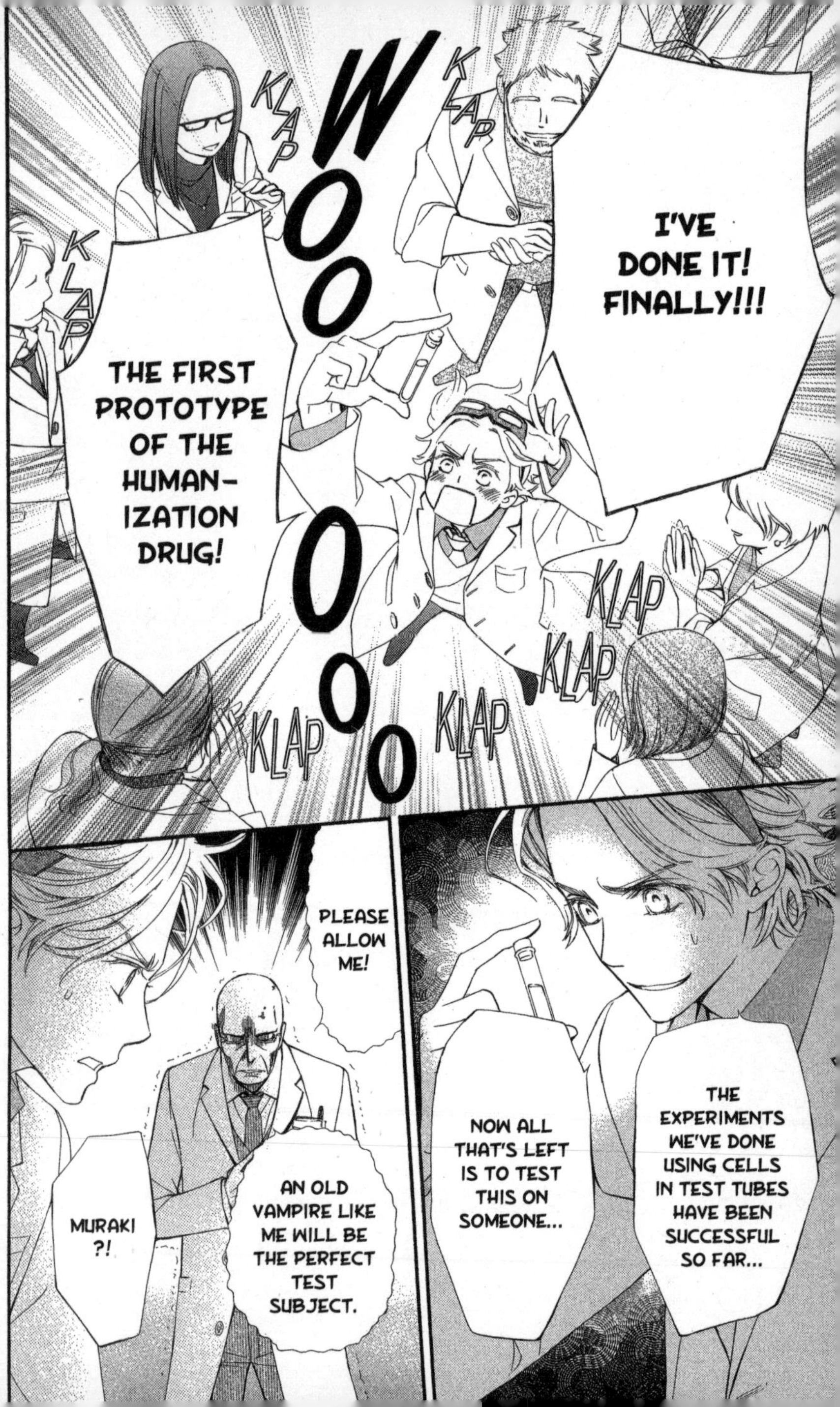
I'VE DONE IT! FINALLY!!!
KLAP
WOOOOOO
KLAP
KLAP
THE FIRST PROTOTYPE OF THE HUMAN-IZATION DRUG!
KLAP
KLAP
KLAP
KLAP
THE EXPERIMENTS WE'VE DONE USING CELLS IN TEST TUBES HAVE BEEN SUCCESSFUL SO FAR...
NOW ALL THAT'S LEFT IS TO TEST THIS ON SOMEONE...
PLEASE ALLOW ME!
AN OLD VAMPIRE LIKE ME WILL BE THE PERFECT TEST SUBJECT.
MURAKI ?!

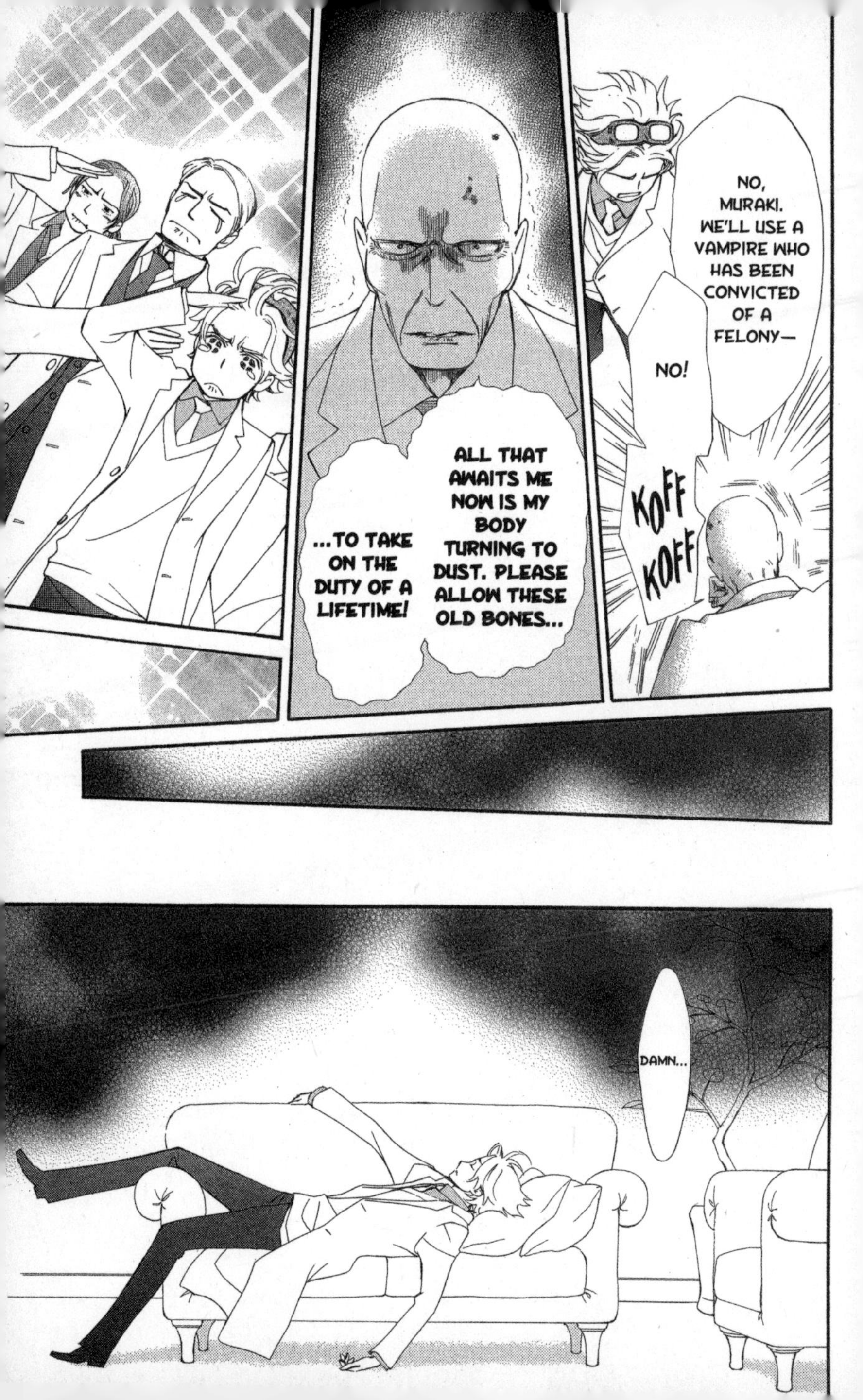
NO, MURAKI. WE'LL USE A VAMPIRE WHO HAS BEEN CONVICTED OF A FELONY—
NO!
KOFF KOFF
ALL THAT AWAITS ME NOW IS MY BODY TURNING TO DUST. PLEASE ALLOW THESE OLD BONES...
...TO TAKE ON THE DUTY OF A LIFETIME!
DAMN...

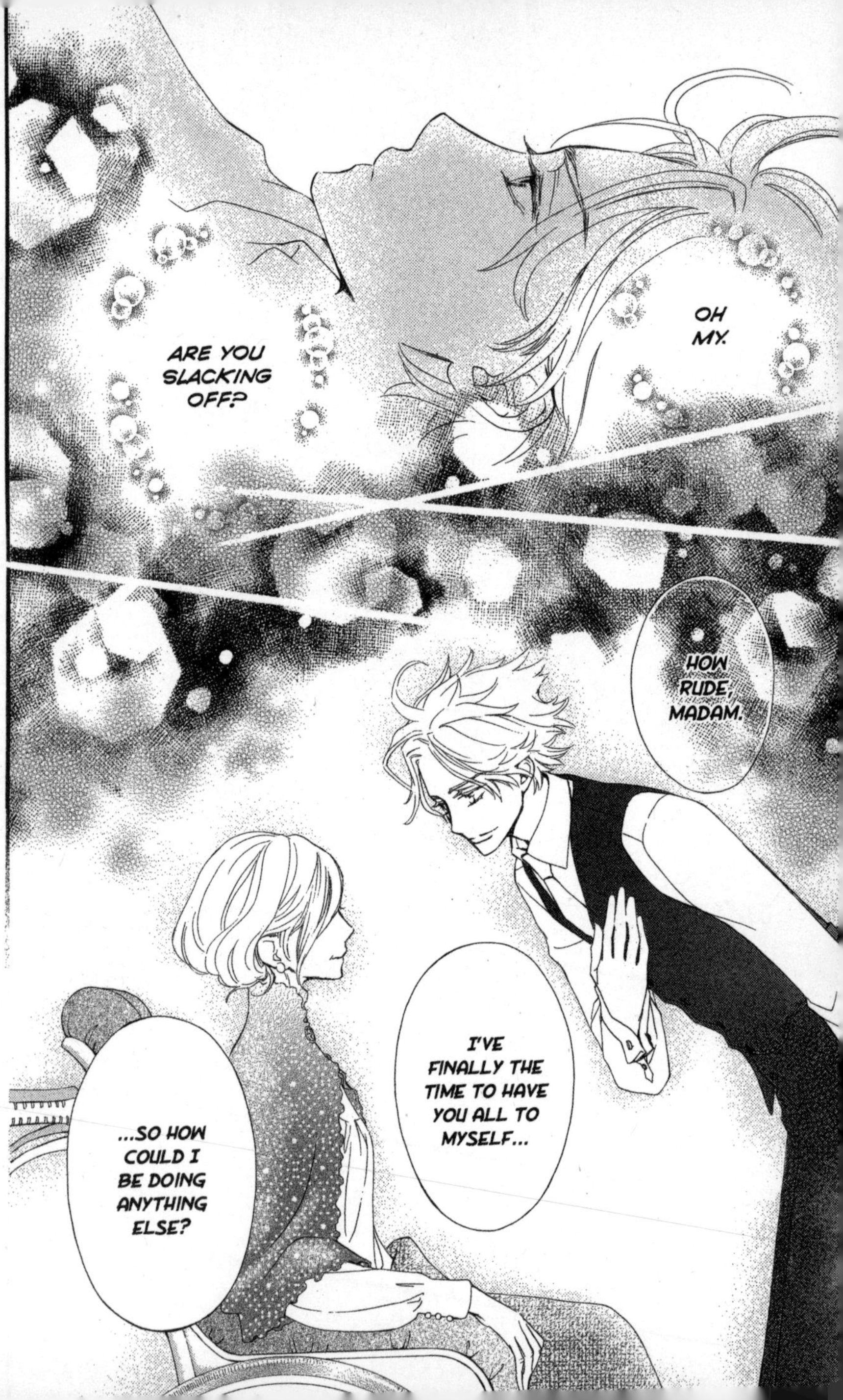
OH MY.
ARE YOU SLACKING OFF?
HOW RUDE, MADAM.
I'VE FINALLY THE TIME TO HAVE YOU ALL TO MYSELF...
...SO HOW COULD I BE DOING ANYTHING ELSE?

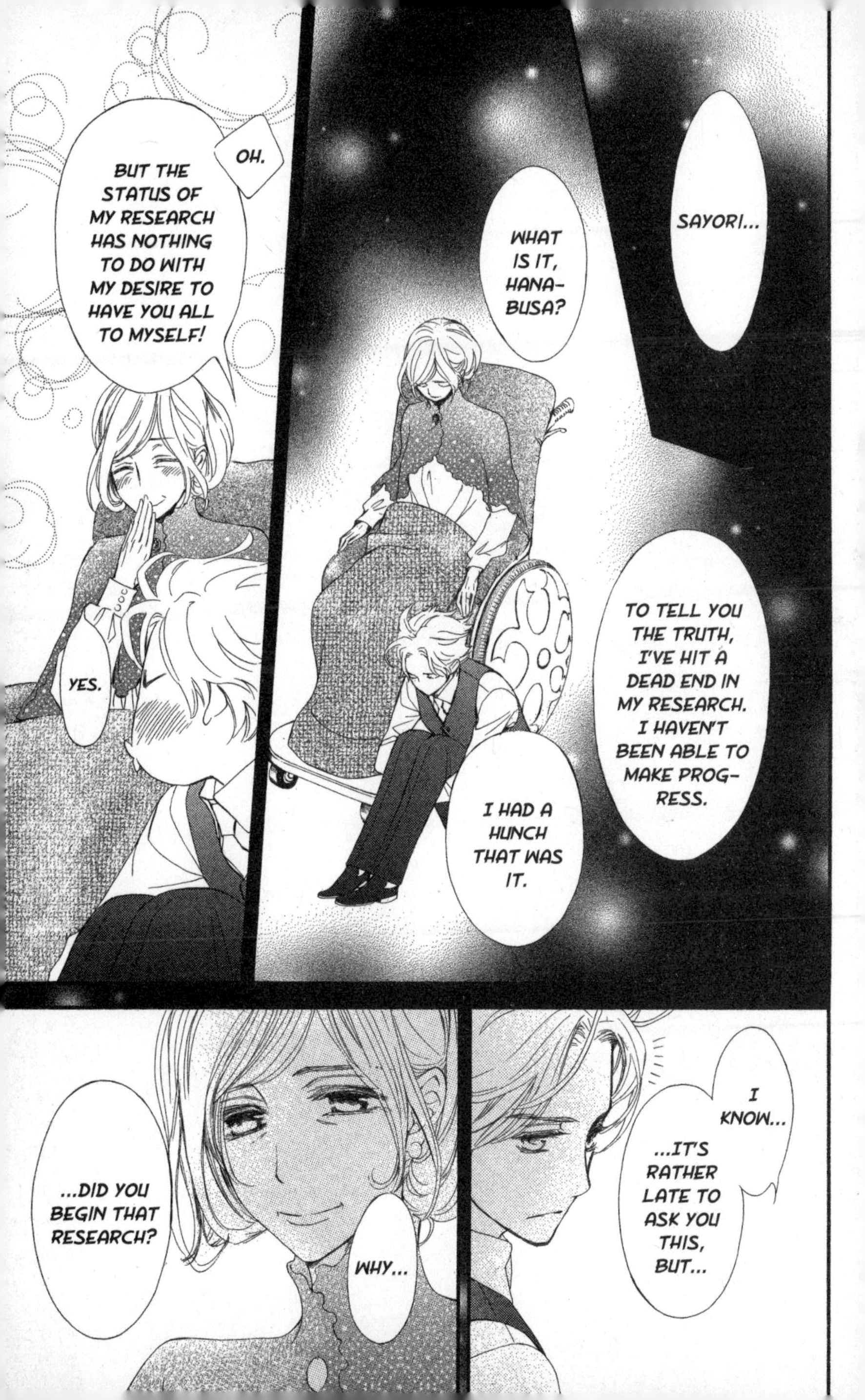
SAYORI...
WHAT IS IT, HANA-BUSA?
TO TELL YOU THE TRUTH, I'VE HIT A DEAD END IN MY RESEARCH. I HAVEN'T BEEN ABLE TO MAKE PROG-RESS.
I HAD A HUNCH THAT WAS IT.
OH.
BUT THE STATUS OF MY RESEARCH HAS NOTHING TO DO WITH MY DESIRE TO HAVE YOU ALL TO MYSELF!
YES.
I KNOW...
...IT'S RATHER LATE TO ASK YOU THIS, BUT...
WHY...
...DID YOU BEGIN THAT RESEARCH?

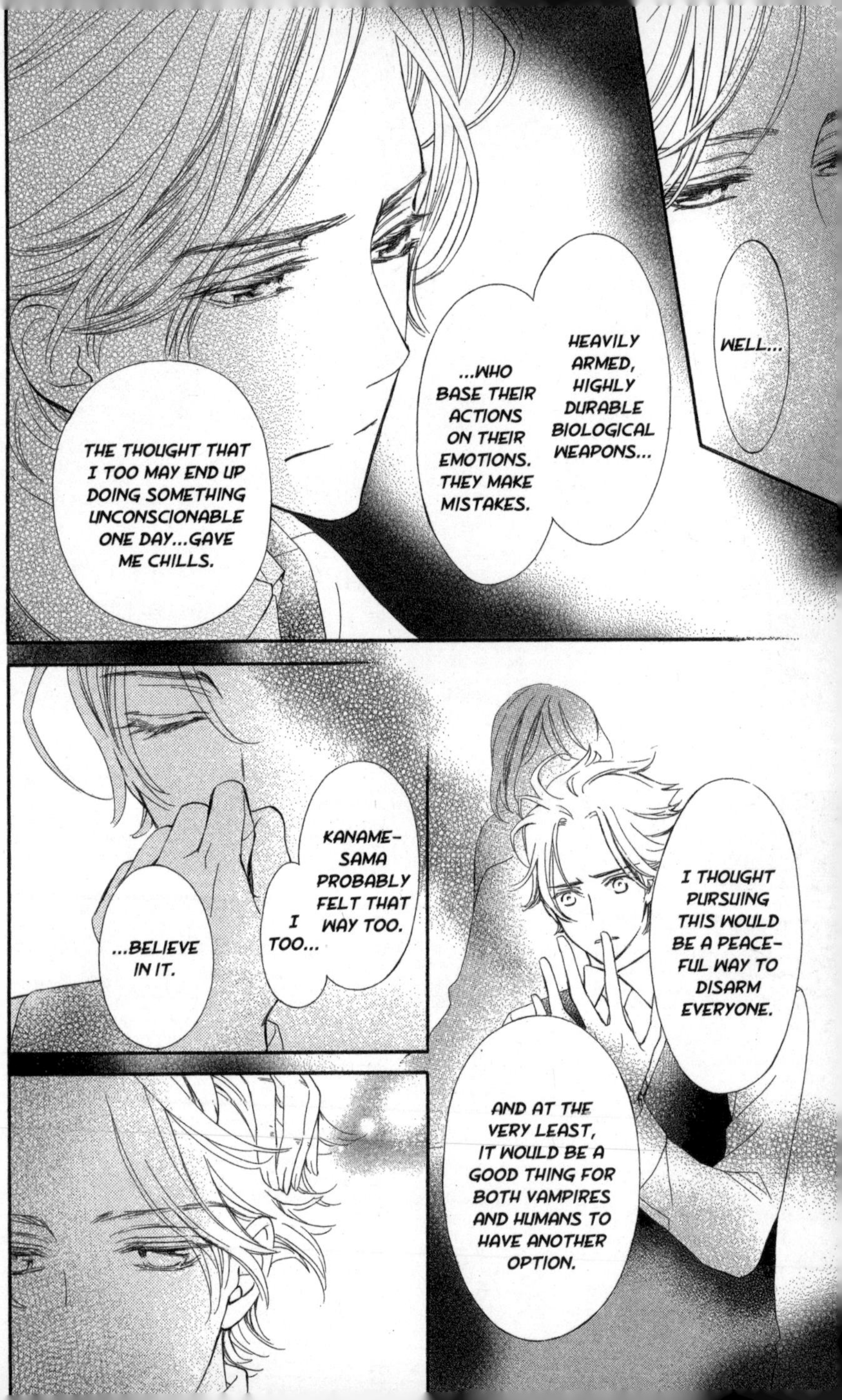
WELL...
HEAVILY ARMED, HIGHLY DURABLE BIOLOGICAL WEAPONS...
...WHO BASE THEIR ACTIONS ON THEIR EMOTIONS. THEY MAKE MISTAKES.
THE THOUGHT THAT I TOO MAY END UP DOING SOMETHING UNCONSCIONABLE ONE DAY...GAVE ME CHILLS.
I THOUGHT PURSUING THIS WOULD BE A PEACE-FUL WAY TO DISARM EVERYONE.
AND AT THE VERY LEAST, IT WOULD BE A GOOD THING FOR BOTH VAMPIRES AND HUMANS TO HAVE ANOTHER OPTION.
KANAME-SAMA PROBABLY FELT THAT WAY TOO.
I TOO...
...BELIEVE IN IT.

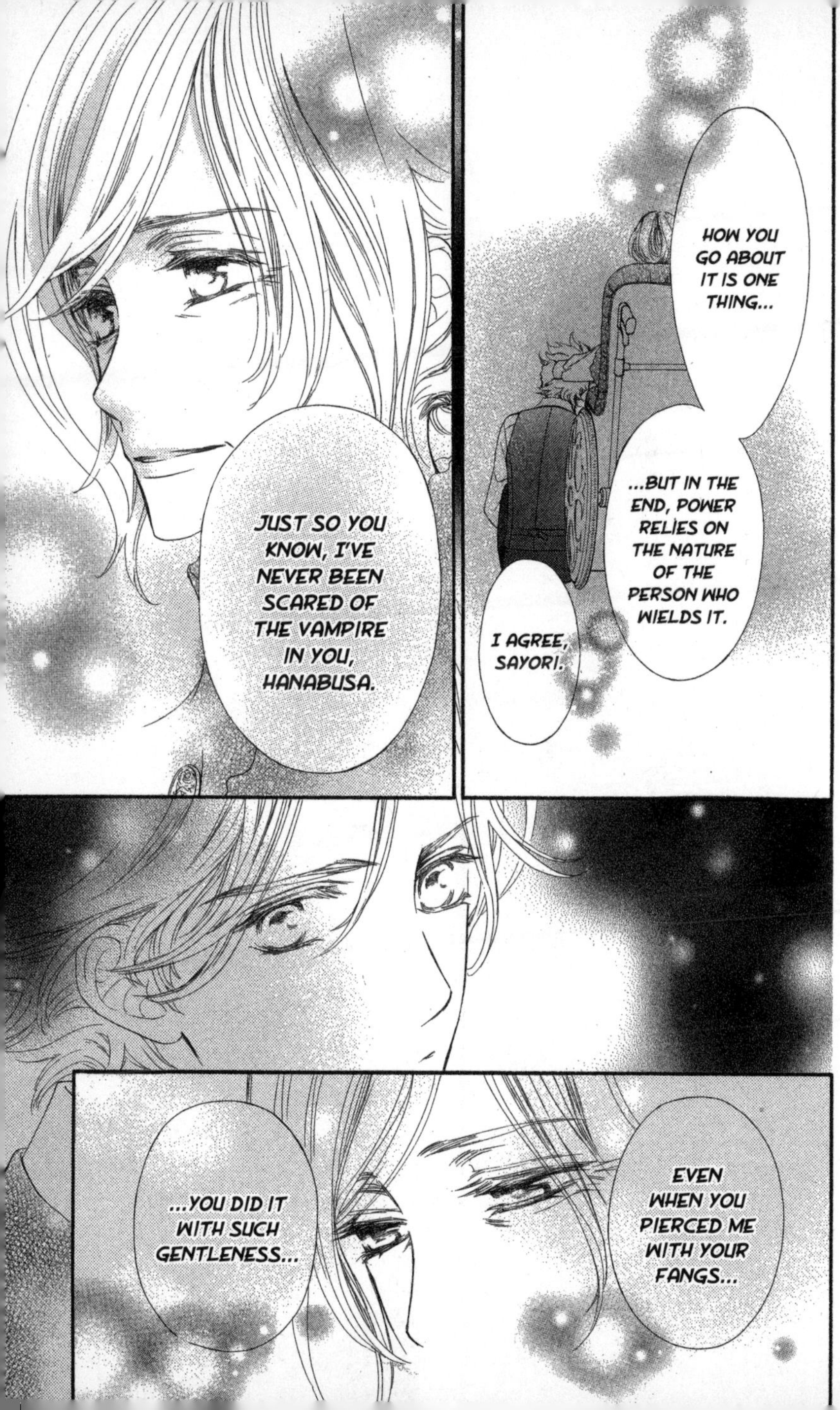
HOW YOU GO ABOUT IT IS ONE THING...
...BUT IN THE END, POWER RELIES ON THE NATURE OF THE PERSON WHO WIELDS IT.
I AGREE, SAYORI.
JUST SO YOU KNOW, I'VE NEVER BEEN SCARED OF THE VAMPIRE IN YOU, HANABUSA.
EVEN WHEN YOU PIERCED ME WITH YOUR FANGS...
...YOU DID IT WITH SUCH GENTLENESS...

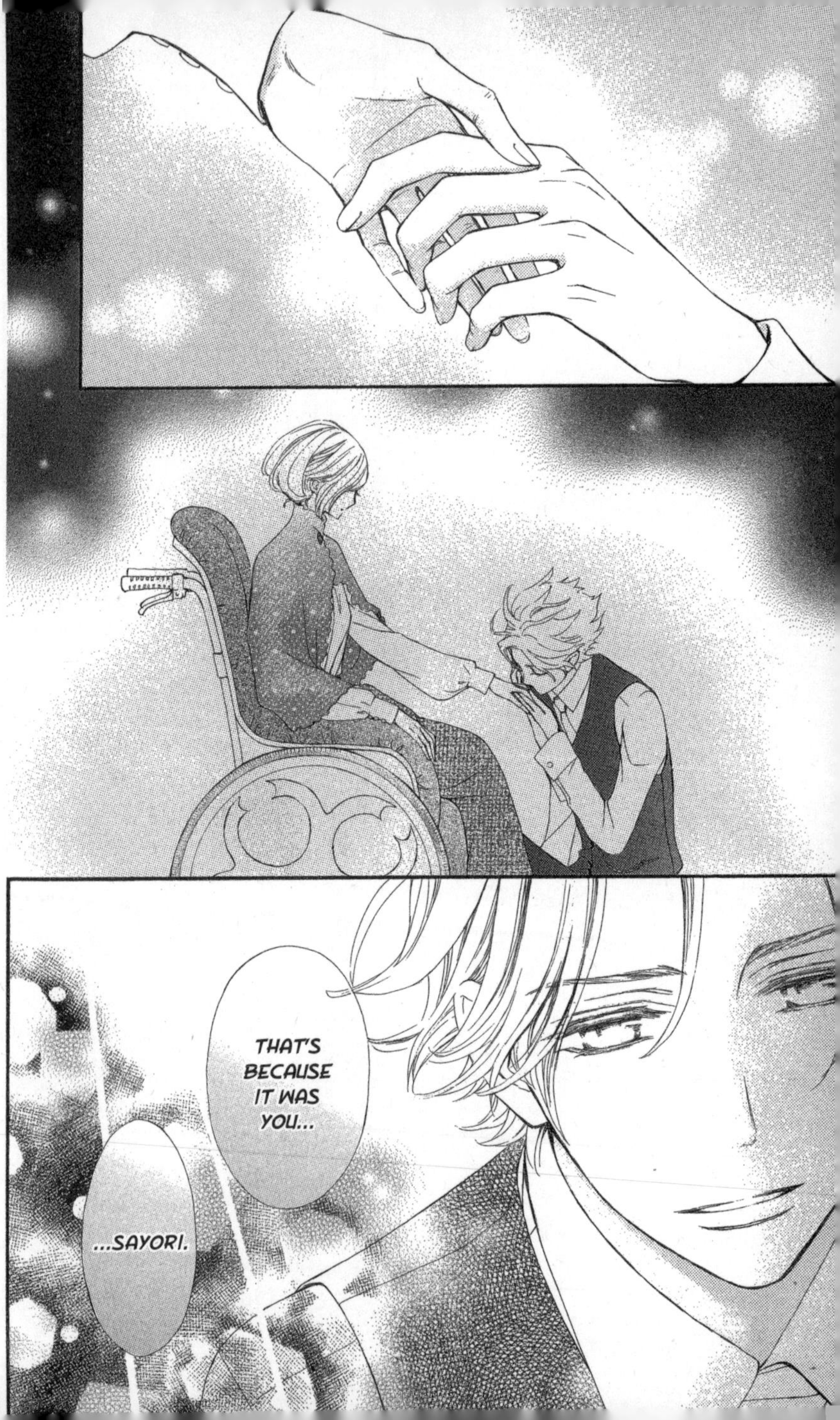
THAT'S BECAUSE IT WAS YOU...
...SAYORI.

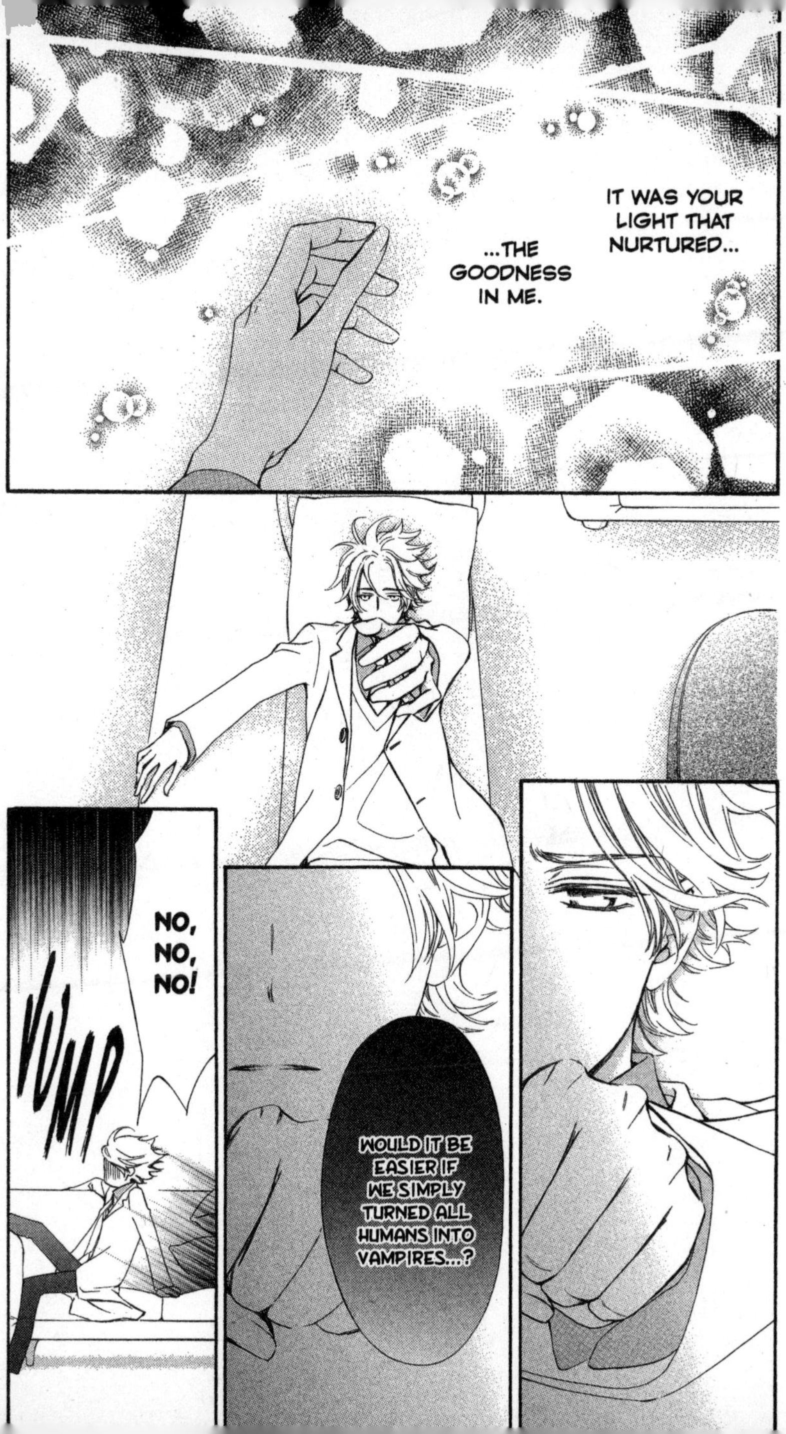
IT WAS YOUR LIGHT THAT NURTURED...
...THE GOODNESS IN ME.
NO, NO, NO!
VUMP
WOULD IT BE EASIER IF WE SIMPLY TURNED ALL HUMANS INTO VAMPIRES...?

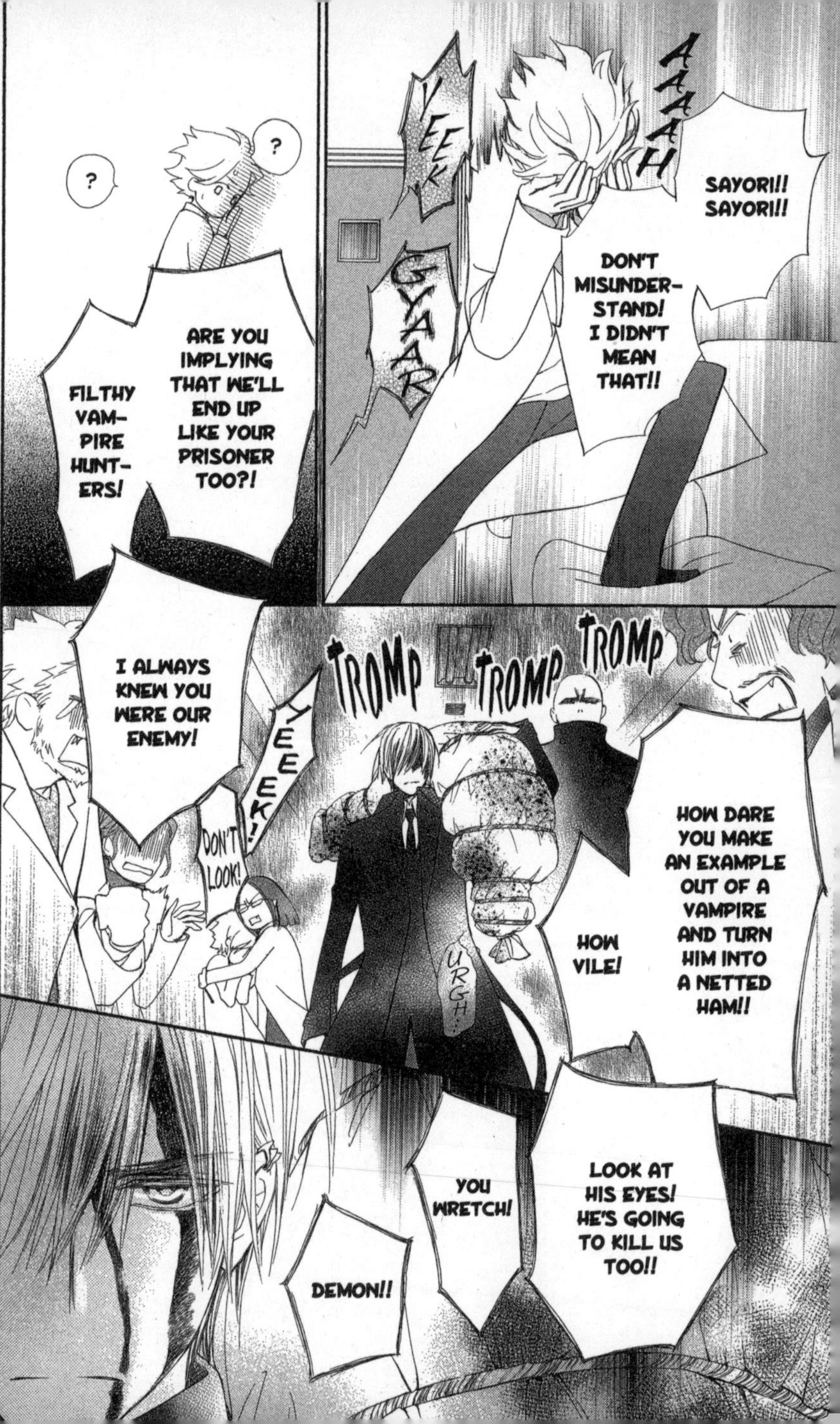
AAAAH
SAYORI!! SAYORI!!
YEEK
DON'T MISUNDER-STAND! I DIDN'T MEAN THAT!!
GYAAR
?
?
ARE YOU IMPLYING THAT WE'LL END UP LIKE YOUR PRISONER TOO?!
FILTHY VAM-PIRE HUNT-ERS!
HOW DARE YOU MAKE AN EXAMPLE OUT OF A VAMPIRE AND TURN HIM INTO A NETTED HAM!!
TROMP TROMP TROMP
HOW VILE!
I ALWAYS KNEW YOU WERE OUR ENEMY!
YEEEK!
DON'T LOOK!
URGH...
LOOK AT HIS EYES! HE'S GOING TO KILL US TOO!!
YOU WRETCH!
DEMON!!

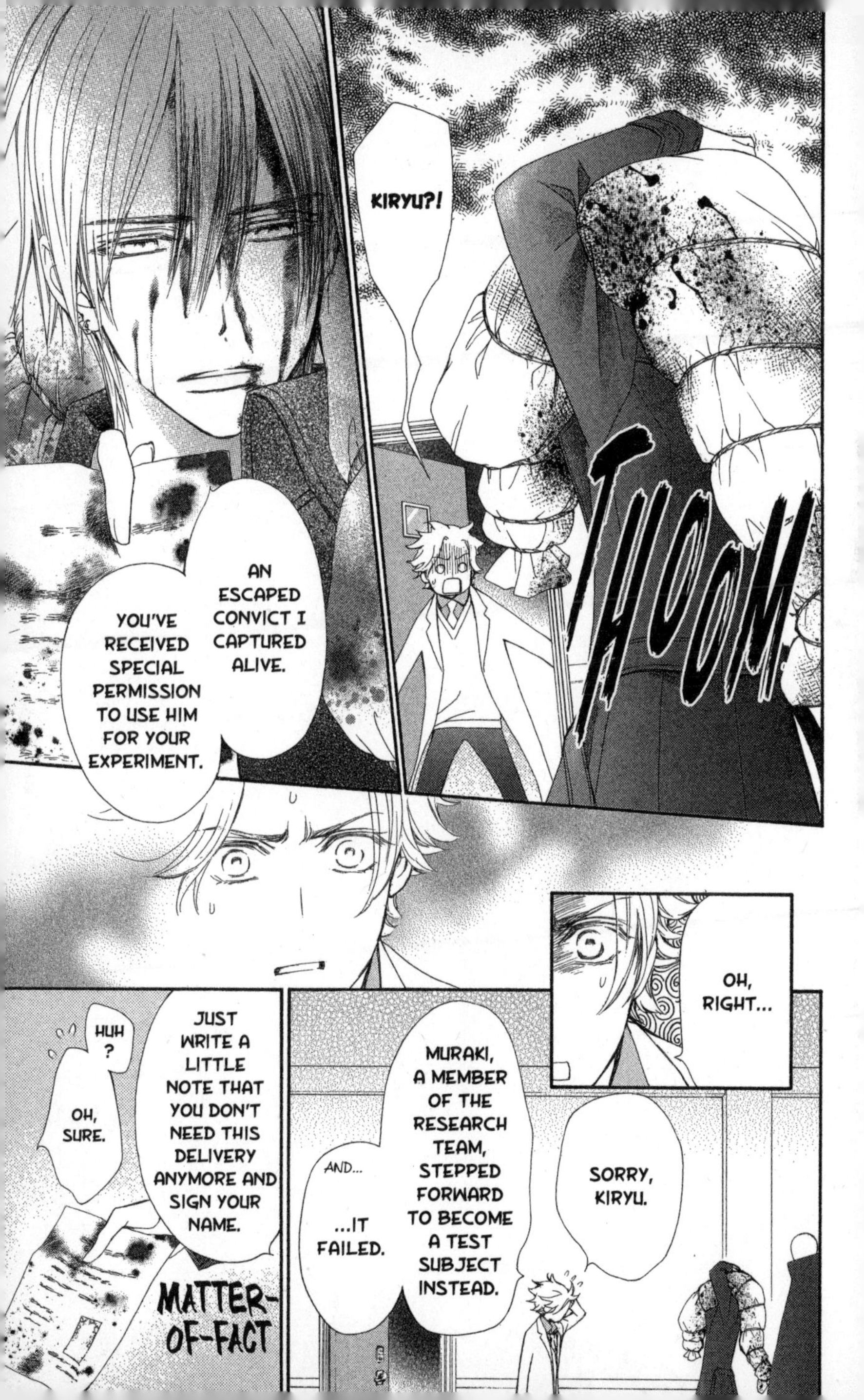
KIRYU?!
THOOM
AN ESCAPED CONVICT I CAPTURED ALIVE.
YOU'VE RECEIVED SPECIAL PERMISSION TO USE HIM FOR YOUR EXPERIMENT.
OH, RIGHT...
SORRY, KIRYU.
MURAKI, A MEMBER OF THE RESEARCH TEAM, STEPPED FORWARD TO BECOME A TEST SUBJECT INSTEAD.
AND...
...IT FAILED.
JUST WRITE A LITTLE NOTE THAT YOU DON'T NEED THIS DELIVERY ANYMORE AND SIGN YOUR NAME.
HUH?
OH, SURE.
MATTER-OF-FACT

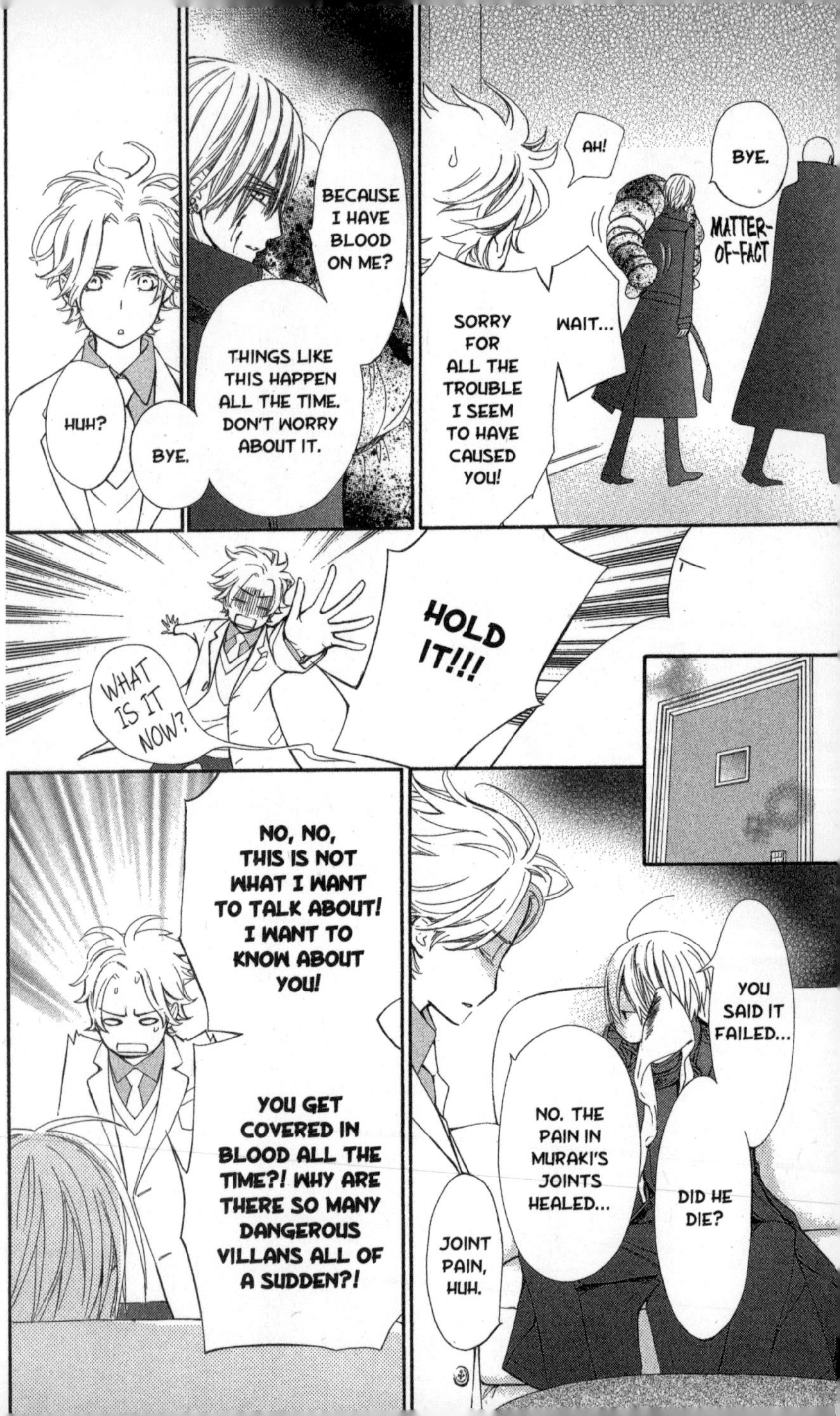
BYE.
MATTER-OF-FACT
AH!
WAIT...
SORRY FOR ALL THE TROUBLE I SEEM TO HAVE CAUSED YOU!
BECAUSE I HAVE BLOOD ON ME?
THINGS LIKE THIS HAPPEN ALL THE TIME. DON'T WORRY ABOUT IT.
BYE.
HUH?
HOLD IT!!!
WHAT IS IT NOW?
YOU SAID IT FAILED...
DID HE DIE?
NO. THE PAIN IN MURAKI'S JOINTS HEALED...
JOINT PAIN, HUH.
NO, NO, THIS IS NOT WHAT I WANT TO TALK ABOUT! I WANT TO KNOW ABOUT YOU!
YOU GET COVERED IN BLOOD ALL THE TIME?! WHY ARE THERE SO MANY DANGEROUS VILLANS ALL OF A SUDDEN?!

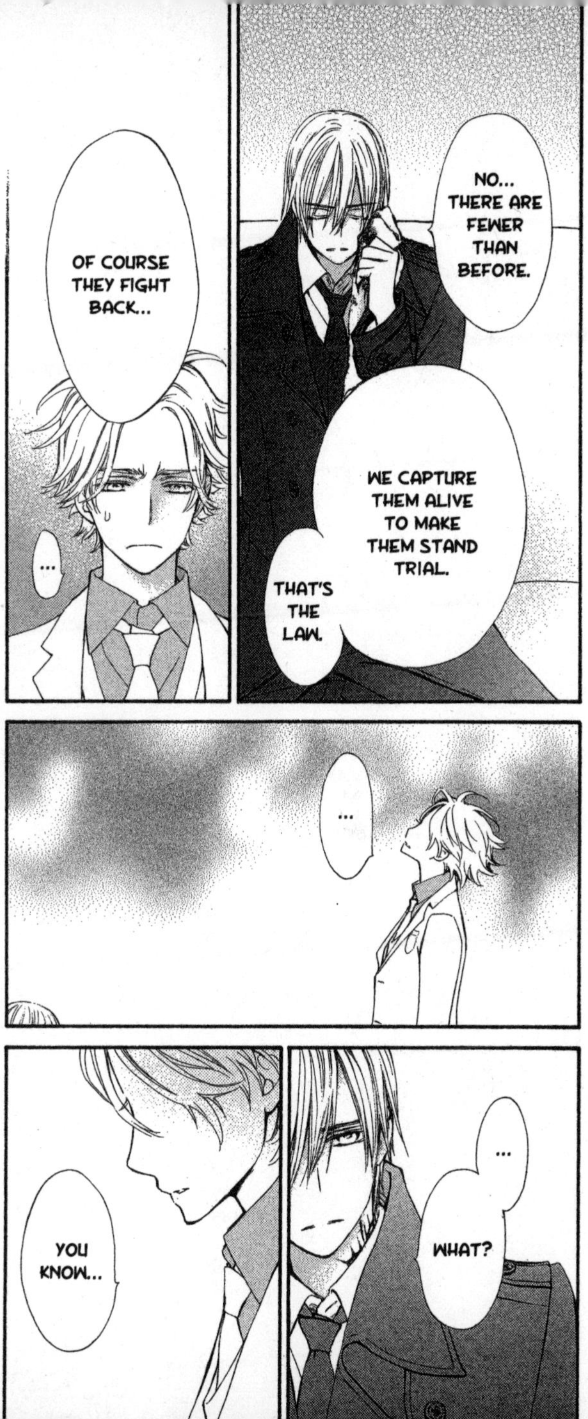
NO... THERE ARE FEWER THAN BEFORE.
WE CAPTURE THEM ALIVE TO MAKE THEM STAND TRIAL.
THAT'S THE LAW.
OF COURSE THEY FIGHT BACK...
...
...
...
WHAT?
YOU KNOW...

— 5 —

(continued ↓)

In my twenties I learned that it was very difficult to balance work and medical treatment.

But time has passed, and now there is a limit to how much I can bear. I had another stomach you-know-what, and I've had various other troubles, so nowadays I go with the "trying not to overdo anything so it doesn't get out of hand" plan. Health-wise, I should be able to keep drawing for a little longer.

My drawing and thinking speed has slowed down too, so I am very grateful for the current work pace.

Next time I would like to reveal some exciting news. (If they give me the go-ahead.)

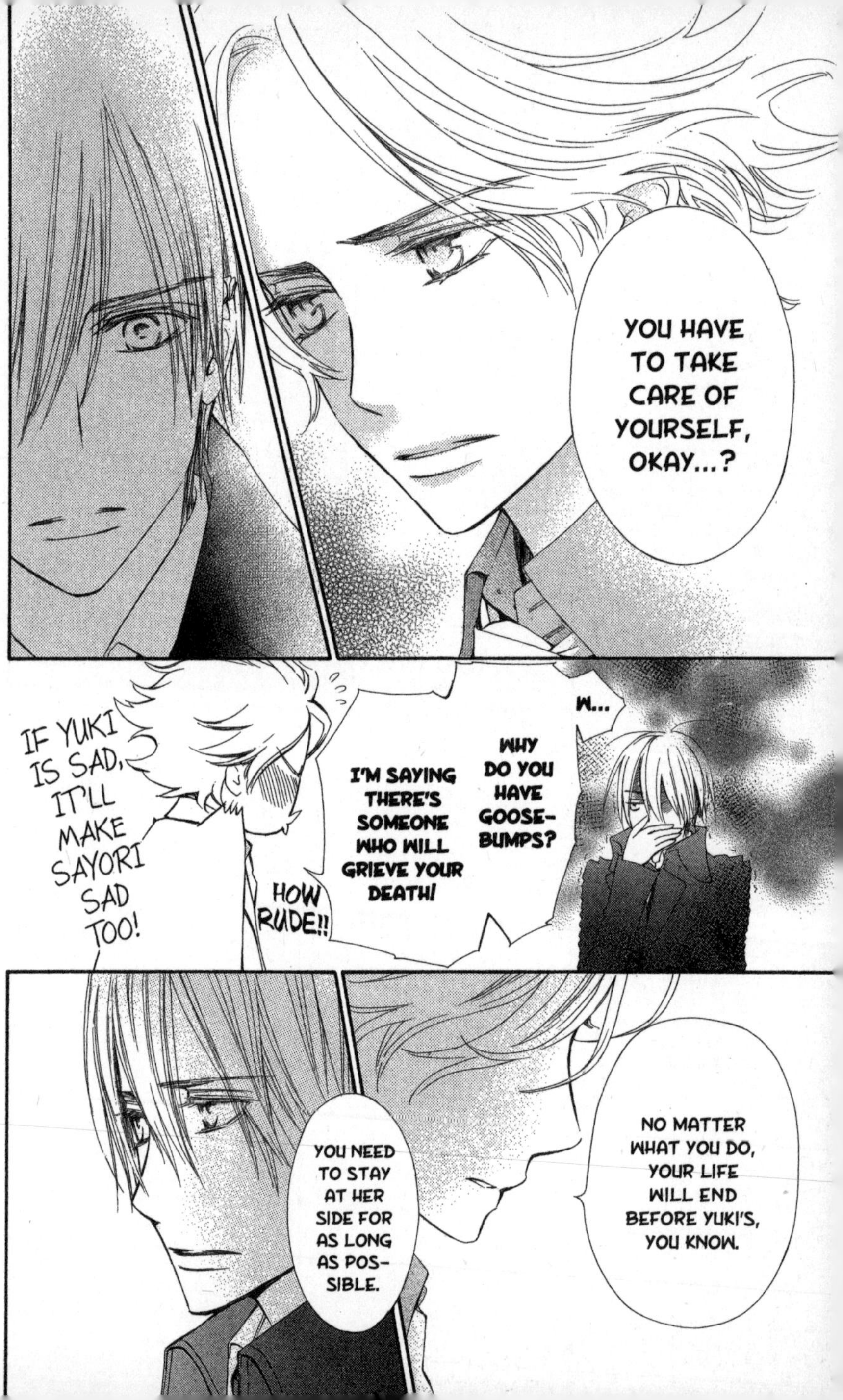
YOU HAVE TO TAKE CARE OF YOURSELF, OKAY...?
W...
WHY DO YOU HAVE GOOSE-BUMPS?
I'M SAYING THERE'S SOMEONE WHO WILL GRIEVE YOUR DEATH!
HOW RUDE!!
IF YUKI IS SAD, IT'LL MAKE SAYORI SAD TOO!
NO MATTER WHAT YOU DO, YOUR LIFE WILL END BEFORE YUKI'S, YOU KNOW.
YOU NEED TO STAY AT HER SIDE FOR AS LONG AS POS-SIBLE.

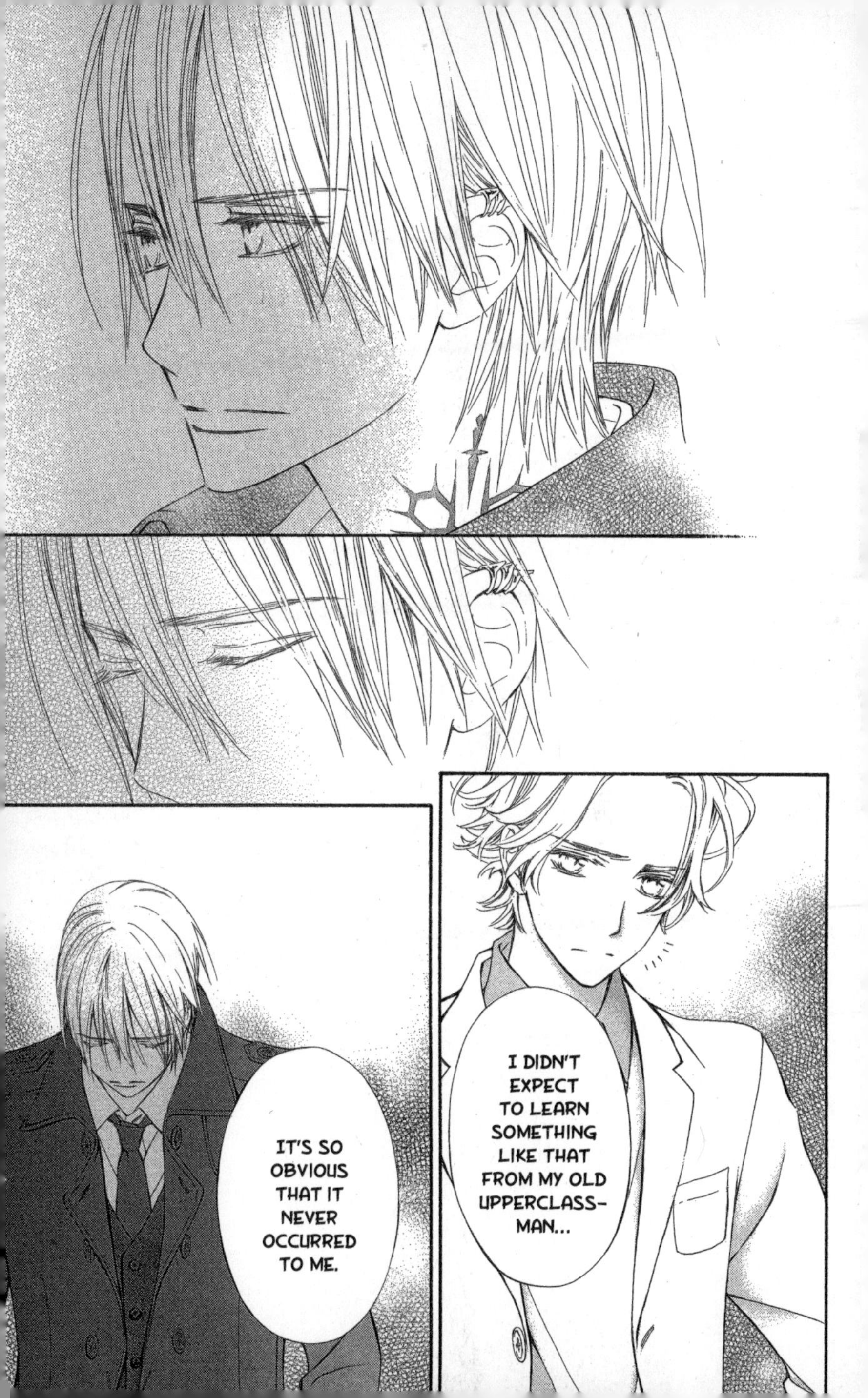
I DIDN'T EXPECT TO LEARN SOMETHING LIKE THAT FROM MY OLD UPPERCLASS-MAN...
IT'S SO OBVIOUS THAT IT NEVER OCCURRED TO ME.

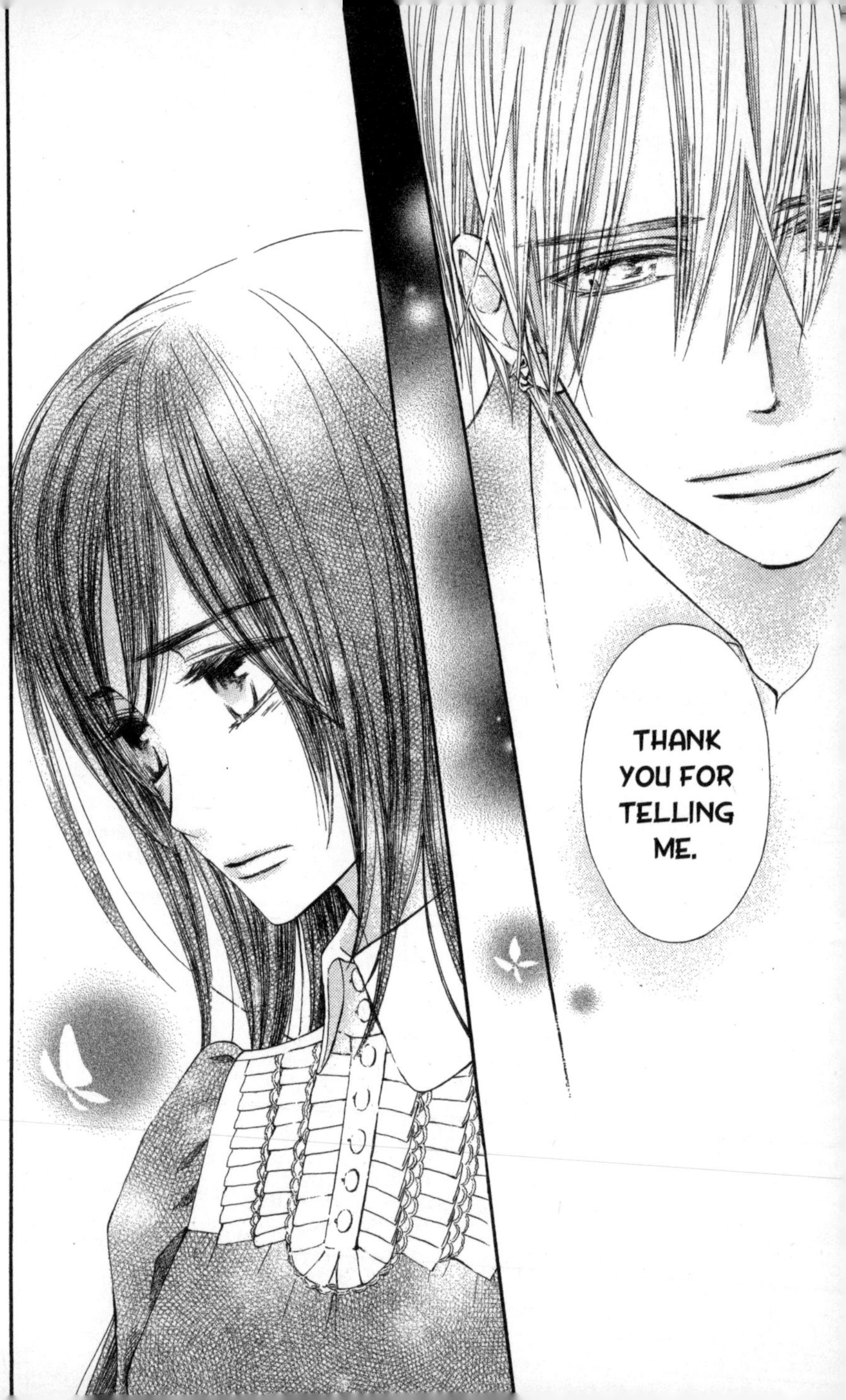
THANK YOU FOR TELLING ME.

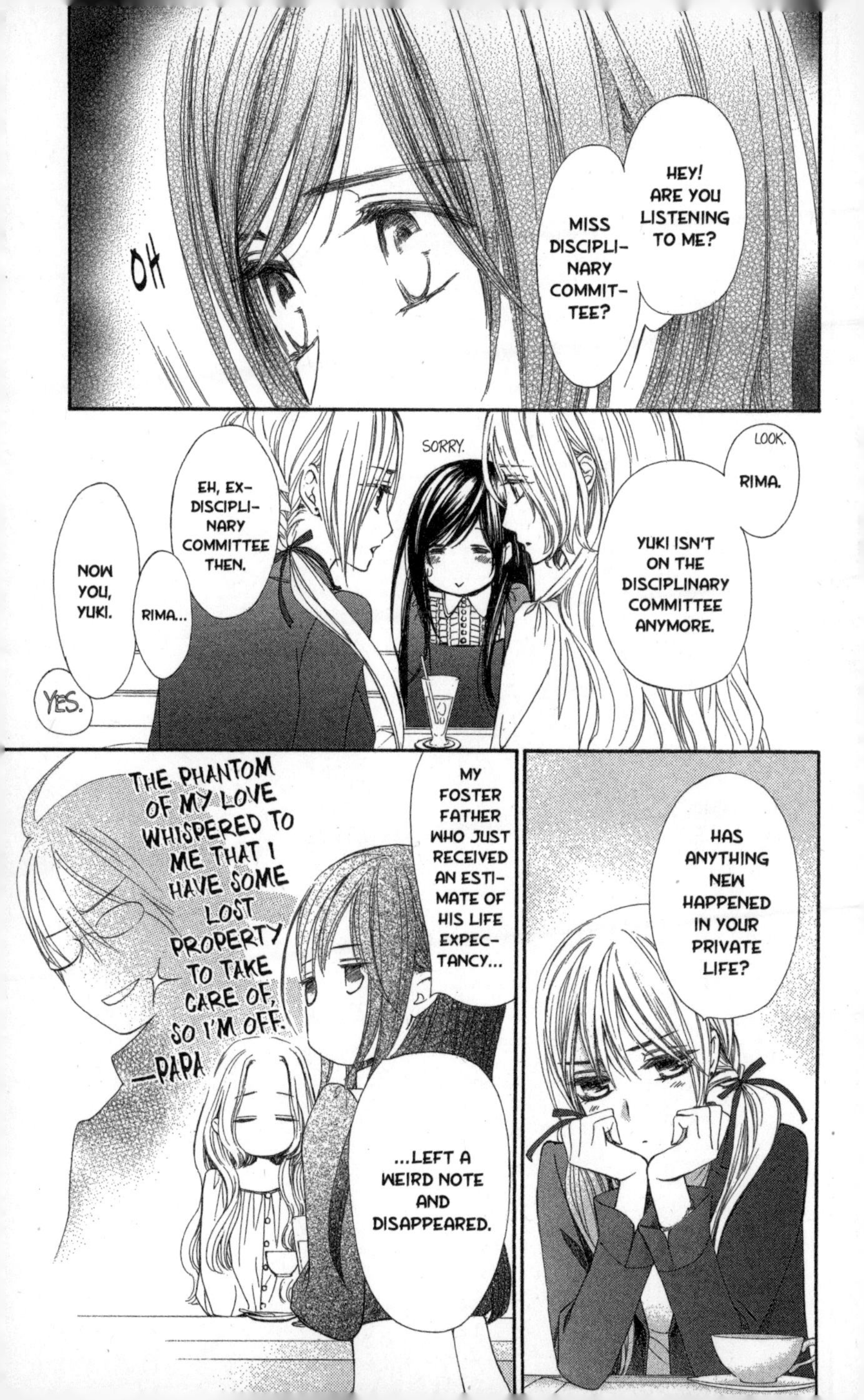
HEY! ARE YOU LISTENING TO ME?
MISS DISCIPLINARY COMMITTEE?
OH
LOOK.
RIMA.
YUKI ISN'T ON THE DISCIPLINARY COMMITTEE ANYMORE.
SORRY.
EH, EX-DISCIPLINARY COMMITTEE THEN.
RIMA...
NOW YOU, YUKI.
YES.
HAS ANYTHING NEW HAPPENED IN YOUR PRIVATE LIFE?
MY FOSTER FATHER WHO JUST RECEIVED AN ESTIMATE OF HIS LIFE EXPECTANCY...
THE PHANTOM OF MY LOVE WHISPERED TO ME THAT I HAVE SOME LOST PROPERTY TO TAKE CARE OF, SO I'M OFF. —PAPA
...LEFT A WEIRD NOTE AND DISAPPEARED.

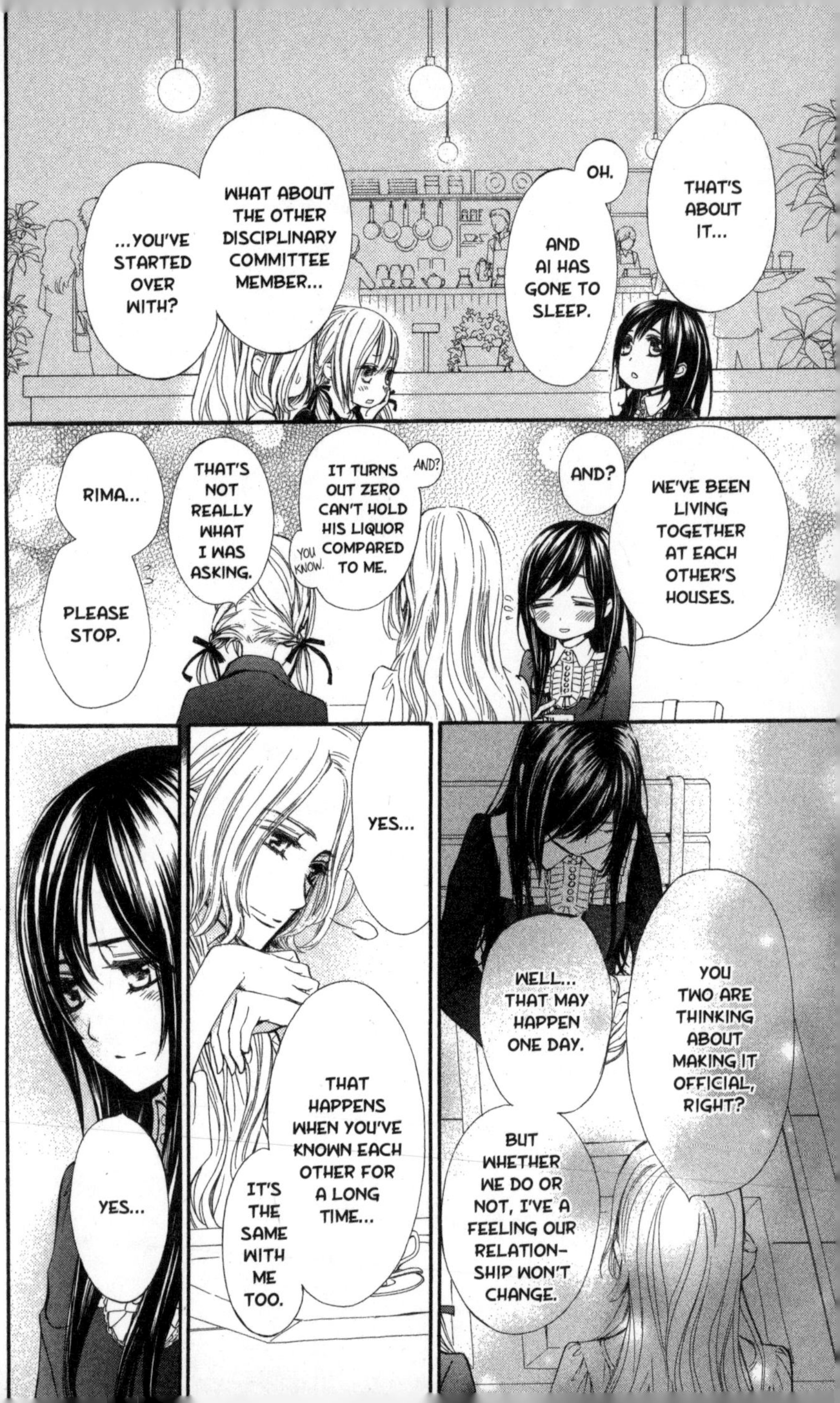
THAT'S ABOUT IT...
OH.
AND AI HAS GONE TO SLEEP.
WHAT ABOUT THE OTHER DISCIPLINARY COMMITTEE MEMBER...
...YOU'VE STARTED OVER WITH?
WE'VE BEEN LIVING TOGETHER AT EACH OTHER'S HOUSES.
AND?
AND?
IT TURNS OUT ZERO CAN'T HOLD HIS LIQUOR COMPARED TO ME.
YOU KNOW.
THAT'S NOT REALLY WHAT I WAS ASKING.
RIMA...
PLEASE STOP.
YOU TWO ARE THINKING ABOUT MAKING IT OFFICIAL, RIGHT?
WELL... THAT MAY HAPPEN ONE DAY.
BUT WHETHER WE DO OR NOT, I'VE A FEELING OUR RELATION-SHIP WON'T CHANGE.
YES...
THAT HAPPENS WHEN YOU'VE KNOWN EACH OTHER FOR A LONG TIME...
IT'S THE SAME WITH ME TOO.
YES...

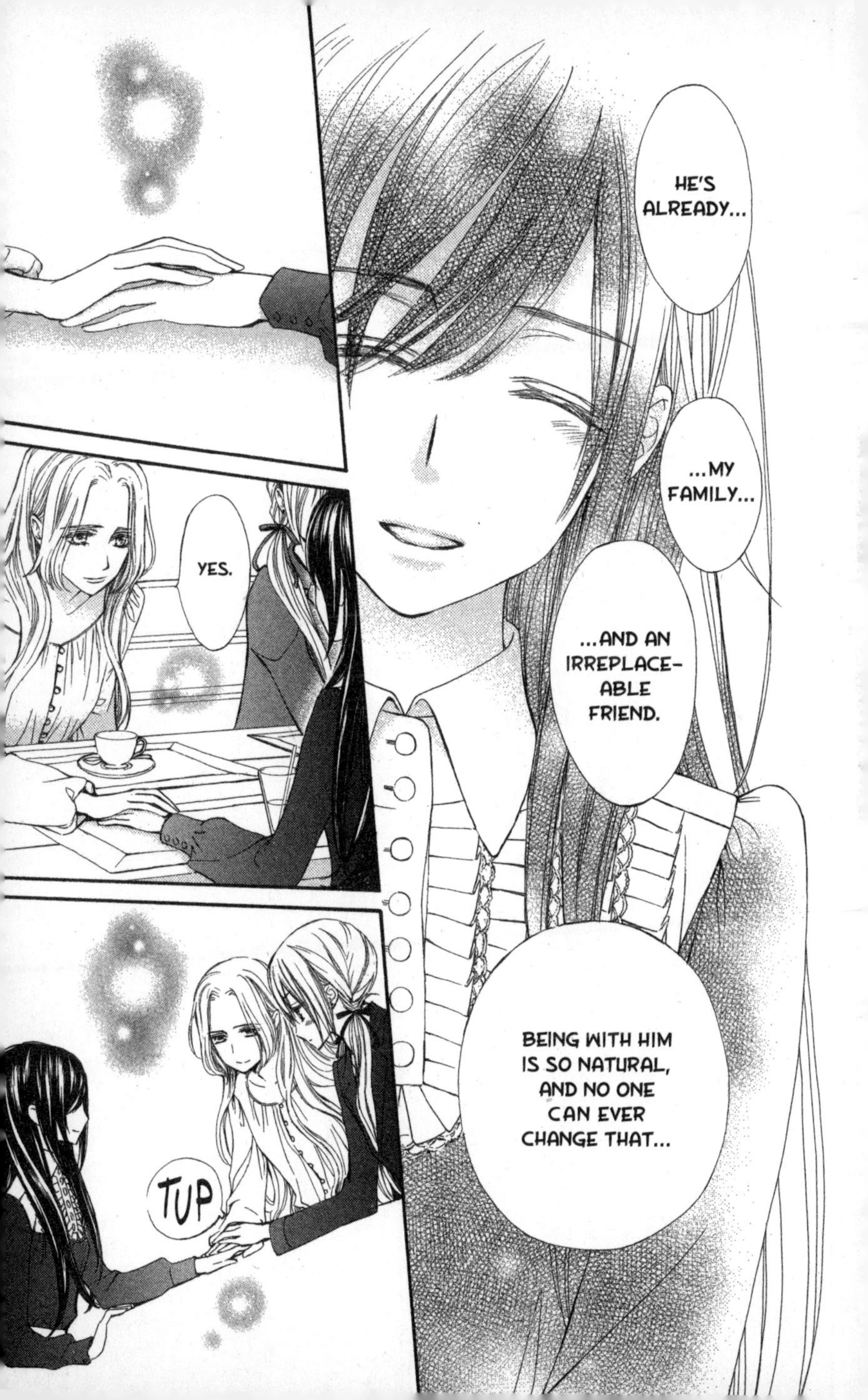
HE'S ALREADY...
...MY FAMILY...
...AND AN IRREPLACE-ABLE FRIEND.
BEING WITH HIM IS SO NATURAL, AND NO ONE CAN EVER CHANGE THAT...
YES.
TUP

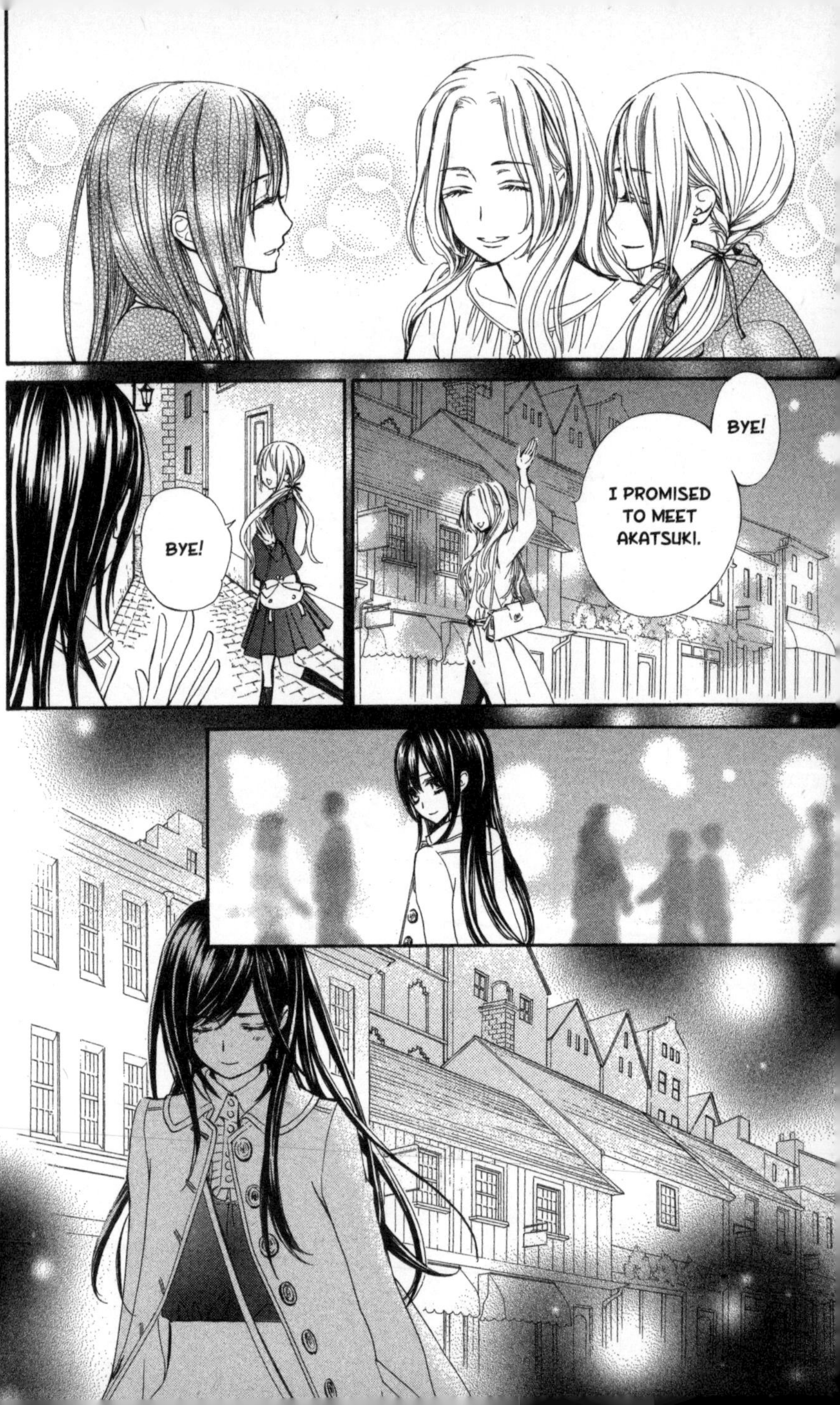
BYE!
I PROMISED TO MEET AKATSUKI.
BYE!

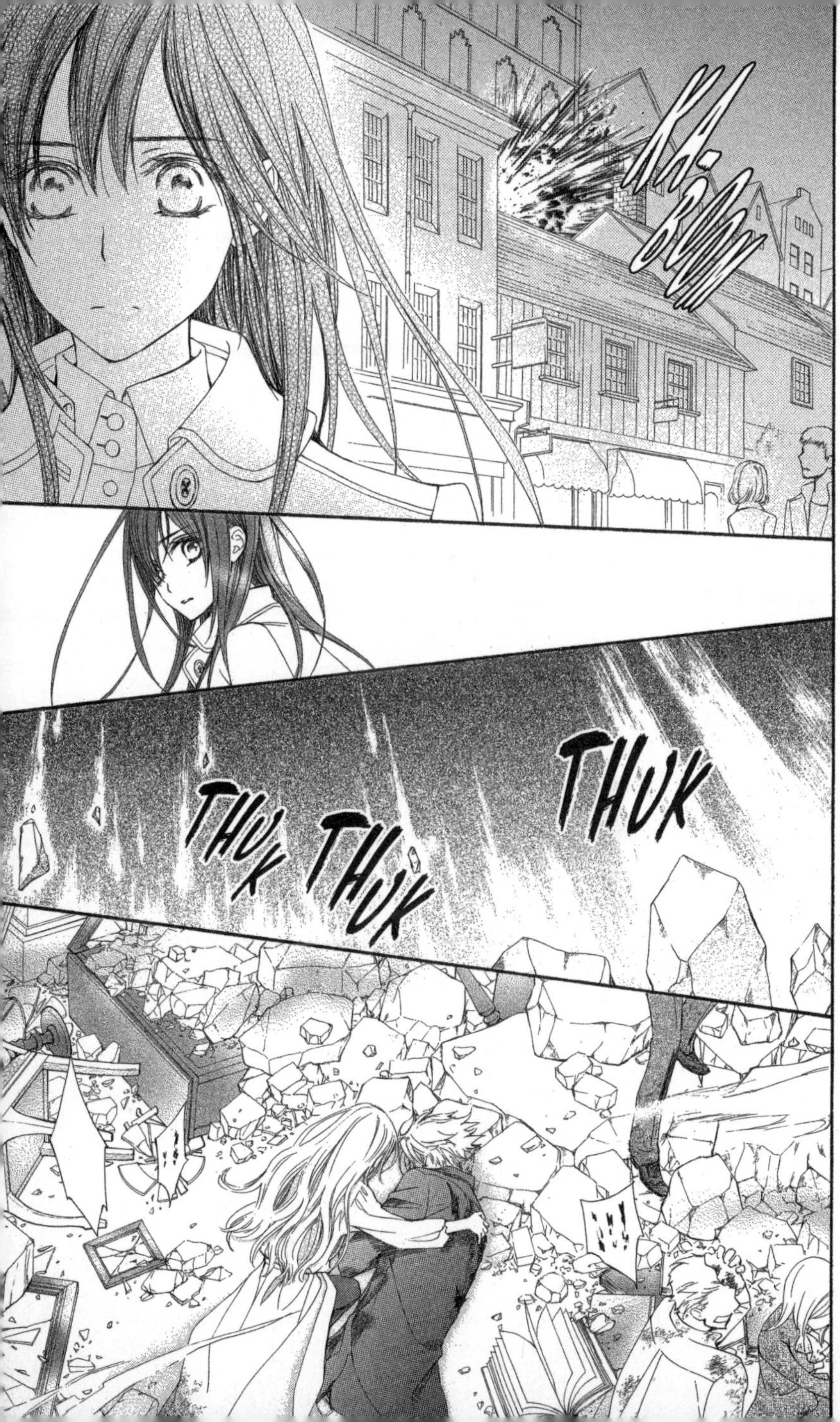
KA-BOOM
THUK
THUK
THUK

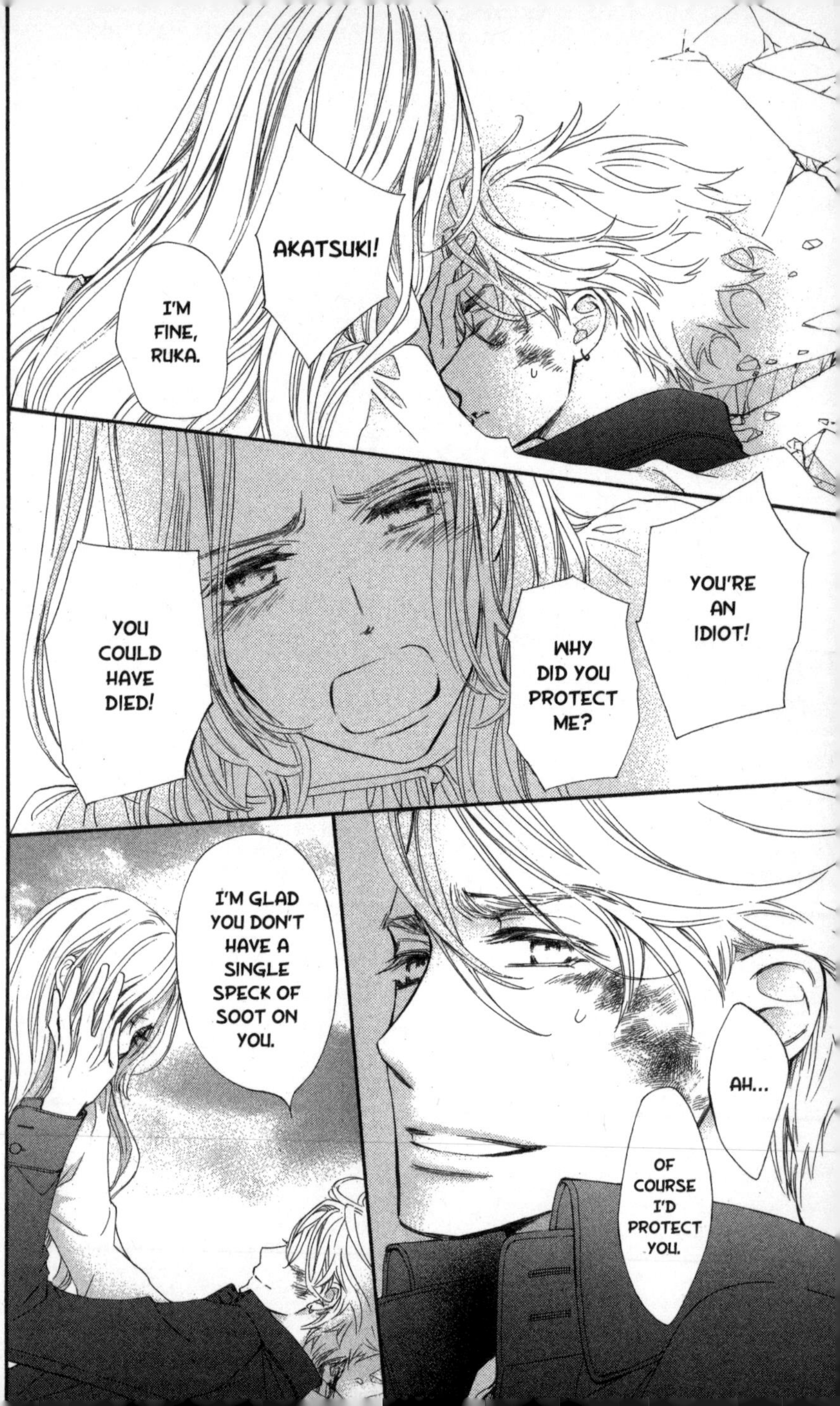
AKATSUKI!
I'M FINE, RUKA.
YOU'RE AN IDIOT!
WHY DID YOU PROTECT ME?
YOU COULD HAVE DIED!
AH...
OF COURSE I'D PROTECT YOU.
I'M GLAD YOU DON'T HAVE A SINGLE SPECK OF SOOT ON YOU.

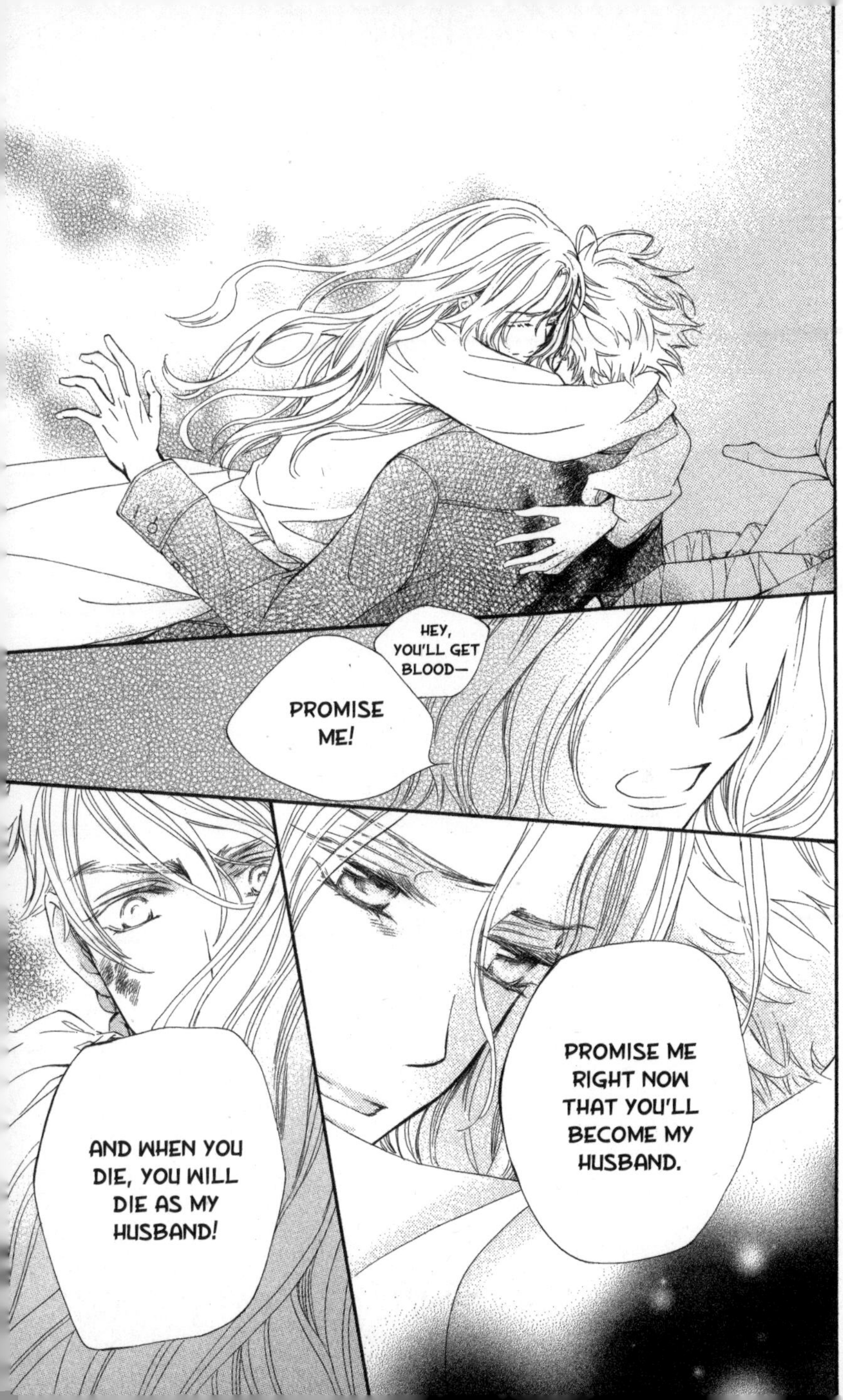
HEY, YOU'LL GET BLOOD—
PROMISE ME!
PROMISE ME RIGHT NOW THAT YOU'LL BECOME MY HUSBAND.
AND WHEN YOU DIE, YOU WILL DIE AS MY HUSBAND!

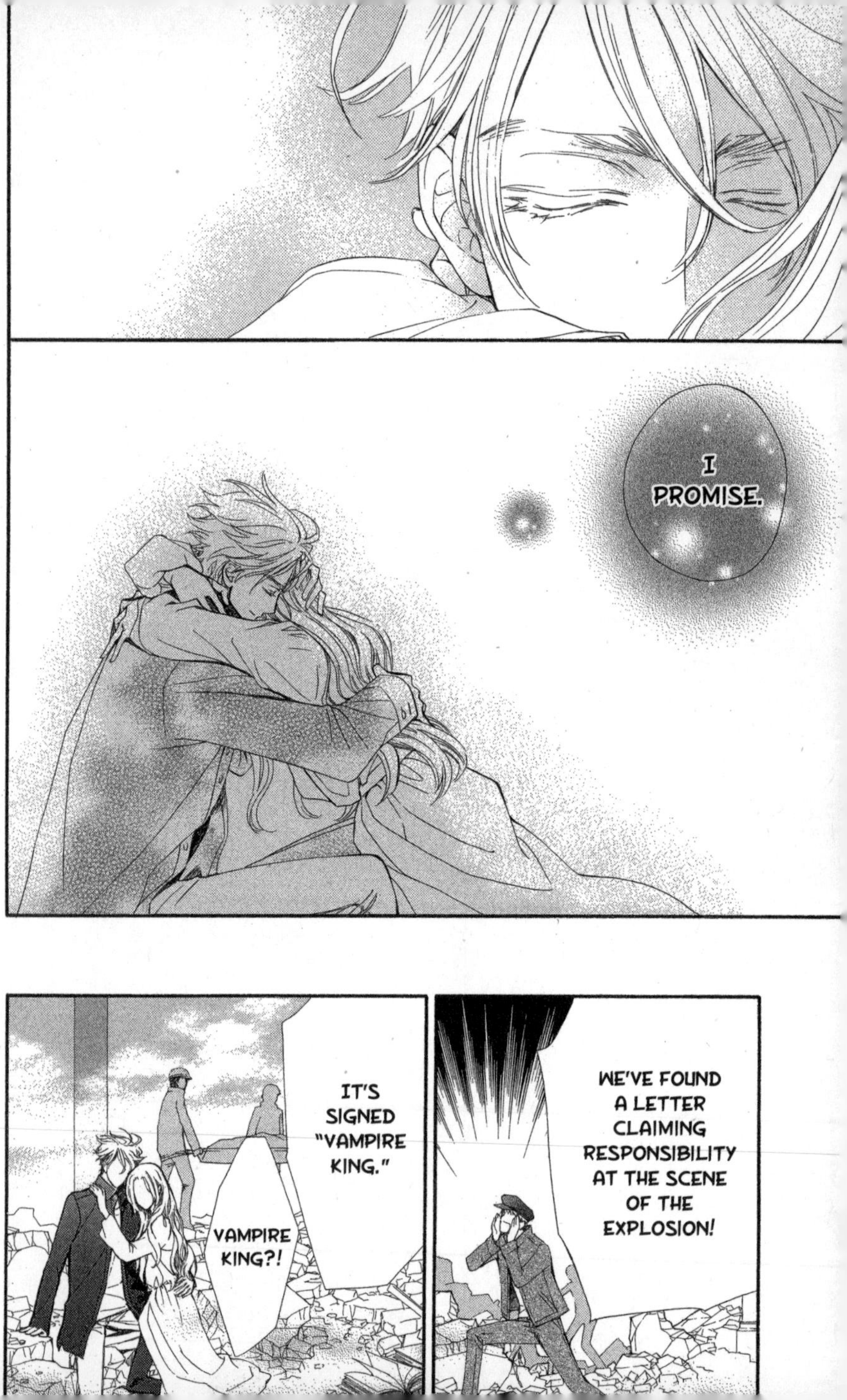
I PROMISE.
WE'VE FOUND A LETTER CLAIMING RESPONSIBILITY AT THE SCENE OF THE EXPLOSION!
IT'S SIGNED "VAMPIRE KING."
VAMPIRE KING?!

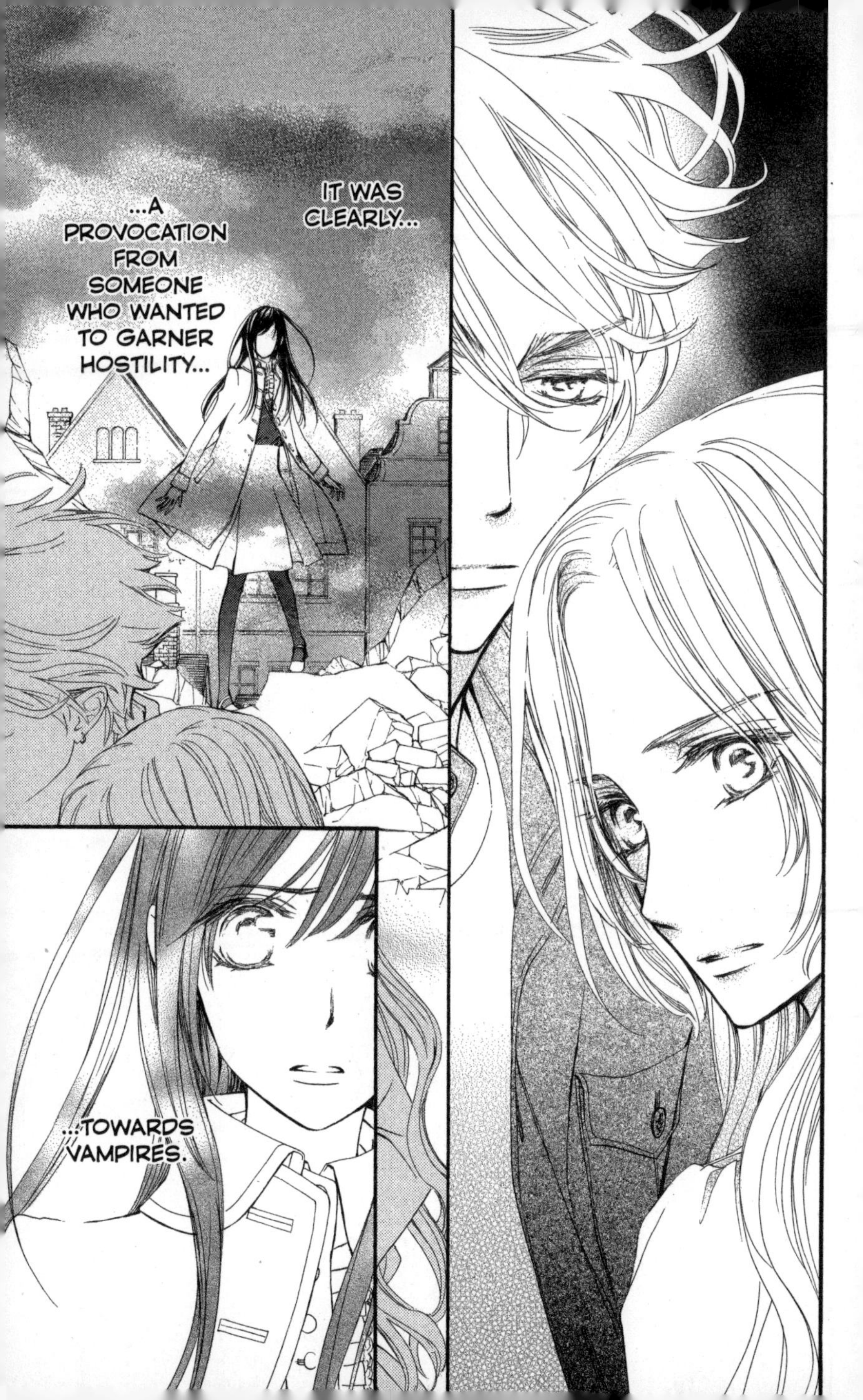
IT WAS CLEARLY...
...A PROVOCATION FROM SOMEONE WHO WANTED TO GARNER HOSTILITY...
...TOWARDS VAMPIRES.

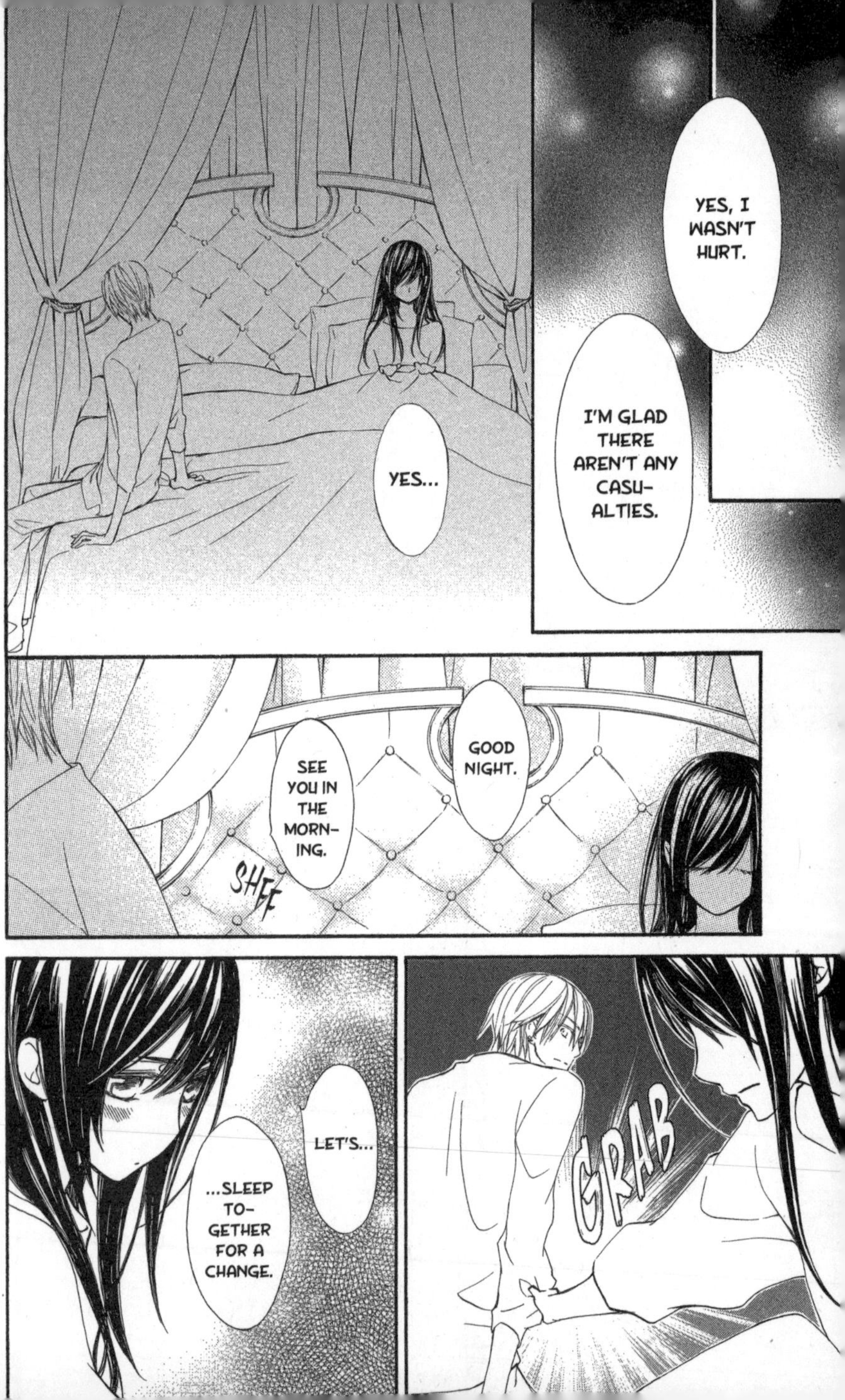
YES, I WASN'T HURT.
I'M GLAD THERE AREN'T ANY CASU-ALTIES.
YES...
GOOD NIGHT.
SEE YOU IN THE MORN-ING.
SHFF
GRAB
LET'S...
...SLEEP TO-GETHER FOR A CHANGE.

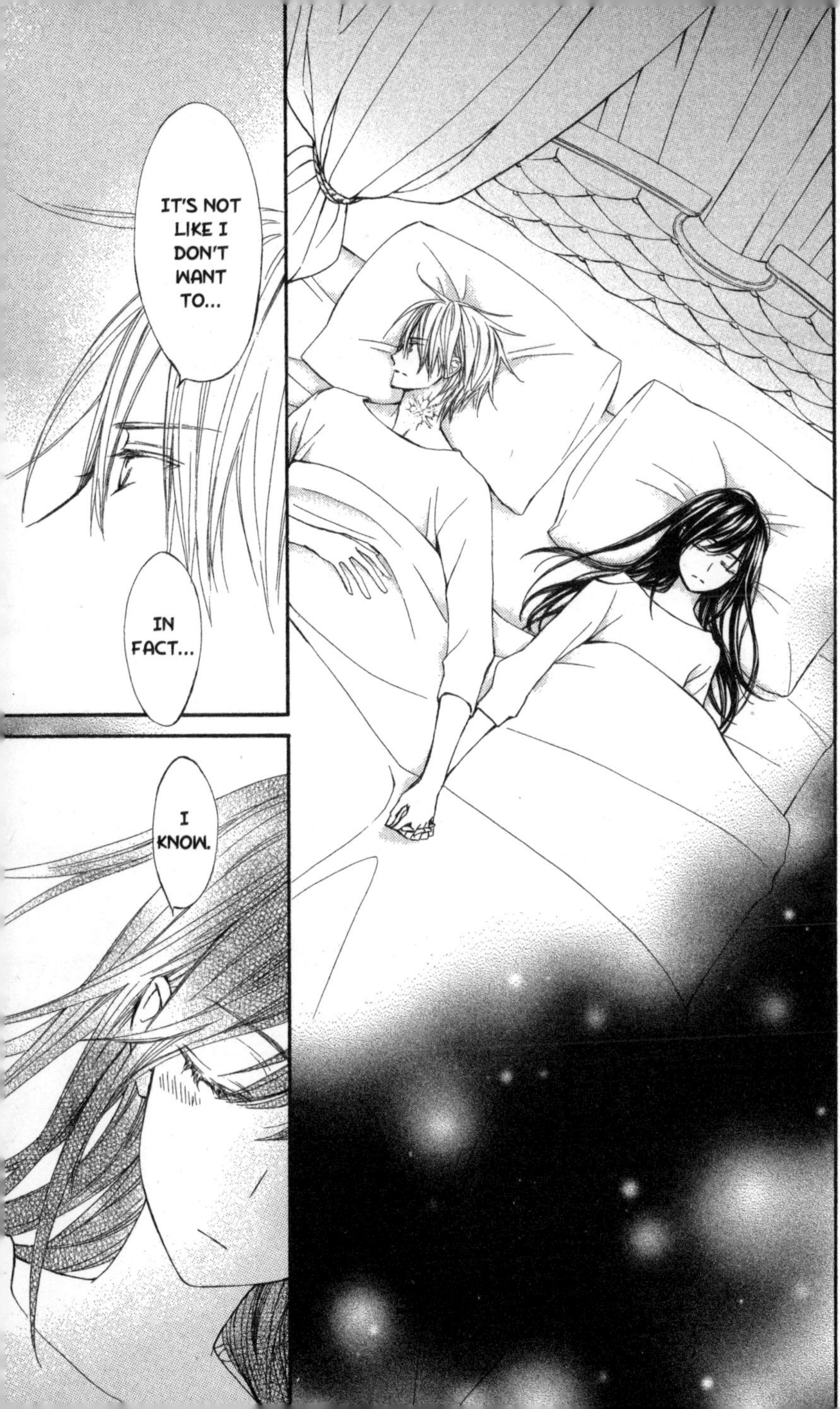
IT'S NOT LIKE I DON'T WANT TO...
IN FACT...
I KNOW.

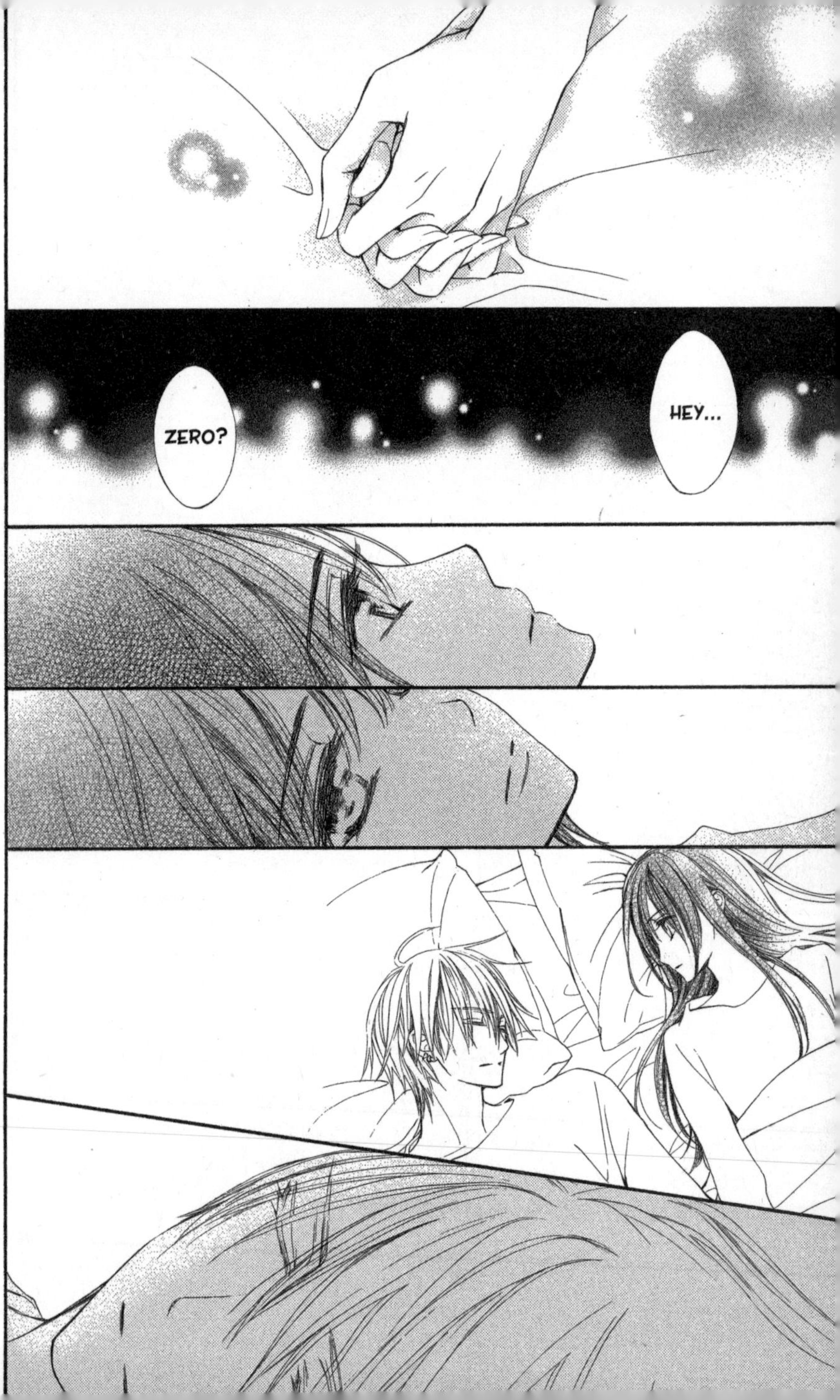
HEY...
ZERO?

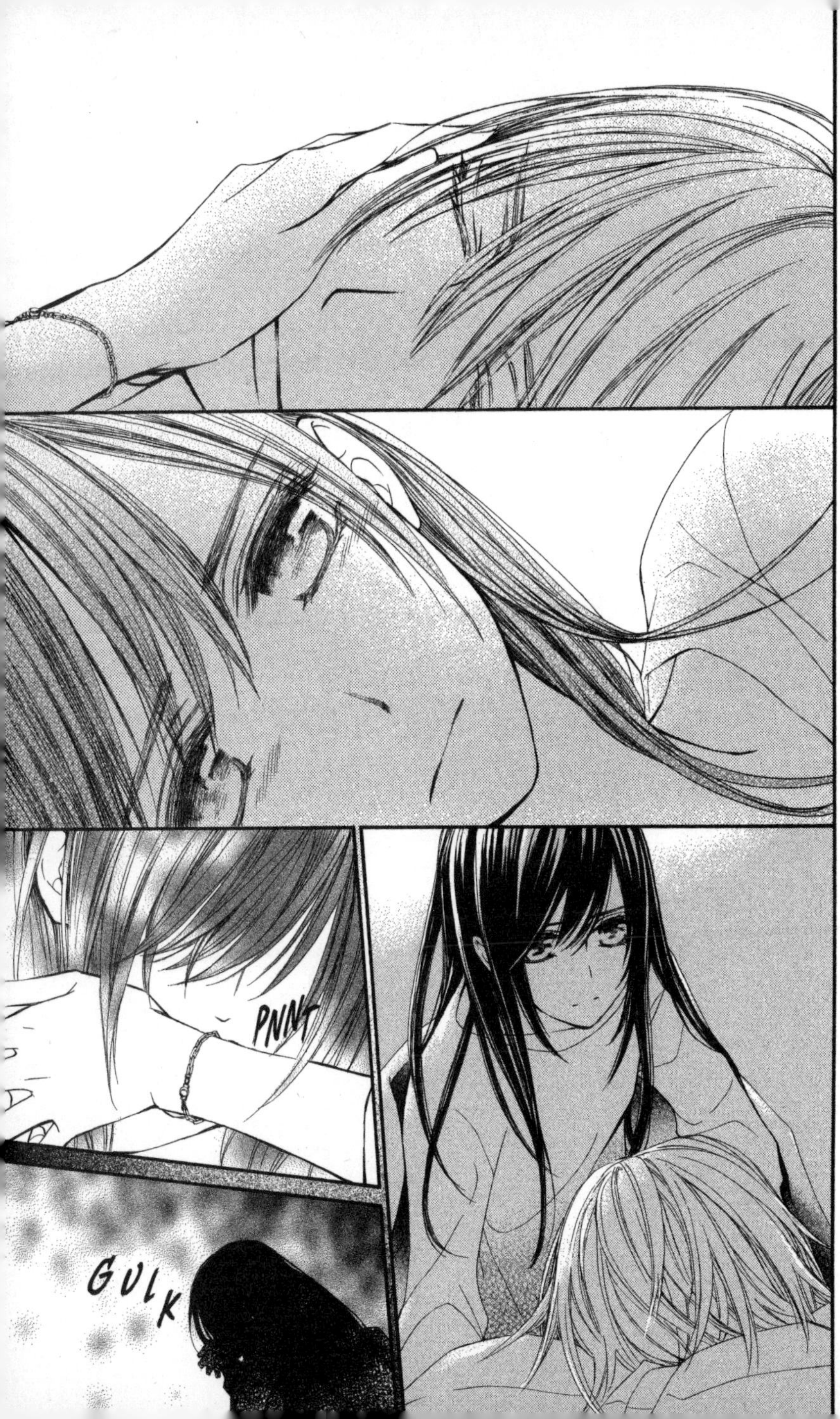
PNNT
GULK

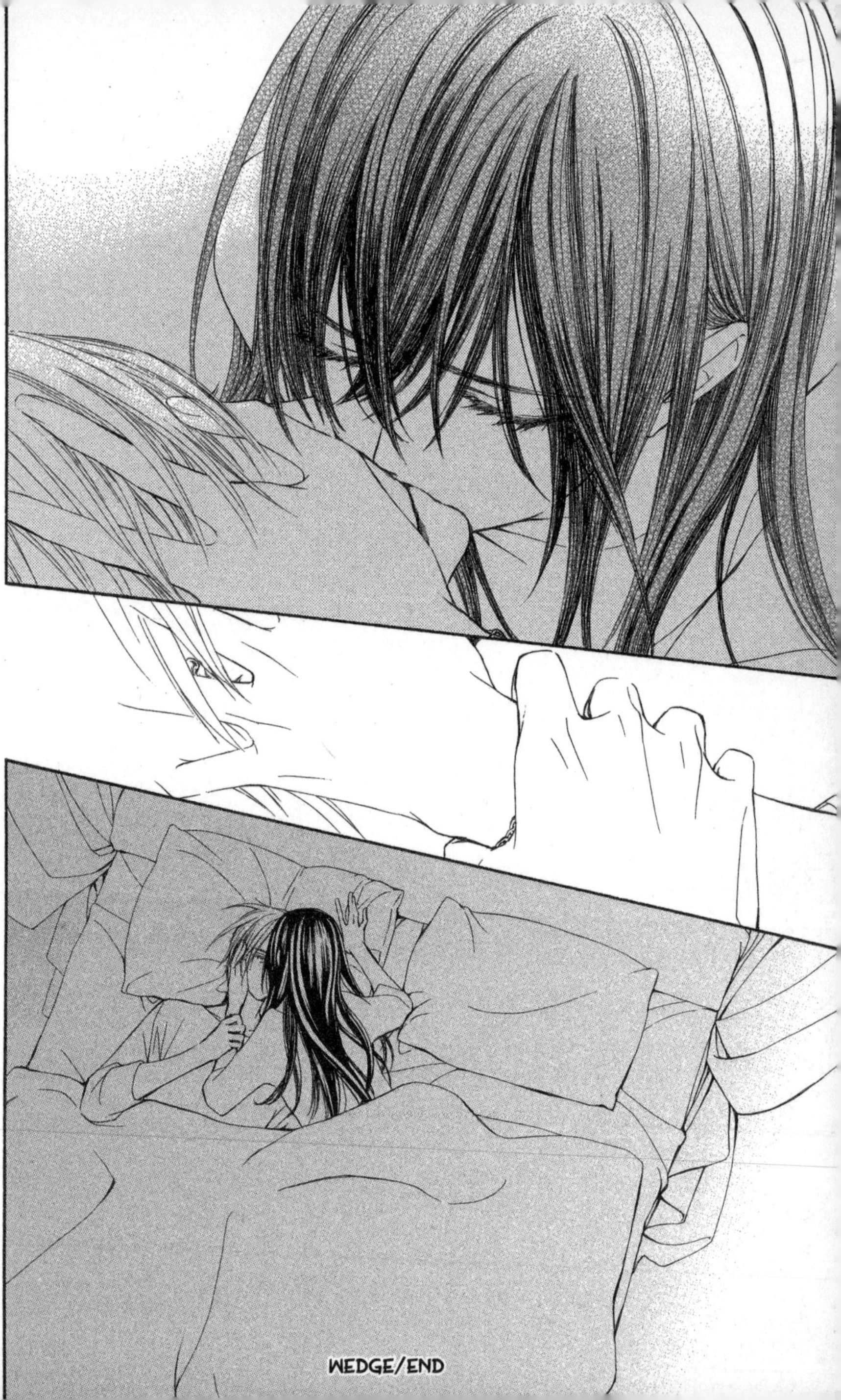
WEDGE/END

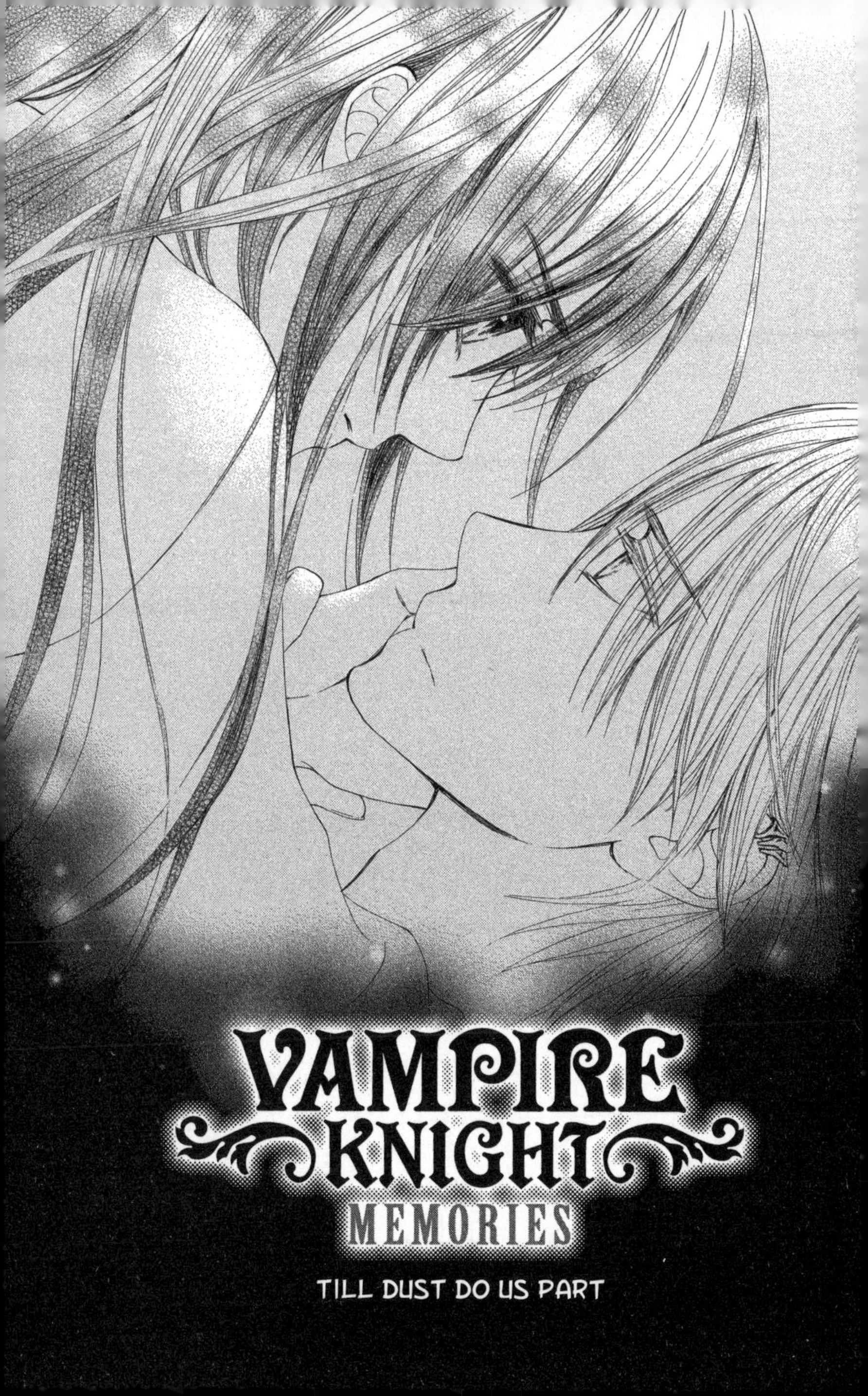

VAMPIRE KNIGHT MEMORIES

TILL DUST DO US PART

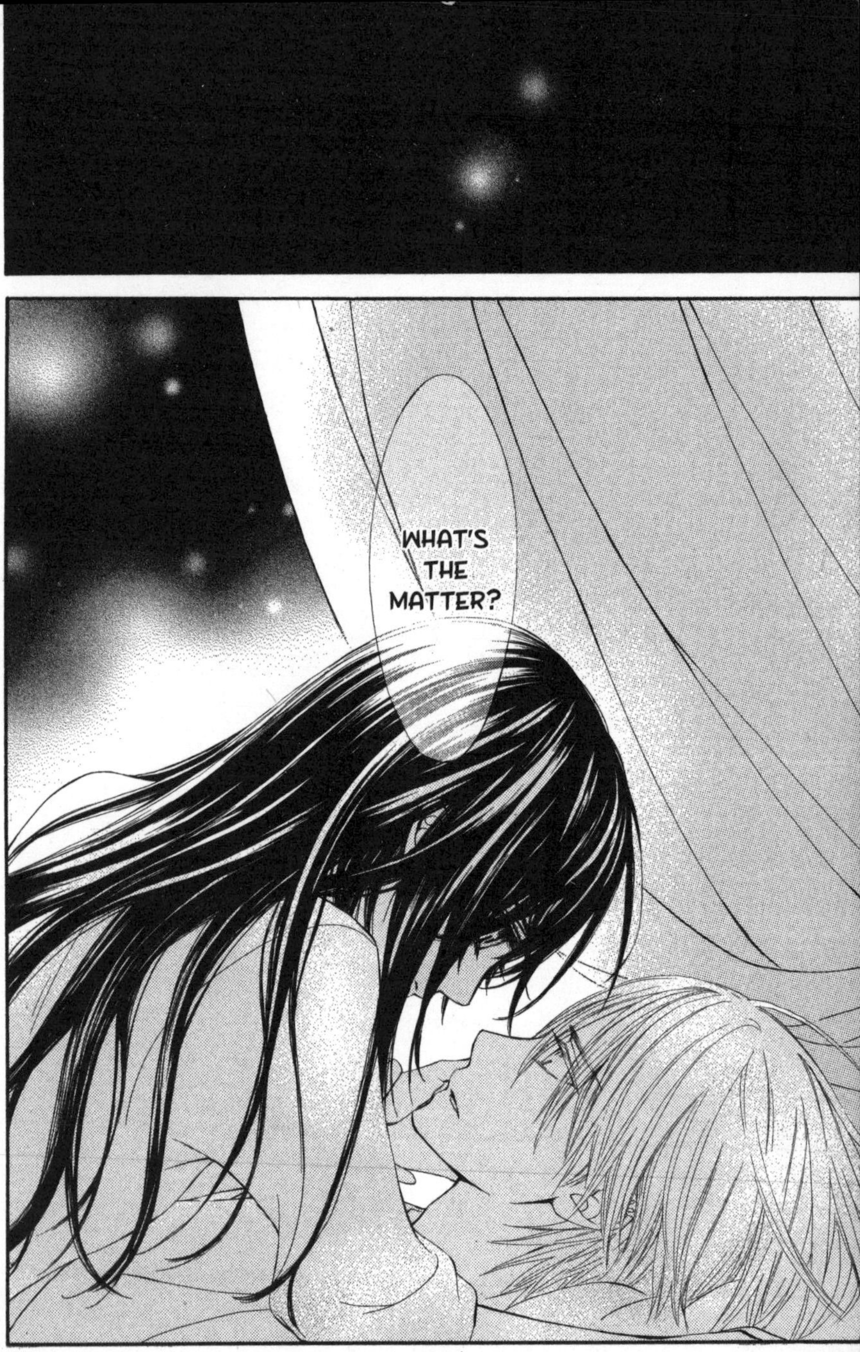
WHAT'S THE MATTER?

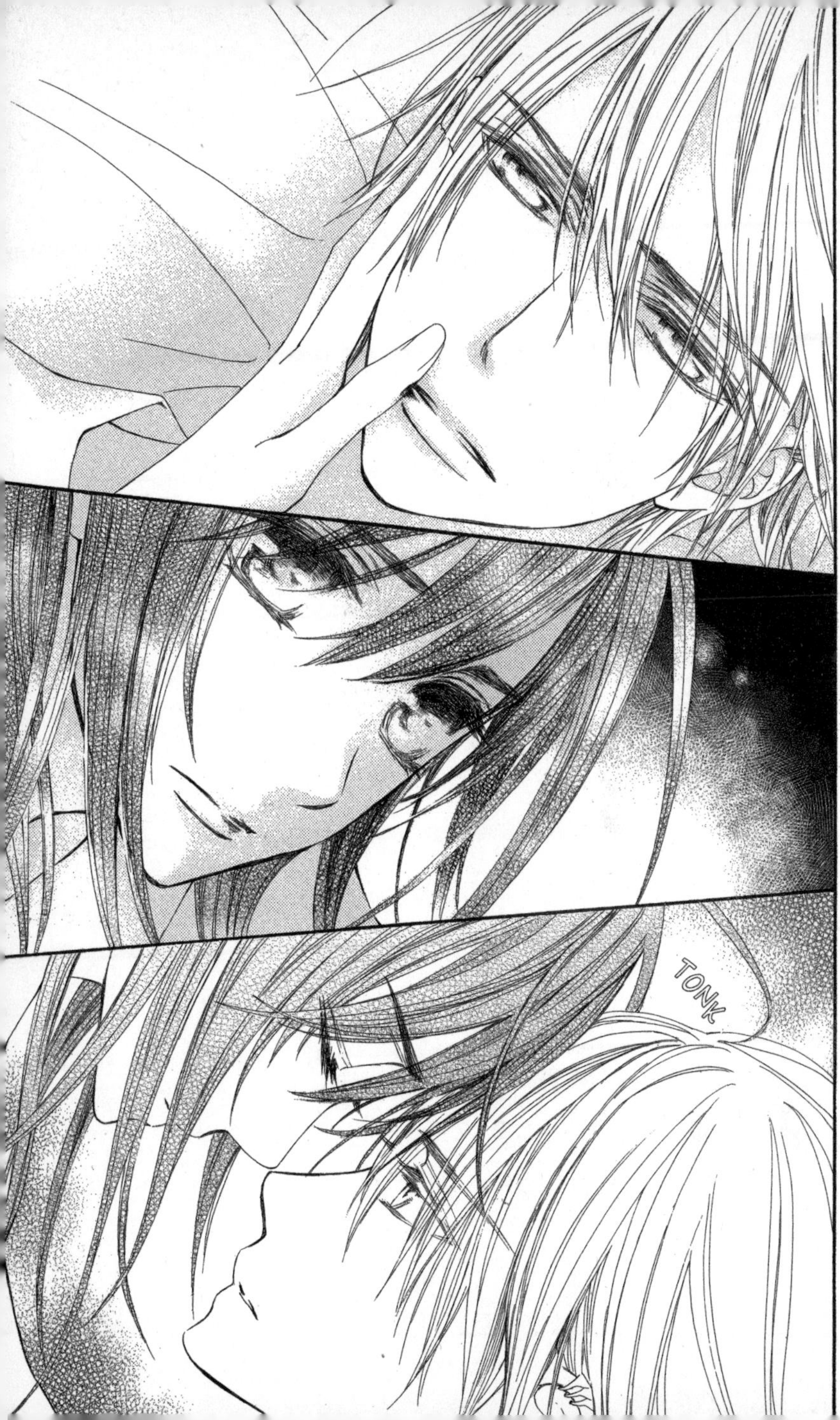
TONK

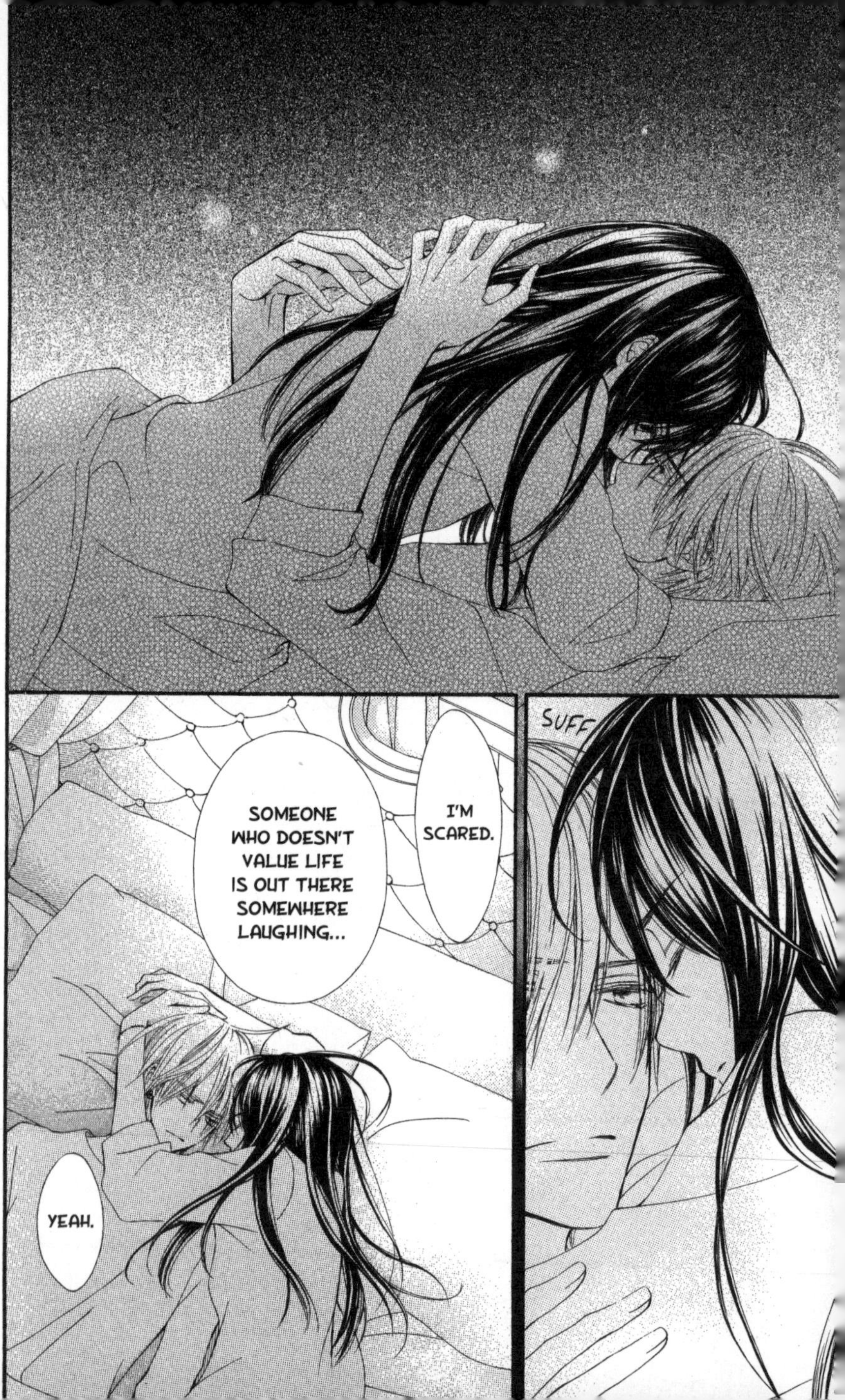
SUFF
I'M SCARED.
SOMEONE WHO DOESN'T VALUE LIFE IS OUT THERE SOMEWHERE LAUGHING...
YEAH.

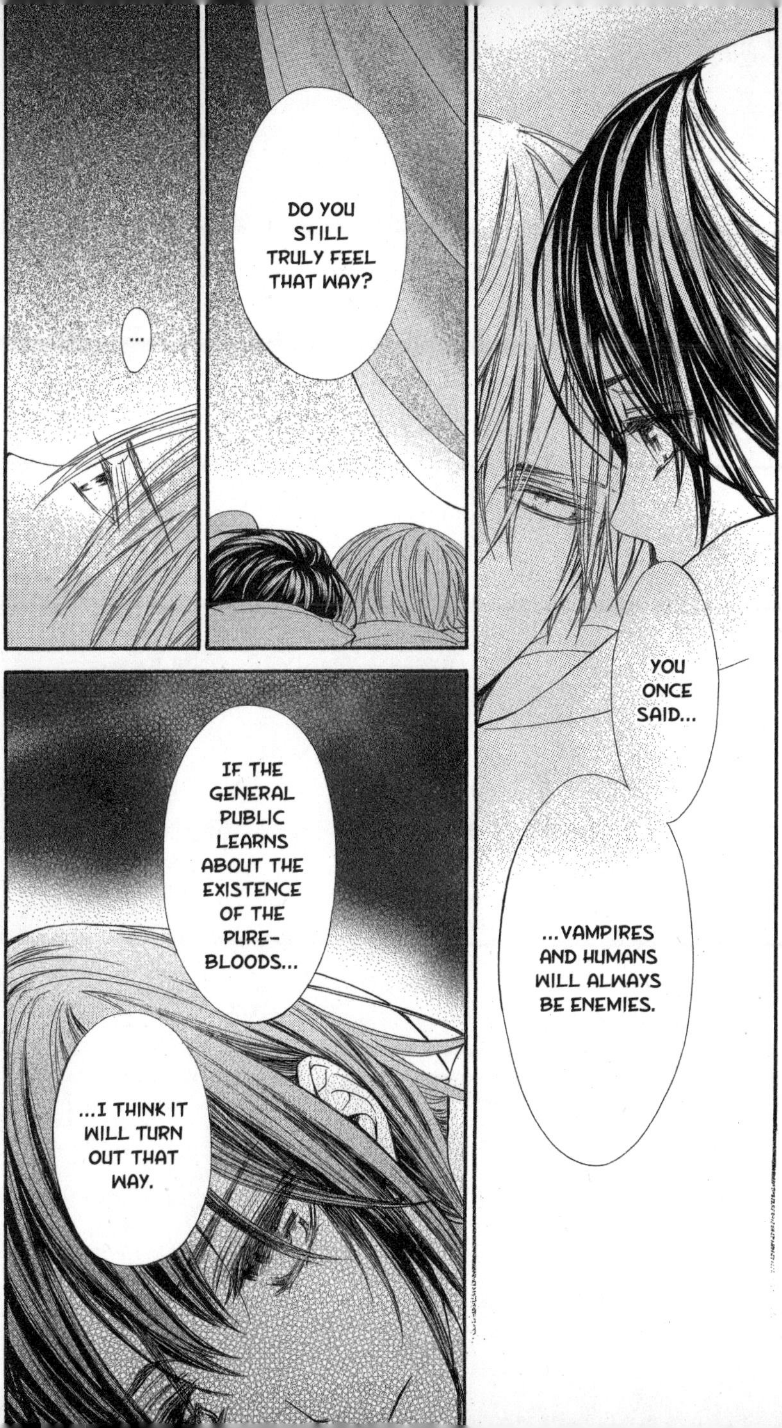
YOU ONCE SAID...
...VAMPIRES AND HUMANS WILL ALWAYS BE ENEMIES.
DO YOU STILL TRULY FEEL THAT WAY?
...
IF THE GENERAL PUBLIC LEARNS ABOUT THE EXISTENCE OF THE PURE-BLOODS...
...I THINK IT WILL TURN OUT THAT WAY.

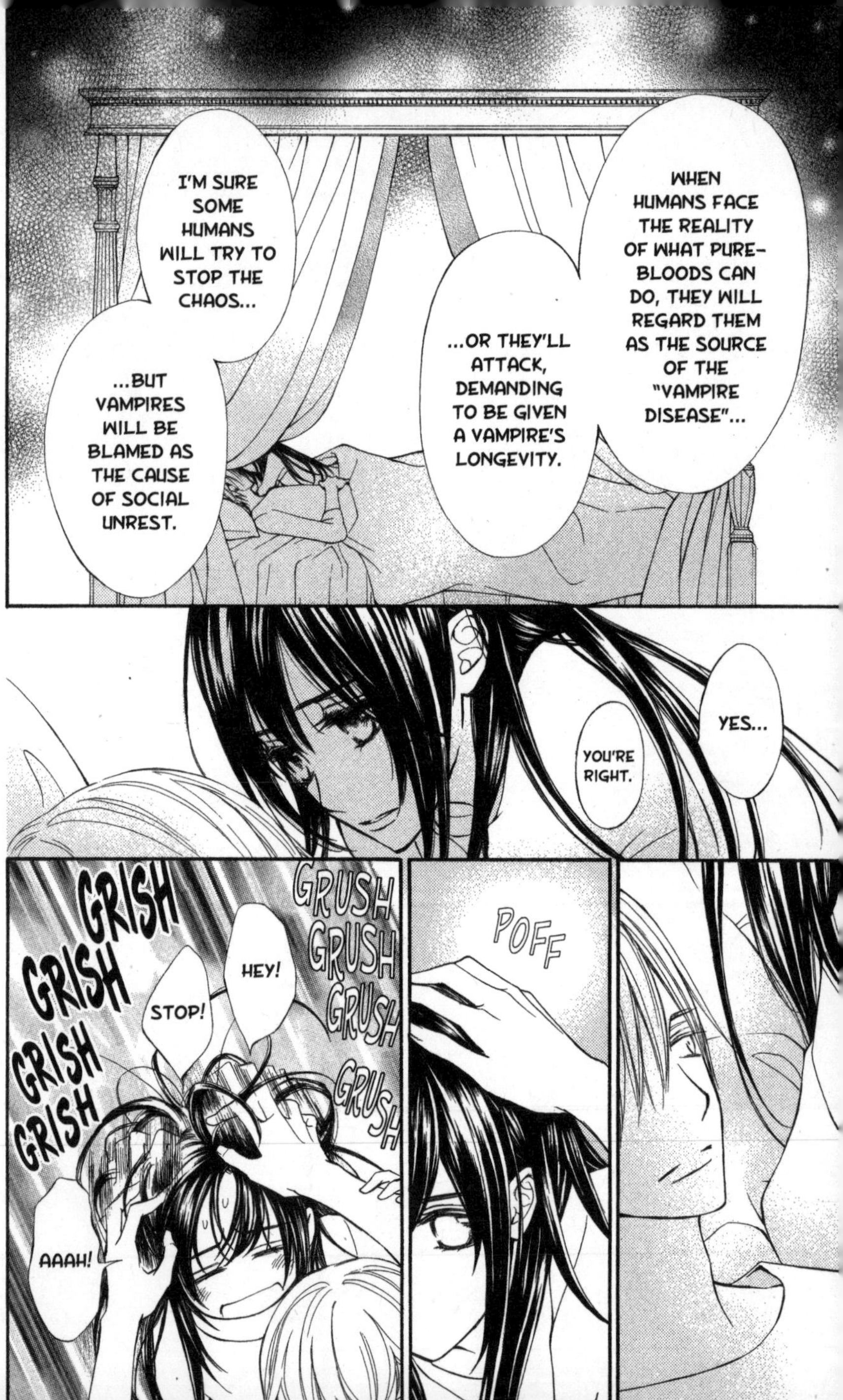
WHEN HUMANS FACE THE REALITY OF WHAT PURE-BLOODS CAN DO, THEY WILL REGARD THEM AS THE SOURCE OF THE "VAMPIRE DISEASE"...
...OR THEY'LL ATTACK, DEMANDING TO BE GIVEN A VAMPIRE'S LONGEVITY.
I'M SURE SOME HUMANS WILL TRY TO STOP THE CHAOS...
...BUT VAMPIRES WILL BE BLAMED AS THE CAUSE OF SOCIAL UNREST.
YES...
YOU'RE RIGHT.
POFF
GRUSH GRUSH GRUSH GRUSH
HEY!
STOP!
GRISH GRISH GRISH GRISH
AAAH!

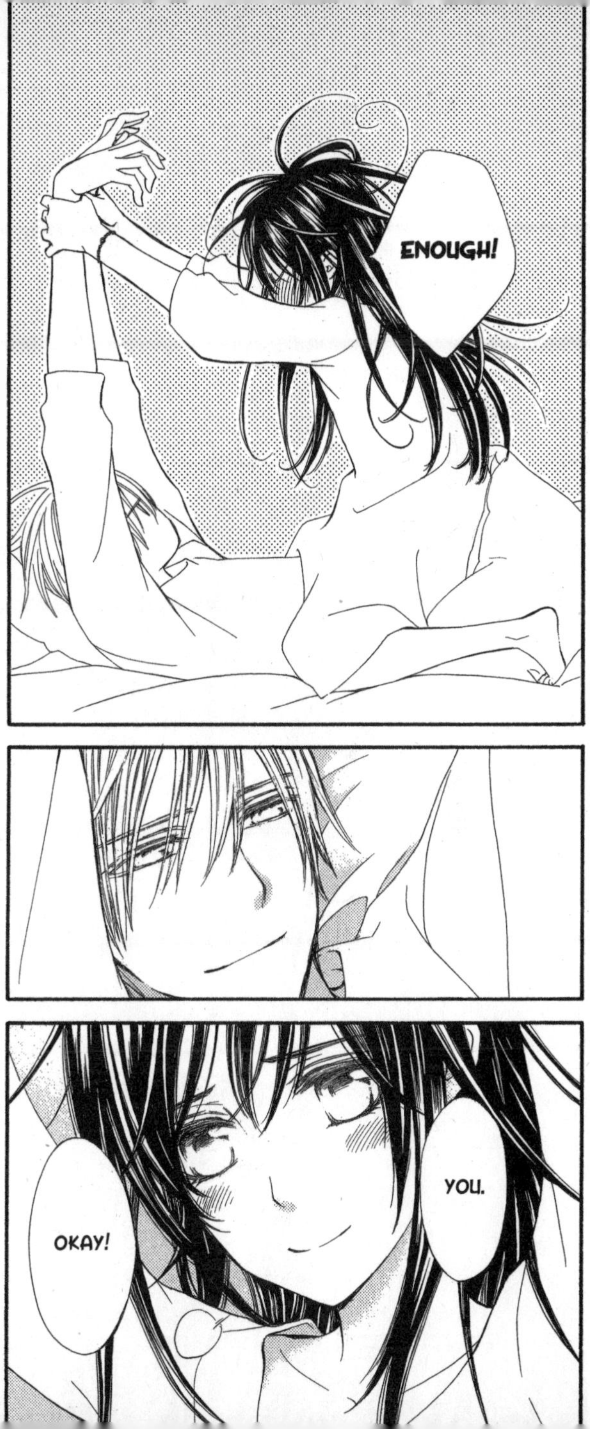
ENOUGH!
YOU.
OKAY!

— 6 —

In recent years, many of my regular drawing tools have gone out of production.

Honestly speaking, I've felt more cornered by this than when I was working on that final draft in the hospital room...

My greatest despair was Tachikawa changing the specifications of the mapping pen I had been using. It no longer had the same drawing and feel of the previous model. Because of that, I could no longer ink the pencil lines with the mapping pen. So for two years or so, I'd ink with a standard drawing pen, which seemed to have helped reset my drawing skills.

Then one day I realized I no longer had any trouble inking with the new mapping pen. As a matter of fact, the new pen felt better to draw with. So I'll continue using it...!

(continues ↓)

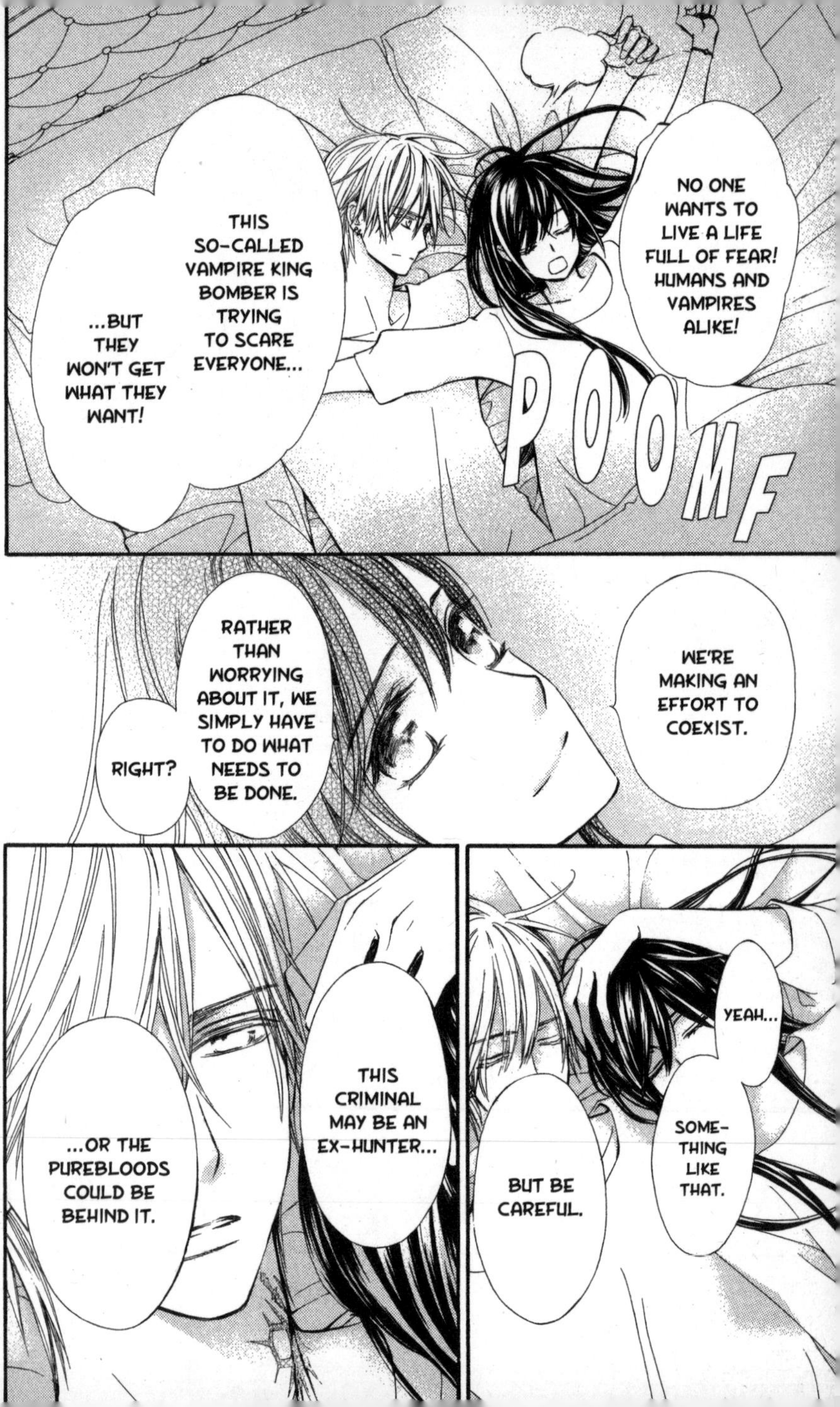
NO ONE WANTS TO LIVE A LIFE FULL OF FEAR! HUMANS AND VAMPIRES ALIKE!
POOMF
THIS SO-CALLED VAMPIRE KING BOMBER IS TRYING TO SCARE EVERYONE...
...BUT THEY WON'T GET WHAT THEY WANT!
WE'RE MAKING AN EFFORT TO COEXIST.
RATHER THAN WORRYING ABOUT IT, WE SIMPLY HAVE TO DO WHAT NEEDS TO BE DONE.
RIGHT?
YEAH...
SOME-THING LIKE THAT.
BUT BE CAREFUL.
THIS CRIMINAL MAY BE AN EX-HUNTER...
...OR THE PUREBLOODS COULD BE BEHIND IT.

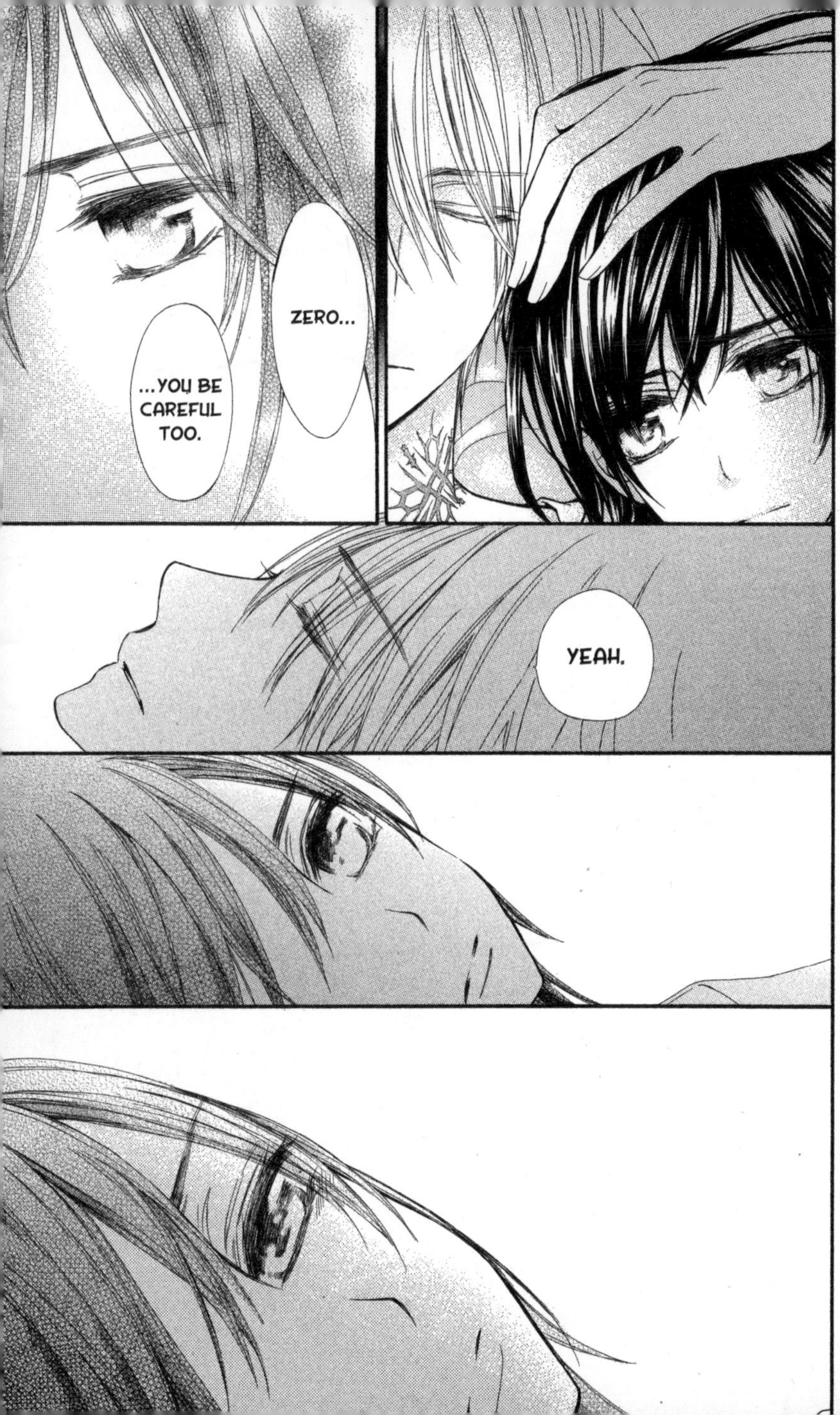
ZERO...
...YOU BE CAREFUL TOO.
YEAH.

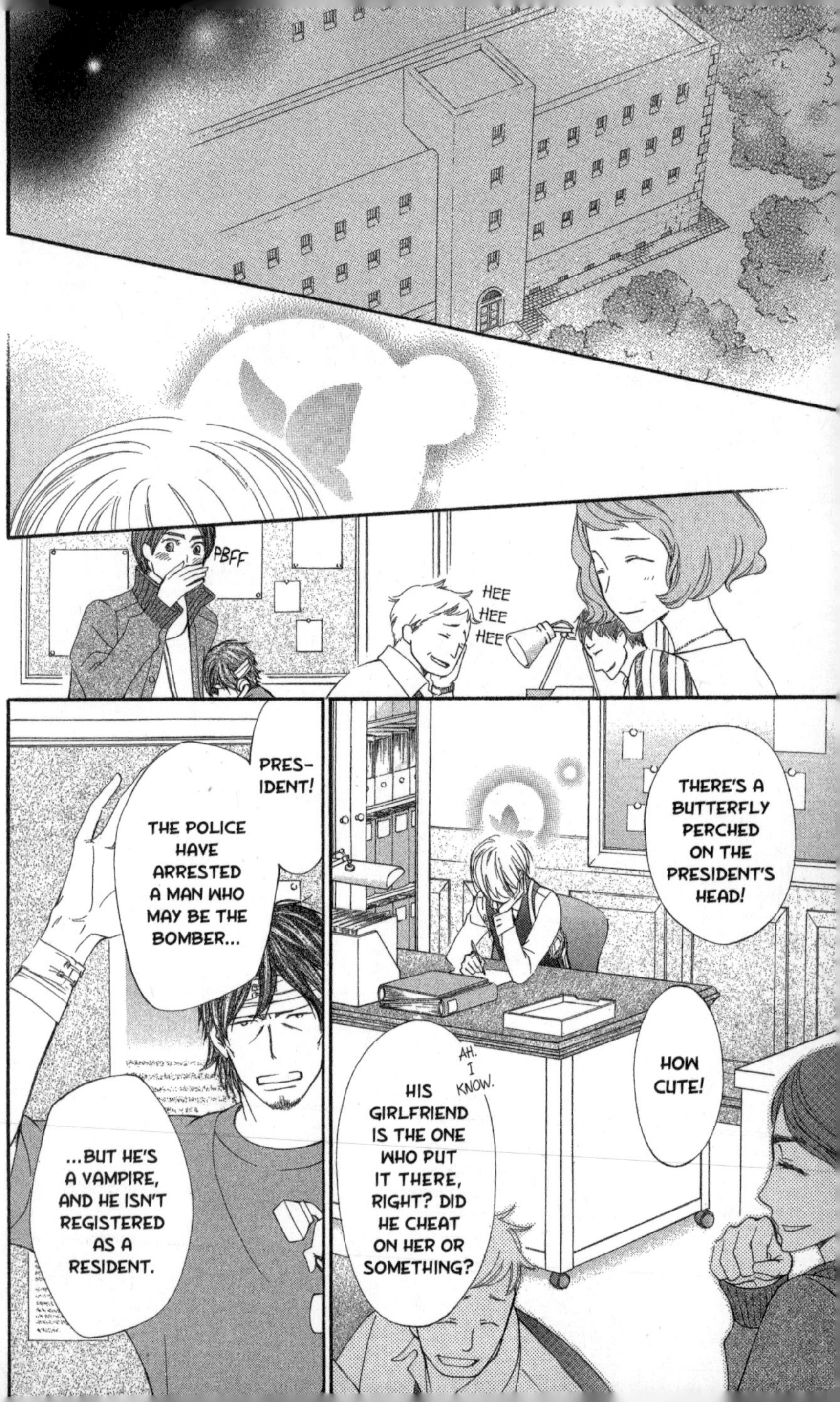
HEE HEE HEE
PBFF
THERE'S A BUTTERFLY PERCHED ON THE PRESIDENT'S HEAD!
HOW CUTE!
AH. I KNOW.
HIS GIRLFRIEND IS THE ONE WHO PUT IT THERE, RIGHT? DID HE CHEAT ON HER OR SOMETHING?
PRES-IDENT!
THE POLICE HAVE ARRESTED A MAN WHO MAY BE THE BOMBER...
...BUT HE'S A VAMPIRE, AND HE ISN'T REGISTERED AS A RESIDENT.

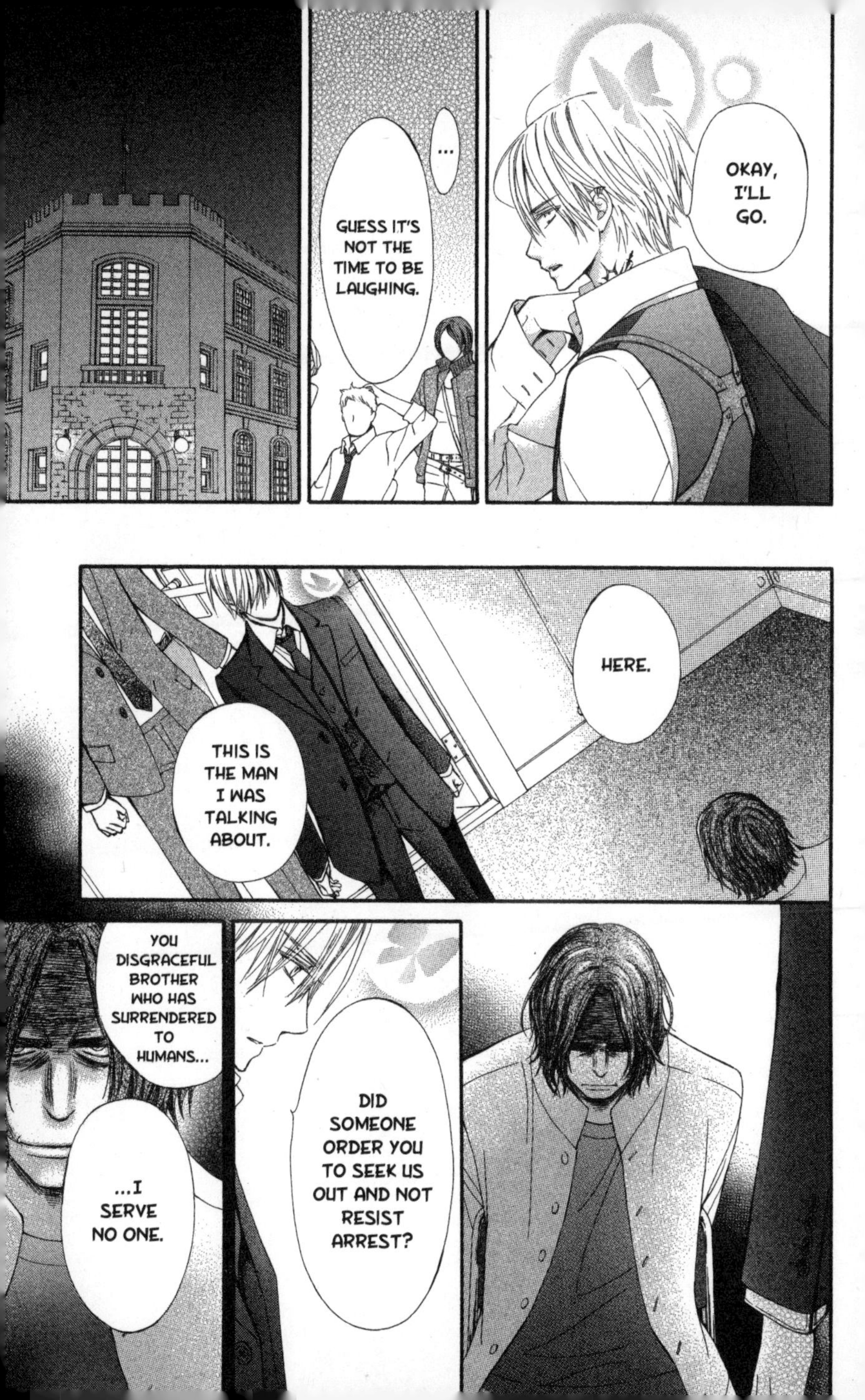
OKAY, I'LL GO.
...
GUESS IT'S NOT THE TIME TO BE LAUGHING.
HERE.
THIS IS THE MAN I WAS TALKING ABOUT.
DID SOMEONE ORDER YOU TO SEEK US OUT AND NOT RESIST ARREST?
YOU DISGRACEFUL BROTHER WHO HAS SURRENDERED TO HUMANS...
...I SERVE NO ONE.

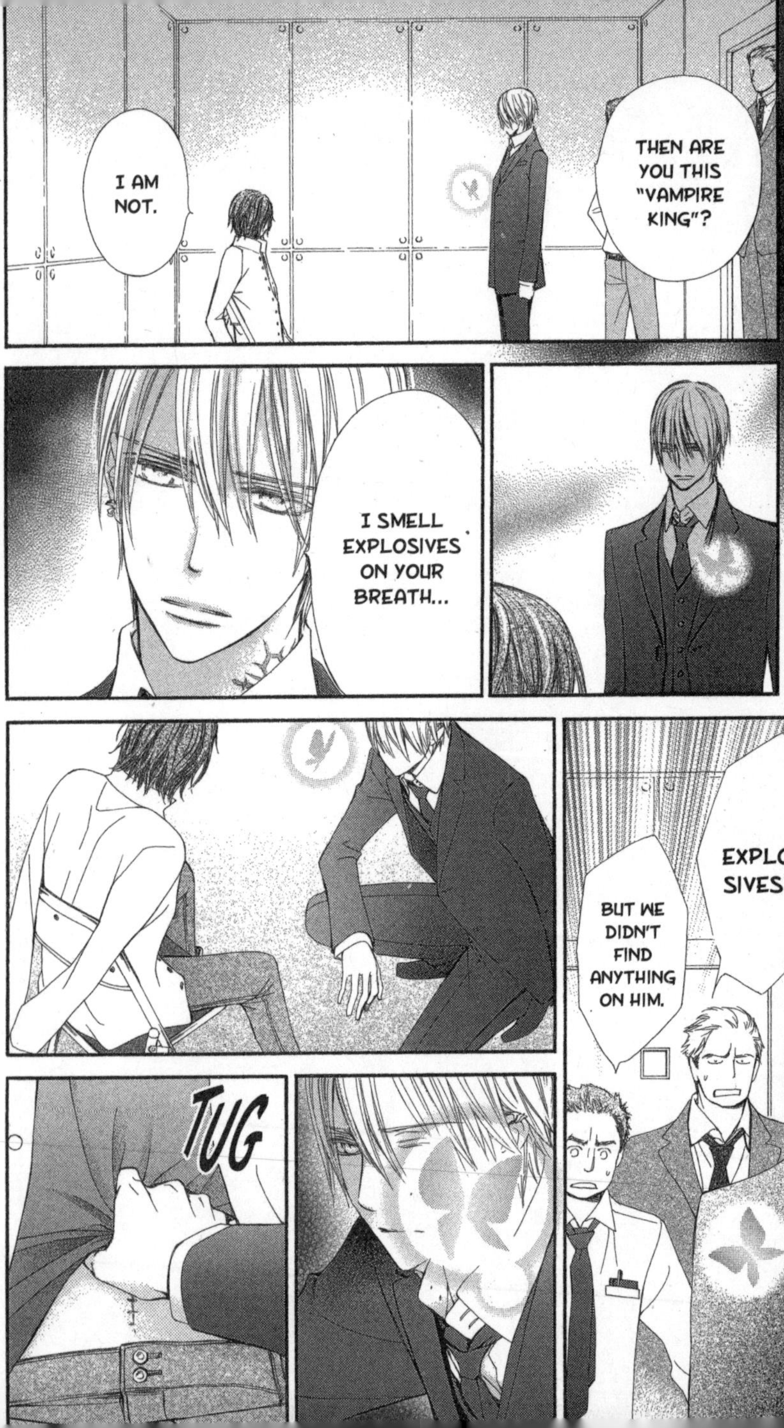
THEN ARE YOU THIS "VAMPIRE KING"?
I AM NOT.
I SMELL EXPLOSIVES ON YOUR BREATH...
EXPLO-SIVES?!
BUT WE DIDN'T FIND ANYTHING ON HIM.
TUG

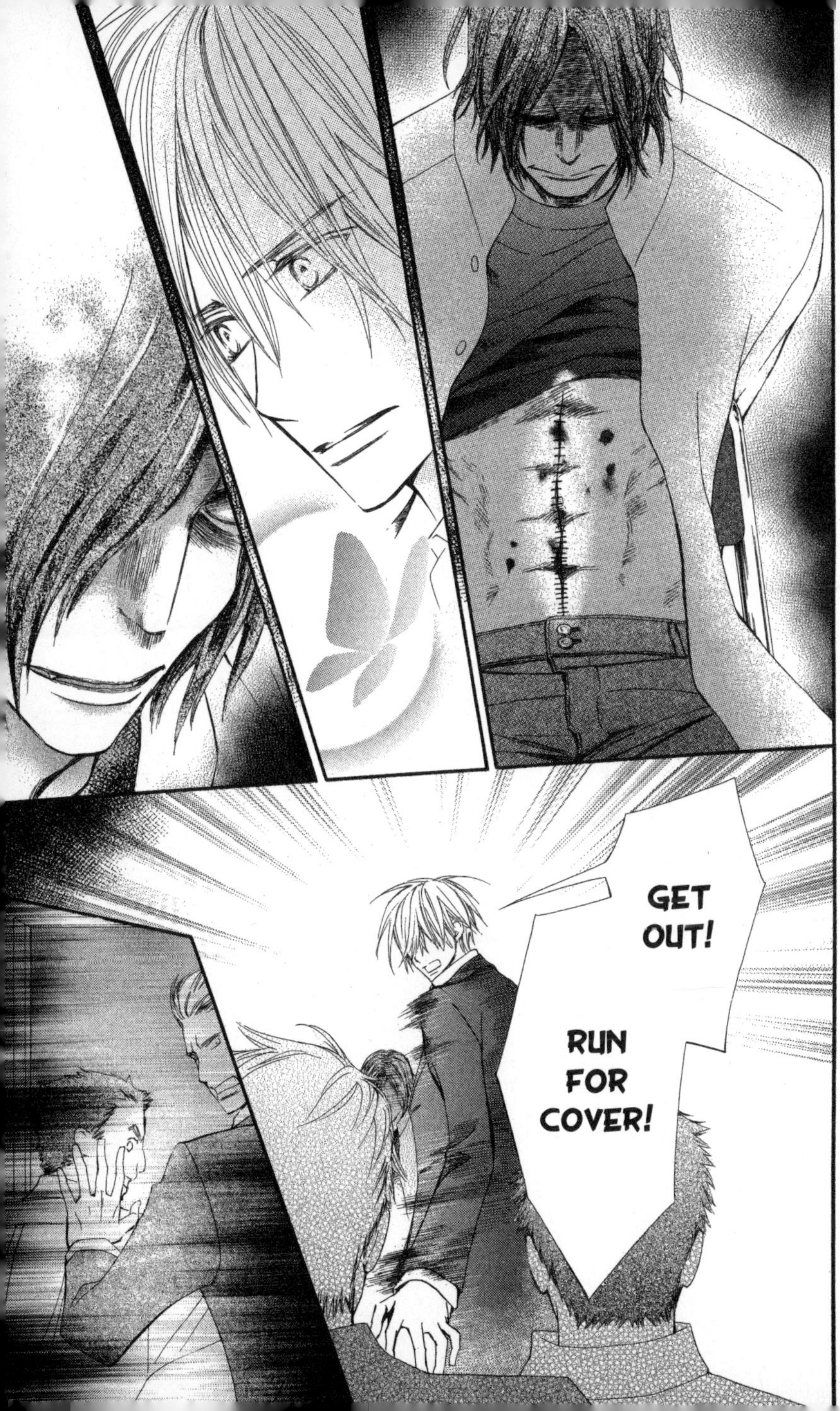
GET OUT!
RUN FOR COVER!

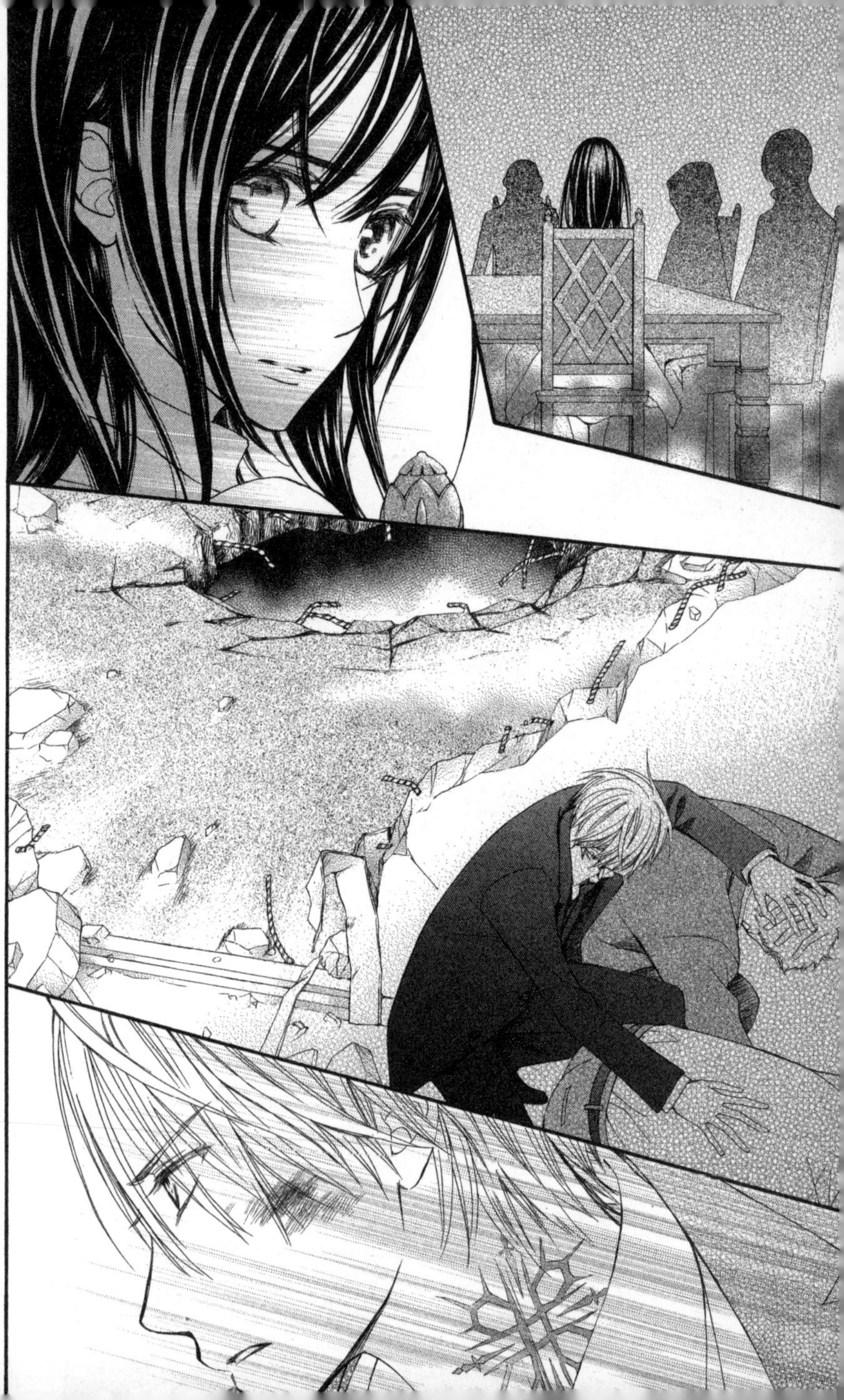

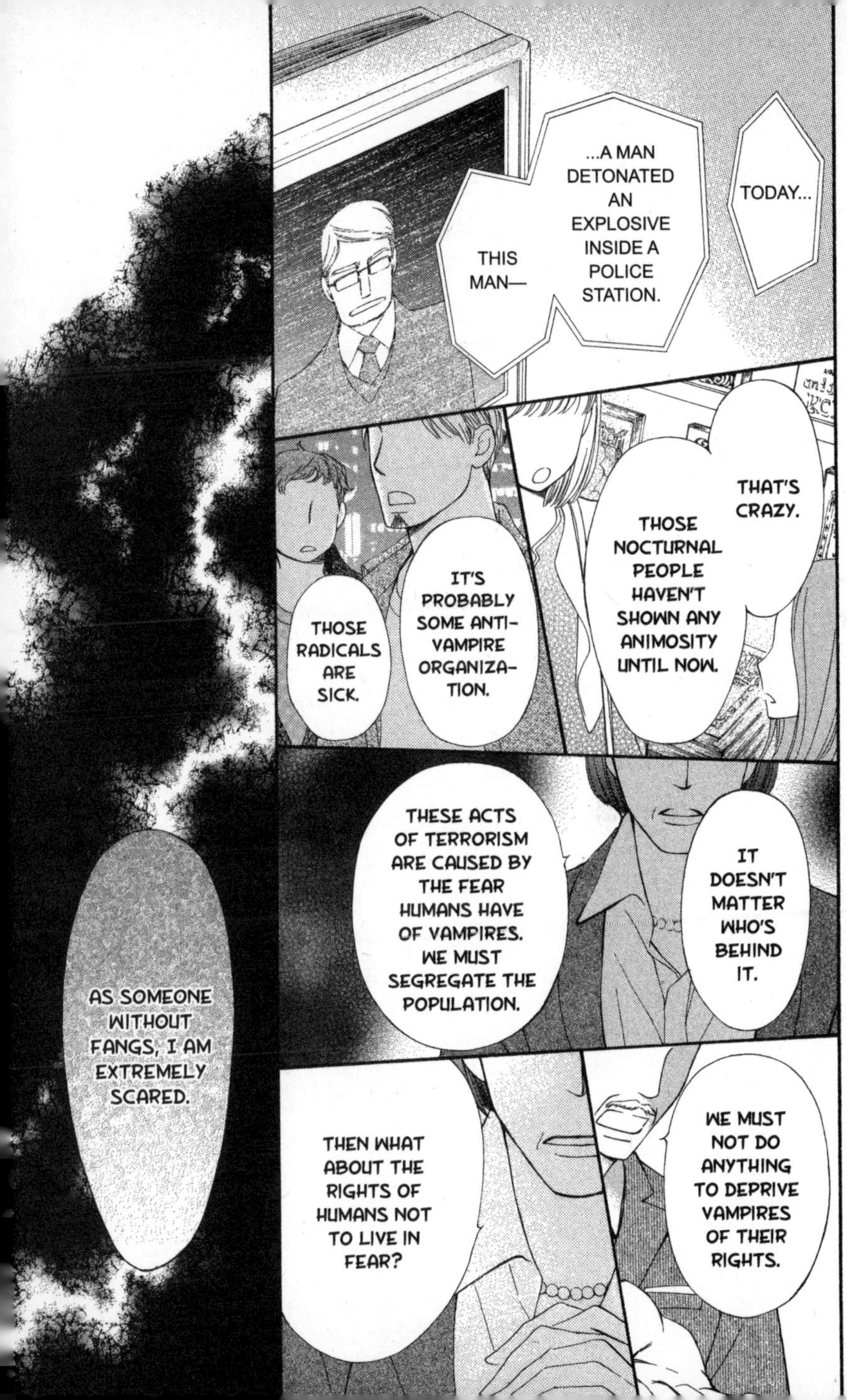
TODAY...
...A MAN DETONATED AN EXPLOSIVE INSIDE A POLICE STATION.
THIS MAN—
THAT'S CRAZY.
THOSE NOCTURNAL PEOPLE HAVEN'T SHOWN ANY ANIMOSITY UNTIL NOW.
IT'S PROBABLY SOME ANTI-VAMPIRE ORGANIZATION.
THOSE RADICALS ARE SICK.
IT DOESN'T MATTER WHO'S BEHIND IT.
THESE ACTS OF TERRORISM ARE CAUSED BY THE FEAR HUMANS HAVE OF VAMPIRES. WE MUST SEGREGATE THE POPULATION.
WE MUST NOT DO ANYTHING TO DEPRIVE VAMPIRES OF THEIR RIGHTS.
THEN WHAT ABOUT THE RIGHTS OF HUMANS NOT TO LIVE IN FEAR?
AS SOMEONE WITHOUT FANGS, I AM EXTREMELY SCARED.

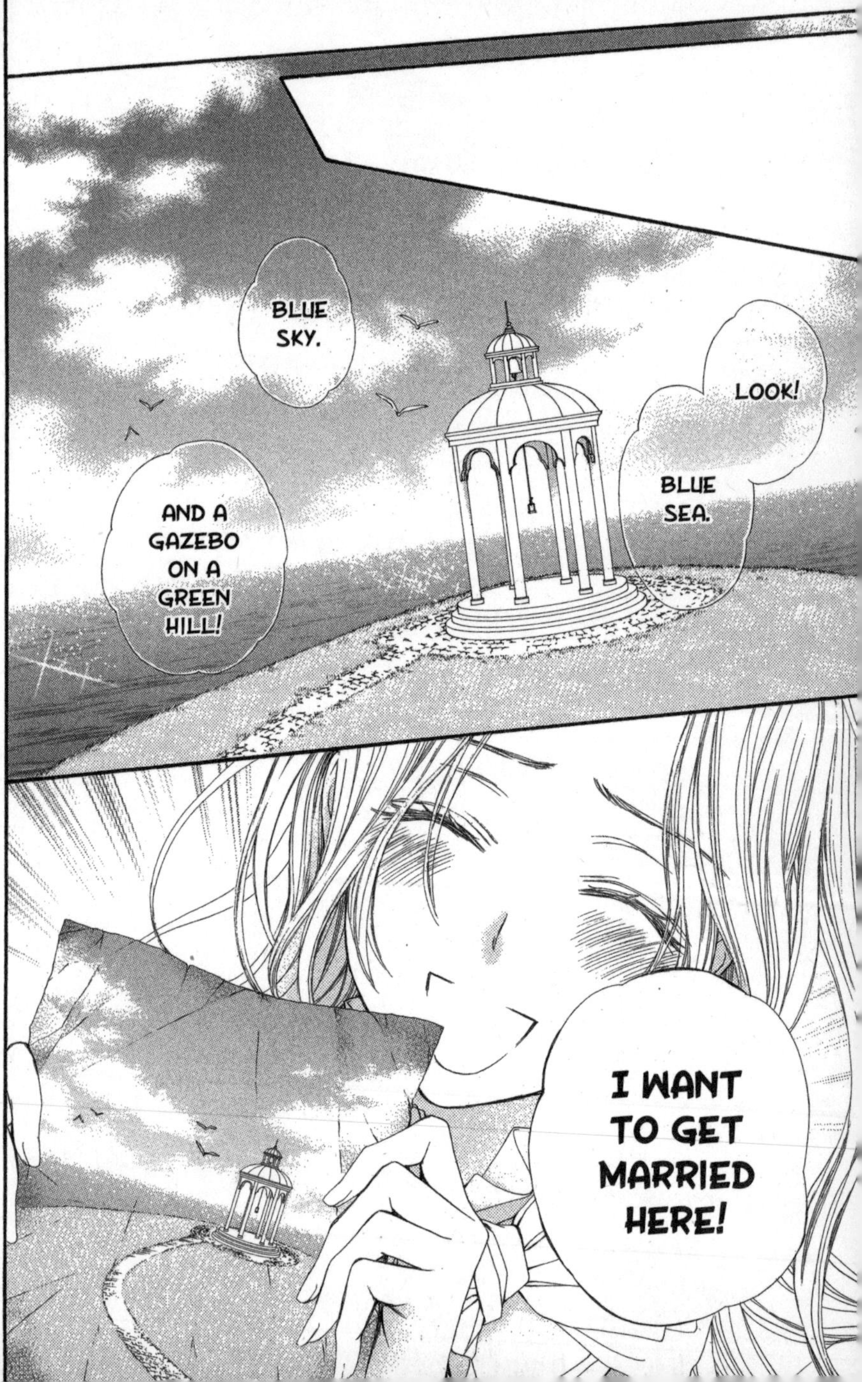
LOOK!
BLUE SKY.
BLUE SEA.
AND A GAZEBO ON A GREEN HILL!
I WANT TO GET MARRIED HERE!

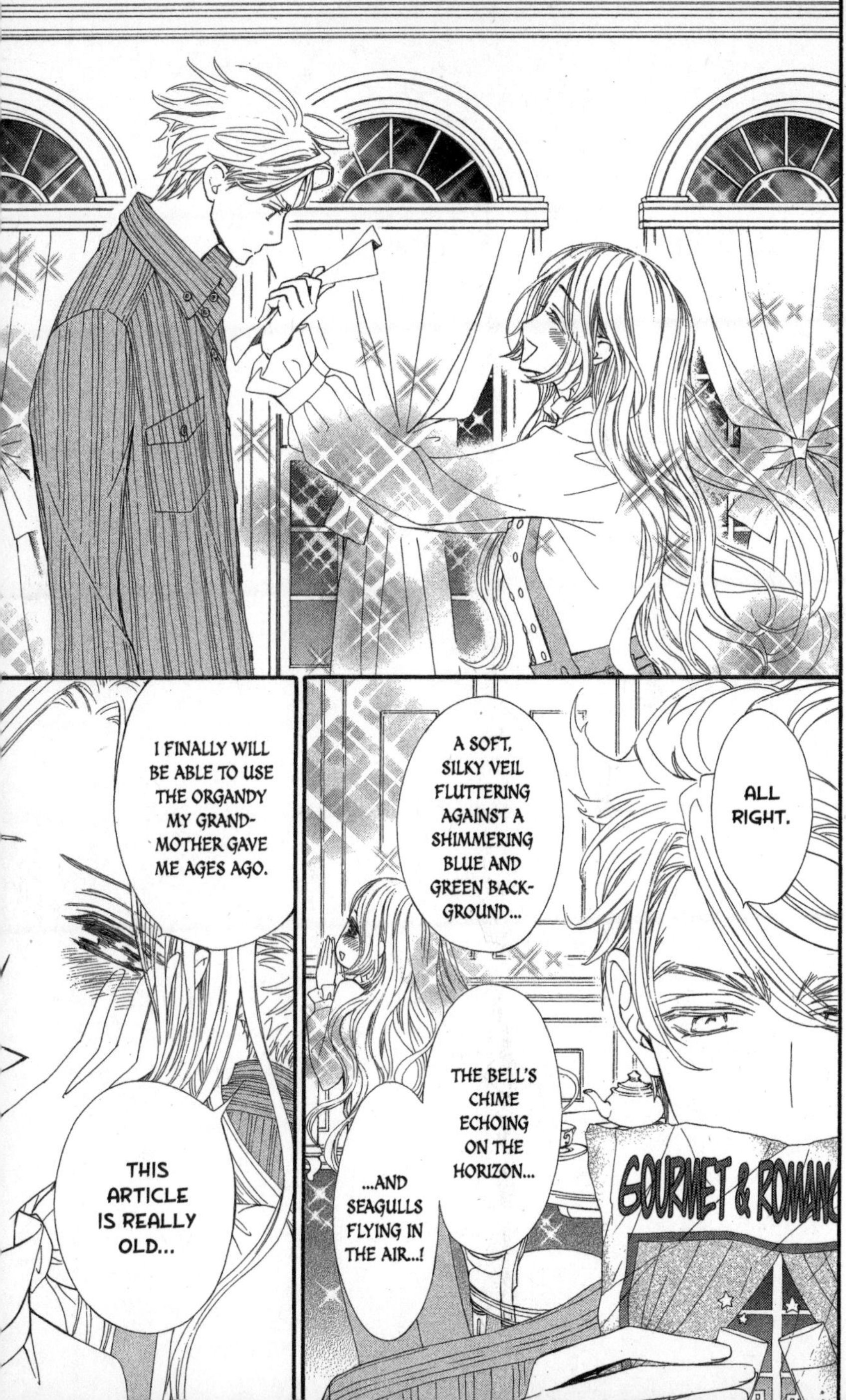
ALL RIGHT.
A SOFT, SILKY VEIL FLUTTERING AGAINST A SHIMMERING BLUE AND GREEN BACK-GROUND...
THE BELL'S CHIME ECHOING ON THE HORIZON...
...AND SEAGULLS FLYING IN THE AIR...!
GOURMET & ROMANC
I FINALLY WILL BE ABLE TO USE THE ORGANDY MY GRAND-MOTHER GAVE ME AGES AGO.
THIS ARTICLE IS REALLY OLD...

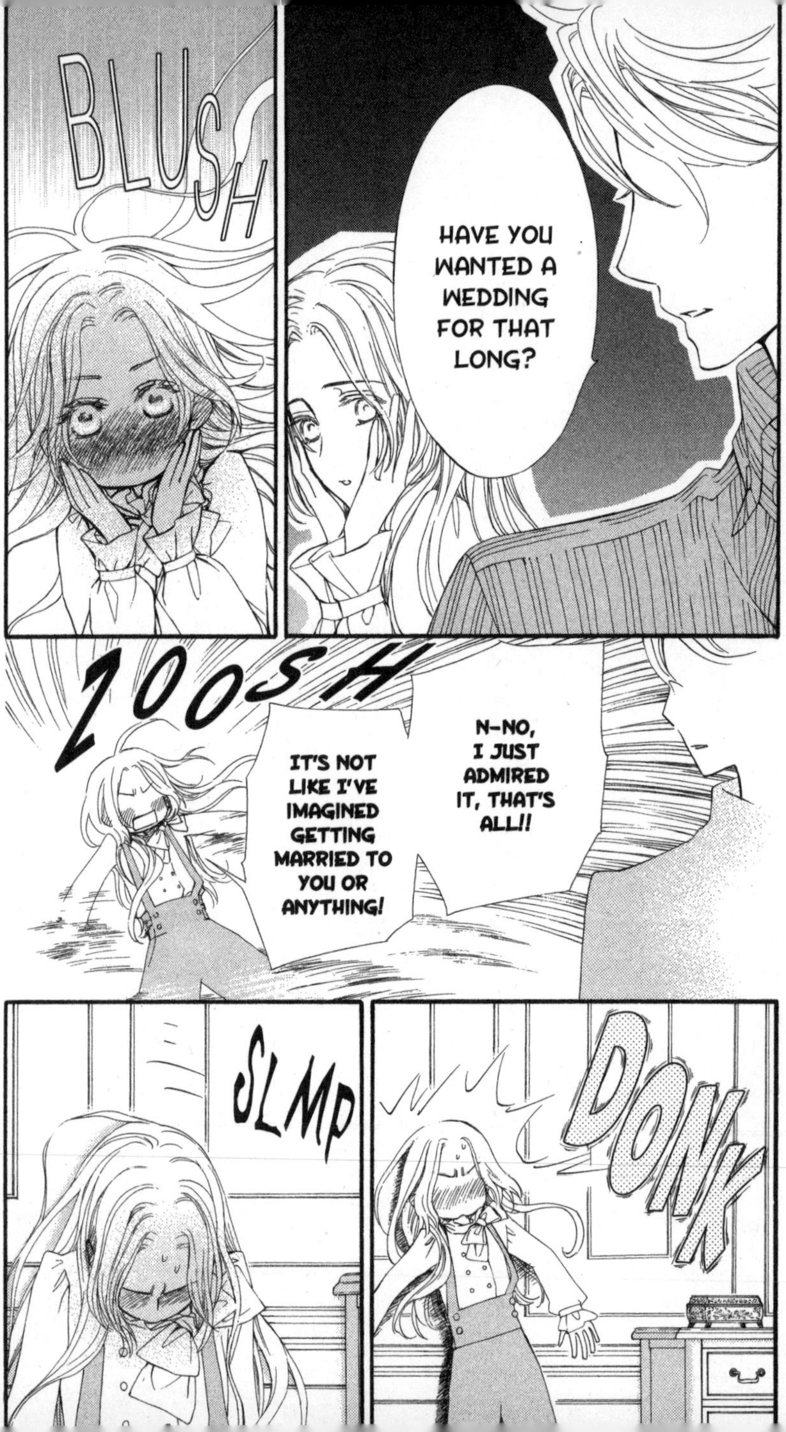
HAVE YOU WANTED A WEDDING FOR THAT LONG?
BLUSH
N-NO, I JUST ADMIRED IT, THAT'S ALL!!
IT'S NOT LIKE I'VE IMAGINED GETTING MARRIED TO YOU OR ANYTHING!
ZOOSH
DONK
SLMP

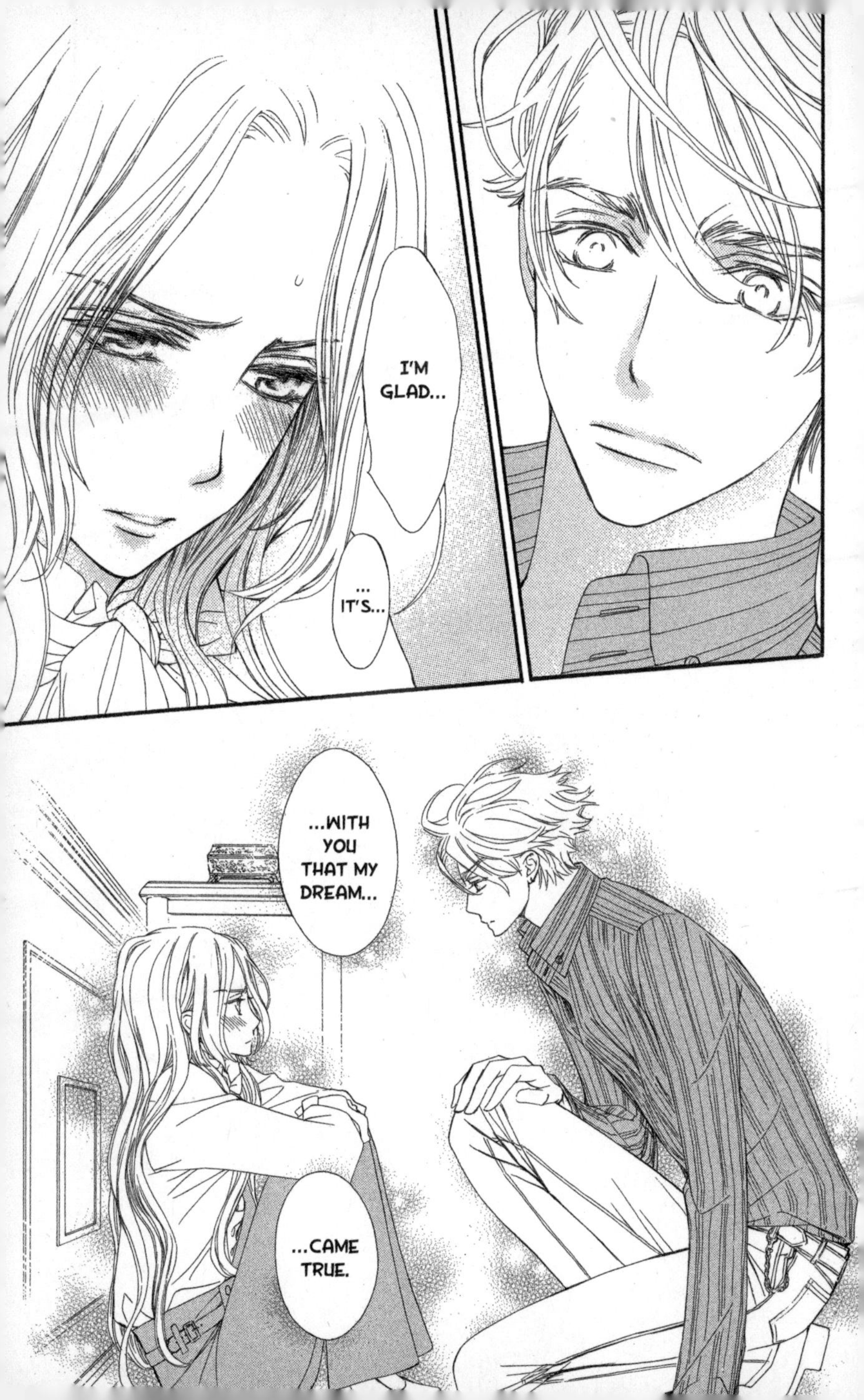
I'M GLAD...
... IT'S...
...WITH YOU THAT MY DREAM...
...CAME TRUE.

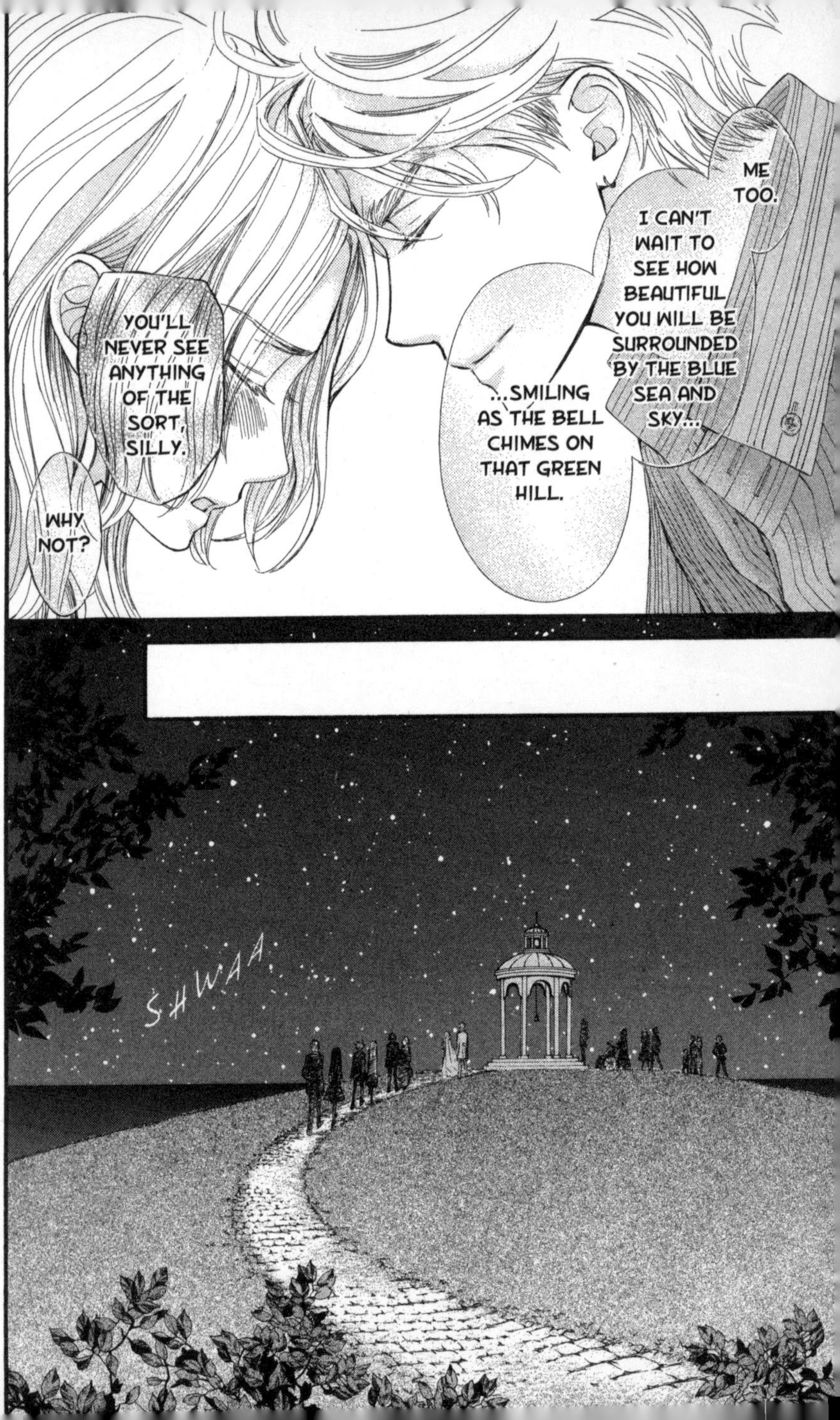
ME TOO.
I CAN'T WAIT TO SEE HOW BEAUTIFUL YOU WILL BE SURROUNDED BY THE BLUE SEA AND SKY...
...SMILING AS THE BELL CHIMES ON THAT GREEN HILL.
YOU'LL NEVER SEE ANYTHING OF THE SORT, SILLY.
WHY NOT?
SHWAA

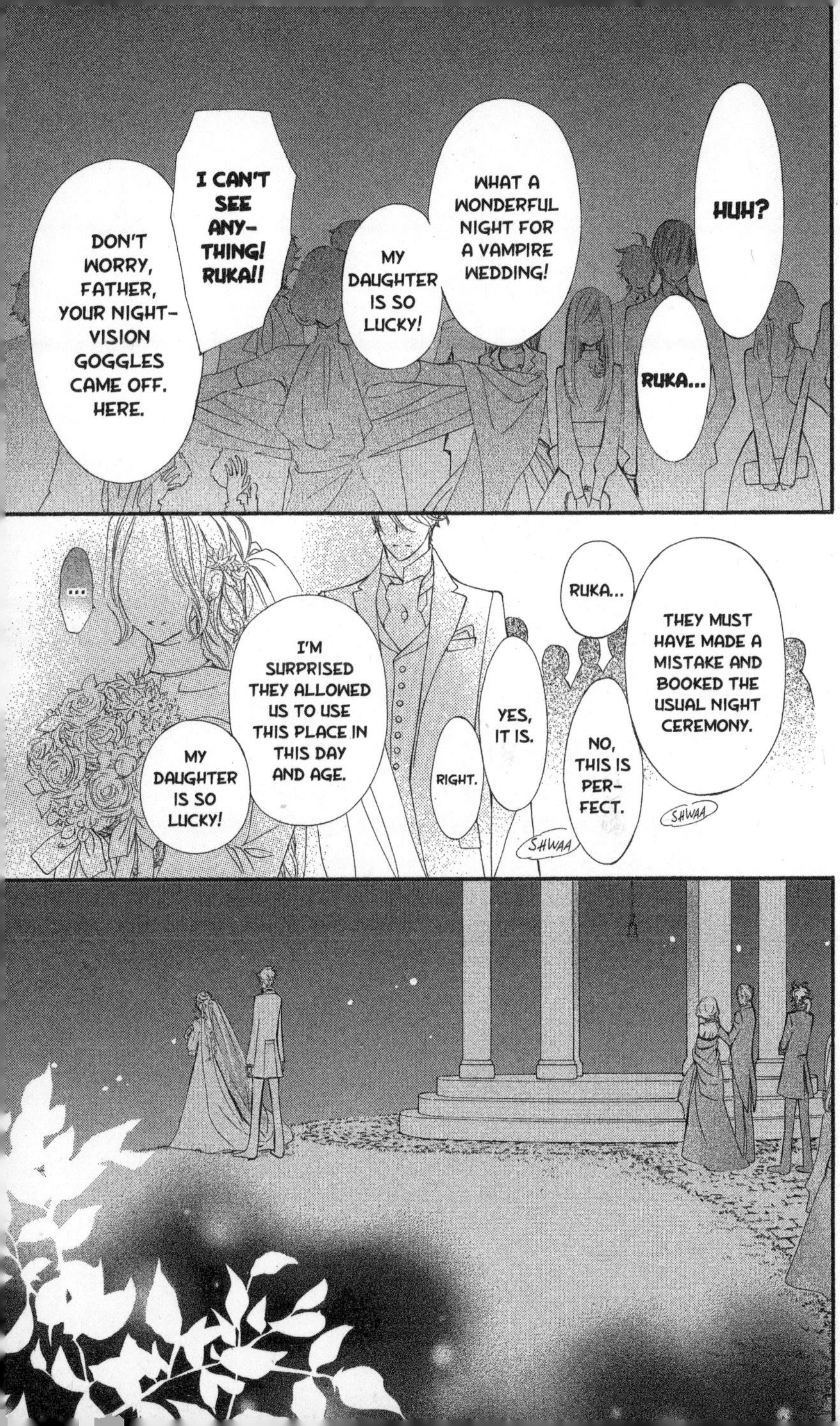
HUH?
RUKA...
WHAT A WONDERFUL NIGHT FOR A VAMPIRE WEDDING!
MY DAUGHTER IS SO LUCKY!
I CAN'T SEE ANYTHING! RUKA!!
DON'T WORRY, FATHER, YOUR NIGHT-VISION GOGGLES CAME OFF. HERE.
RUKA...
THEY MUST HAVE MADE A MISTAKE AND BOOKED THE USUAL NIGHT CEREMONY.
SHWAA
NO, THIS IS PERFECT.
YES, IT IS.
RIGHT.
SHWAA
I'M SURPRISED THEY ALLOWED US TO USE THIS PLACE IN THIS DAY AND AGE.
MY DAUGHTER IS SO LUCKY!
...

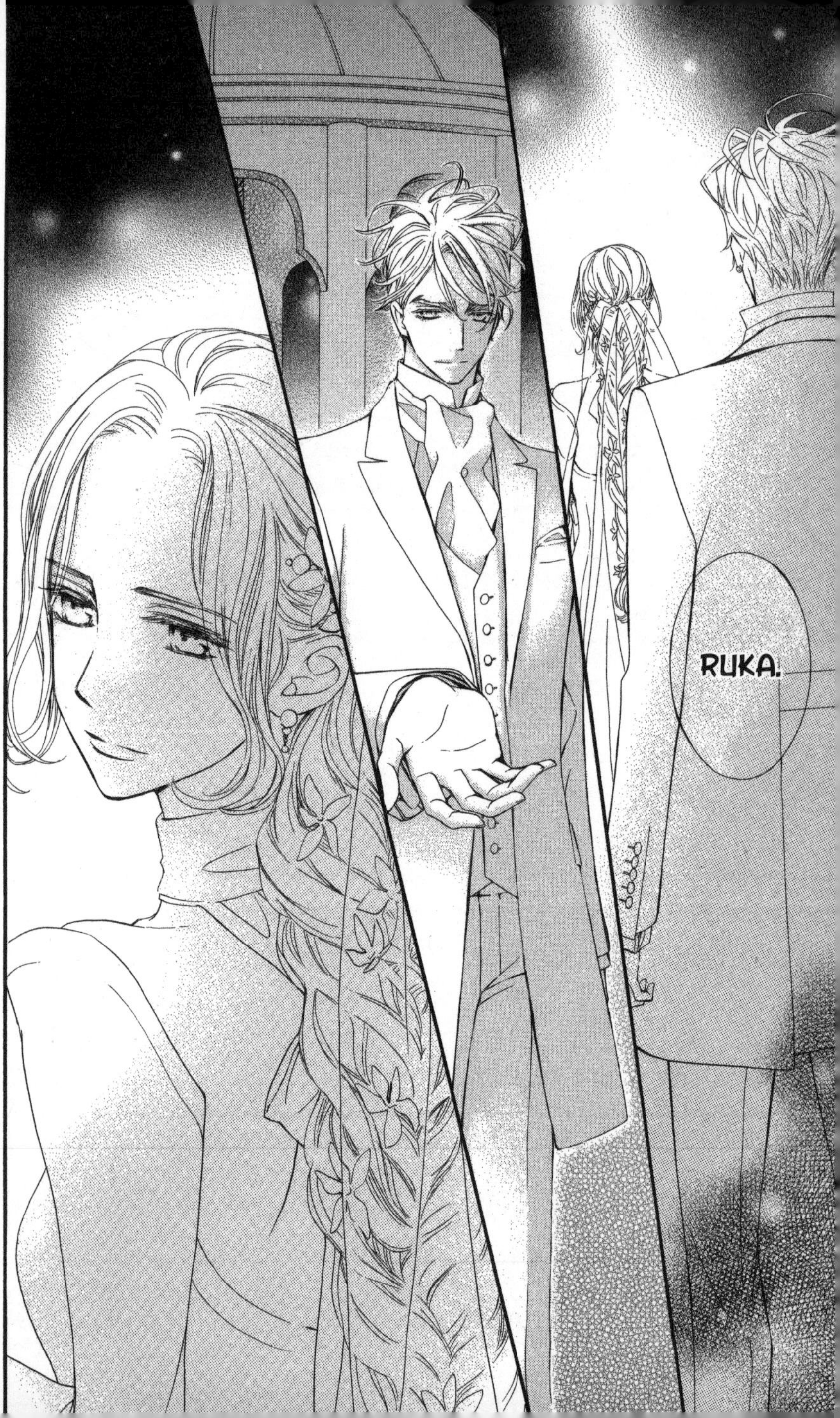
RUKA.

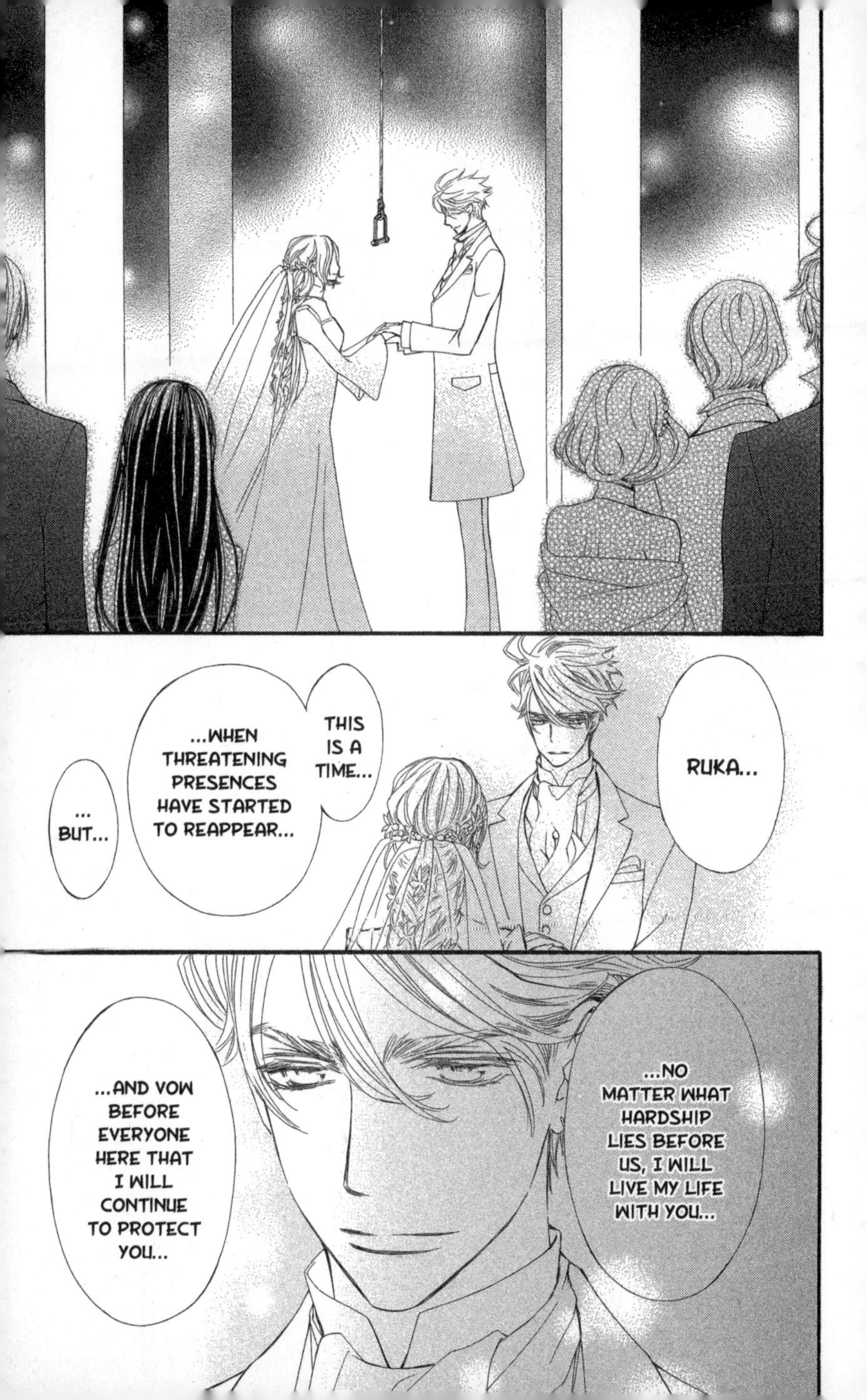
RUKA...
THIS IS A TIME...
...WHEN THREATENING PRESENCES HAVE STARTED TO REAPPEAR...
... BUT...
...NO MATTER WHAT HARDSHIP LIES BEFORE US, I WILL LIVE MY LIFE WITH YOU...
...AND VOW BEFORE EVERYONE HERE THAT I WILL CONTINUE TO PROTECT YOU...

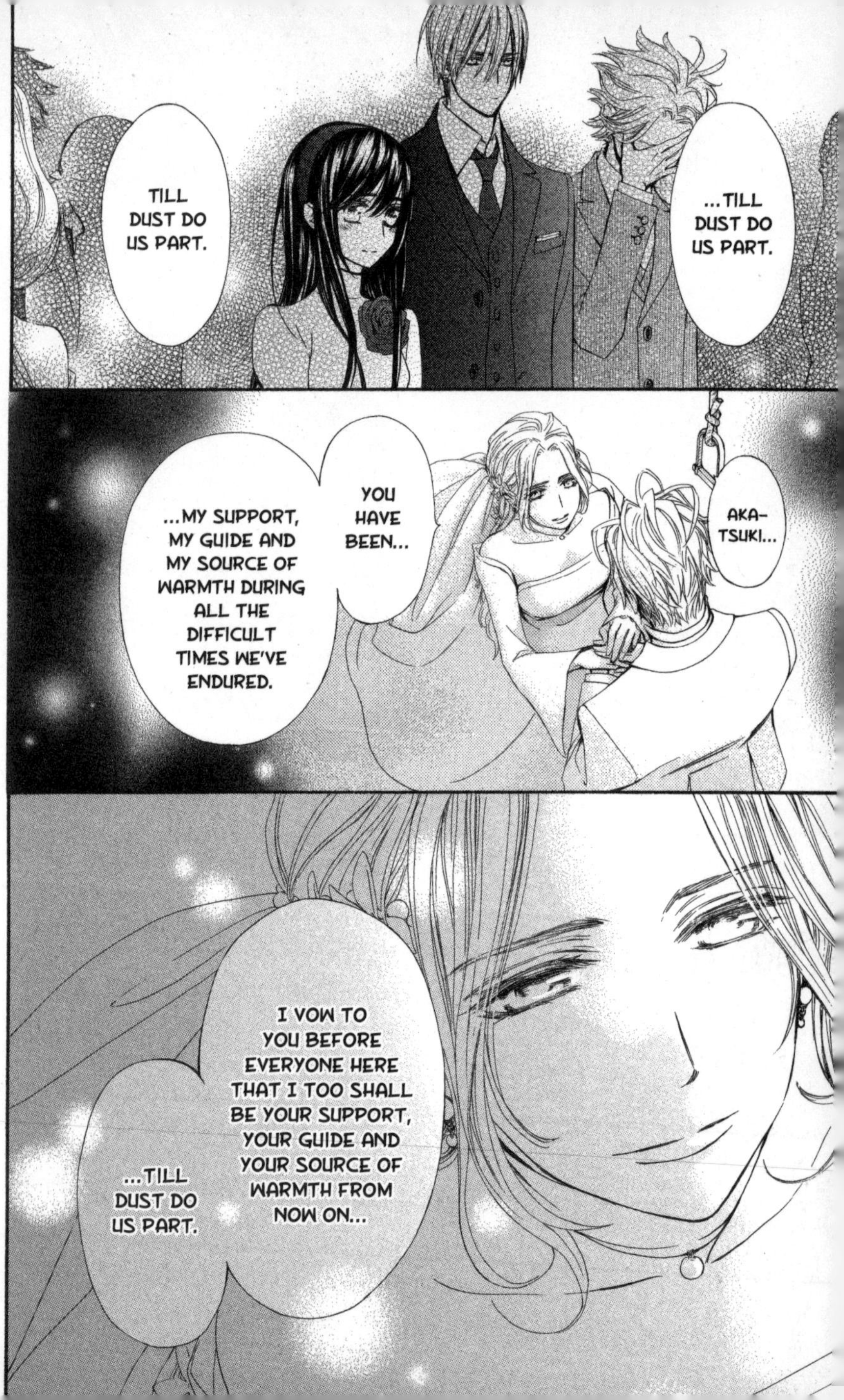
...TILL DUST DO US PART.
TILL DUST DO US PART.
AKA-TSUKI...
YOU HAVE BEEN...
...MY SUPPORT, MY GUIDE AND MY SOURCE OF WARMTH DURING ALL THE DIFFICULT TIMES WE'VE ENDURED.
I VOW TO YOU BEFORE EVERYONE HERE THAT I TOO SHALL BE YOUR SUPPORT, YOUR GUIDE AND YOUR SOURCE OF WARMTH FROM NOW ON...
...TILL DUST DO US PART.

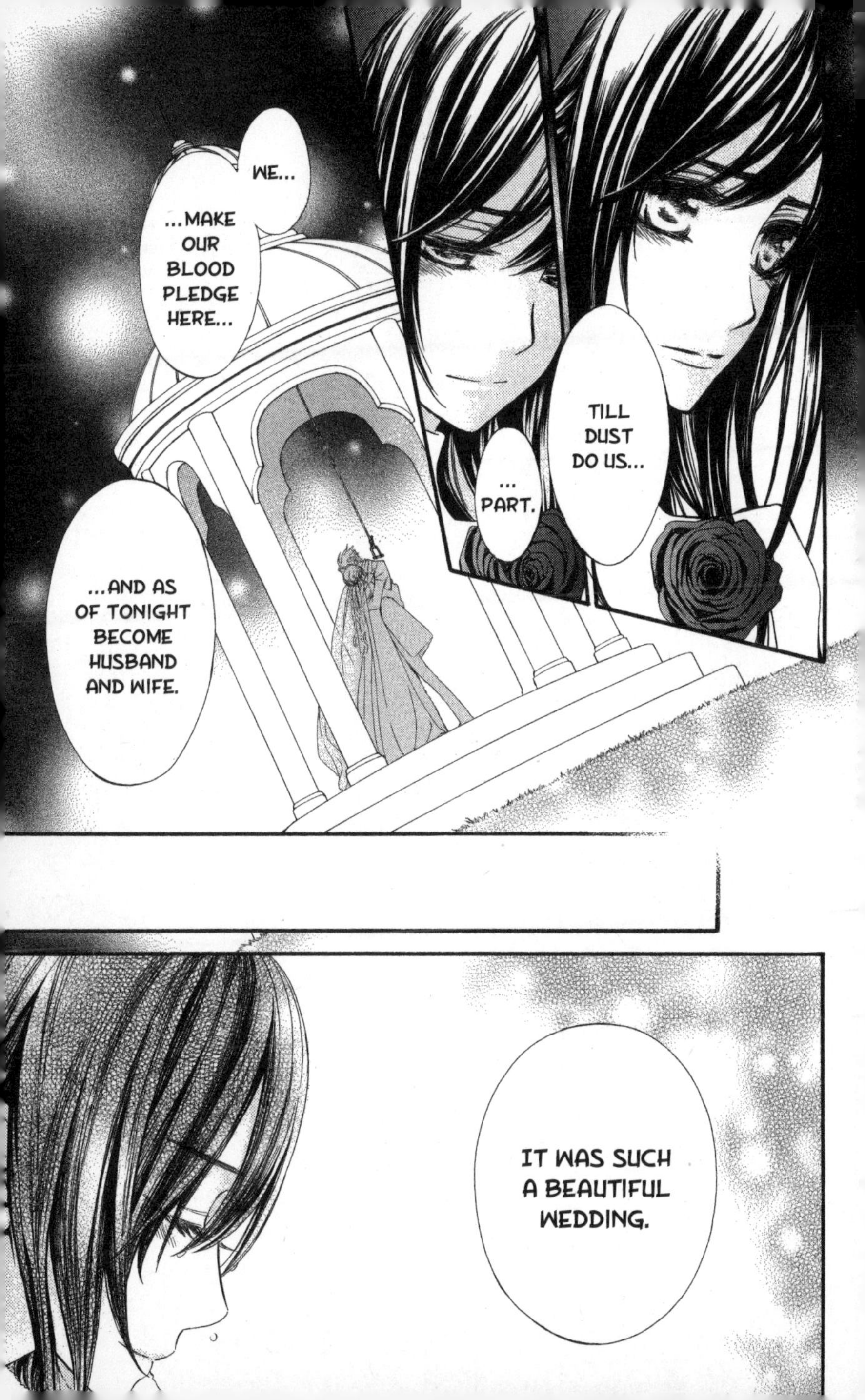
WE...
...MAKE OUR BLOOD PLEDGE HERE...
...AND AS OF TONIGHT BECOME HUSBAND AND WIFE.
TILL DUST DO US...
...PART.
IT WAS SUCH A BEAUTIFUL WEDDING.

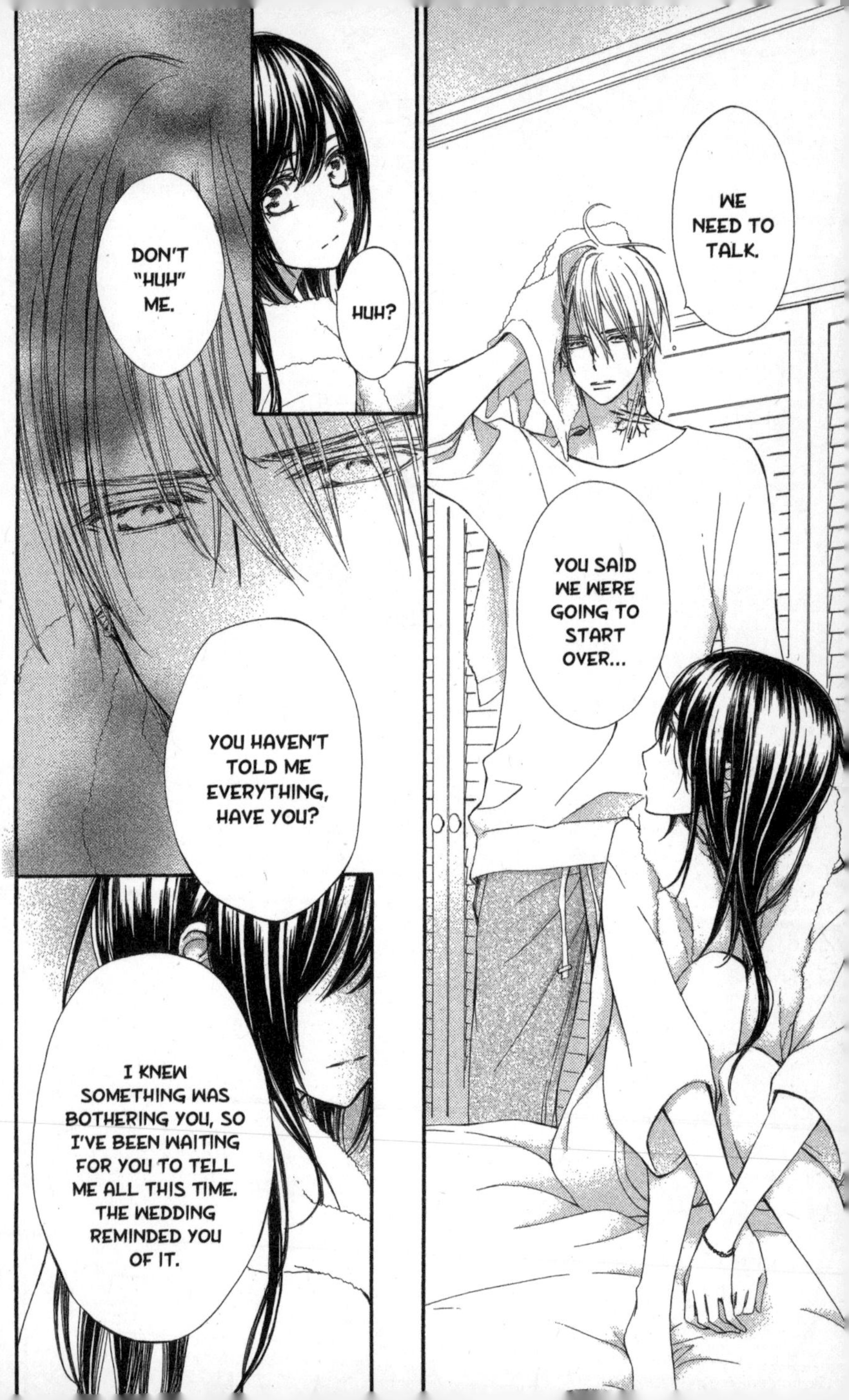
WE NEED TO TALK.
YOU SAID WE WERE GOING TO START OVER...
HUH?
DON'T "HUH" ME.
YOU HAVEN'T TOLD ME EVERYTHING, HAVE YOU?
I KNEW SOMETHING WAS BOTHERING YOU, SO I'VE BEEN WAITING FOR YOU TO TELL ME ALL THIS TIME. THE WEDDING REMINDED YOU OF IT.

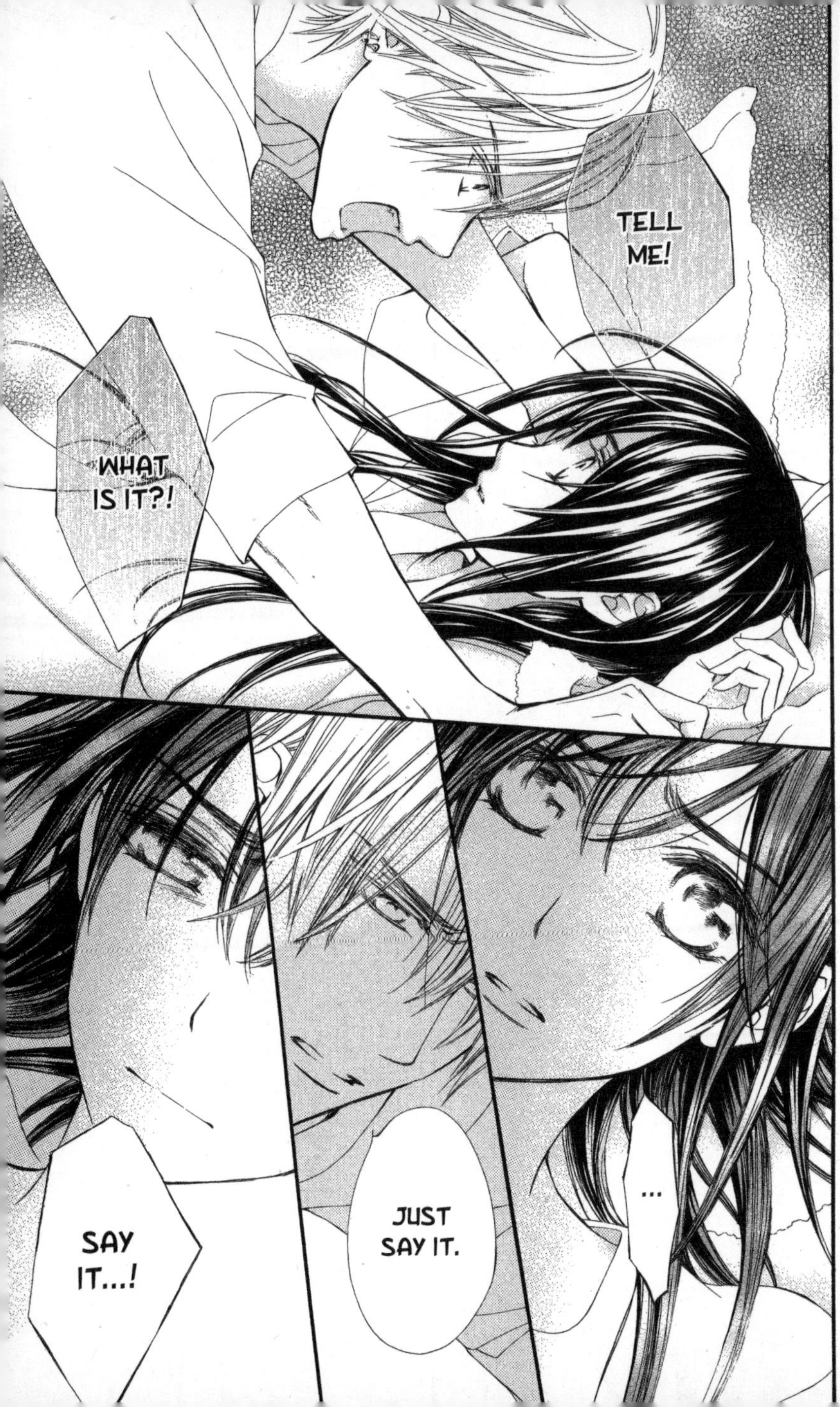
TELL ME!
WHAT IS IT?!
...
JUST SAY IT.
SAY IT...!

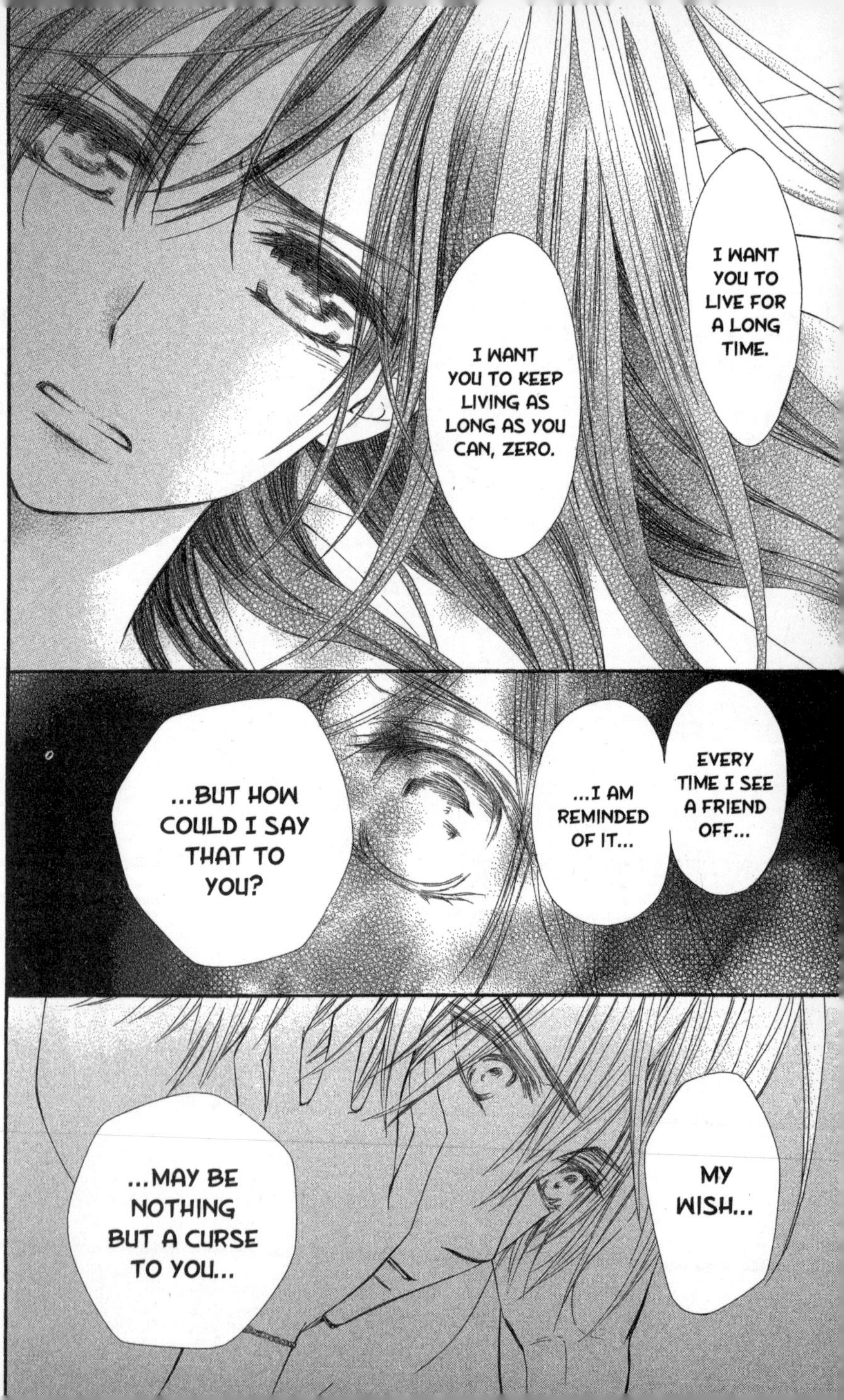
I WANT YOU TO LIVE FOR A LONG TIME.
I WANT YOU TO KEEP LIVING AS LONG AS YOU CAN, ZERO.
EVERY TIME I SEE A FRIEND OFF...
...I AM REMINDED OF IT...
...BUT HOW COULD I SAY THAT TO YOU?
MY WISH...
...MAY BE NOTHING BUT A CURSE TO YOU...

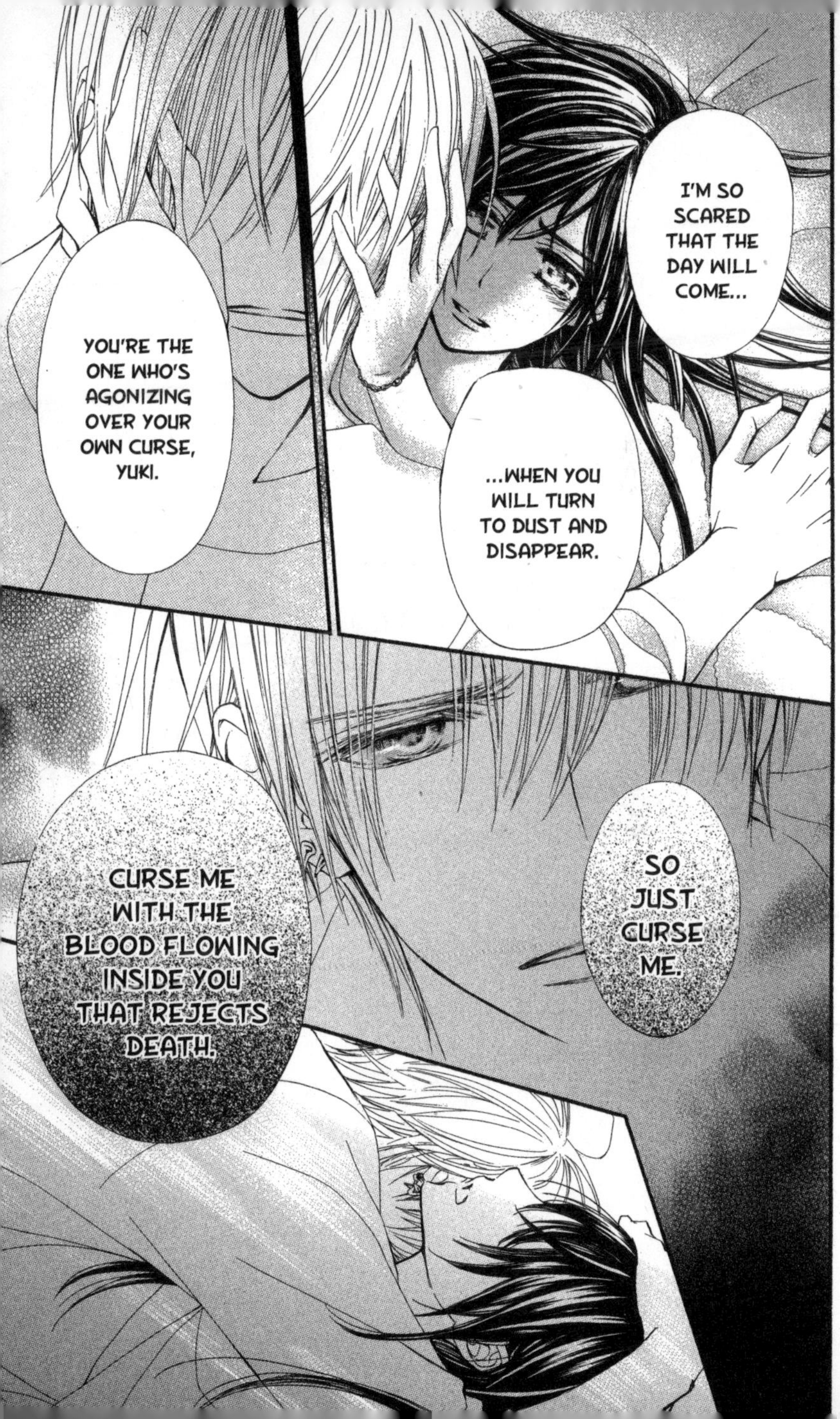
I'M SO SCARED THAT THE DAY WILL COME...
...WHEN YOU WILL TURN TO DUST AND DISAPPEAR.
YOU'RE THE ONE WHO'S AGONIZING OVER YOUR OWN CURSE, YUKI.
SO JUST CURSE ME.
CURSE ME WITH THE BLOOD FLOWING INSIDE YOU THAT REJECTS DEATH.

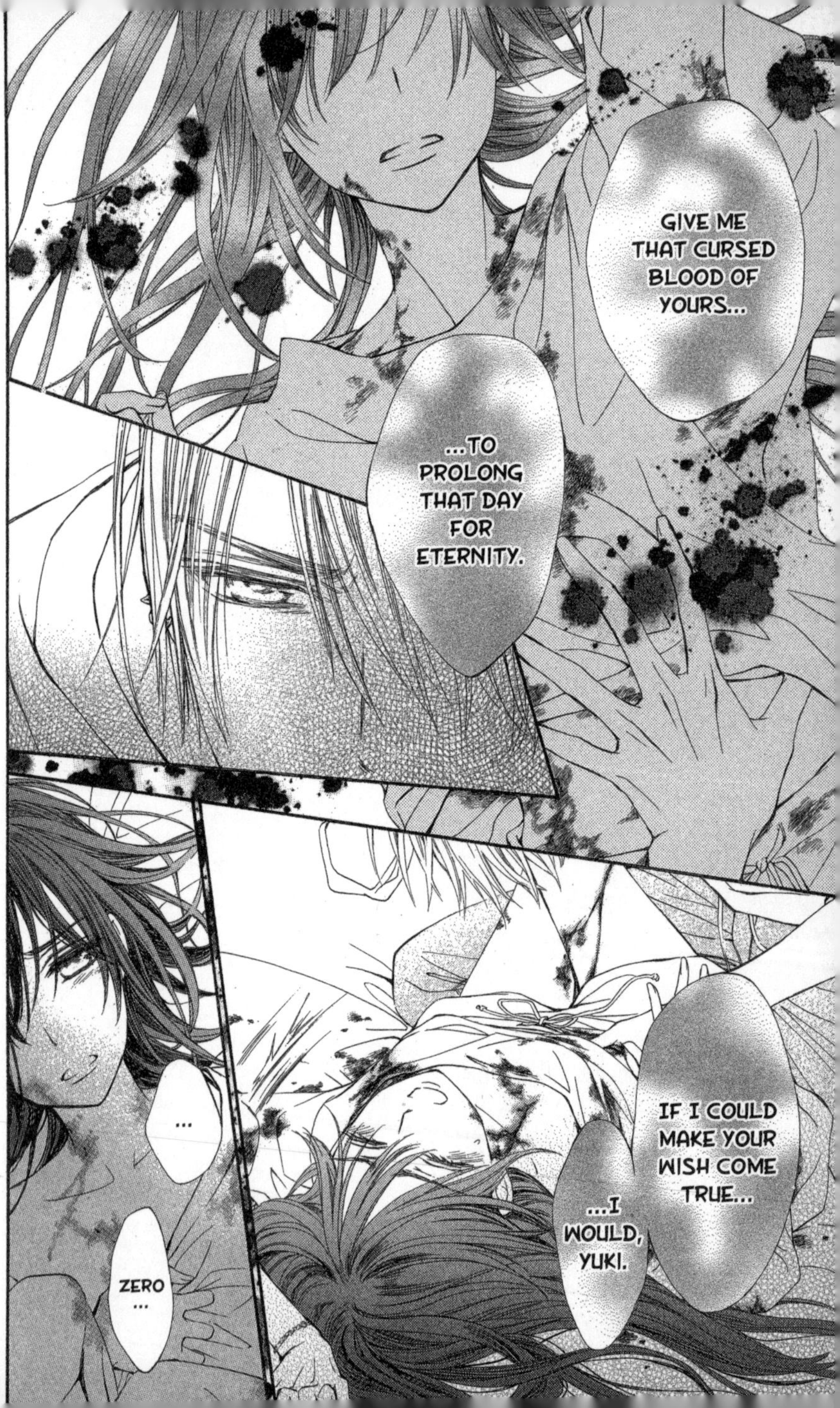
GIVE ME THAT CURSED BLOOD OF YOURS...
...TO PROLONG THAT DAY FOR ETERNITY.
IF I COULD MAKE YOUR WISH COME TRUE...
...I WOULD, YUKI.
...
ZERO ...

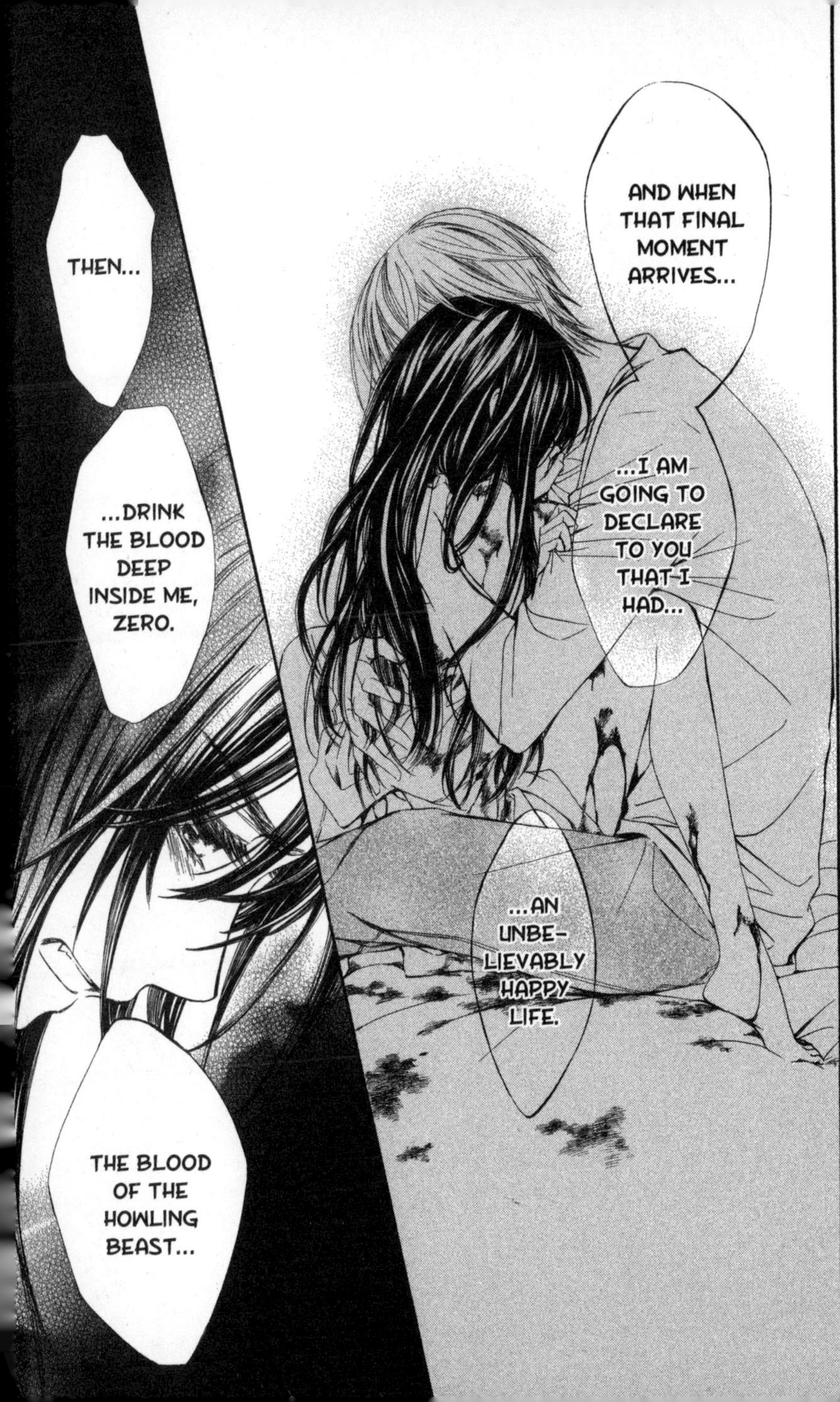
AND WHEN THAT FINAL MOMENT ARRIVES...
...I AM GOING TO DECLARE TO YOU THAT I HAD...
...AN UNBE- LIEVABLY HAPPY LIFE.
THEN...
...DRINK THE BLOOD DEEP INSIDE ME, ZERO.
THE BLOOD OF THE HOWLING BEAST...

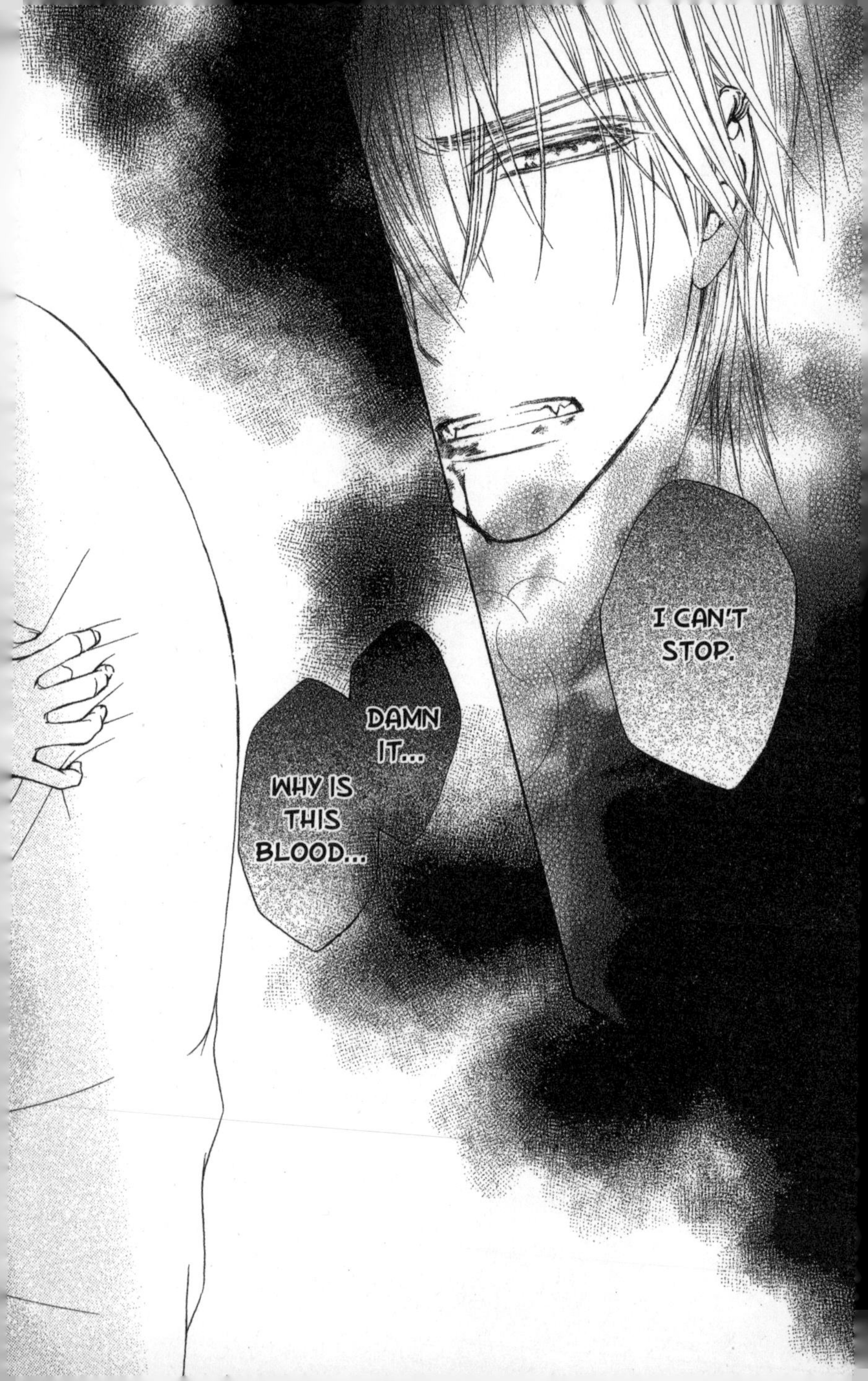
I CAN'T STOP.
DAMN IT...
WHY IS THIS BLOOD...

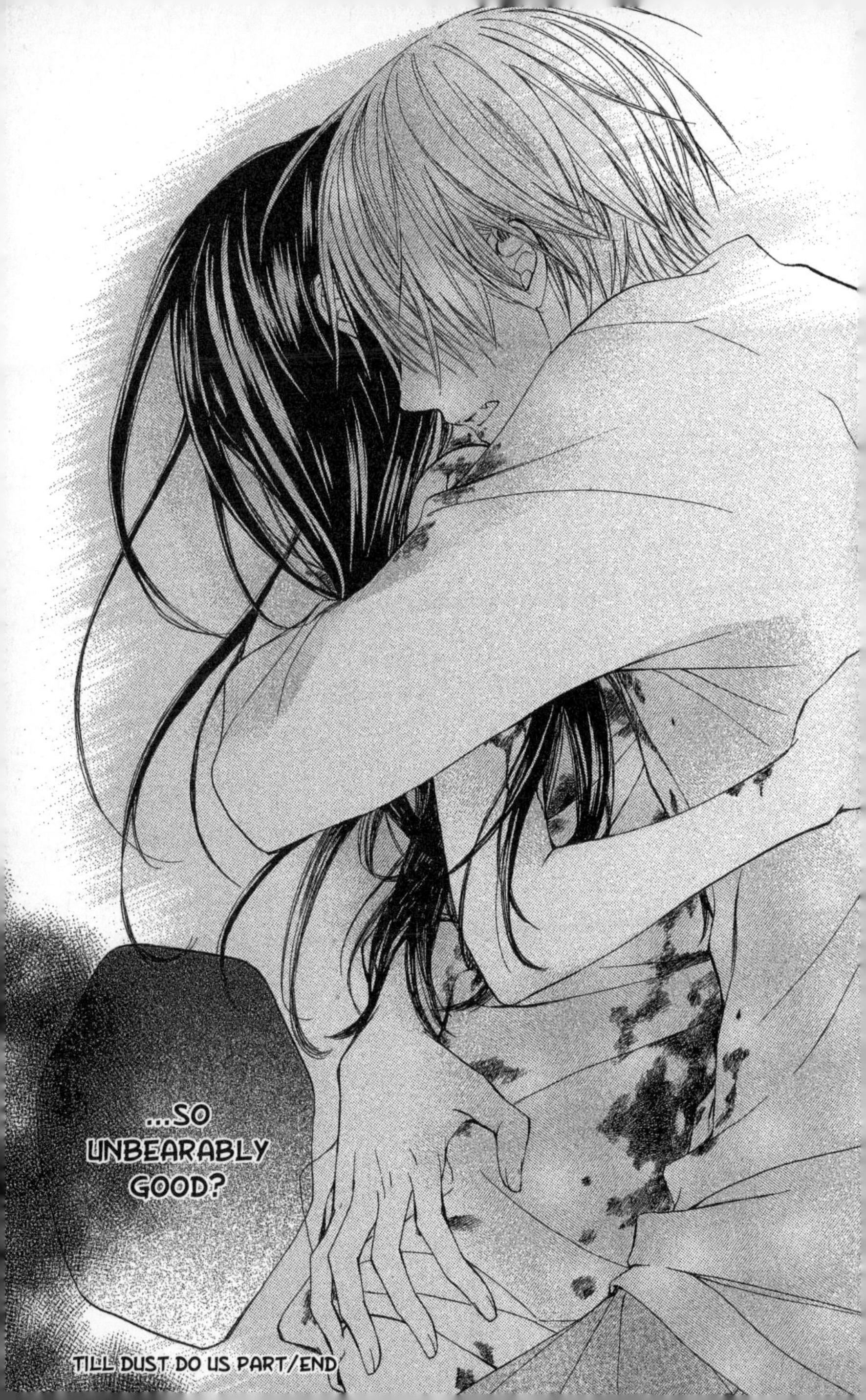
...SO UNBEARABLY GOOD?
TILL DUST DO US PART/END

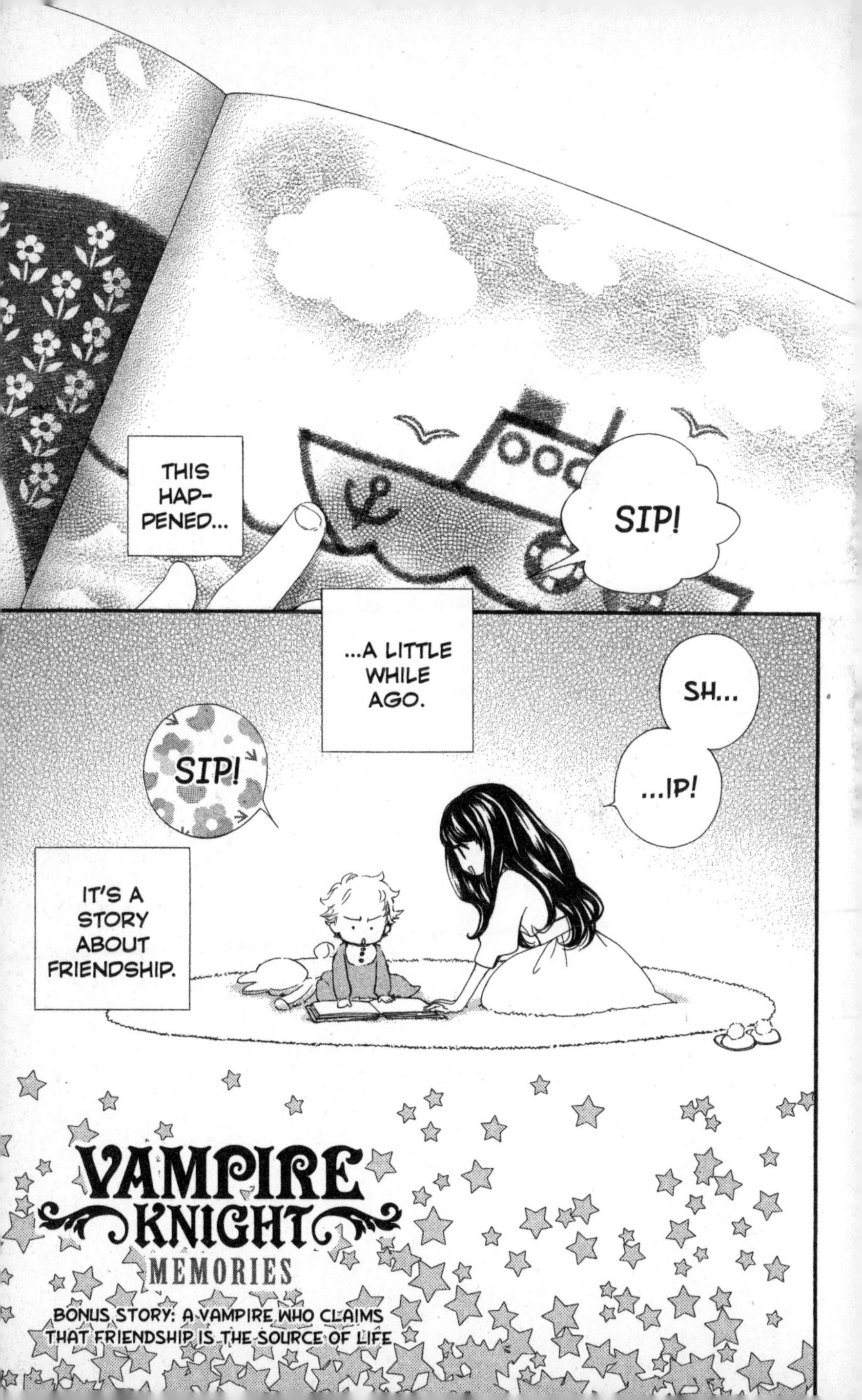
SIP!
THIS HAPPENED...
...A LITTLE WHILE AGO.
SH...
...IP!
SIP!
IT'S A STORY ABOUT FRIENDSHIP.
VAMPIRE KNIGHT MEMORIES
BONUS STORY: A VAMPIRE WHO CLAIMS THAT FRIENDSHIP IS THE SOURCE OF LIFE

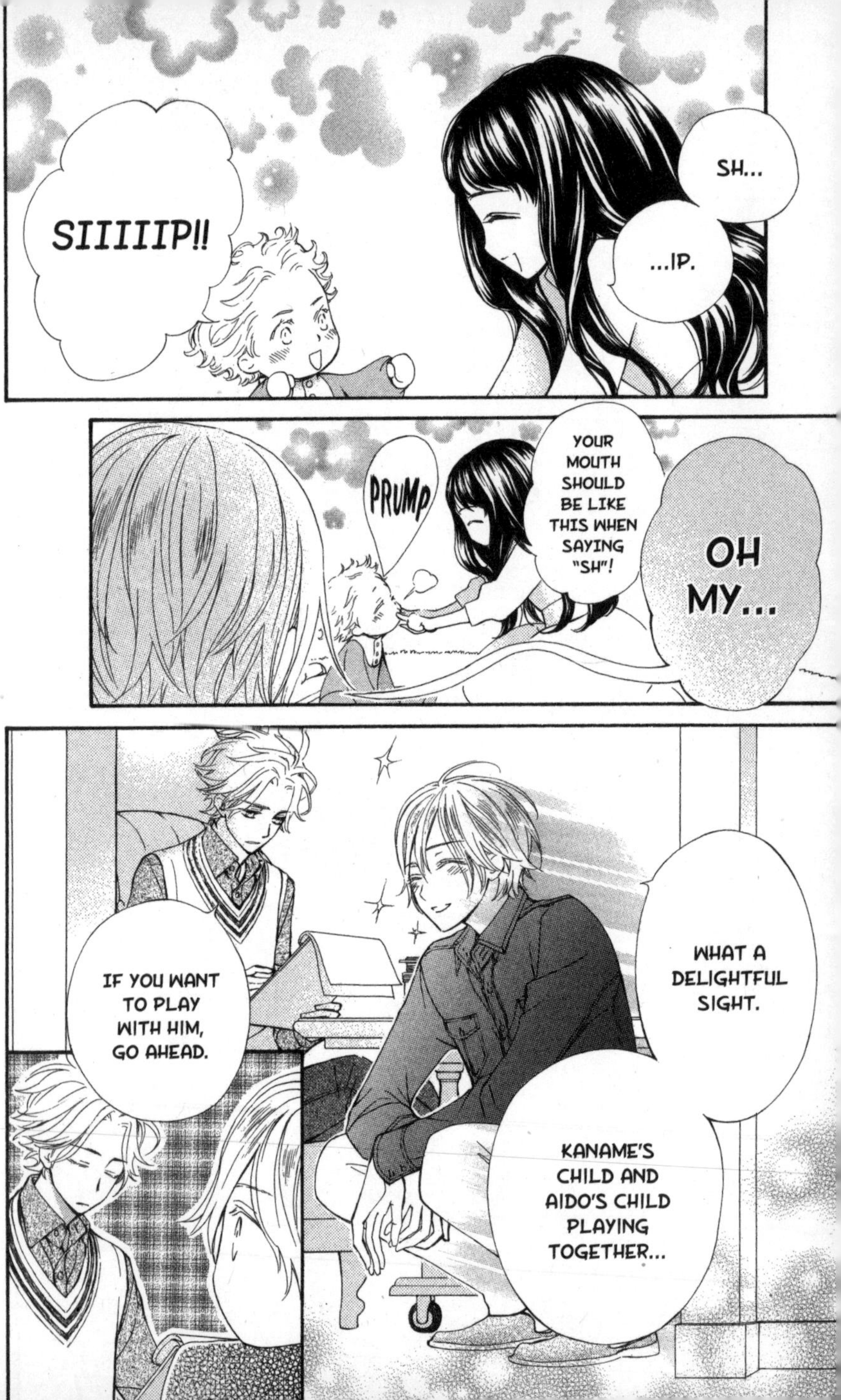
SH...
...IP.
SIIIIIP!!
OH MY...
YOUR MOUTH SHOULD BE LIKE THIS WHEN SAYING "SH"!
PRUMP
WHAT A DELIGHTFUL SIGHT.
KANAME'S CHILD AND AIDO'S CHILD PLAYING TOGETHER...
IF YOU WANT TO PLAY WITH HIM, GO AHEAD.

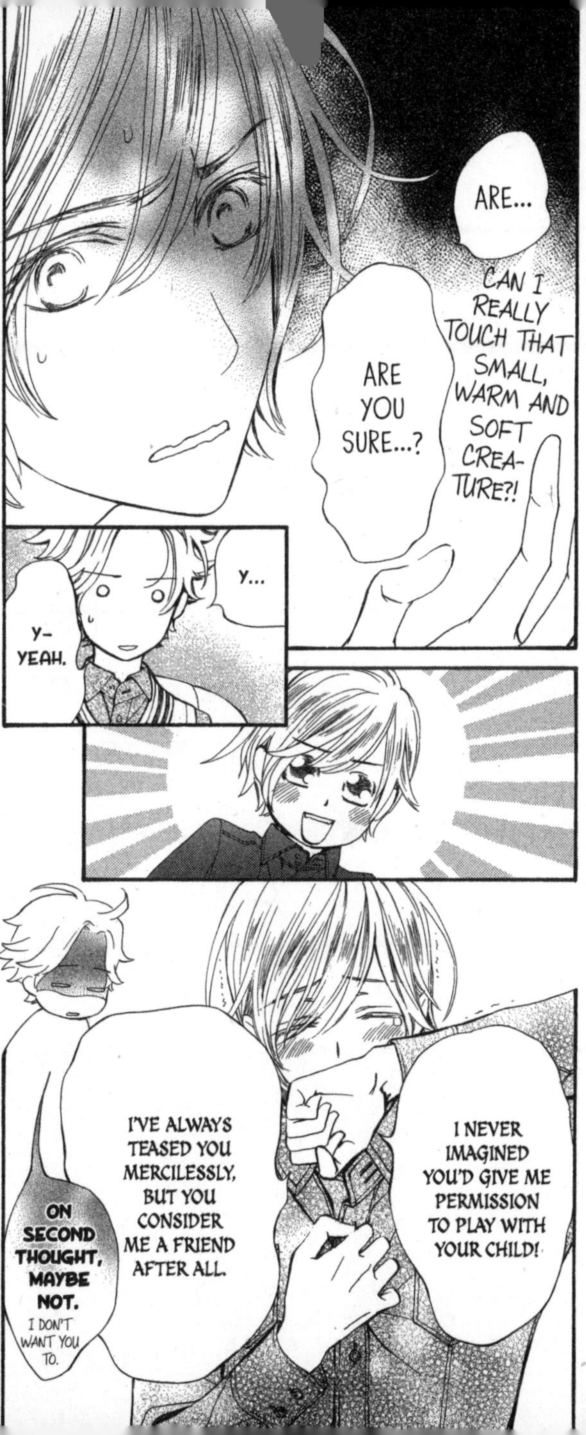
ARE...
CAN I REALLY TOUCH THAT SMALL, WARM AND SOFT CREATURE?!
ARE YOU SURE...?
Y...
Y-YEAH.
I NEVER IMAGINED YOU'D GIVE ME PERMISSION TO PLAY WITH YOUR CHILD!
I'VE ALWAYS TEASED YOU MERCILESSLY, BUT YOU CONSIDER ME A FRIEND AFTER ALL.
ON SECOND THOUGHT, MAYBE NOT.
I DON'T WANT YOU TO.

— 7 —

(continued ↓)

Tokyo Slider's cork penholder was a must-have for me too, but sadly I had to part with it. I liked the thickness, weight... And most of all, it did not slip in my sweaty hand because it was made of cork. It had just the right cushion to it too. It was a super-trustworthy partner, so it came as a huge shock when I learned that it had gone out of production. Thank you for all those years, cork penholder...!

It's farewell to Pilot's pigment ink brush pen with the small soft tip as well. It was a wonderfully easy-to-use pen. It really is a pity.

I've revamped a penholder from a different maker, and as for the brush pen... I still haven't been able to find anything new. I've tried out so many in hopes of finding a perfect match for me, but... (*laugh*)

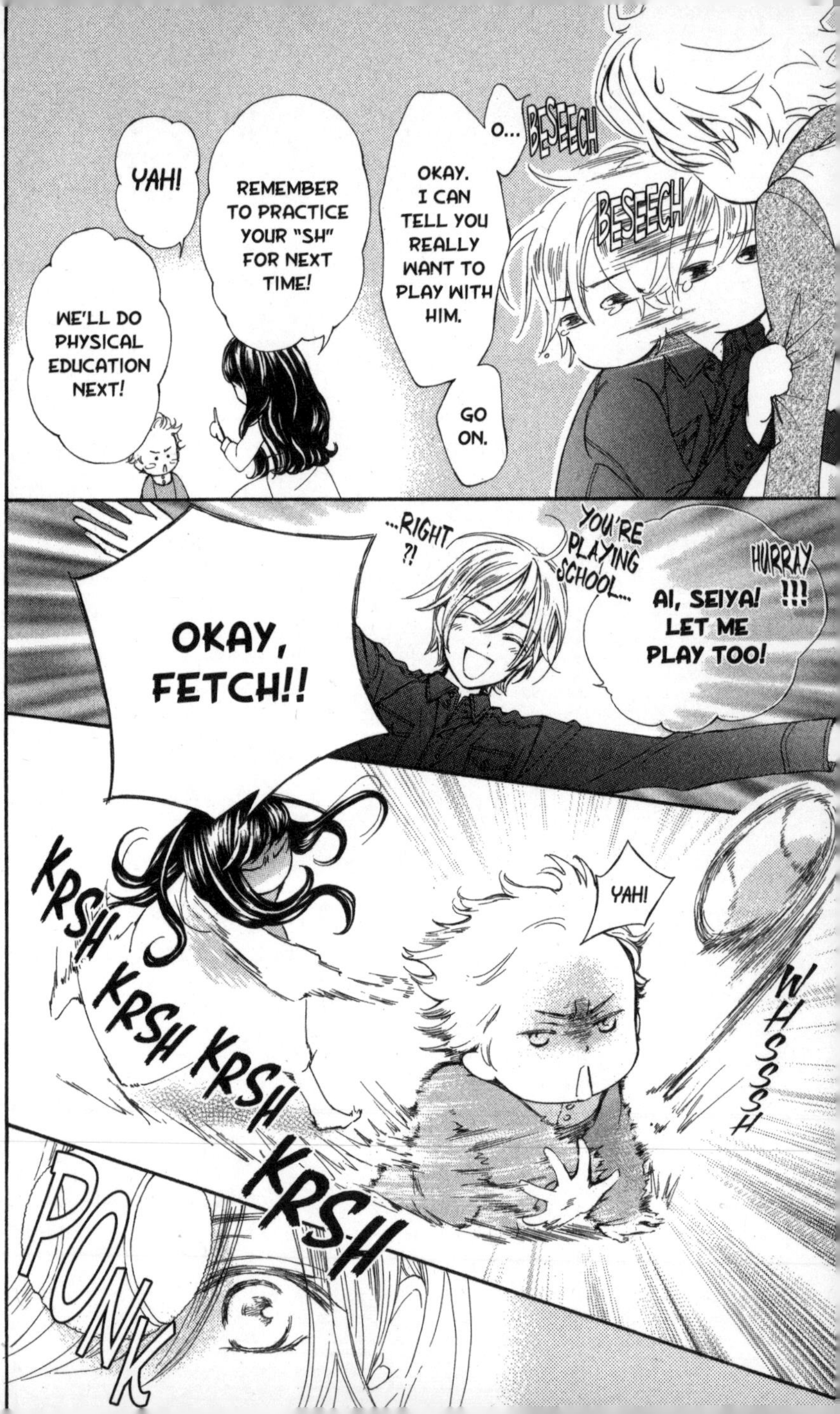
O... BESEECH
BESEECH
OKAY. I CAN TELL YOU REALLY WANT TO PLAY WITH HIM.
GO ON.
REMEMBER TO PRACTICE YOUR "SH" FOR NEXT TIME!
YAH!
WE'LL DO PHYSICAL EDUCATION NEXT!
HURRAY!!!
AI, SEIYA! LET ME PLAY TOO!
YOU'RE PLAYING SCHOOL...
...RIGHT?!
OKAY, FETCH!!
WHSSSH
YAH!
KRSH KRSH KRSH KRSH KRSH
PONK

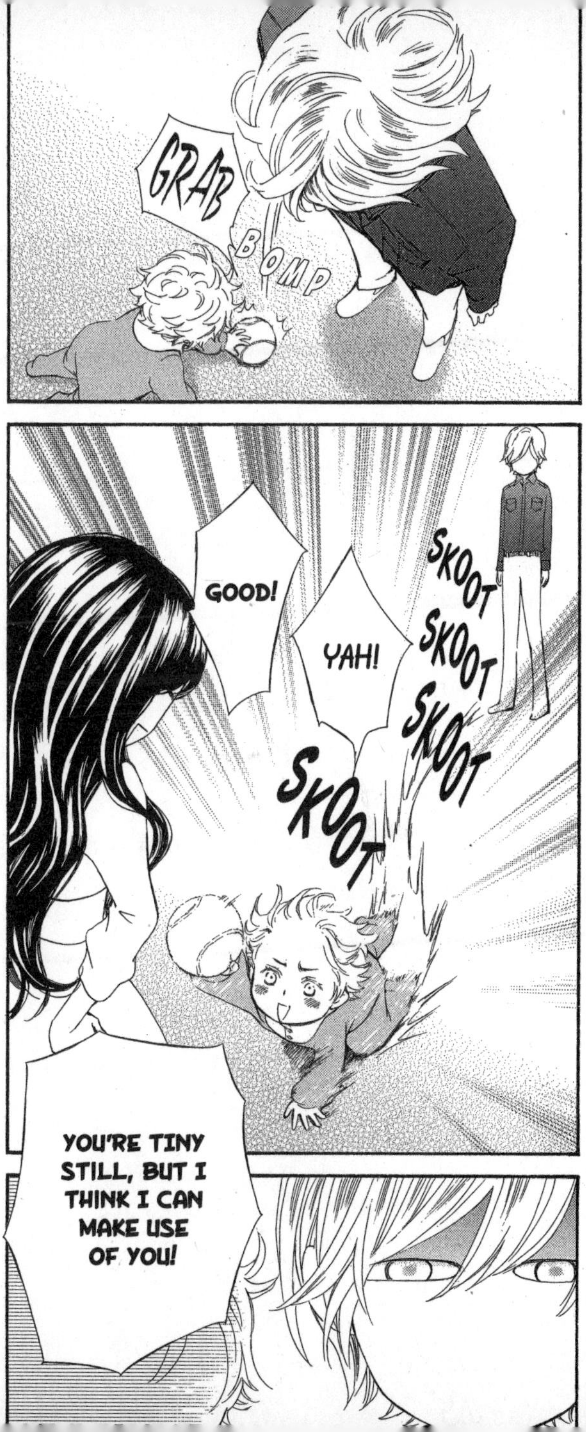
GRAB
BOMP
SKOOT SKOOT SKOOT
GOOD!
YAH!
SKOOT
YOU'RE TINY STILL, BUT I THINK I CAN MAKE USE OF YOU!

— 8 —

Those who follow the magazine must already know, but the last two chapters contained another short about Shiki and Rima. This manga volume did not have enough space to include it, so that story about them will be included in the next volume. (I decided on writing short stories just so they could be divided up...) And so, this will be the last sidebar in this volume.

Thank you very much for reading volume 3 too! I hope we will meet again in volume 4...!

I would also like to thank my editor, my family and everyone involved in creating this volume. And last but not least...

O. Mio-sama
K. Midori-sama
A. Ichiya-sama

Thank you very much!

樋野まつり
Matsuri Hino

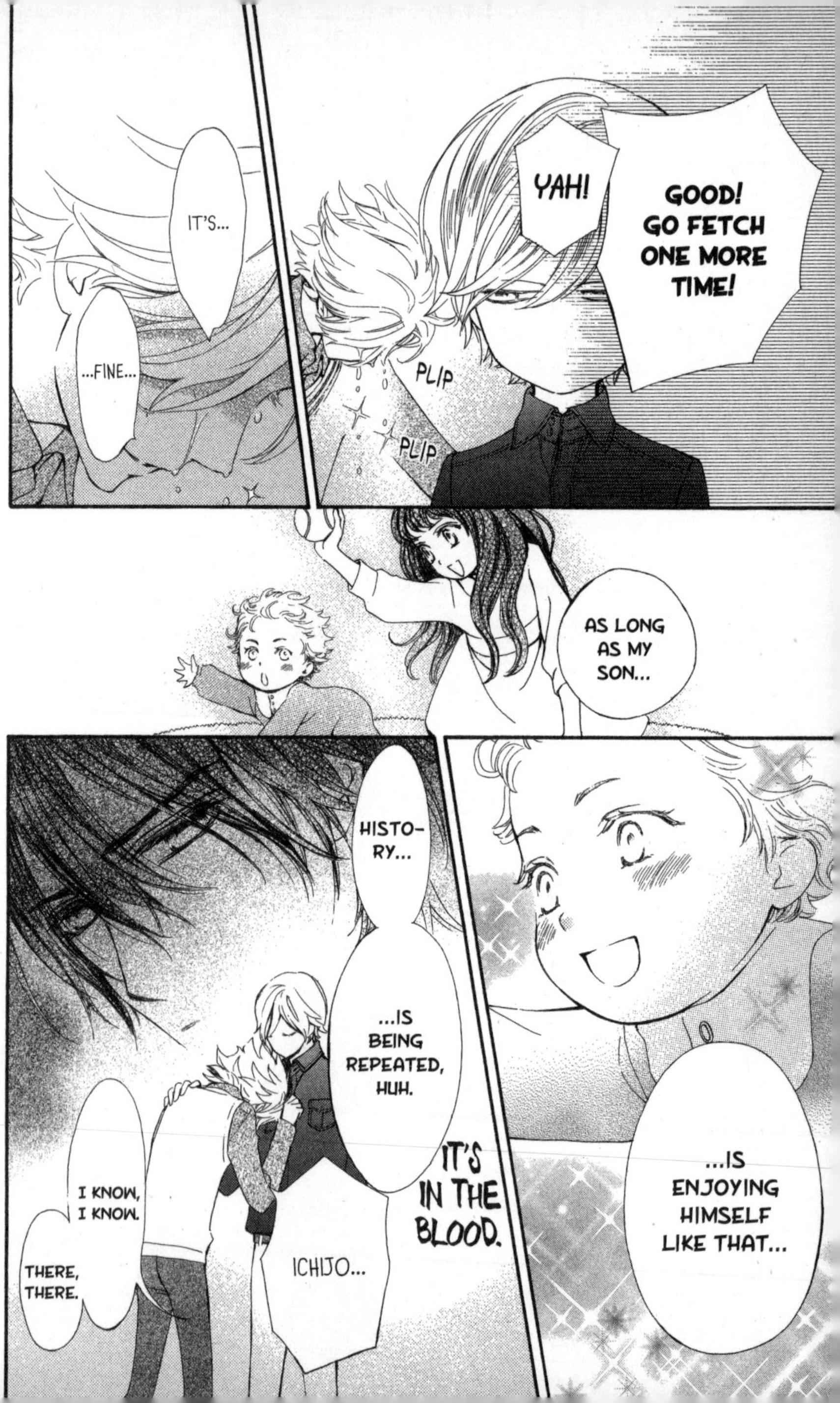
GOOD! GO FETCH ONE MORE TIME!
YAH!
PLIP
PLIP
IT'S...
...FINE...
AS LONG AS MY SON...
...IS ENJOYING HIMSELF LIKE THAT...
HISTORY...
...IS BEING REPEATED, HUH.
IT'S IN THE BLOOD.
ICHIJO...
I KNOW, I KNOW.
THERE, THERE.

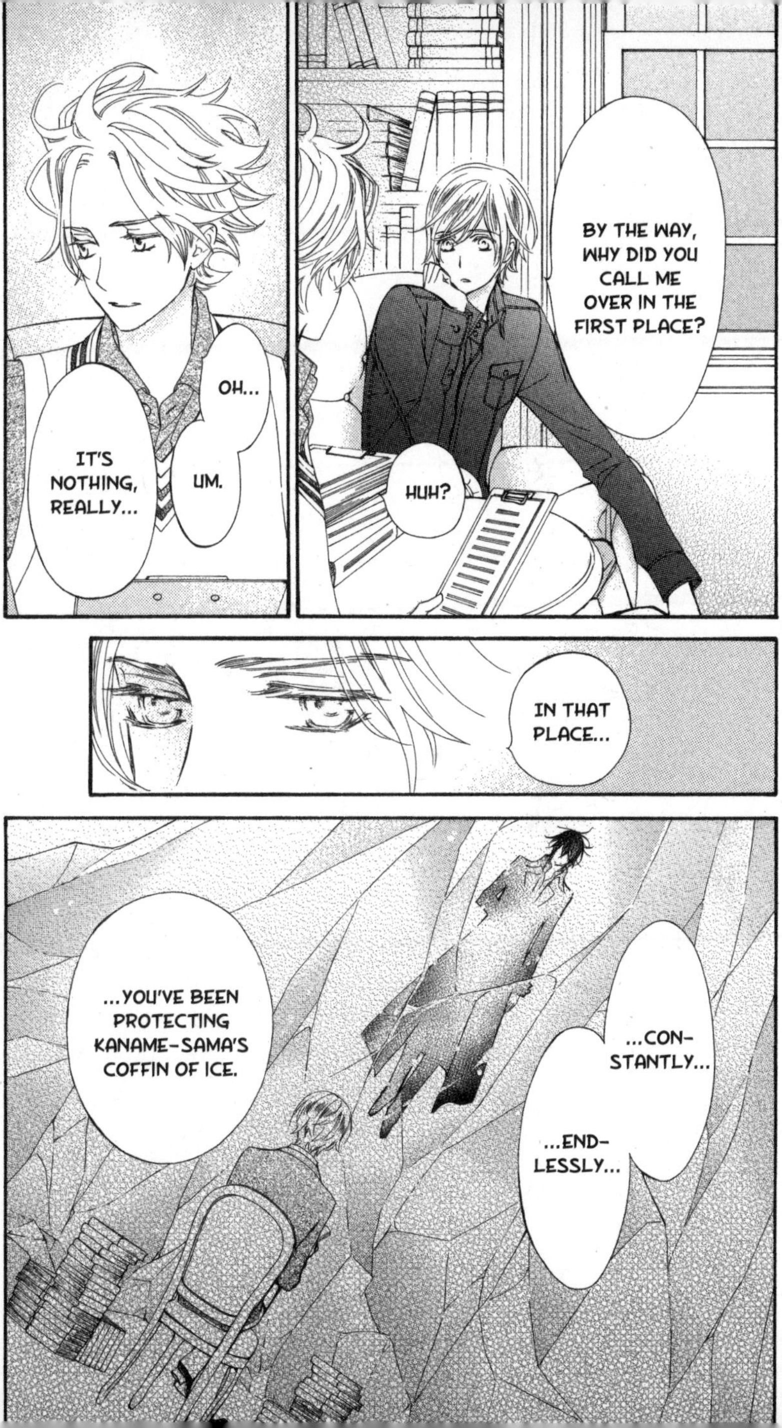
BY THE WAY, WHY DID YOU CALL ME OVER IN THE FIRST PLACE?
HUH?
OH...
UM.
IT'S NOTHING, REALLY...
IN THAT PLACE...
...CON-STANTLY...
...END-LESSLY...
...YOU'VE BEEN PROTECTING KANAME-SAMA'S COFFIN OF ICE.

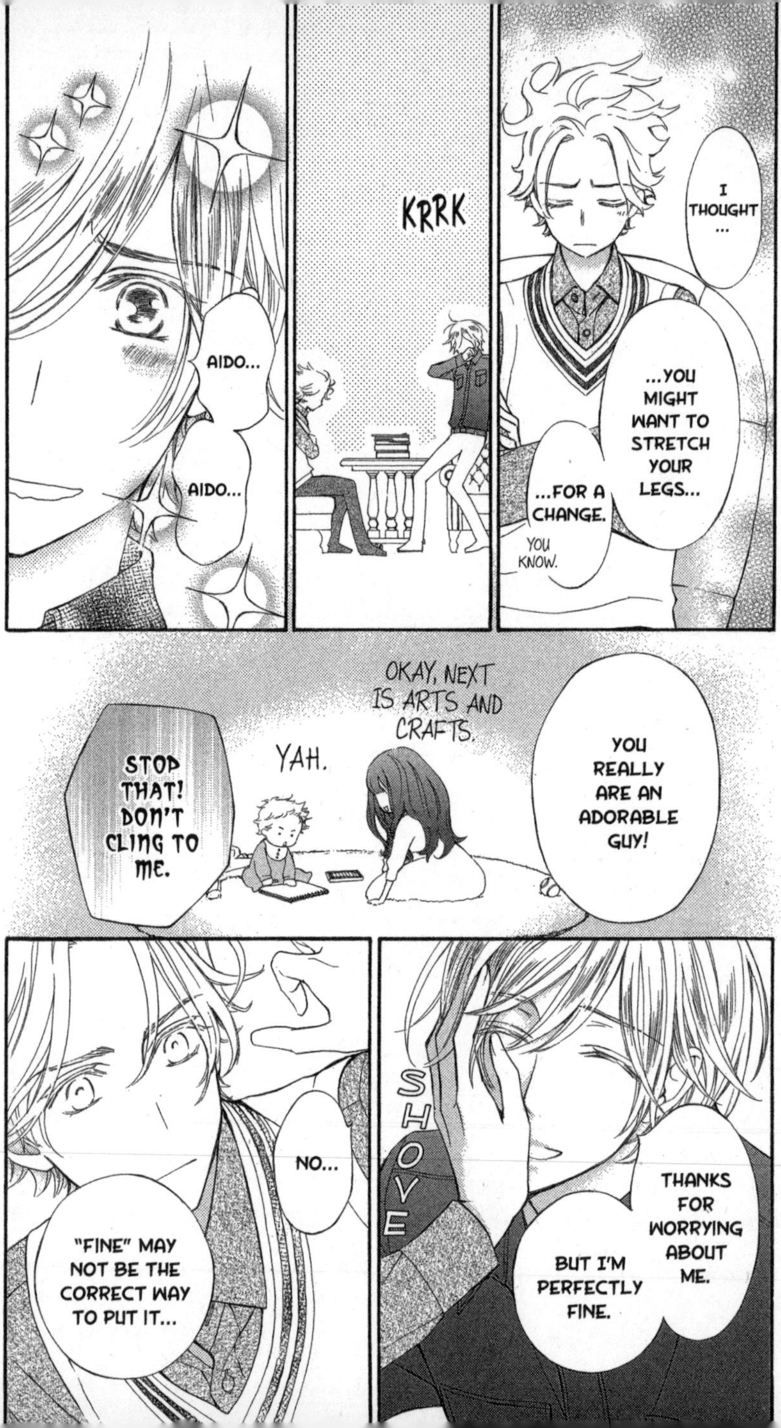
I THOUGHT...
...YOU MIGHT WANT TO STRETCH YOUR LEGS...
...FOR A CHANGE.
YOU KNOW.
KRRK
AIDO...
AIDO...
YOU REALLY ARE AN ADORABLE GUY!
OKAY, NEXT IS ARTS AND CRAFTS.
YAH.
STOP THAT! DON'T CLING TO ME.
SHOVE
THANKS FOR WORRYING ABOUT ME.
BUT I'M PERFECTLY FINE.
NO...
"FINE" MAY NOT BE THE CORRECT WAY TO PUT IT...

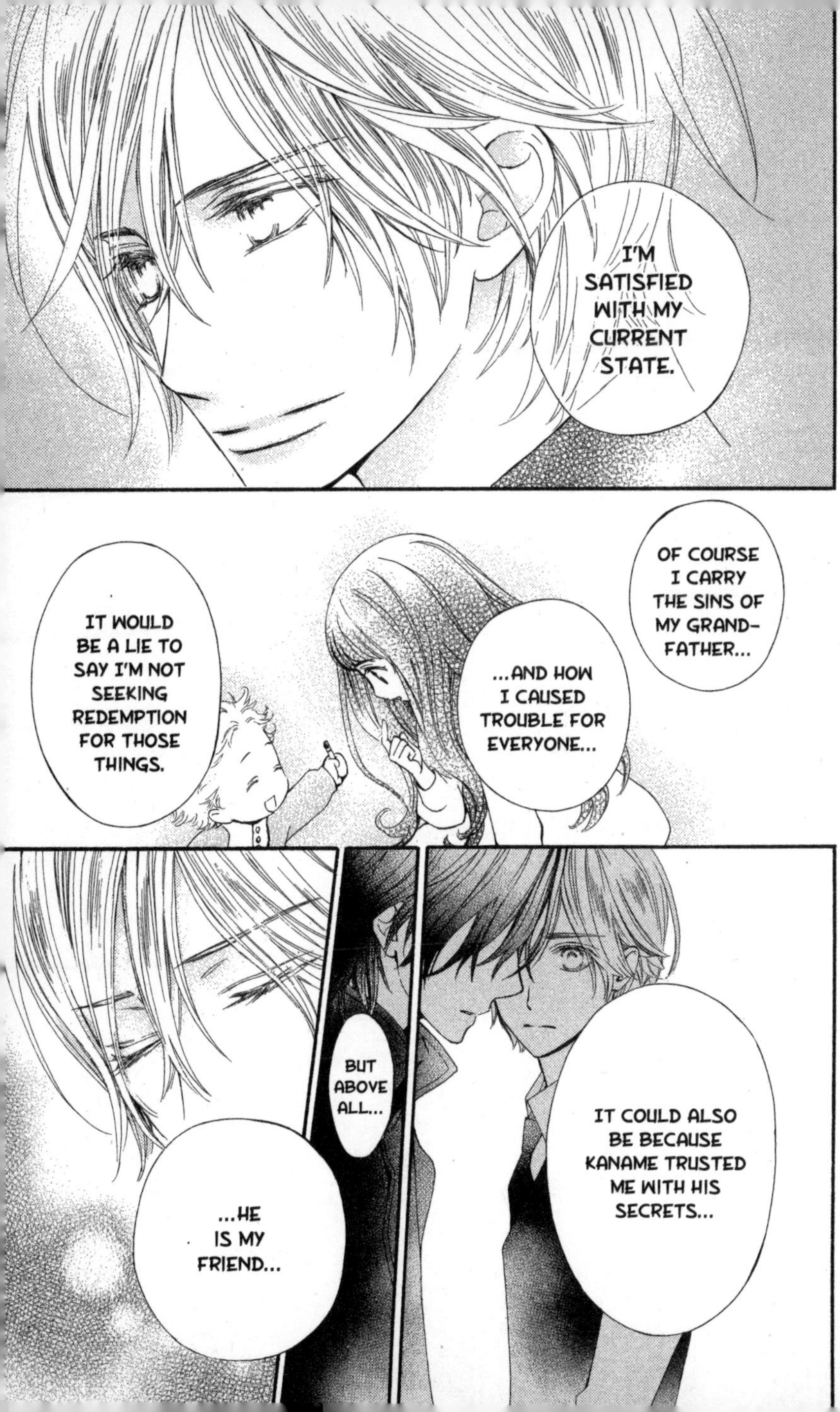
I'M SATISFIED WITH MY CURRENT STATE.
OF COURSE I CARRY THE SINS OF MY GRAND-FATHER...
...AND HOW I CAUSED TROUBLE FOR EVERYONE...
IT WOULD BE A LIE TO SAY I'M NOT SEEKING REDEMPTION FOR THOSE THINGS.
IT COULD ALSO BE BECAUSE KANAME TRUSTED ME WITH HIS SECRETS...
BUT ABOVE ALL...
...HE IS MY FRIEND...

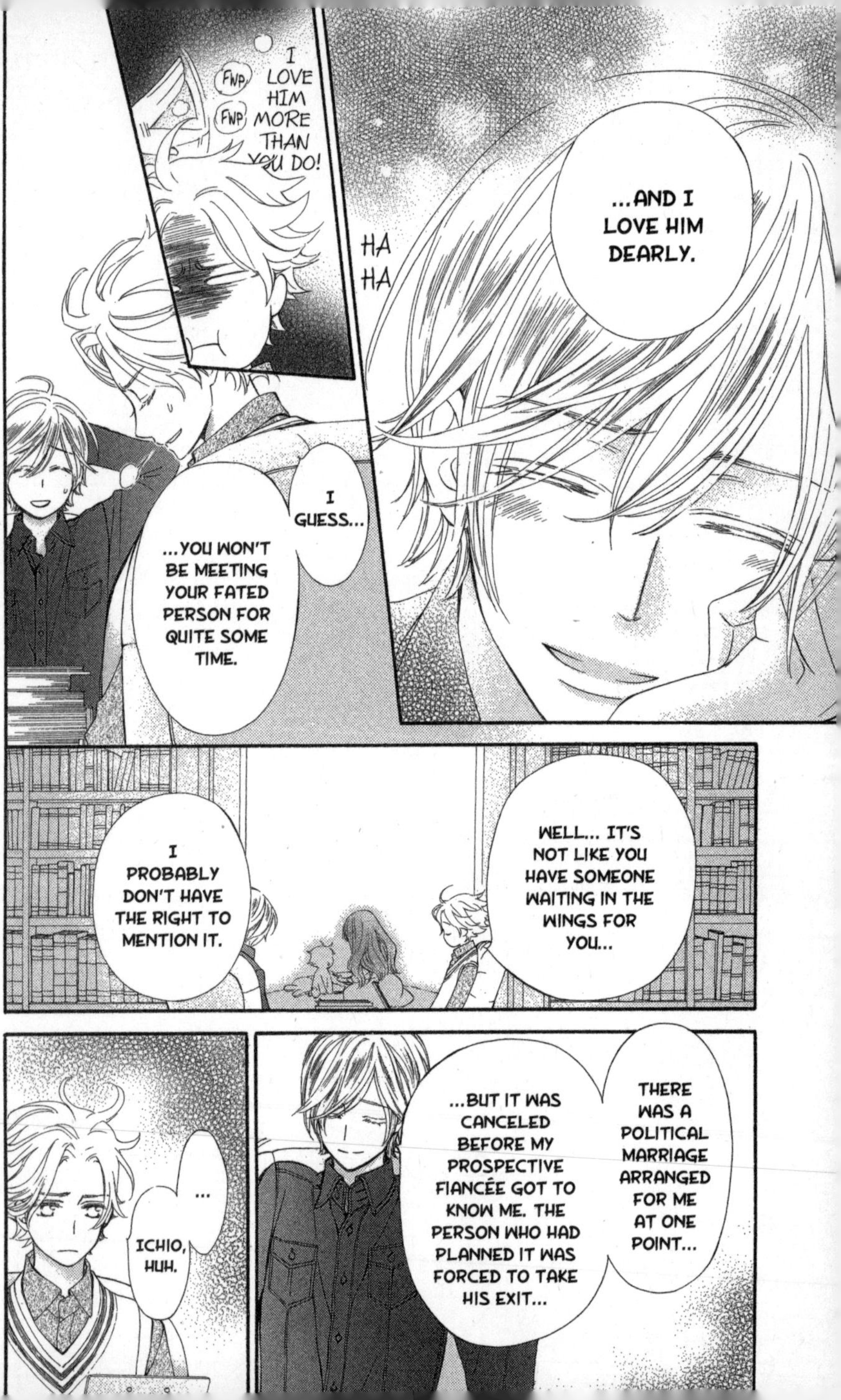
...AND I LOVE HIM DEARLY.
I LOVE HIM MORE THAN YOU DO!
FWP
FWP
HA HA
I GUESS...
...YOU WON'T BE MEETING YOUR FATED PERSON FOR QUITE SOME TIME.
WELL... IT'S NOT LIKE YOU HAVE SOMEONE WAITING IN THE WINGS FOR YOU...
I PROBABLY DON'T HAVE THE RIGHT TO MENTION IT.
THERE WAS A POLITICAL MARRIAGE ARRANGED FOR ME AT ONE POINT...
...BUT IT WAS CANCELED BEFORE MY PROSPECTIVE FIANCÉE GOT TO KNOW ME. THE PERSON WHO HAD PLANNED IT WAS FORCED TO TAKE HIS EXIT...
...
ICHIO, HUH.

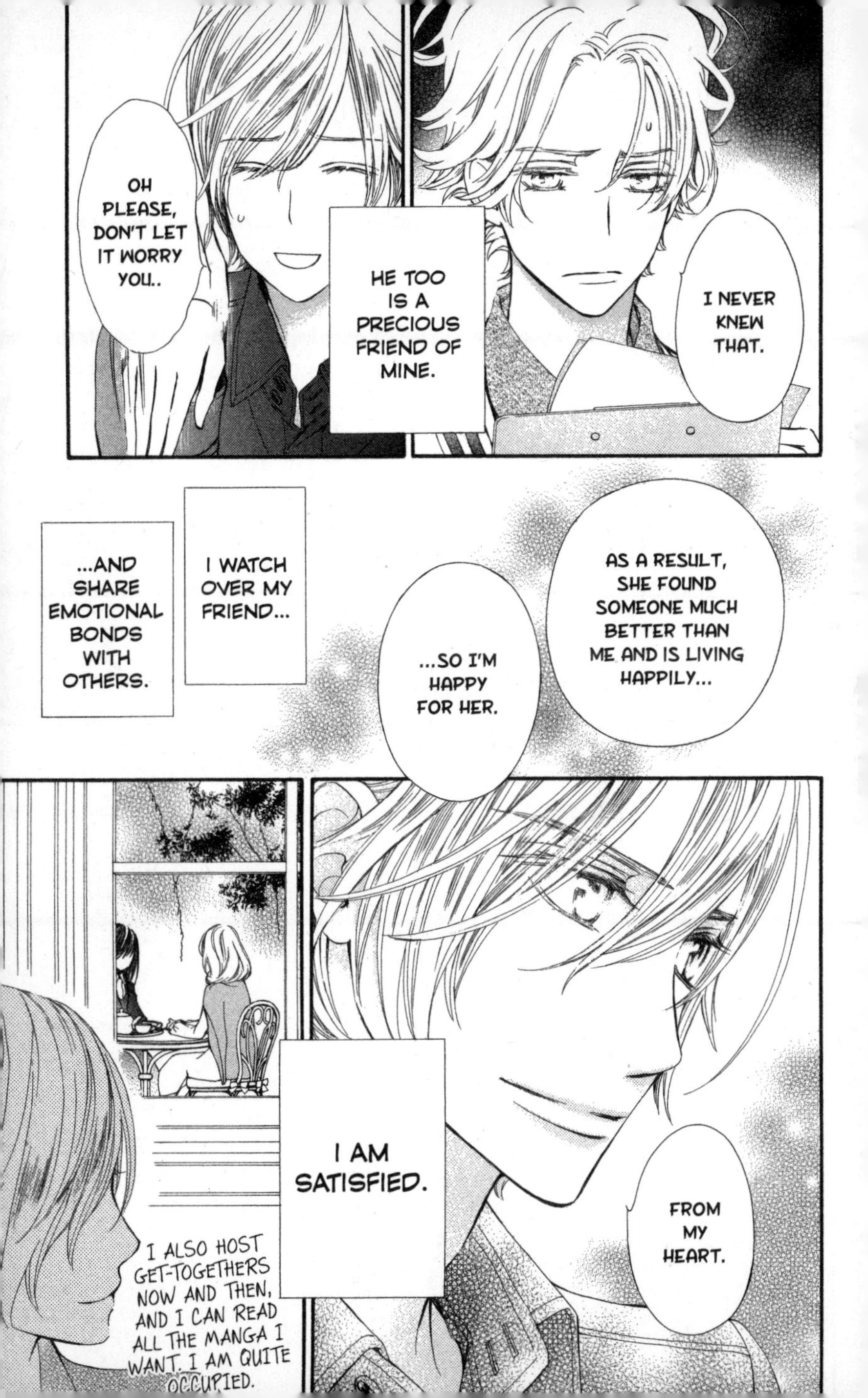
I NEVER KNEW THAT.
HE TOO IS A PRECIOUS FRIEND OF MINE.
OH PLEASE, DON'T LET IT WORRY YOU..
AS A RESULT, SHE FOUND SOMEONE MUCH BETTER THAN ME AND IS LIVING HAPPILY...
...SO I'M HAPPY FOR HER.
I WATCH OVER MY FRIEND...
...AND SHARE EMOTIONAL BONDS WITH OTHERS.
FROM MY HEART.
I AM SATISFIED.
I ALSO HOST GET-TOGETHERS NOW AND THEN, AND I CAN READ ALL THE MANGA I WANT. I AM QUITE OCCUPIED.

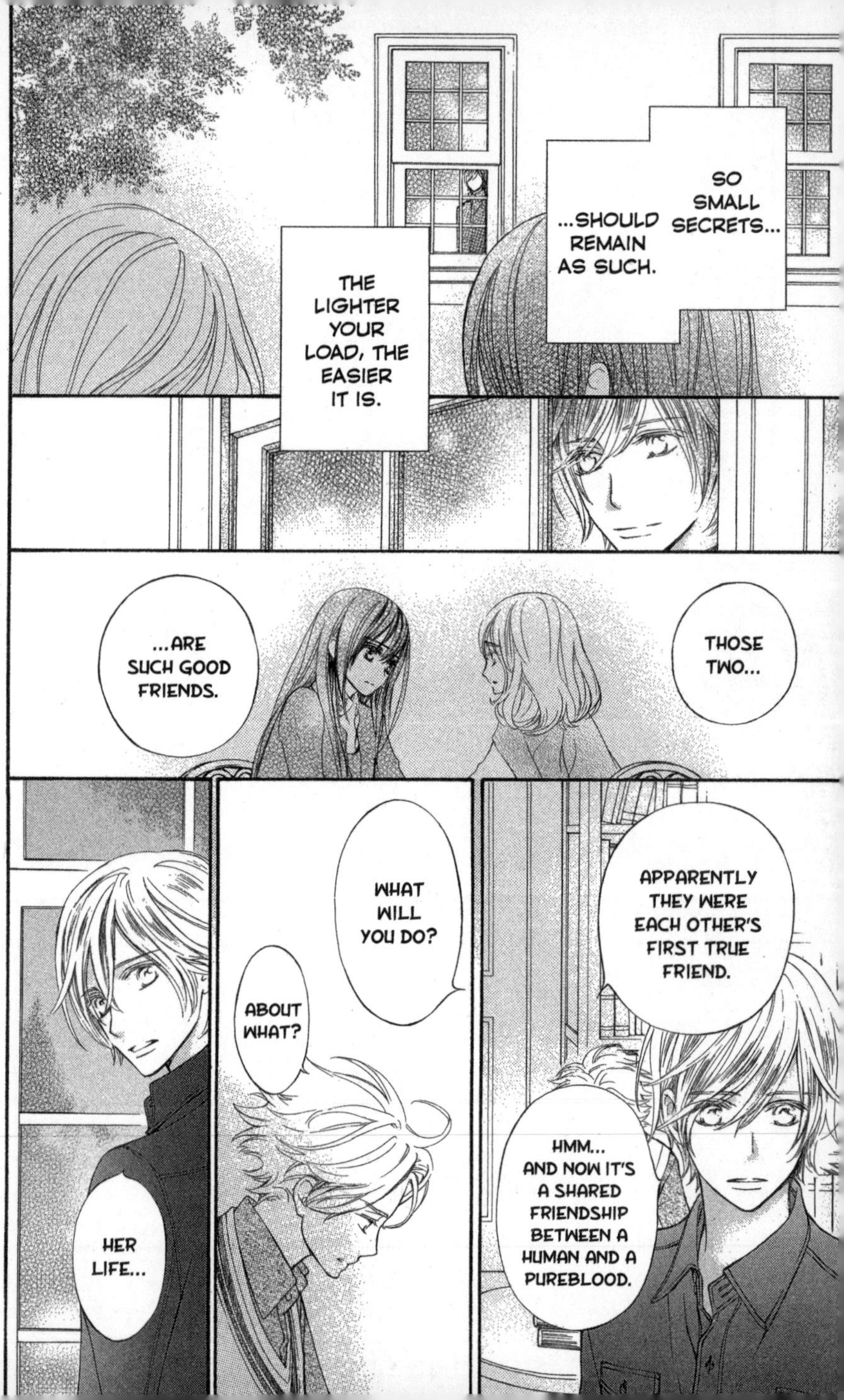
SO SMALL SECRETS...
...SHOULD REMAIN AS SUCH.
THE LIGHTER YOUR LOAD, THE EASIER IT IS.
THOSE TWO...
...ARE SUCH GOOD FRIENDS.
APPARENTLY THEY WERE EACH OTHER'S FIRST TRUE FRIEND.
HMM... AND NOW IT'S A SHARED FRIENDSHIP BETWEEN A HUMAN AND A PUREBLOOD.
WHAT WILL YOU DO?
ABOUT WHAT?
HER LIFE...

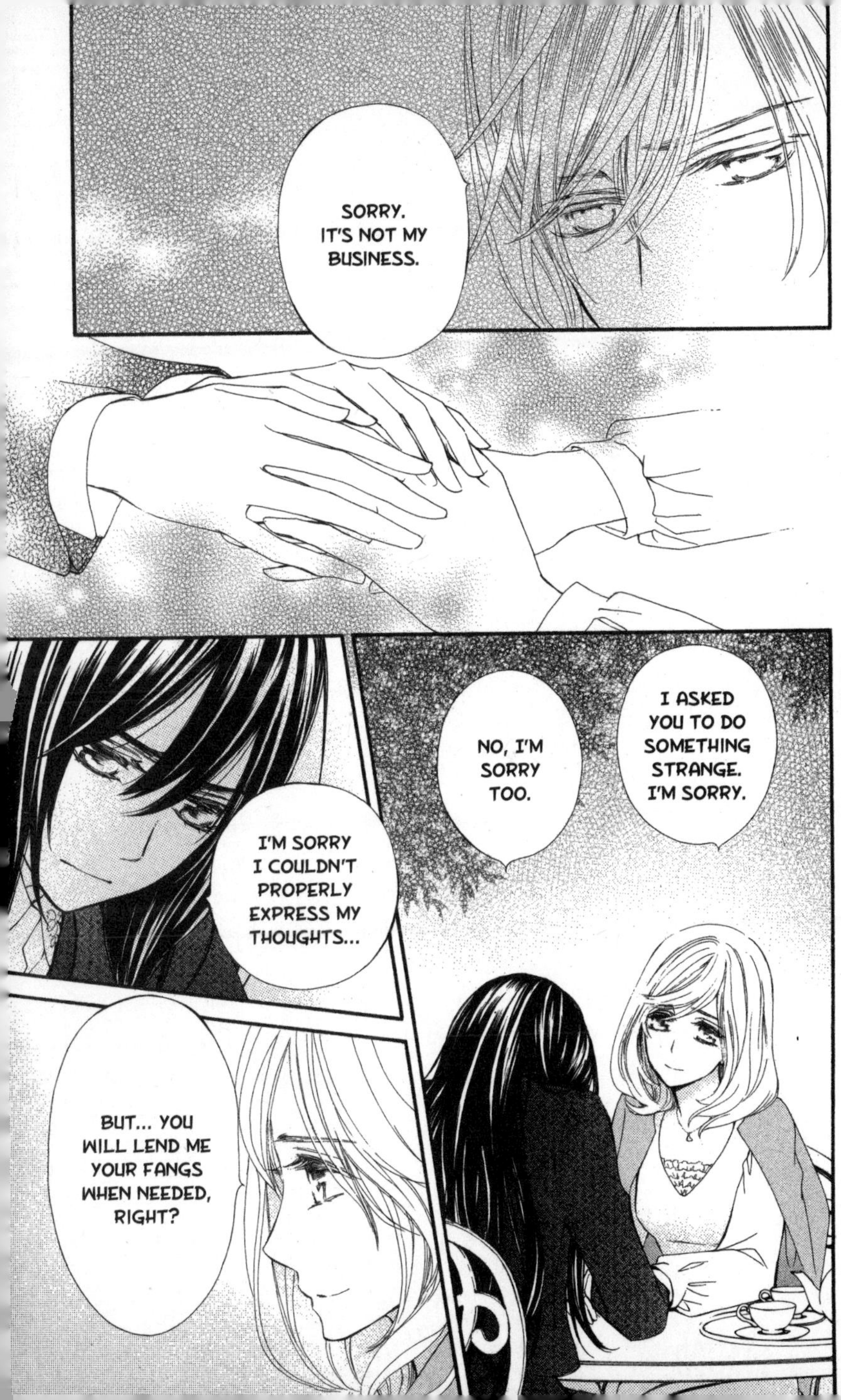
SORRY. IT'S NOT MY BUSINESS.
I ASKED YOU TO DO SOMETHING STRANGE. I'M SORRY.
NO, I'M SORRY TOO.
I'M SORRY I COULDN'T PROPERLY EXPRESS MY THOUGHTS...
BUT... YOU WILL LEND ME YOUR FANGS WHEN NEEDED, RIGHT?

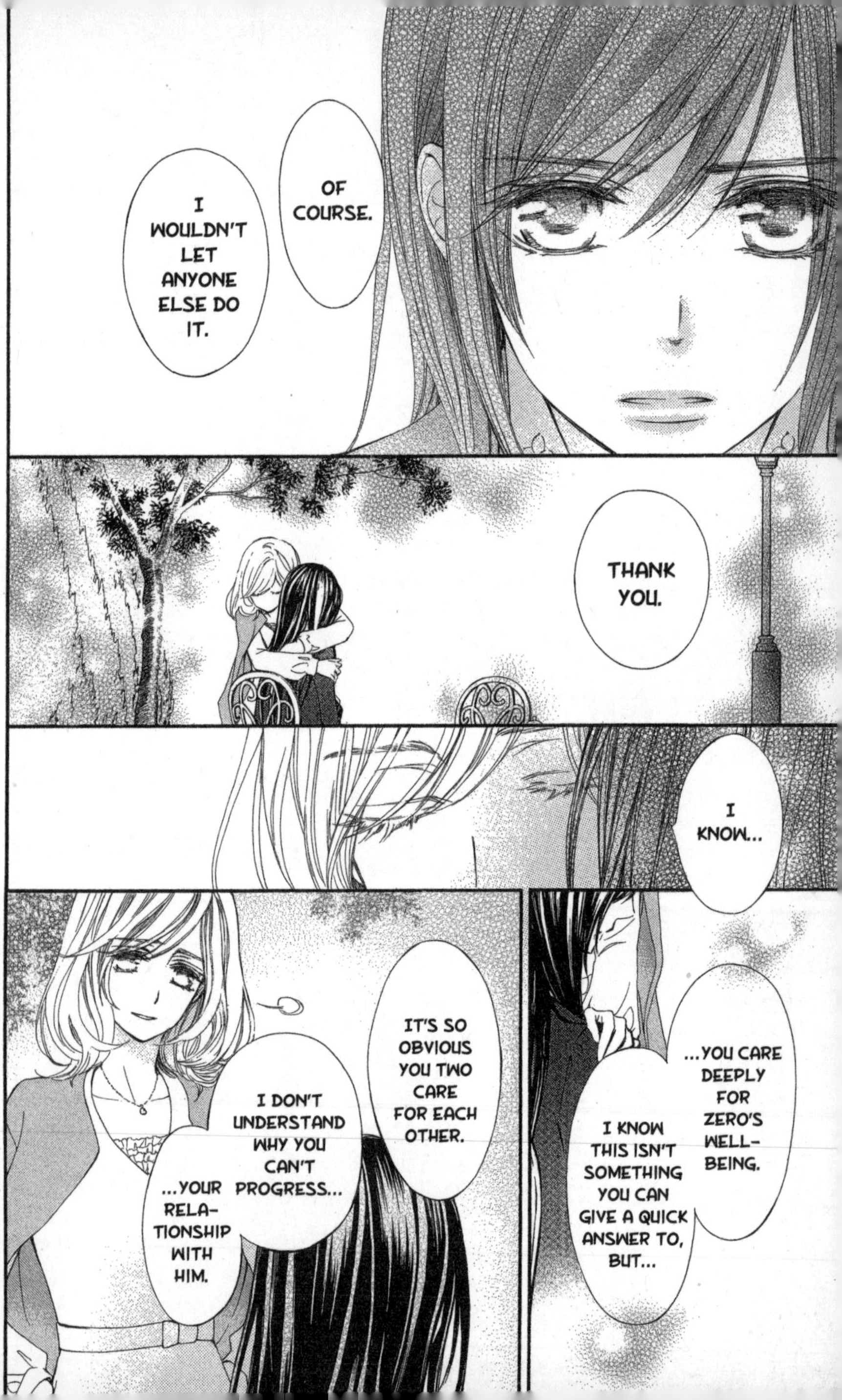
OF COURSE.
I WOULDN'T LET ANYONE ELSE DO IT.
THANK YOU.
I KNOW...
...YOU CARE DEEPLY FOR ZERO'S WELL-BEING.
I KNOW THIS ISN'T SOMETHING YOU CAN GIVE A QUICK ANSWER TO, BUT...
IT'S SO OBVIOUS YOU TWO CARE FOR EACH OTHER.
I DON'T UNDERSTAND WHY YOU CAN'T PROGRESS...
...YOUR RELA-TIONSHIP WITH HIM.

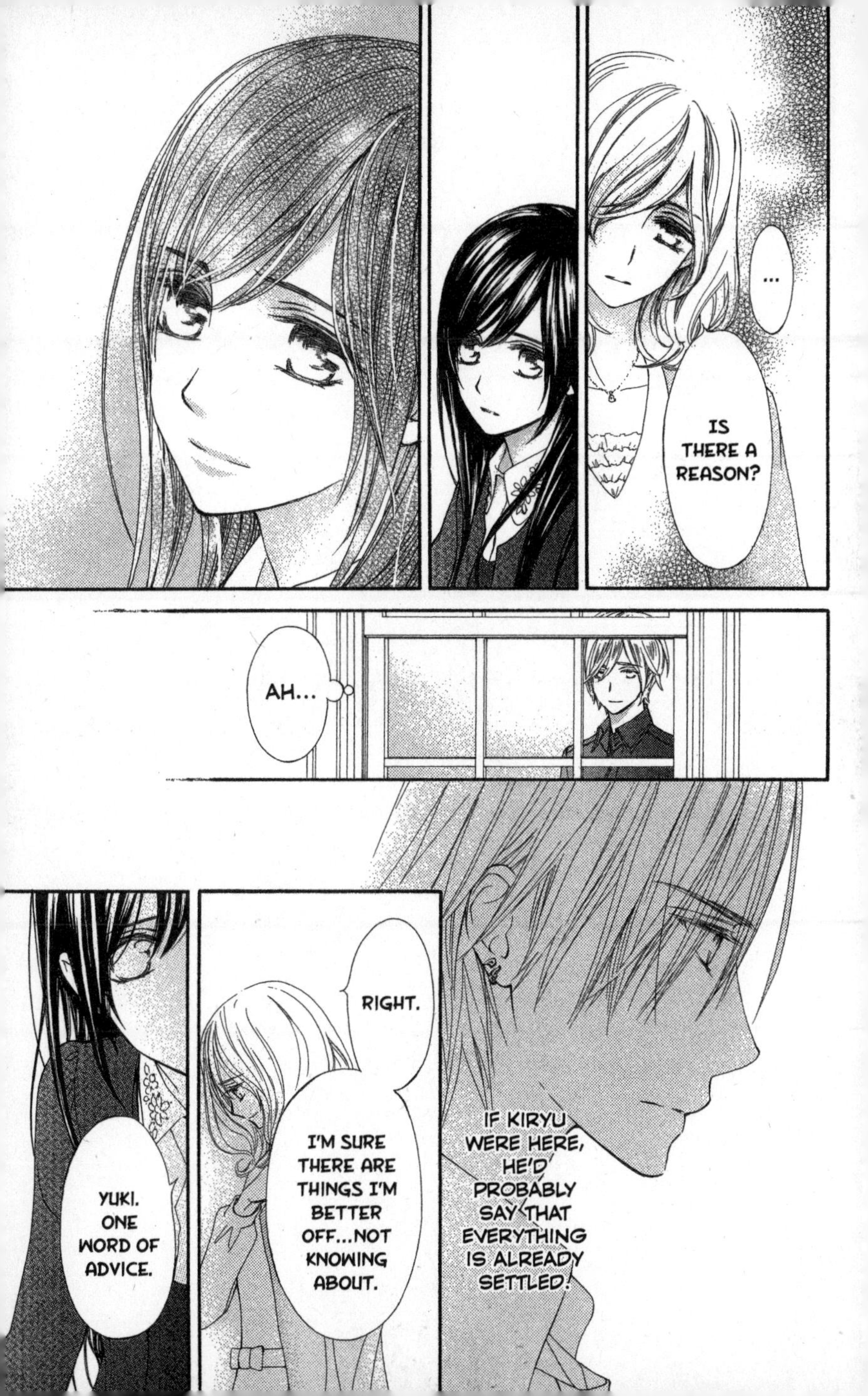
...
IS THERE A REASON?
AH...
IF KIRYU WERE HERE, HE'D PROBABLY SAY THAT EVERYTHING IS ALREADY SETTLED.
RIGHT.
I'M SURE THERE ARE THINGS I'M BETTER OFF...NOT KNOWING ABOUT.
YUKI. ONE WORD OF ADVICE.

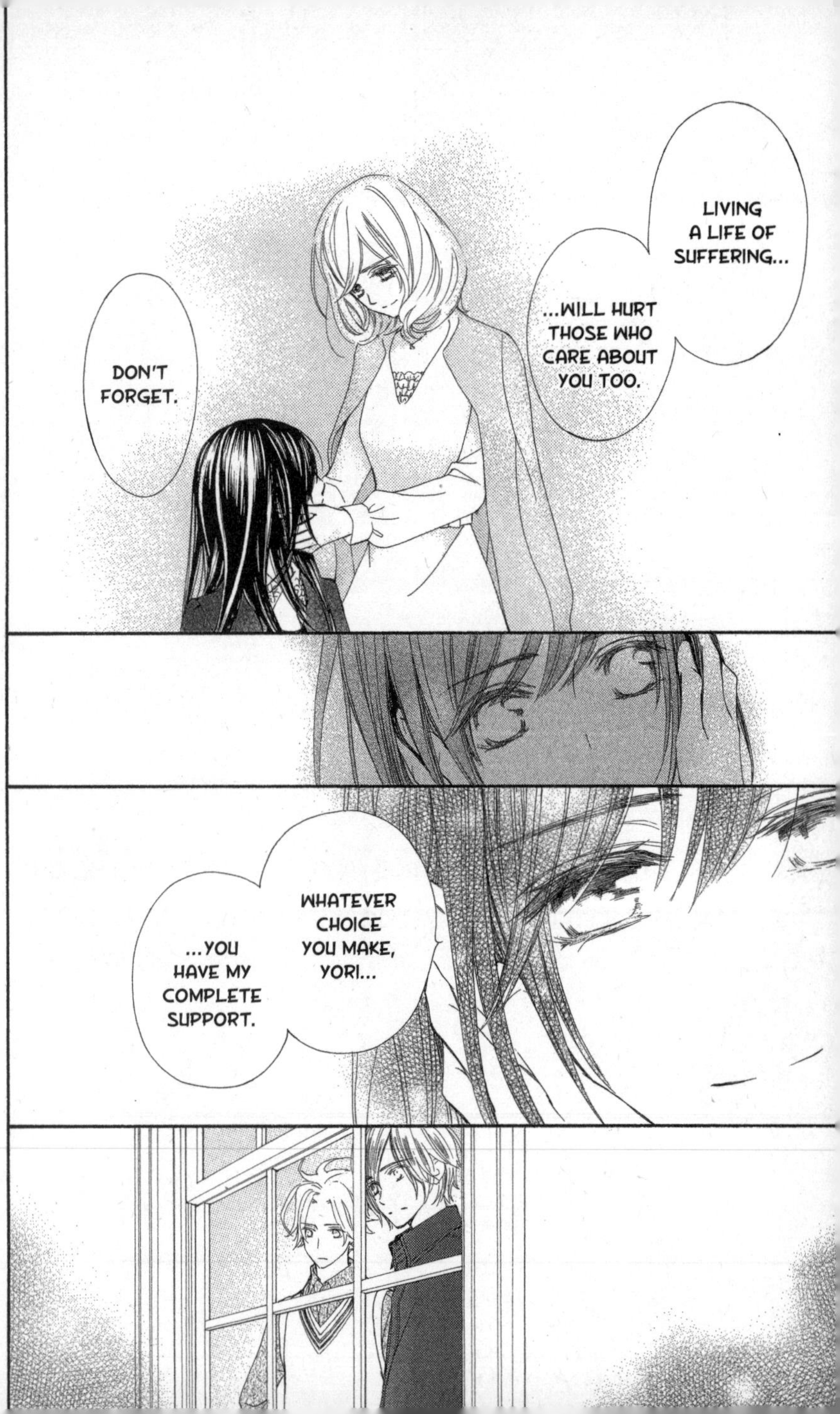
LIVING A LIFE OF SUFFERING...
...WILL HURT THOSE WHO CARE ABOUT YOU TOO.
DON'T FORGET.
WHATEVER CHOICE YOU MAKE, YORI...
...YOU HAVE MY COMPLETE SUPPORT.

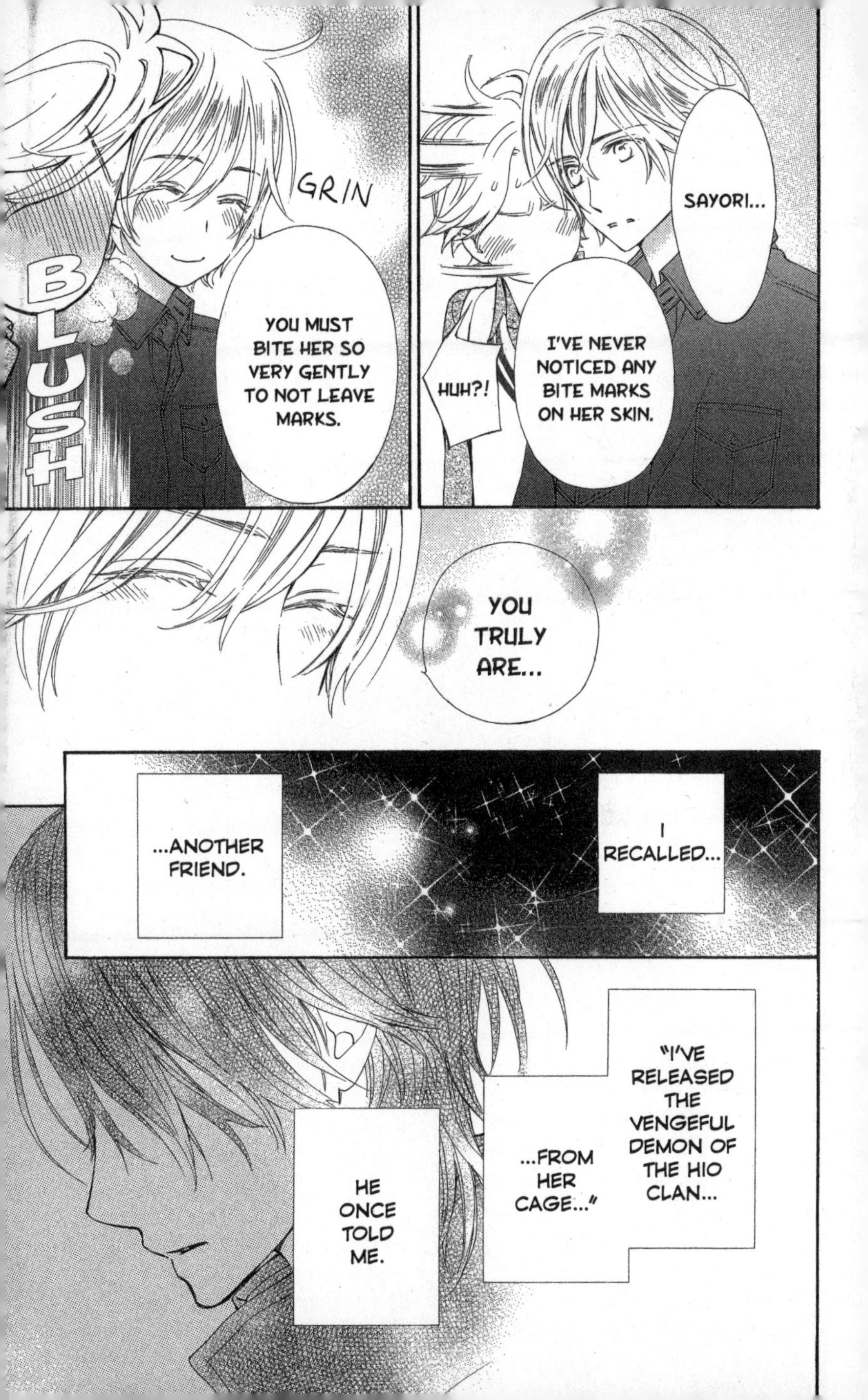
SAYORI...
HUH?!
I'VE NEVER NOTICED ANY BITE MARKS ON HER SKIN.
GRIN
YOU MUST BITE HER SO VERY GENTLY TO NOT LEAVE MARKS.
BLUSH
YOU TRULY ARE...
I RECALLED...
...ANOTHER FRIEND.
"I'VE RELEASED THE VENGEFUL DEMON OF THE HIO CLAN...
...FROM HER CAGE..."
HE ONCE TOLD ME.

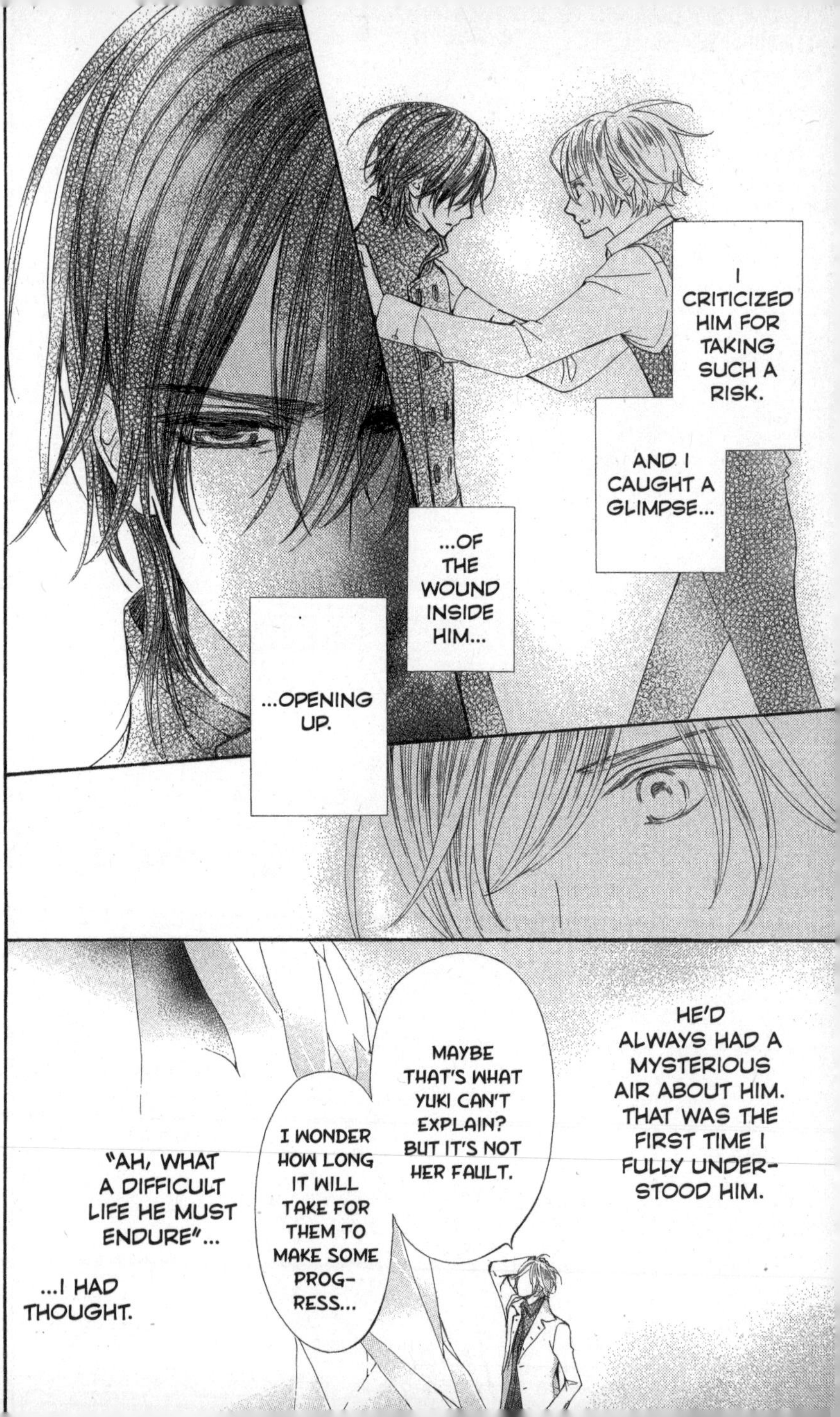
I CRITICIZED HIM FOR TAKING SUCH A RISK.
AND I CAUGHT A GLIMPSE...
...OF THE WOUND INSIDE HIM...
...OPENING UP.
HE'D ALWAYS HAD A MYSTERIOUS AIR ABOUT HIM. THAT WAS THE FIRST TIME I FULLY UNDER-STOOD HIM.
MAYBE THAT'S WHAT YUKI CAN'T EXPLAIN? BUT IT'S NOT HER FAULT.
I WONDER HOW LONG IT WILL TAKE FOR THEM TO MAKE SOME PROG-RESS...
"AH, WHAT A DIFFICULT LIFE HE MUST ENDURE"...
...I HAD THOUGHT.

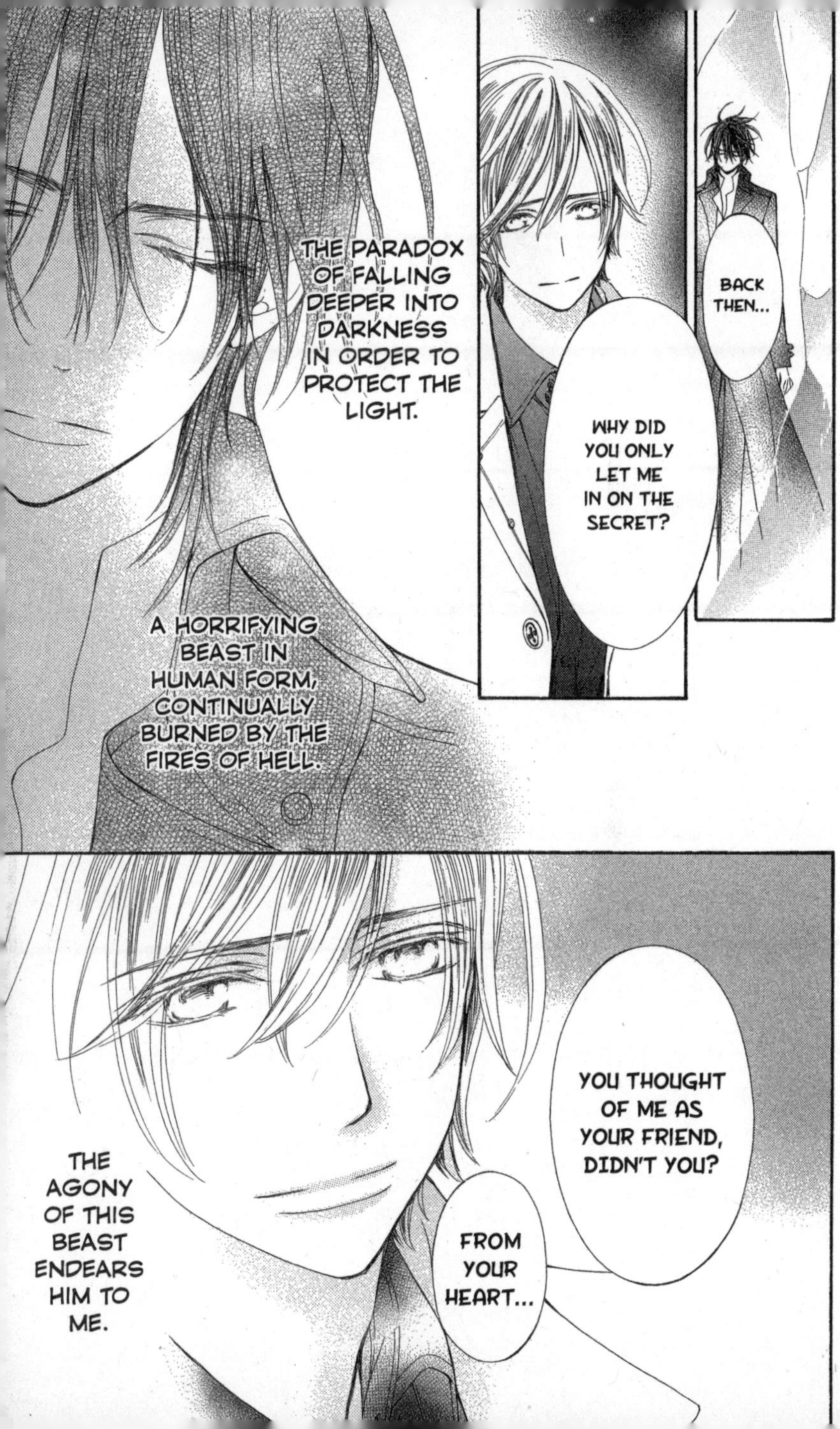
BACK THEN...
WHY DID YOU ONLY LET ME IN ON THE SECRET?
THE PARADOX OF FALLING DEEPER INTO DARKNESS IN ORDER TO PROTECT THE LIGHT.
A HORRIFYING BEAST IN HUMAN FORM, CONTINUALLY BURNED BY THE FIRES OF HELL.
YOU THOUGHT OF ME AS YOUR FRIEND, DIDN'T YOU?
FROM YOUR HEART...
THE AGONY OF THIS BEAST ENDEARS HIM TO ME.

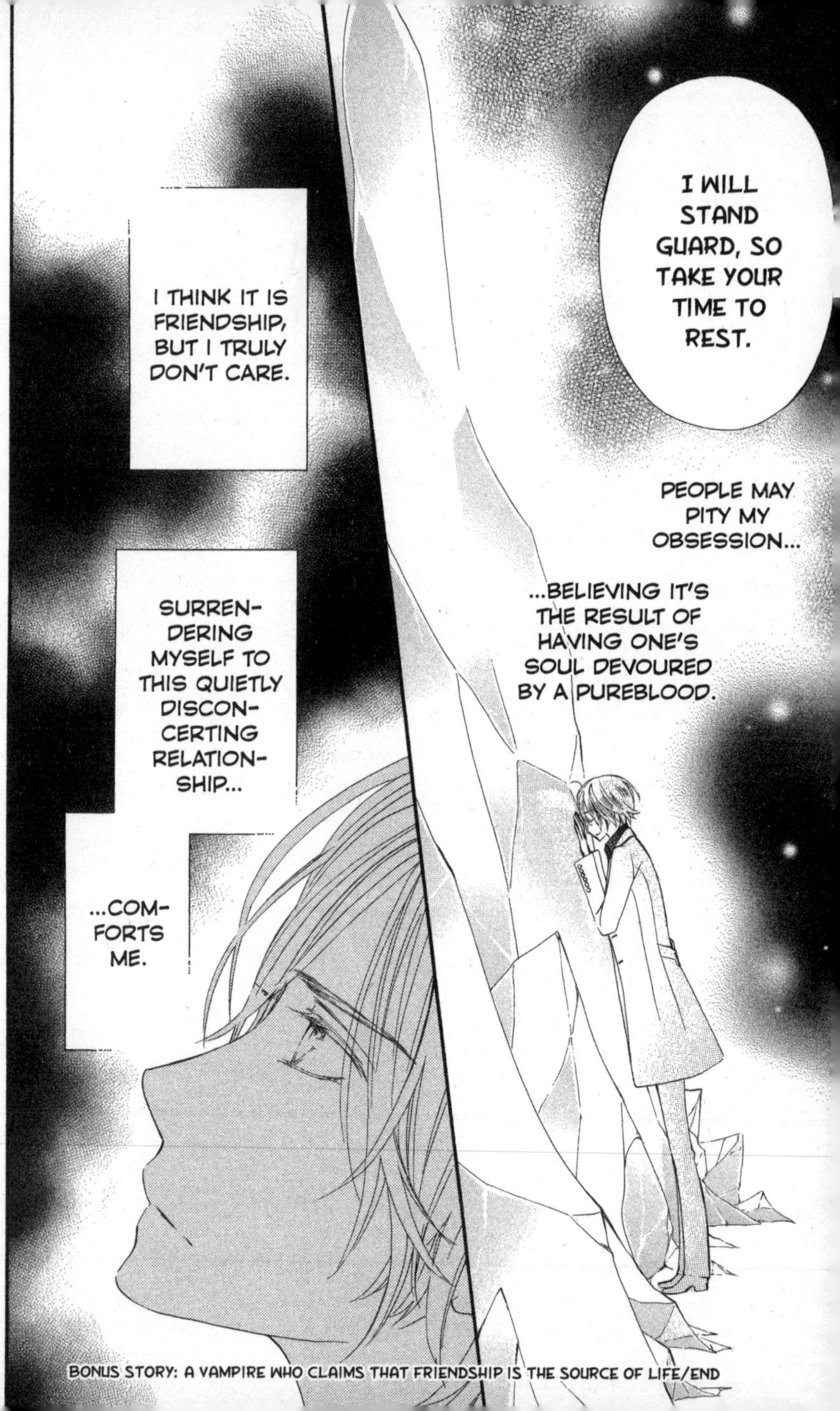
I WILL STAND GUARD, SO TAKE YOUR TIME TO REST.
PEOPLE MAY PITY MY OBSESSION...
...BELIEVING IT'S THE RESULT OF HAVING ONE'S SOUL DEVOURED BY A PUREBLOOD.
I THINK IT IS FRIENDSHIP, BUT I TRULY DON'T CARE.
SURREN-DERING MYSELF TO THIS QUIETLY DISCON-CERTING RELATION-SHIP...
...COM-FORTS ME.

BONUS STORY: A VAMPIRE WHO CLAIMS THAT FRIENDSHIP IS THE SOURCE OF LIFE/END

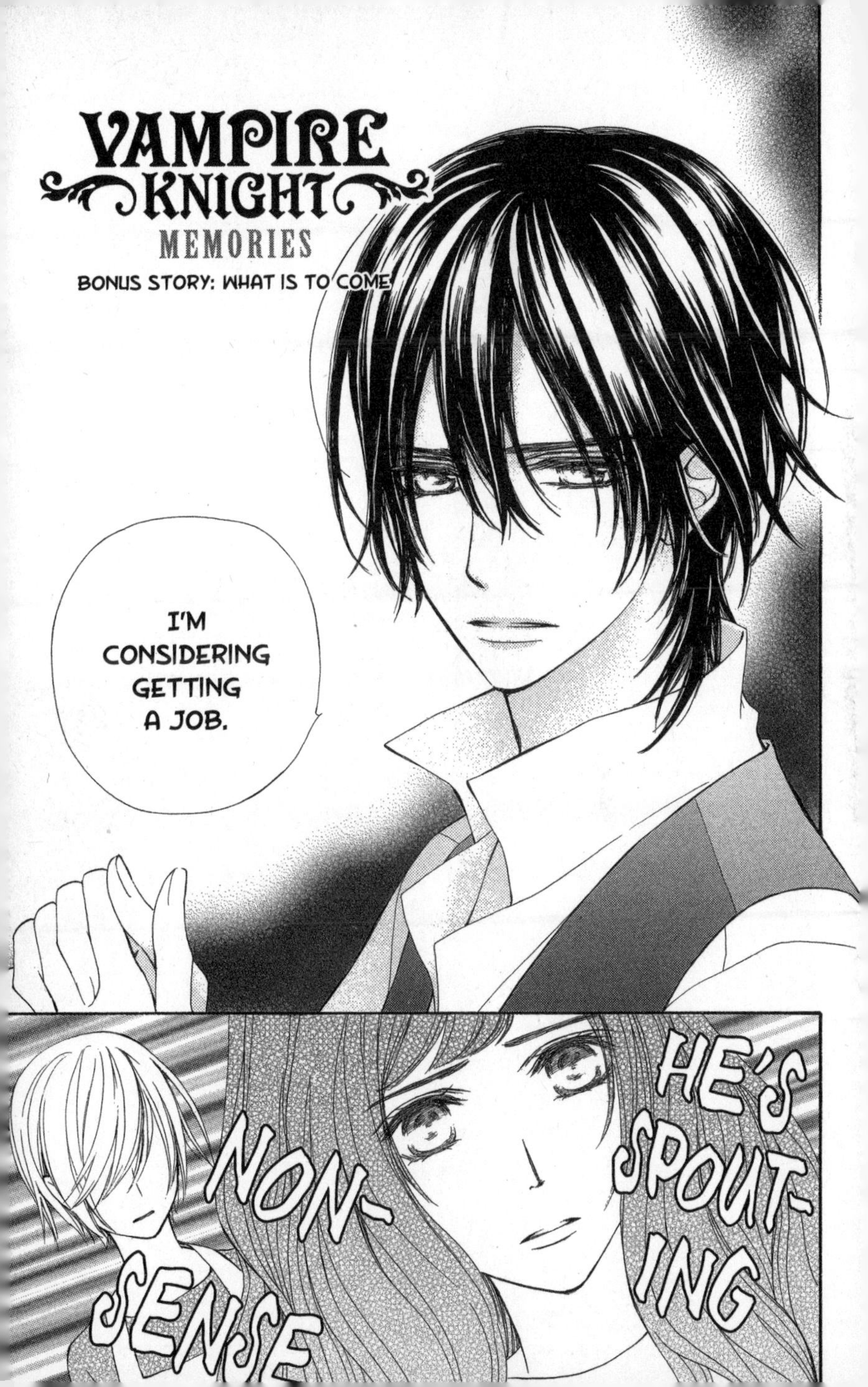
VAMPIRE KNIGHT
MEMORIES
BONUS STORY: WHAT IS TO COME
I'M CONSIDERING GETTING A JOB.
HE'S SPOUTING
NONSENSE

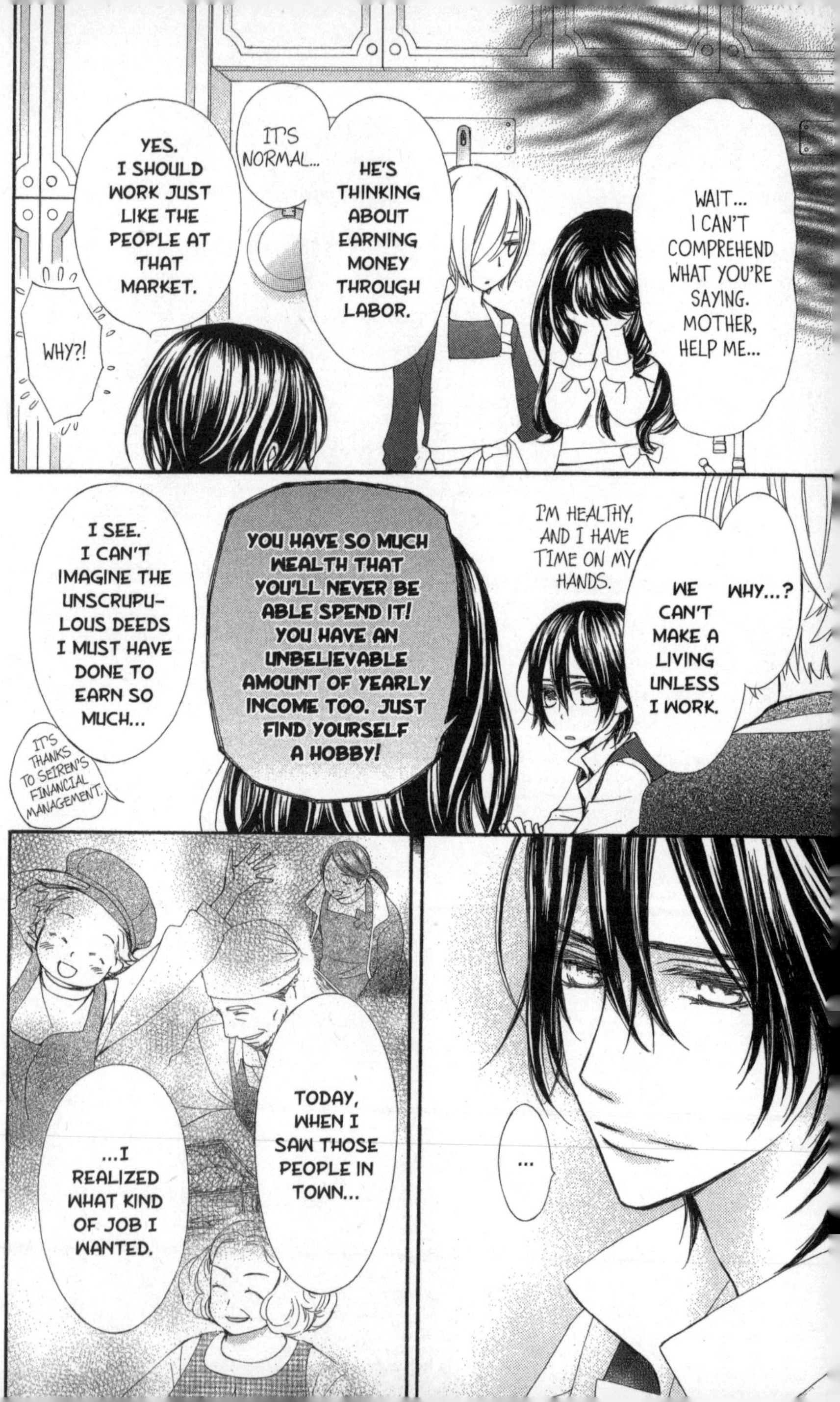
WAIT... I CAN'T COMPREHEND WHAT YOU'RE SAYING. MOTHER, HELP ME...
HE'S THINKING ABOUT EARNING MONEY THROUGH LABOR.
IT'S NORMAL...
YES. I SHOULD WORK JUST LIKE THE PEOPLE AT THAT MARKET.
WHY?!
WHY...?
WE CAN'T MAKE A LIVING UNLESS I WORK.
I'M HEALTHY, AND I HAVE TIME ON MY HANDS.
YOU HAVE SO MUCH WEALTH THAT YOU'LL NEVER BE ABLE SPEND IT! YOU HAVE AN UNBELIEVABLE AMOUNT OF YEARLY INCOME TOO. JUST FIND YOURSELF A HOBBY!
I SEE. I CAN'T IMAGINE THE UNSCRUPULOUS DEEDS I MUST HAVE DONE TO EARN SO MUCH...
IT'S THANKS TO SEIREN'S FINANCIAL MANAGEMENT.
...
TODAY, WHEN I SAW THOSE PEOPLE IN TOWN...
...I REALIZED WHAT KIND OF JOB I WANTED.

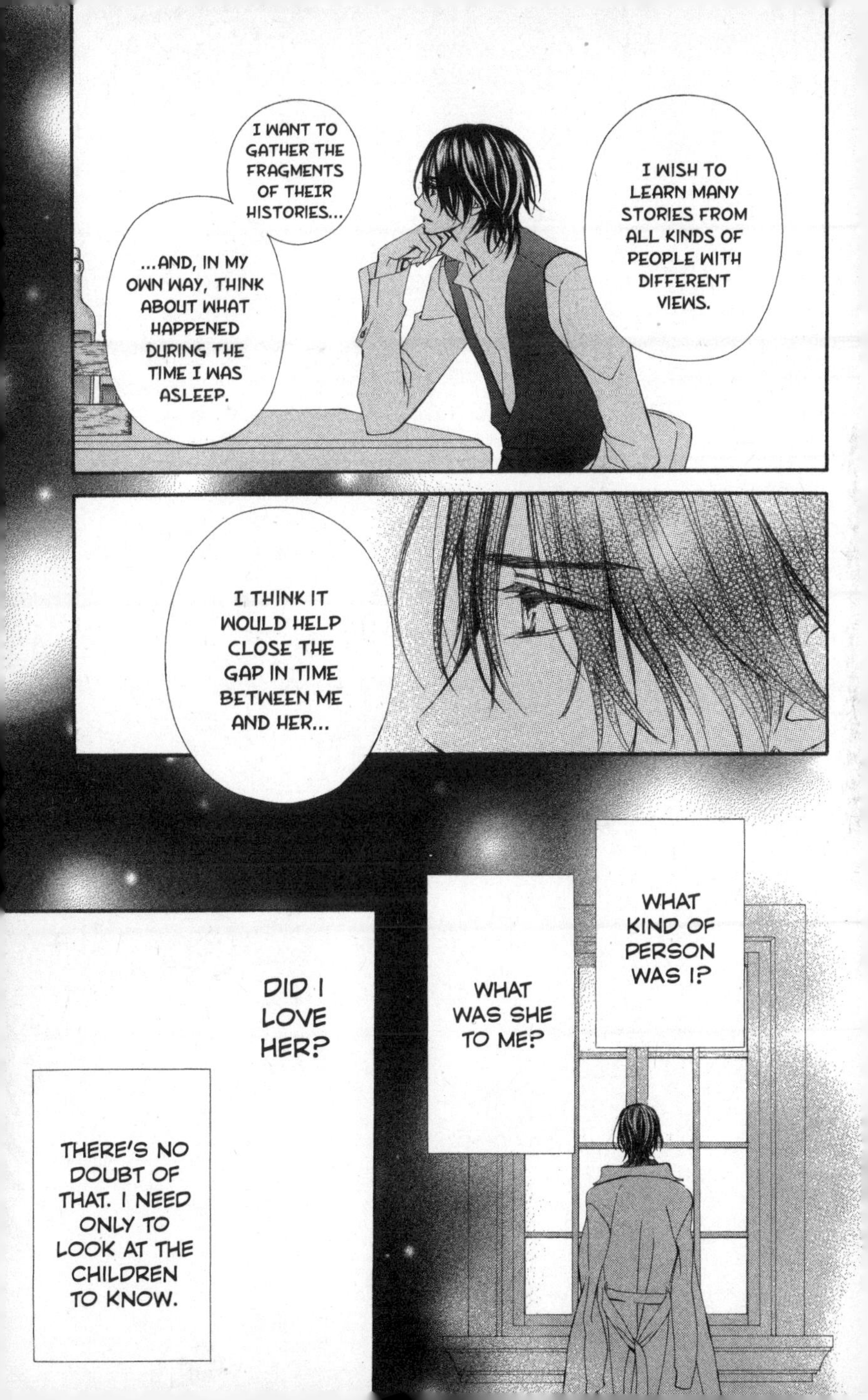
I WISH TO LEARN MANY STORIES FROM ALL KINDS OF PEOPLE WITH DIFFERENT VIEWS.
I WANT TO GATHER THE FRAGMENTS OF THEIR HISTORIES...
...AND, IN MY OWN WAY, THINK ABOUT WHAT HAPPENED DURING THE TIME I WAS ASLEEP.
I THINK IT WOULD HELP CLOSE THE GAP IN TIME BETWEEN ME AND HER...
WHAT KIND OF PERSON WAS I?
WHAT WAS SHE TO ME?
DID I LOVE HER?
THERE'S NO DOUBT OF THAT. I NEED ONLY TO LOOK AT THE CHILDREN TO KNOW.

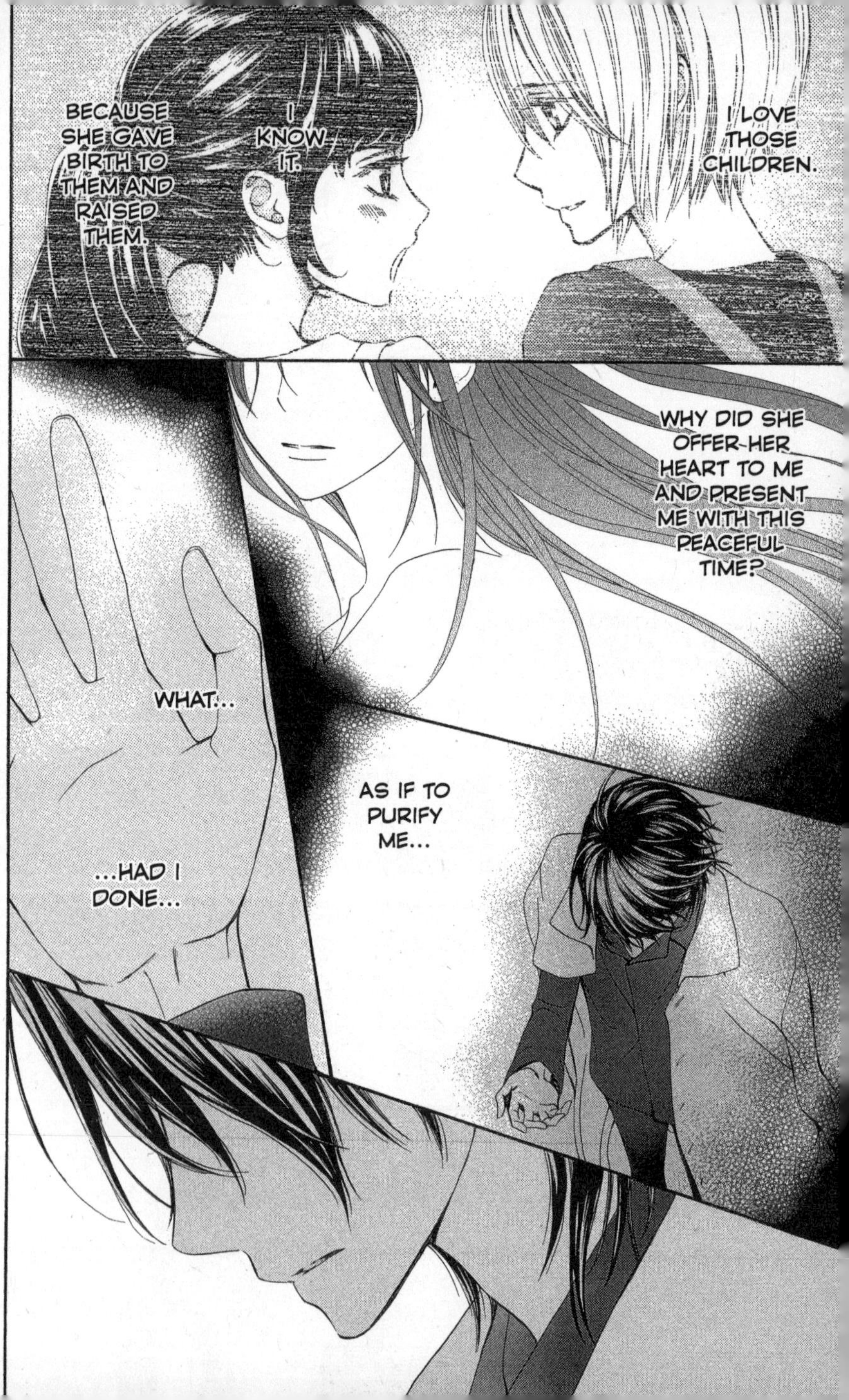
I LOVE THOSE CHILDREN.
I KNOW IT.
BECAUSE SHE GAVE BIRTH TO THEM AND RAISED THEM.
WHY DID SHE OFFER HER HEART TO ME AND PRESENT ME WITH THIS PEACEFUL TIME?
AS IF TO PURIFY ME...
WHAT...
...HAD I DONE...

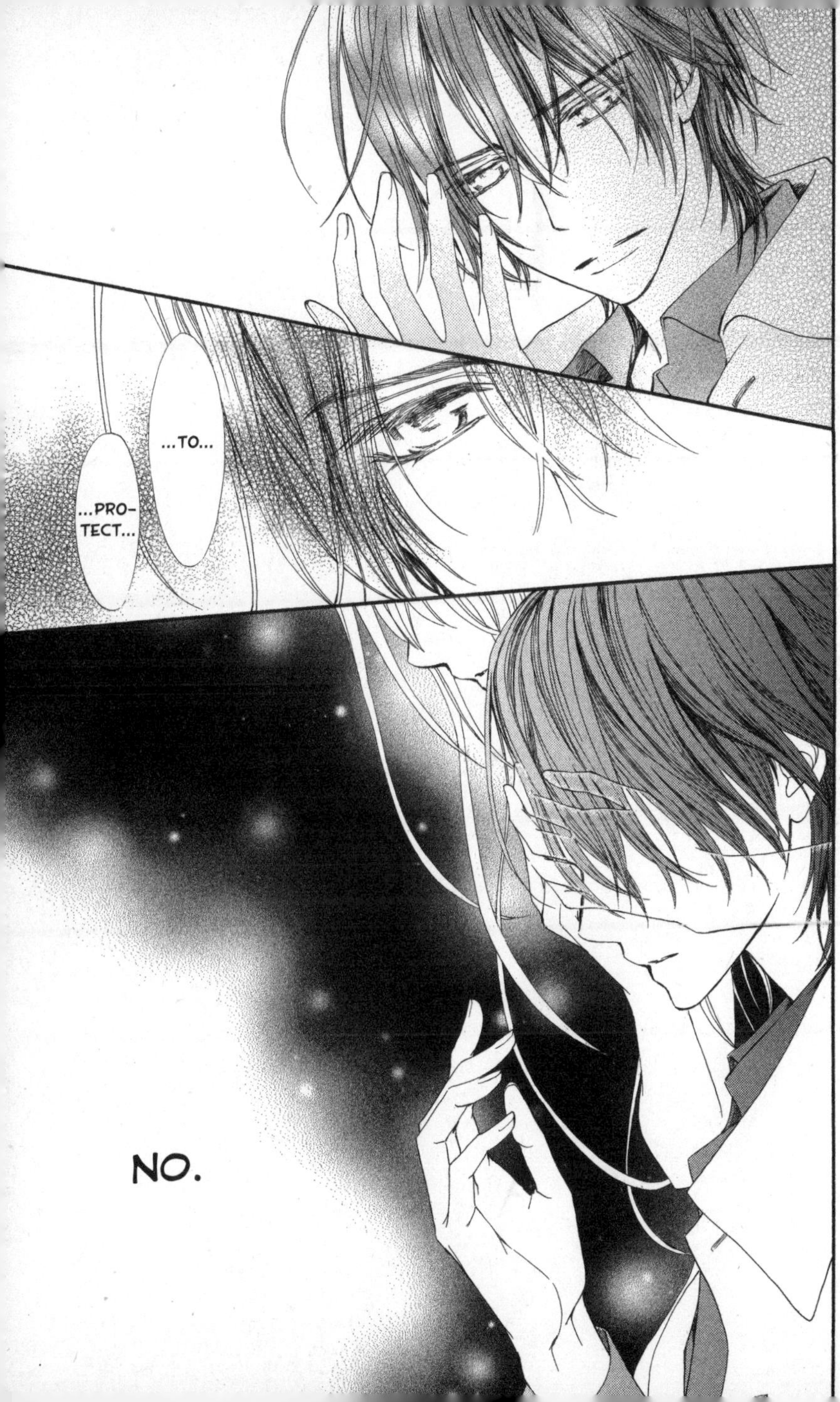
...TO...
...PRO-TECT...
NO.

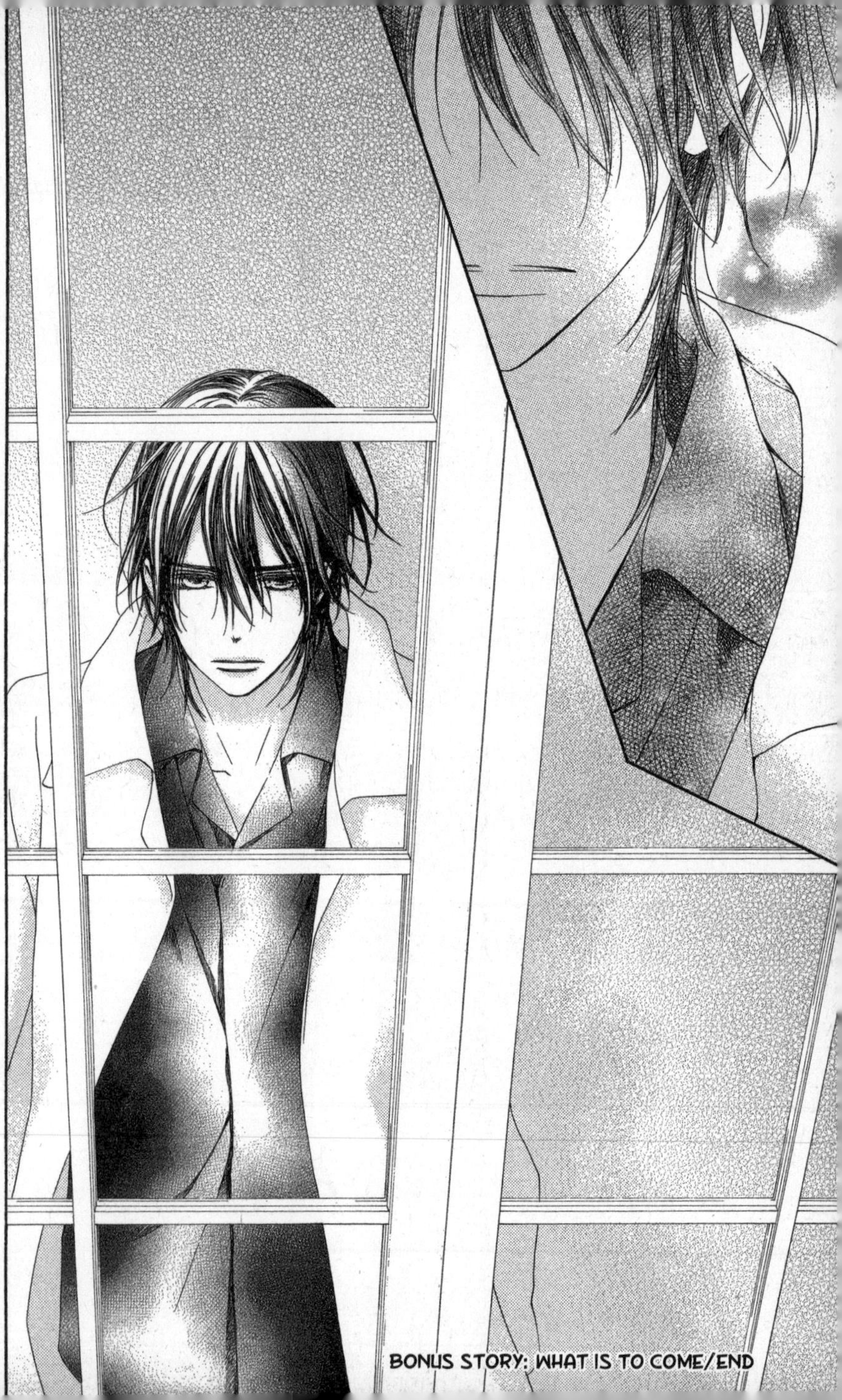
BONUS STORY: WHAT IS TO COME/END

MEMORIES OF LITTLE CONSEQUENCE

LOOK!
HEY, I THINK?!
THERE!
I'M SURE HIS HAIR HAS GROWN LONGER!
THE OTHER DAY...
...I THOUGHT I SAW HIM BLINK FOR A MOMENT.
HE MOVED THE MOMENT I TOOK MY EYES OFF HIM!!
LIKE THIS!!
THE USUAL SPOOKY TALES ABOUT OLD THINGS WITH A STORY BEHIND THEM...
KEEN KEEN
DO A BACKFLIP.
ROLL YOUR EYES BACK.

EDITOR'S NOTES

CHARACTERS

Matsuri Hino puts careful thought into the names of her characters in *Vampire Knight*. Below is the collection of characters throughout the manga. Each character's name is presented family name first, per the kanji reading.

黒主優姫

Cross Yuki

Yuki's last name, *Kurosu*, is the Japanese pronunciation of the English word "cross." However, the kanji has a different meaning—*kuro* means "black" and *su* means "master." Her first name is a combination of *yuu*, meaning "tender" or "kind," and *ki*, meaning "princess."

錐生零

Kiryu Zero

Zero's first name is the kanji for *rei*, meaning "zero." In his last name, *Kiryu*, the *ki* means "auger" or "drill" and the *ryu* means "life."

玖蘭枢

Kuran Kaname

Kaname means "hinge" or "door." The kanji for his last name is a combination of the old-fashioned way of writing *ku*, meaning "nine," and *ran*, meaning "orchid": "nine orchids."

藍堂英

Aido Hanabusa

Hanabusa means "petals of a flower." *Aido* means "indigo temple." In Japanese, the pronunciation of *Aido* is very close to the pronunciation of the English word *idol*.

架院暁

Kain Akatsuki

Akatsuki means "dawn" or "daybreak." In *Kain, ka* is a base or support, while *in* denotes a building that has high fences around it, such as a temple or school.

早園瑠佳

Souen Ruka

In *Ruka*, the *ru* means "lapis lazuli" while the *ka* means "good-looking" or "beautiful." The *sou* in Ruka's surname, *Souen*, means "early," but this kanji also has an obscure meaning of "strong fragrance." The *en* means "garden."

一条拓麻

Ichijo Takuma

Ichijo can mean a "ray," or "streak." The kanji for *Takuma* is a combination of *taku*, meaning "to cultivate," and *ma*, which is the kanji for *asa*, meaning "hemp" or "flax," a plant with blue flowers.

支葵千里

Shiki Senri

Shiki's last name is a combination of *shi*, meaning "to support" and *ki*, meaning "mallow"—a flowering plant with pink or white blossoms. The *ri* in *Senri* is a traditional Japanese unit of measure for distance, and one *ri* is about 2.44 miles. *Senri* means "1,000 *ri*."

夜刈十牙

Yagari Toga

Yagari is a combination of *ya*, meaning "night," and *gari*, meaning "to harvest." *Toga* means "ten fangs."

一条麻遠，一翁

Ichijo Asato, a.k.a. "Ichio"

Ichijo can mean a "ray" or "streak." Asato's first name is comprised of *asa*, meaning "hemp" or "flax," and *tou*, meaning "far-off." His nickname is *ichi*, or "one," combined with *ou*, which can be used as an honorific when referring to an older man.

若葉沙頼

Wakaba Sayori

Yori's full name is Sayori Wakaba. *Wakaba* means "young leaves." Her given name, *Sayori*, is a combination of *sa*, meaning "sand," and *yori*, meaning "trust."

星煉

Seiren

Sei means "star" and ren means
"to smelt" or "to refine." *Ren* is also
the same kanji used in *rengoku*, or
"purgatory." Her previous name,
Hoshino, uses the same kanji for
"star" (*hoshi*) and *no*, which can mean
"from" and is often used at the end of
traditional female names.

遠矢莉磨

Toya Rima

Toya means a "far-reaching arrow."
Rima's first name is a combination
of *ri*, or "jasmine," and *ma*, which
signifies enhancement by wearing
away, such as by polishing
or scouring.

紅まり亜

Kurenai Maria

Kurenai means "crimson." The kanji
for the last *a* in Maria's first name is
the same that is used in "Asia."

錐生壱縷

Kiryu Ichiru

Ichi is the old-fashioned way of writing "one" and *ru* means "thread." In *Kiryu*, the *ki* means "auger" or "drill" and the *ryu* means "life."

緋桜閑, 狂咲姫

Hio Shizuka, Kuruizaki-hime

Shizuka means "calm and quiet." In Shizuka's family name, *hi* is "scarlet" and *ou* is "cherry blossoms." Shizuka Hio is also referred to as the "Kuruizaki-hime." *Kuruizaki* means "flowers blooming out of season" and *hime* means "princess."

藍堂月子

Aido Tsukiko

Aido means "indigo temple." *Tsukiko* means "moon child."

白蕗更

Shirabuki Sara

Shira is "white" and *buki* is "butterbur," a plant with white flowers. *Sara* means "to renew."

黒主灰閻

Cross Kaien

Cross, or *Kurosu*, means "black master." *Kaien* is a combination of *kai*, meaning "ashes," and *en*, meaning "village gate." The kanji for *en* is also used for Enma, the ruler of the underworld in Buddhist mythology.

玖蘭李土

Kuran Rido

Kuran means "nine orchids." In *Rido*, *ri* means "plum" and *do* means "earth."

玖蘭樹里

Kuran Juri

Kuran means "nine orchids." In her first name, *ju* means "tree" and a *ri* is a traditional Japanese unit of measure for distance. The kanji for *ri* is the same as in Senri's name.

玖蘭悠

Kuran Haruka

Kuran means "nine orchids." *Haruka* means "distant" or "remote."

鷹宮海斗

Takamiya Kaito

Taka means "hawk" and *miya* means "imperial palace" or "shrine." *Kai* is "sea" and *to* means "to measure" or "grid."

菖藤依砂也

Shoto Isaya

Sho means "Siberian iris" and *to* is "wisteria." The *I* in *Isaya* means "to rely on" while the *sa* means "sand." *Ya* is a suffix used for emphasis.

橙茉

Toma

In the family name *Toma*, *to* means "Seville orange" and *ma* means "jasmine flower."

藍堂永路

Aido Nagamichi

The name *Nagamichi* is a combination of *naga*, which means "long" or "eternal," and *michi*, which is the kanji for "road" or "path." *Aido* means "indigo temple."

縹木

Hanadagi

In this family name, *hanada* means "bright light blue" and *gi* means "tree."

影山霞

Kageyama Kasumi

In the Class Rep's family name, *kage* means "shadow" and *yama* means "mountain." His first name, *Kasumi*, means "haze" or "mist."

愛

Ai

Ai means "love." It is used in terms of unconditional, unending love and affection.

恋

Ren

Ren means "love." It is used in terms of a romantic love or crush.

星夜

Seiya

Sei means "star" and *ya* means "night": "starry night."

Terms

-sama: The suffix *-sama* is used in formal address for someone who ranks higher in the social hierarchy. The vampires call their leader "Kaname-sama" only when they are among their own kind.

Renai: The combination of Ren's and Ai's names (恋愛) means "romantic love."

Matsuri Hino burst onto the manga scene with her title
Kono Yume ga Sametara (When This Dream Is Over), which
was published in *LaLa DX* magazine. Hino was a manga artist
a mere nine months after she decided to become one.

With the success of her popular series *Captive Hearts*,
MeruPuri and *Vampire Knight*, Hino is a major player in the
world of shojo manga.

Hino enjoys creative activities and has commented that
she would have been either an architect or an apprentice to
traditional Japanese craftsmasters if she had not become a
manga artist.

VAMPIRE KNIGHT: MEMORIES
Vol. 3
Shojo Beat Manga Edition

STORY AND ART BY
MATSURI HINO

Adaptation/Nancy Thistlethwaite
Translation/Tetsuichiro Miyaki
Touch-Up Art & Lettering/Inori Fukuda Trant
Graphic Design/Alice Lewis
Editor/Nancy Thistlethwaite

Vampire Knight memories by Matsuri Hino © Matsuri Hino 2018
All rights reserved. First published in Japan in 2018 by HAKUSENSHA,
Inc., Tokyo. English language translation rights arranged with
HAKUSENSHA, Inc., Tokyo.

The stories, characters and incidents mentioned in this publication are
entirely fictional.

Printed in the U.S.A.

Published by VIZ Media, LLC
P.O. Box 77010
San Francisco, CA 94107

10 9 8 7 6 5 4 3 2 1
First printing, July 2019

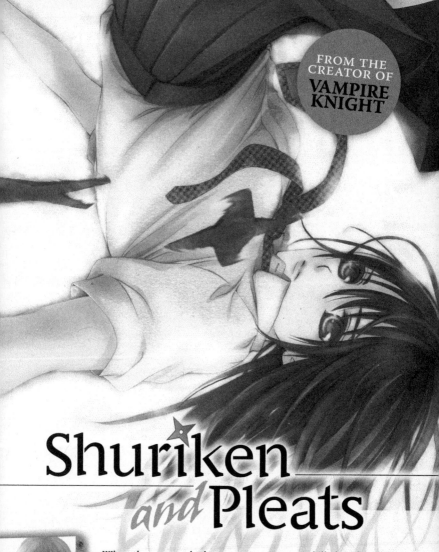

Shuriken
and Pleats

When the master she has sworn to protect is killed, Mikage Kirio, a skilled ninja, travels to Japan to start a new, peaceful life for herself. But as soon as she arrives, she finds herself fighting to protect the life of Mahito Wakashimatsu, a man who is under attack by a band of ninja. From that time on, Mikage is drawn deeper into the machinations of his powerful family.

www.viz.com

ratings.viz.com

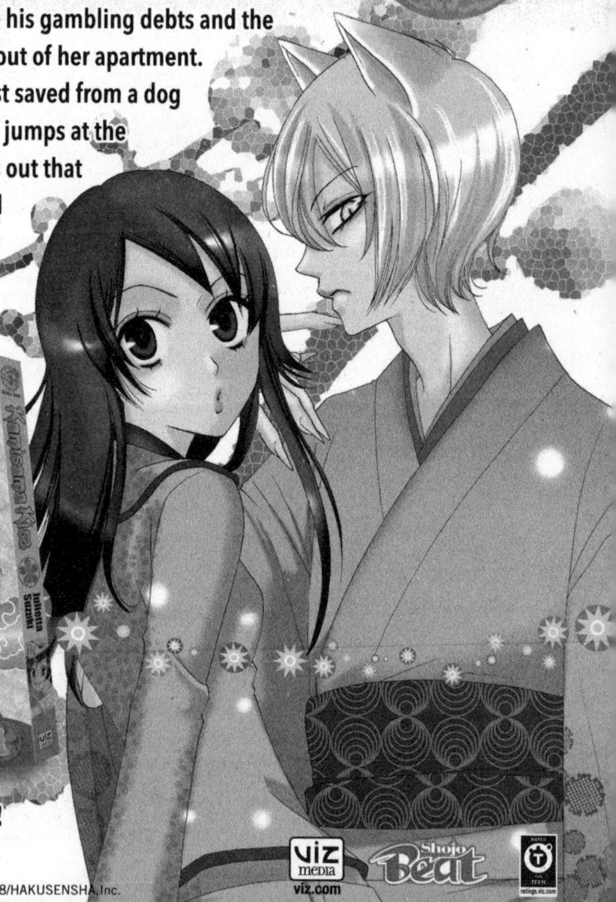

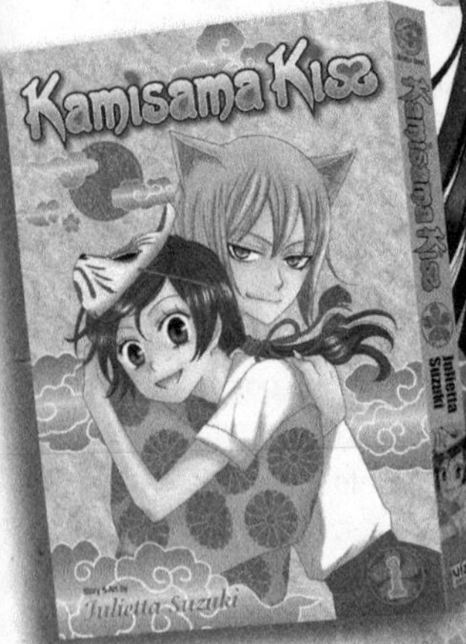

Kamisama Kiss
Julietta Suzuki

Behind the Scenes!!

STORY AND ART BY BISCO HATORI

From the creator of *Ouran High School Host Club*

Ranmaru Kurisu comes from a family of hardy, rough-and-tumble fisherfolk and he sticks out at home like a delicate, artistic sore thumb. It's given him a raging inferiority complex and a permanently pessimistic outlook. Now that he's in college, he's hoping to find a sense of belonging. But after a whole life of being left out, does he even know how to fit in?!

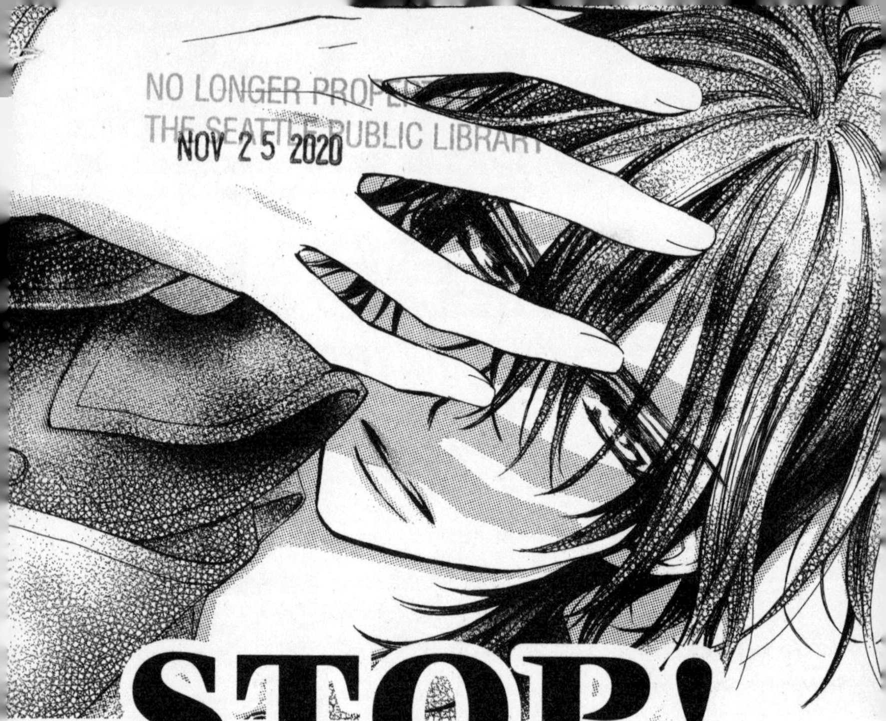

STOP!

You may be reading the wrong way!

In keeping with the original Japanese comic format, this book reads from right to left—so word balloons, action and sound effects and are reversed to preserve the orientation of the original artwork.

Check out the diagram shown here to get the hang of things, and then turn to the other side of the book to get started!

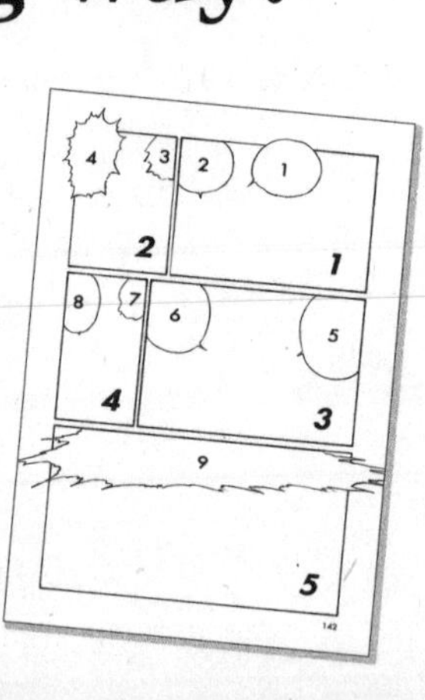
1
2
3
4
1
2
5
6
7
8
3
4
9
5
142